MULTICULTURAL JURISPRUDENCE

As individuals travel across borders, societies have become more and more pluralistic. The result of increased migration is the interaction among cultural communities and inevitably clashes between state law and customary law. These cultural conflicts have given rise to a new multicultural jurisprudence. In this volume scholars grapple with the immense challenges judges are currently experiencing everywhere. To what extent can and should courts accommodate litigants' requests by taking their cultural backgrounds into account?

This collection brings together powerful examples of the cultural defense in many countries in Western Europe, North America, and elsewhere. It shows the ubiquity of this defense, contrary to the mistaken impression that it has been invoked principally in the United States. This book makes the case for undertaking studies of the use of the cultural defense in jurisdictions all over the world where this has not been previously documented.

Many of the chapters concentrate on criminal cases including homicide in the context of honour crimes, provocation based on 'loss of face' or witchcraft killings. Some deal with other areas of law such as asylum jurisprudence, family law and housing policy. They show in concrete cases how cultural claims have arisen and how legal systems wrestle with these arguments. It is clear that judges have had considerable difficulty handling many of the cultural claims.

The authors demonstrate persuasively the need to reconsider the proper use of cultural evidence in legal proceedings. Those interested in the ways in which expertise influences the disposition of cases will find this book compelling.

Oñati International Series in Law and Society

A SERIES PUBLISHED FOR THE OÑATI INSTITUTE FOR THE SOCIOLOGY OF LAW

General Editors

William LF Felstiner   Judy Fudge

Founding Editors

William LF Felstiner   Johannes Feest

Board of General Editors

Rosemary Hunter, University of Kent, United Kingdom
Carlos Lugo, Hostos Law School, Puerto Rico
David Nelken, Macerata University, Italy
Jacek Kurczewski, Warsaw University, Poland
Marie-Claire Foblets, Leuven University, Belgium
Roderick Macdonald, McGill University, Canada

Titles in this Series

Social Dynamics of Crime and Control: New Theories for a World in Transition edited by Susanne Karstedt and Kai Bussmann

Criminal Policy in Transition edited by Andrew Rutherford and Penny Green

Making Law for Families edited by Mavis Maclean

Poverty and the Law edited by Peter Robson and Asbjørn Kjønstad

Adapting Legal Cultures edited by Johannes Feest and David Nelken

Rethinking Law Society and Governance: Foucault's Bequest edited by Gary Wickham and George Pavlich

Rules and Networks edited by Richard Appelbaum, Bill Felstiner and Volkmar Gessner

Women in the World's Legal Professions edited by Ulrike Schultz and Gisela Shaw

Healing the Wounds edited by Marie-Claire Foblets and Trutz von Trotha

Imaginary Boundaries of Justice edited by Ronnie Lippens

Family Law and Family Values edited by Mavis Maclean

Contemporary Issues in the Semiotics of Law
edited by Anne Wagner, Tracey Summerfield and Farid Benavides Vanegas

The Geography of Law: Landscapes, Identity and Regulation
edited by Bill Taylor

Theory and Method in Socio-Legal Research edited by Reza Banakar and
Max Travers

Luhmann on Law and Politics edited by Michael King
and Chris Thornhill

*Precarious Work, Women and the New Economy: The Challenge to Legal
Norms* edited by Judy Fudge and Rosemary Owens

*Juvenile Law Violators, Human Rights, and the Development of New
Juvenile Justice Systems* edited by Eric L Jensen and Jørgen Jepsen

*The Language Question in Europe and Diverse Societies: Political, Legal
and Social Perspectives* edited by Dario Castiglione and Chris Longman

European Ways of Law: Towards A European Sociology of Law
edited by Volkmar Gessner and David Nelken

*Crafting Transnational Policing: Police Capacity-Building and Global
Policing Reform* edited by Andrew Goldsmith and James Sheptycki

*Constitutional Politics in the Middle East: With special reference to
Turkey, Iraq, Iran and Afghanistan* edited by Saïd Amir Arjomand

Parenting after Partnering: Containing Conflict after Separation
edited by Mavis Maclean

*Responsible Business: Self-Governance and Law in Transnational
Economic Transactions* edited by Olaf Dilling, Martin Herberg
and Gerd Winter

Rethinking Equality Projects in Law edited by Rosemary Hunter

Multicultural Jurisprudence

Comparative Perspectives on the Cultural Defense

Edited by
Marie-Claire Foblets
and
Alison Dundes Renteln

Oñati International Series in Law and Society

A SERIES PUBLISHED FOR THE OÑATI INSTITUTE
FOR THE SOCIOLOGY OF LAW

·HART·
PUBLISHING

OXFORD AND PORTLAND OREGON
2009

Published in North America (US and Canada)
by Hart Publishing
c/o International Specialized Book Services
920 NE 58th Avenue, Suite 300
Portland, OR 97213-3786
USA
Tel: +1 503 287 3093 or toll-free: (1) 800 944 6190
Fax: +1 503 280 8832
E-mail: orders@isbs.com
Website: www.isbs.com

Hart Publishing Ltd, 16c Worcester Place, Oxford, OX1 2JW
Telephone: +44 (0)1865 517530 Fax: +44 (0)1865 510710
E-mail: mail@hartpub.co.uk
Website: http://www.hartpub.co.uk

British Library Cataloguing in Publication Data
Data Available

l͡ɔɔ5767436
ISBN: 978-1-84113-895-4 (hardback)
ISBN: 978-1-84113- 896-1 (paperback)

Typeset by Compuscript, Shannon
Printed by the MPG Books Group in the UK

Contents

Part IV   Legal Actors

List of Contributors

Kumaralingam Amirthalingam is Professor and Vice Dean (International Programmes), Faculty of Law, National University of Singapore; Director, Asian Law Institute. He has a PhD, LLB (Hons) from Australian National University. His research interests include criminal law, torts, multiculturalism, international human rights, vulnerability and criminal law. Recent publications relevant to this area include 'Free Speech and Religious Sensitivity' (2007) 29 *Media, Culture and Society* 509; 'Women's Rights, International Norms and Domestic Violence: Asian Perspectives' (2005) 27 *Human Rights Quarterly* 683.

César Arjona, LLB (ESADE, Barcelona, 1999), LLM (European Academy of Legal Theory, Brussels, 2000), JSD (Cornell University, 2004). Professor in the Department of Public Law at ESADE. He teaches in the fields of legal philosophy, social sciences and professional ethics. His main publications are in the field of jurisprudence. They include *Roscoe Pound and the Problems of Contemporary Jurisprudence* (UMI, 2004) and the Spanish edition of *The Dissenting Opinions of Oliver Wendell Holmes* (Iustel, 2006).

Simon H Bronitt is Professor at ANU College of Law; Director, National Europe Centre, Research School of Humanities, ANU College of Arts and Social Sciences. He has LLB (Hons) from University of Bristol, and LLM (Hons) from University of Cambridge. His interests include criminal law procedure and criminal justice and criminology, evidence, human rights, European and comparative law. Main publications related to the topic of this volume include S Bottomley and S Bronitt, *Law in Context*, 3rd edn (Sydney, Federation Press, 2006) and S Bronitt and B McSherry, *Principles of Criminal Law*, 2nd edn (Sydney, LBC, 2005).

Pieter A Carstens holds BLC (1980), LLB (1982), LLD (1996) from the University of Pretoria, South Africa. He is presently Professor of criminal and medical law at the University of Pretoria. He also holds an appointment as Extraordinary Professor in the Department of Forensic Medicine, Faculty of Health Sciences at the University of Pretoria. He is an associate member of the Pretoria Bar. He has defended many people accused of witchcraft and muti-murders, hence his interest in the 'cultural defence'. He is presently the chairperson of the Unit for Medicine and Law, a joint venture between the University of Pretoria and the University of South Africa. He is a past member of the ethics committee of the Faculty of Health Sciences of the University of Pretoria and a member of the Hospital Board of Weskoppies

Mental Hospital. He has published widely in criminal and medical law, nationally and internationally, and is the co-author of *Foundational Principles of South African Medical Law* (2007). He is a member of the World Association for Medical Law.

John L Caughey is Professor at the Department of American Studies, Affiliate Professor at the Department of Anthropology and co-director of the The Life Writing Project, University of Maryland, College Park. His main research and teaching interests are ethnography and life history research, psychological anthropology, contemporary American individuals and their cultures, South Asian and US cultures. Some of his publications include *Negotiating Cultures and Identities: Life History Issues, Methods, and Readings* (Lincoln, University of Nebraska Press, 2006); with Mac Marshall, *Culture, Kin, and Cognition in Oceania: Essays in Honor of Ward H. Goodenough*, American Anthropological Association Special Publications, Scholarly Series no 25 (Washington, DC, 1989); 'Introduction' in John L Caughey and Mac Marshall, *Imaginary Social Worlds: a Cultural Approach* (Lincoln, University of Nebraska Press, 1984) pp 1–16; *Faanakkar: Cultural Values in a Micronesian Society*, University of Pennsylvania Publications in Anthropology no 2 (Philadelphia, Department of Anthropology, University of Pennsylvania, 1977).

Erik Claes is Professor of Law at the Faculty of Law, University of Leuven. His main research areas are theory of adjudication, philosophy of criminal law, penal theory and restorative justice. His PhD thesis in law, defended at the University of Leuven, *Legality and Adjudication in the Criminal Law* (Leuven, Universitaire Pers Leuven, 2003) was awarded the Fernand Collin Prize for Law in 2002. He is contributing editor with R Foqué and T Peters of *Punishment, Restorative Justice and the Rule of Law* (Antwerp/Oxford, Intersentia, 2004) and recently with A Duff and S Gutwirth of *Privacy and the Criminal Law* (Antwerp/Oxford, Intersentia, 2006).

Maneesha Deckha received her BA in Anthropology and Political Science with a minor in Women's Studies (Hons) from McGill University, her LLB from the University of Toronto and her LLM from Columbia University. She was called to the Bar in Ontario (2000), practised with the Ministry of the Attorney General until 2001, and is currently a non-practising member of the Law Society of Upper Canada. She joined the University of Victoria Faculty of Law in Victoria, Canada, as an Assistant Professor in 2002 after completing her graduate thesis on gender and cultural equality at Columbia Law School. Her research interests include feminist legal theories, law and culture, bioethics, and the boundaries between property and personhood, especially as they relate to non-human animals. Her work has been published in the *Canadian Journal of Women and the Law, Osgoode Hall Law*

Journal, Hastings Women's Law Journal, UCLA Women's Law Journal, Harvard Journal of Gender and Law and *Journal of Animal Law and Ethics*. She teaches bioethics, personhood and the law, feminist legal theories, property, administrative law and legal process. In 2006, her seminar on Animals, Culture and the Law received the US Humane Society's Animal and Society New Course Award. She is a member of several academic associations as well as serving as part of the National Steering Committee for the National Association of Women and the Law.

Alison Dundes Renteln is a Professor of Political Science and Anthropology at the University of Southern California where she teaches law and public policy. She has a BA from Harvard (History and Literature), a PhD in Jurisprudence and Social Policy from Boalt Hall at the University of California, Berkeley, and a JD from the USC Law School. She served as the Director of the Jesse Unruh Institute of Politics at USC 2005–07. Her publications include three books, *International Human Rights: Universalism Versus Relativism* (1990), *Folk Law: Essays in the Theory and Practice of Lex Non Scripta* (1994) and *The Cultural Defense* (Oxford University Press, 2004) and numerous articles. She was a core member of the Law and Culture Working Group of the Social Science Research Council. She also worked with the United Nations on the new treaty guaranteeing the rights of persons with disabilities. Renteln has taught judicial and legal ethics in the Philippines and Thailand through the American Bar Association Asia Law Project. Since the early 1990s, she has taught seminars on the rights of ethnic minorities for judges, lawyers, court interpreters and police officers. She also served on several California civil rights commissions and the California Committee for Human Rights Watch. She is a member of the American Political Science Association, American Society of International Law, the Commission on Folk Law and Legal Pluralism, the International Law Association, the Law and Society Association and the American Society of Comparative Law.

Marie-Claire Foblets Lic Iur, Lic Phil, PhD Anthrop (Leuven, Belgium). She is Professor ordinarius of Law and Anthropology at the Universities of Leuven, Brussels and Antwerp, member of the Flemish Royal Academy of Sciences (Vlaamse Koninklijke Academie voor Wetenschappen) and honorary member of the Brussels Bar. She received the Francqui Prize 2004 (Human Sciences). She has done extensive research and published widely on issues of immigration, integration and nationality law in Belgium. In the field of anthropology of law, her research focuses on the application of Islamic family laws in Europe, including M-C Foblets, *Les familles maghrébines et la justice en Belgique. Anthropologie juridique et immigration* (Paris, Karthala, 1994); M-C Foblets (ed), *Familles—Islam—Europe. Le droit confronté au changement* (coll Musulmans d'Europe) (Paris,

L'Harmattan, 1996); M-C Foblets (ed), *Femmes marocaines et conflits familiaux en immigration. Quelles solutions juridiques appropriées?* (Antwerp, Maklu, 1998); M-C Foblets and JY Carlier, *Le nouveau Code marocain de la famille. Son application en Europe (The Family Code in Morocco: its Application in Europe)* (Brussels, Bruylant, 2005); M-C Foblets, *Culturen voor de rechter (Cultures Before the Courts)* (Antwerp, Maklu, forthcoming)

Joke Kusters has a Masters in Law from the University of Antwerp and the Uppsala Universitet and also a Master in Social and Cultural Anthropology from the KU Leuven. She is a PhD researcher at the University of Antwerp and Member of the Migration and Minority Research Centre (IMMRC) at the KU Leuven. Publications related to the topic of this volume include 'Het gebrek aan plaats voor de woonwagenbewoners. Bestaat er een recht op nomadisme als onderdeel van het recht op culturele identiteitsbeleving? Een analyse binnen het kader van het EVRM (Does the Right to Nomadism Exists as Part of the Right to Cultural Identity? An Analysis within the Frame of the ECHR) (2003) *Tijdschrift voor Vreemdelingenrecht* 197; 'Het recht op huisvesting voor woonwagenbewoners (The Right to Housing for Nomadic People)' (2004) *Juristenkrant* 11; 'De marge van de samenleving in (rechts)historisch perspectief, bespreking van F. Vanhemelryck (The Margin of Society in (Legal-)Historical Perspective, Review of F Vanhemelryck, *Marginalen in de geschiedenis: over beulen, joden, hoeren, zigeuners en andere zondebokken* (Davidsfonds, Leuven, 2004))' (2005) 4 *T Gesch* 604; 'Met de Roma op café: culturele predisposities onderzocht, bespreking van I Pogany (Having a Coffee with the Roma: Cultural Predispositions Examined, Review of I Pogany, *The Roma Café: Human Rights and the Plight of the Romani People* (London, Pluto Press, 2004))' (2005) 1 *Recht der Werkelijkheid* 79.

Sylvia Maier is Assistant Professor/Faculty Fellow at the Center for European and Mediterranean Studies at New York University. She received her MA (1999) and PhD (2001) from the University of Southern California in Los Angeles. Her research interests concern the legal accommodation of Muslim minority rights in Western Europe, the emergence of an Islamic feminism in Saudi Arabia, and the use of information and communication technologies for the empowerment of disadvantaged groups in the Global South. She has published articles, book chapters and op-ed pieces on honour killings in Germany, sex-trafficking, and the use of ICTs for women's empowerment in India. She is currently completing a book-length manuscript 'Mainstreaming Muslims: Culture, Islam and the Law in France and Germany'.

Brenda Carina Oude Breuil is Assistant Professor of Anthropology (Faculty of Social Sciences) at Utrecht University. Her interests include the role of cultural differences in multicultural law enforcement and, more broadly, the consequences of globalisation and migration for children and youth. Main publications related to the topic of this volume include *De Raad voor de Kinderbescherming in een multiculturele samenleving (The Council for Child Protection in a Multicultural Society)* (Dissertation, The Hague, Boom Juridische Uitgevers) and 'De Raad voor de Kinderbescherming (The Council of Child Protection)' in F Bovenkerk, M Komen and Y Yeşilgöz (eds), *Multiculturaliteit in de strafrechtspleging (Multiculturality in Criminal Law Practice)* (The Hague, Boom Juridische Uitgevers). She currently conducts research on the phenomenon of 'child trafficking' from Eastern Europe to Western European cities.

Mirjam Siesling. After graduating from high school in 1995, she read law at Utrecht University. In the academic year 1999–2000 she studied at Edinburgh University in Scotland (courses: Social Anthropology, Jurisprudence and Criminology). In 2000 she became a PhD fellow at Utrecht University. Her research was titled 'Multiculturality and Defense in Dutch Criminal Law', which explores to what extent the defendant's cultural background is taken into account in Dutch criminal law. She defended her PhD thesis successfully on 23 November 2006. Since February 2005, she has been an Assistant Professor of Criminal Law and Criminology at the Willem Pompe Institute for Criminal Law and Criminology of Utrecht University.

Jeroen ten Voorde. After graduating from high school in 1996 he read law at Erasmus University in Rotterdam and became a PhD fellow at this university in 2001. His research was titled 'Culture as a Defense' and was a legal and legal-philosophical research into the possibilities and limits of cultural diversity in Dutch criminal law. This research was funded by the Netherlands Organisation for Scientific Research (NWO). He defended his PhD thesis successfully on 28 June 2007. Since September 2005, he has been Assistant Professor of Criminal Law and Criminal Procedure in Department of Criminal Law and Criminology, Leiden University. Since September 2007, he has also been a part-time judge at Haarlem District Court.

Barbara Truffin has a Degree in Law, a Master in International Law and a PhD in Anthropology from the Université libre de Bruxelles and also a Master of Arts in Social Sciences from the University of Chicago. She is a FRS-FNRS (National Research Foundation) postdoctoral researcher and a lecturer at the Law Faculty of the Université libre de Bruxelles (legal anthropology). Her publications include 'Droits autochtones amazoniens et droit officiel équatorien: une opposition culturelle? Le cas des Runa et des Shiwiars (Indigenous Rights and Ecuadorian State Law in the Amazon: a Cultural Opposition? The Case of Runa and Shiwiar Peoples)' (2006)

Civilisations 143; 'Des règles du jeux en action: l'élaboration réglementaire des droits des peuples autochtone en tension (Rules in Action: the Tense Regulation of Indigenous Rights)' in *Cahiers d'anthropologie du droit 2006—Le droit en action* (Paris, Karthala—Laboratoire d'anthropologie juridique de Paris I, 2006) 199–243.

Jogchum Vrielink is PhD researcher at the University of Leuven. His research areas include discrimination law, racism, antisemitism and homophobia and the law, freedom of speech and hate speech. Amongst other things he co-authored a *Handbook on Discrimination Law* (Mechelen, Kluwer, 2005).

Cher Weixia Chen received her doctorate in Politics and International Relations from the University of Southern California. She holds an LLB from Beijing University, LLM from National University of Singapore, and MA from University of Southern California. Currently she is working at her dissertation on gender pay equity. Her research interests include culture and law, human rights, comparative law and East Asian studies.

Gordon R Woodman studied law at the University of Cambridge (BA 1960, LLM 1961, PhD 1966). He then worked in Law Faculties in Ghana and Nigeria until 1976, when he joined the Birmingham Law School, University of Birmingham, where he is now Emeritus Professor of Comparative Law. He has studied and written extensively about customary laws, the common law and legal pluralism, and is the editor-in-chief of the *Journal of Legal Pluralism*. His recent publications include *Customary Land Law in the Ghanaian Courts* (Accra, Ghana Universities Press, 1994); 'Ideological Combat and Social Observation: Recent Debate about Legal Pluralism' (1998) 42 *Journal of Legal Pluralism* 21; 'Droit comparé général' in W Capeller and T Kitmura (eds), *Une introduction aux cultures juridiques non occidentales* (Brussels, Bruylant, 1998); with U Wanitzek, 'Relating Local Legal Activity to Global Influences: a Theoretical Survey' in GR Woodman, U Wanitzek and H Sippel (eds), *Local Land Law and Globalization: a Comparative Study of Peri-Urban Areas in Benin, Ghana and Tanzania* (Münster, LIT Verlag, 2004) 1; 'The Involvement of English Common Law with Other Laws' in C Eberhard and G Vernicos (eds), *La quête anthropologique du droit: autour de la démarche d'Étienne Le Roy* (Paris, Éditions Karthala, 2006) 477.

Introduction

ALISON DUNDES RENTELN AND MARIE-CLAIRE FOBLETS

I N THIS BOOK we have gathered together analytic essays demonstrating the widespread use of the cultural defence in many countries around the world. This monograph contains illustrations from Australia, Belgium, Canada, England, Germany, the Netherlands, Singapore, Spain, South Africa and the United States. The data prove irrefutably that courts are increasingly expected to resolve conflicts that require substantial cultural expertise, despite their lack of familiarity with ethnography and other tools of cultural analysis. We regard this as a serious problem.

This project was designed to provide a comparative analysis of the cultural defence. By focusing on the trial strategy of referring to litigants' cultural background in the courtroom, we aimed to show the range of possible situations in which attorneys may invoke this defence. We had several goals in mind: to document the range of experiences individuals have in presenting cultural evidence in legal systems; to encourage scholars to undertake research projects investigating uses of the cultural defences in other jurisdictions; and to inspire practitioners to consider the possibility of raising cultural defences in appropriate cases. An overriding concern of ours was to question whether there is sufficient expertise to handle the numerous cases in which cultural issues arise.

It was not our intent to develop a new theoretical model for analysing cultural defences in legal systems around the world. Nor did we expect that the contributors to this work would have a common conception of the cultural defence. Realising that there are various interpretations of the defence, we were interested in trying to find different approaches to the study of culture conflict in legal proceedings. Moreover, it was our hope that the research inspired by the meeting would reveal a broad range of possible uses of cultural arguments in court. By raising awareness of the ubiquity and variation in the forms, we aim to encourage others to identify the historic and contemporary practice in additional legal systems. We trust that the illustrations contained in this book will pave the way for others who wish to engage in further consideration of the phenomenon. This book is only the beginning of this project.

The volume is based on papers given at the Onati International Institute of the Sociology of Law in June 2005. The colloquium 'Multicultural Jurisprudence: Comparative Perspectives on the Cultural Defense' was convened in order to shift the discussion of the cultural defence from the United States only to other countries which have also witnessed the rise of cultural defences.[1] We perceived a need to include scholars from these places in the conversation. We attempted to bring together our colleagues from different academic disciplines, including some who had already published on the subject, as well as individuals who had not previously carried out research in this area. By involving new scholars in the investigation of the phenomenon, we would gain new insights. Although we invited scholars from many continents, the challenges of travel and ill-health prevented some of our colleagues from joining us. We recognise that the bulk of the essays concentrate on cultural defences in Western Europe and wish we had obtained essays from even more countries. In the future, more research is needed to examine how cultural defences figure into legal proceedings in other parts of the world.

The essays in this collection do not share a common conceptual framework. Indeed, some of the contributors have different ideas about what constitutes a cultural defence. While some view it as primarily a criminal law matter, others consider the role of cultural factors in other fields of law, eg, child welfare, housing codes and asylum jurisprudence. We left it to the participants to analyse the role of cultural factors in legal processes as they saw fit. It will be up to the reader to decide if some went too far in what they included as relevant cultural defence cases in their data collection. However, our goal was not to offer a definitive statement about what the cultural defence encompasses. Rather, we were interested in finding out more about the range of possible uses of cultural evidence and divergent scholarly approaches to this important issue. Insofar as our purpose was to document the phenomenon in countries where little or no data existed, this work is a success.

As the scholars who contributed to this volume take differing views of the benefits of the cultural defence, we wish to emphasise here that we are not advancing any argument in particular in this book. We recognise that the cultural defence is a mechanism which can protect certain aspects of cultures. Although some may acknowledge the factual existence of this strategy, they may argue strongly that the accommodation of cultural differences should occur in extra-legal contexts. While conceding that it may be preferable to safeguard traditions in other institutional settings, we contend that sometimes the only way to help individuals belonging to ethnic minority groups is in a court of law.

The first set of essays examines definitional questions, as well as theoretical issues that arise in debates that centre on questions concerning if and

---

[1] Reading the English language commentary, one might have the misimpression that the cultural defense is employed exclusively in the United States.

when use of the cultural defence is legitimate. Although these chapters do contain concrete cases, their primary objective is to offer conceptual clarification of the parameters of the strategy. Part II is comprised of country studies that discuss various contexts in which cultural defences are raised in particular national jurisdictions. The essays in Part III offer analyses of specific issues or particular groups. The final Part contains papers that address the role legal actors play in interpreting cultural issues by legal actors and the tacit assumptions by which they operate. The master bibliography at the end of the collection contains all the sources to which authors refer throughout the book, as well as a number of additional sources with a view to offer the reader an instrument for further research and investigations.

One of the insights in the book is that public officials ought to be cautious about the consideration of culture. There is reason to be concerned about the lack of expertise evident in the behaviour of lawyers, judges and other legal actors. The contributors raise important questions. By what standards should expertise be measured? Should scholars with academic credentials enjoy a privileged status in court as opposed to the representatives of the cultural communities whose traditions are at the centre of the litigation? How should a tradition be evaluated when there is internal disagreement about its continuation? Should experts receive compensation for testifying about cultural practices? Should testifying be compulsory as a form of civic duty? Why it is more difficult to introduce cultural evidence in some legal systems compared to others? Would the adoption of a formal cultural defence address some of these evidentiary challenges?

It is, of course, true that some aspects of culture do not deserve protection. This view is most obvious in the discussion of honour killings. While one ought to limit the influence of culture as a mitigating factor in murder cases, it is important to note that cultural defences are raised in many other kinds of cases besides homicide. Therefore, although cases involving culturally motivated killings receive widespread media attention, we think that as a general practice it is dangerous to base public policy on sensational cases. The reason why scholars tend to focus on murder is not only that these cases enjoy a certain notoriety in the press, but also because the treatment of the cultural defence in law reviews also concentrates on these gory cases.

It is therefore our hope that the analysis of murder cases does not distract the reader from the more general arguments for and against the cultural defence. For in cases in which defendants invoke the cultural defence that do not involve the loss of life, there are, in our view, legitimate uses of this strategy. As always, there is the perennial question of 'where to draw the line'. But this volume is not intended to provide definite solutions to the problems we have identified. We hope that these provocative essays will spark interest in the subject, so that others will conduct further research on the potential uses of the cultural defences, as well as formulate policies concerning the limitations to their usage.

We are deeply indebted to all of the scholars who shared their thought-provoking scholarship with us. It is an honour to include their essays in this volume. We would also like to acknowledge the contributions of workshop participants whose insightful comments enriched our discussions. We thank Alepi Lida-Panagiota, Antonio Peña Jumpa, Odile Van der Vaeren, Hermine Wiersinga, and Unni Wikan. We owe an enormous debt of gratitude to the individuals at the Onati Institute who worked very hard to help us coordinate the travel of scholars from many places. Our special thanks go to Malen Gordoa Mendizabal without whose assistance we could not have organised the workshop. It was a privilege to have the opportunity to meet in such an idyllic setting, a place that gave us the freedom to contemplate a policy without distraction. We also wish to thank Betty Vanden Bavière who prepared the manuscript for publication. Her tremendous expertise, patience and sense of humour were much appreciated.

I

Theoretical Perspectives

1

The Culture Defence in English Common Law: the Potential for Development

GORDON R WOODMAN

DEFINITION OF THE CULTURE DEFENCE

T HE TOPIC FOR discussion in this volume is defined as:

> the question of whether or not people whose conduct conforms to rules of conduct prescribed by their culture are to be considered guilty and thus subject to punishment for the mere reason that their behaviour clashes with the rules of the dominant (national/official) legal system.[1]

However, in the literature on the 'cultural defense' (in this chapter the 'culture defence'),[2] the term is used to designate a variety of different processes, and in some instances to do this quite vaguely. For example, Alison Dundes Renteln's book entitled *The Cultural Defense* states at the outset that it aims 'to examine the nature of the debate surrounding the admissibility of cultural evidence in the courtroom'.[3] This designates clearly an object of debate, but, since the issue of the admissibility of evidence of culture may arise in circumstances other than the advancement of a defence, it is wider

---

[1] Introduction to this volume.

[2] Two minor comments may be made on linguistic questions. (1) The variation in spelling between the 'defence' of the majority of the English-writing world and the 'defense' of North America is unimportant: we should accept cultural diversity here. (2) The use of the adjective 'cultural' in this context seems grammatically erroneous. 'Cultural defence' should designate a defence which is an intrinsic part of a culture, just as a cultural dance and cultural antagonism are parts of cultures. In contrast, the present discussion is concerned with a defence which may exist within a legal system, not within a defendant's culture. It is a legal defence based upon culture. We refer similarly to the provocation defence, a legal defence based upon the fact of provocation of the defendant, and the defence of mistake, a legal defence based upon the fact that the defendant acted on the ground of a mistaken belief. If we speak of the cultural defence, we should refer to these as the provocative defence and the mistaken defence.

[3] AD Renteln, *The Cultural Defense* (New York, Oxford University Press, 2004) 5.

than the book title literally suggests. Moreover, it differs from many other definitions of the concept.[4] Because of this uncertainty it is necessary to begin by considering the meaning which will be given to the concept in this chapter.

If the culture defence is adopted in a legal system, a form of normative pluralism results. In some processes of that legal system, the norms of a certain culture will be applied, whereas in other processes norms derived from different sources such as state legislation and precedent will be exclusively applied. If the norms of the culture can be seen as legal norms, as are the norms of state law, this is an instance of legal pluralism, of the type which has been called 'state law pluralism'.[5]

The issue of the culture defence arises from cultural diversity, or 'multiculturalism', in a state. But the possible field of operation of a culture defence is not as extensive as the possible fields of legal pluralism and of cultural diversity and law. It is noteworthy that in Sebastian Poulter's book on *Ethnicity, Law and Human Rights*, concerned with cultural diversity and law in England, the term 'cultural defence' does not appear in the subject index.[6]

This section attempts to clarify a concept, not to describe an observed social phenomenon. Nevertheless, if the concept is to be helpful in explaining observed legal phenomena it must be defined by reference to the social phenomena of existing laws.

The Notion of Culture

For the present purpose this need not be examined at length. As a general question of social science, the meaning of culture is difficult and controversial. For this discussion it will suffice to take one of the many definitions which represents a widely adopted approach:

> Culture is a dynamic value system of learned elements, with assumptions, conventions, beliefs and rules permitting members of a group to relate to each other and to the world, to communicate and develop their creative potential.[7]

---

[4] See PJ Magnarella, 'Justice in a Culturally Pluralistic Society: the Cultural Defense on Trial' (1991) 19 *Journal of Ethnic Studies* 65, esp at 67; K Maddock, 'Note' (1992) XXI *Commission on Folk Law and Legal Pluralism Newsletter* 64; Law Reform Commission, *Multiculturalism and the Law*, Report no 57 (Sydney NSW, Law Reform Commission, 1992); WI Torry, 'Multicultural Jurisprudence and the Culture Defense' (1999) 44 *Journal of Legal Pluralism* 127; A Phillips, 'When Culture Means Gender: Issues of Cultural Defence in the English Courts' (2003) 66 *Modern Law Review* 510.

[5] GR Woodman, 'Unification or Continuing Pluralism in Family Law in Anglophone Africa: Past Experience, Present Realities, and Future Possibilities' (1988) 4 *Lesotho Law Journal* 33; GR Woodman, 'Ideological Combat and Social Observation: Recent Debate about Legal Pluralism' (1998) 42 *Journal of Legal Pluralism* 21.

[6] S Poulter, *Ethnicity, Law and Human Rights: the English Experience* (Oxford, Oxford University Press, 1998) referred to in Renteln, above n 3 at 222 n 11, as 'the most illuminating work' on multiculturalism and law.

[7] Canadian Commission for UNESCO, 'A Working Definition of "Culture"' (1977) 4 *Cultures* 78, cited and used in AD Renteln, 'Cultural Rights and Culture Defence: Cultural

Culture and its rules may include religion, since conventions, beliefs and rules may be accepted as part of a religious system of thought. It is, however, a condition of inclusion in the category of culture that the system be practised within a group, and not merely believed in by some individuals. In cases where this condition is met, the compulsion felt to observe the rules of a religion may be particularly strong.

The Notion of a Defence

This needs more discussion. It has been elaborated in terms of its use in state laws. Here the term is used to refer to any rule of law which provides that a defendant who would otherwise have been held liable is, because of a certain, defined circumstance, not to be liable.[8] So, for example, the defence of mistake applies if a defendant, who would otherwise be liable, must be acquitted because he or she is found to have done the criminal act as a result of a mistaken belief, and the circumstances are such that, if the belief had been correct, the act would not have been criminal. The defence of duress applies if a defendant would be liable were it not for the fact that he or she was compelled to commit the criminal act.

A defence operates also if a particular circumstance of an offence causes the defendant to be liable not for one wrong but for a lesser wrong included within it, as when in English common law an aspect of a homicide is said to reduce it from murder to manslaughter.[9] Furthermore, it is convenient in the present discussion to treat as a defence an aspect of a wrongful act which does not remove liability for an offence but results in a reduction of the punishment. That is to say, 'defence' includes grounds of mitigation, in the case which Maddock calls the 'weak cultural defence'.[10] The Introduction to this volume implies this, since immediately after the statement quoted

Concerns' in NJ Smelser and PB Baltes (eds), *International Encyclopedia of the Social & Behavioral Sciences* (Oxford, Pergamon, 2001) vol V, 3116, and Renteln, above n 3 at 10. It has been said that '[m]ore than 150 definitions of "culture" have been proposed in the literatures of anthropology, archaeology, sociology, and other disciplines' (MW Feldman, 'Cultural Evolution: Theory and Models' in Smelser and Baltes, *ibid* at 3057) There are surveys of the issues of definition of culture in Feldman, *ibid*, and in RA Schweder, 'Culture: Contemporary Views' in Smelser and Baltes, *ibid* at 3151; J-L Harouel, 'Culture, Sociology of' in Smelser and Baltes, *ibid* at 3179. Perhaps the most often cited definition is in AL Kroeber and C Kluckholn, *Culture: a Critical Review of Concepts and Definitions* (Cambridge, MA, The Museum, 1952) 357, but that is longer and more complex than is required for the present purpose.

[8] 'In casual language, anything that prevents conviction of a defendant is called a "defence", but this term includes doctrines that are very different from one another' (PH Robinson, *Structure and Function in Criminal Law* (Oxford, Clarendon Press, 1997) 11. As Robinson points out (*ibid*), the term is also used for processes such as the so-called 'alibi defence' which 'is not a legal doctrine but a form of factual counterclaim'.
[9] See generally Robinson, *ibid* at 11–12.
[10] Maddock, above n 4.

above, it continues: 'To what extent, if at all, should cultural imperatives mitigate punishment?'

The question arises also whether we should include both criminal and civil law defences in the concept. Although the term 'defence' could in English law refer to arguments which may be presented in both civil and criminal cases, we may wish to separate our discussion of civil actions from criminal. The quotation at the beginning of this chapter identifying the culture defence refers to a question of 'punishment'. Civil actions are aimed at compensation, not at punishment (with minor exceptions, as in the case of where punitive damages are awarded in a civil action). Where compensation is in issue there is a less persuasive ground for permitting a culture defence, so that different arguments need examination in relation to civil law. The present discussion is limited to the defence in criminal law.

It has been pointed out that in other legal systems, especially non-Western systems, the distinction between crime and civil wrong, or tort, is not drawn. However, this is not itself a strong argument for rejecting a reduction of the field of investigation on this ground. The distinction between, on the one hand, rules and processes aimed at punishment and, on the other, those aimed at compensation would appear a realistic distinction with significance for the culture defence.[11] The distinction is not without difficulty or exceptions. There may, for example, be a question whether the processes of restorative justice can be discussed in relation to the culture defence, since their objective appears not to be punishment. Here a more helpful criterion may be that of whether the acts in question are forbidden by the law. However, restorative justice is not at present a major phenomenon in the English legal system.

In discussing specifically the culture defence, there is no suggestion here that it exists only when the rules of state law make explicit reference to a defendant's culture. It is quite possible, as will be argued below, that a defence may be applicable on the occurrence of any instance of a broad category of facts, and some instances of that category may be cases where the criminal act is done as a result of the defendant's culture. Culture may thus be an issue when it is not mentioned in statements of the general rules of law. Whether it would be desirable to develop a rule providing for a defence explicitly and exclusively on the ground of culture is not a question which arises in defining the concept or investigating its application, although no doubt it is of importance for the law-maker.[12]

---

[11] Renteln, above n 7, refers to the use of the culture defence only in the case of 'criminal prosecution'.

[12] This issue is discussed especially fully, with reference primarily to US law, in AD Renteln, 'A Justification of the Cultural Defense as Partial Excuse' (1993) 2 *Southern California Review of Law and Women's Studies* 437.

Function of Culture in Cases of the Defence

The definition of the Introduction states that the circumstances which support the culture defence include the fact that the defendant's act was in accordance with 'rules of conduct prescribed by their culture'. The culture defence is thus seen as arising from the rules, or the normative aspect of a culture.

Two difficulties need mention. First, while the given definition refers only to acts which conform to rules prescribed by a culture, we may wish to consider whether the culture defence is concerned only with action prescribed by a culture, rather than merely permitted, or partly or completely excused by a culture. It is suggested that we should not limit discussion to cases where the actions are prescribed. There are perhaps some cultures which prescribe that, in response to certain insults which in a given state law would not justify any sort of violent reaction, the insulted person must kill the other. But there may also be some cultures in which rules would categorise such a killing as neither obligatory nor forbidden. And there are probably many more cultures which in this situation would classify the killing as wrong but as meriting a reduced punishment. We may wish to include all such cases in a consideration of the culture defence.

Secondly, a more fundamental difficulty is that we may wish to include certain cases where the action giving rise to the defendant's prospective liability may be explicable not so much by the rules as by the 'assumptions, conventions, beliefs' of their culture. For example, cases of witch killings may arise from different perceptions of reality. In some cultures it is believed that there exist people who have the power and the inclination to kill others by magical or supernatural means. If this belief were correct, the killing of a witch might be thought meritorious, and at least in certain circumstances would accord with state law rules about self-defence or the prevention of crime.[13] State laws usually proceed on the basis that these beliefs are mistaken, but it is worthwhile to consider whether there should be a defence available to a defendant who belongs to a culture in which they are generally held. Again, a defendant's actions may be explained in terms of cultural evaluations of others' behaviour, with the result that some forms of behaviour are seen as more insulting and provocative by the culture of a particular defendant than by others. The concept of the culture defence can be usefully extended to cover all cases where the action for which the defendant is presumptively liable follows either from the defendant's adherence to the norms of their culture or from the perceptions or evaluative understandings of that culture.

---

[13] RB Seidman, 'Witch Murder and *Mens Rea*: a Problem of Society under Radical Social Change' (1965) 28 *Modern Law Review* 46.

Types of Cultures in Question[14]

Are minority cultures necessarily in issue? Discussion of the issue in the context of an emphasis on the cultural diversity of many modern states often assumes that the culture defence is to be called upon when the defendant's culture is that of a minority, and differs significantly from that of the dominant majority. The assumptions here again need to be questioned. In the culturally diverse society, there may be no single 'majority' culture, nor is there necessarily one culture which is in all respects 'dominant'. The crucial issue is a clash between the culture followed by the defendant and that followed by the legal system. The question arises because some defendants act from motivation which is produced or influenced by cultures with norms, perceptions and values which differ from those which the law adopts and promotes.

Indeed, the law of a state may embody the values and beliefs of a small minority. Hence a 'dominant' culture may be the professional culture of a small influential elite, rather than the culture of an ethnic majority.[15] Although some law-makers may hold that state law must accord with the culture of the majority of the population,[16] it is not unusual for a small, unrepresentative group which controls the law-making processes of a state to make laws which are designed with the object of changing elements of 'popular' culture. In such a case the administrators of the law are unlikely to be receptive to pleas of a culture defence, for its acceptance might defeat the very purpose for which the law was made, and if accepted it might be raised very frequently. It is also possible that the law of a state may not be imbued throughout with one single culture, but rather that its cultural sources may vary.

For convenience this chapter continues to refer to cultures which are not central to state law as 'minority' cultures. It refers to the culture dominant in state law as the dominant culture. The possibility that there are two or more divergent cultures within state law may be met for the present purpose by noting that a reference to a dominant culture is a reference to the culture embedded in the particular portion of law which is in issue in a particular case.

---

[14] Insightful comments on the issues considered here may be found in JV Broeck, 'Cultural Defence and Culturally Motivated Crimes' (2001) 9 *European Journal of Crime, Criminal Law and Criminal Justice* 1.

[15] It is not necessary here to investigate the concept of legal cultures, which may be 'internal' to a legal profession, or 'external', consisting of public attitudes to a legal system. See further LM Friedman, *The Legal System: a Social Science Perspective* (New York, Russell Sage Foundation, 1975) 223; D Nelken (ed), *Comparing Legal Cultures* (Aldershot, Dartmouth, 1997); GR Woodman, 'Accommodation between Legal Cultures: the Global Encounters the Local in Ghanaian Land Law' (2001) *Recht in Afrika* 57, 58–64.

[16] See, eg, the argument developed in P Devlin, *The Enforcement of Morals* (Oxford, Oxford University Press, 1965).

Those observations prompt another about the use of the concept of culture in the present context. As in the discussion of legal pluralism generally, there may be a danger in treating each culture (or law) as clearly bounded, identifiable and distinct from any other with which it comes into contact.[17] The population of persons who observe a certain culture is not constant. Persons who observe a culture at one time and for one purpose may not observe it at another time or for another purpose. Furthermore, state law is not clearly distinct from other normative orders observed within the boundaries of the state, frequently and constantly deriving its principles from wider cultures. In the case of the culture defence we are by definition concerned with situations in which different cultures are in contact. Cultures in contact tend to interact and to undergo modifications as a result of their interrelations, although the extent of modifications is likely to be unequal as between the cultures affected, and to vary between individual actors within one culture. This should not prevent us from discussing the culture defence, but should caution us against facile conclusions in particular cases, or over-ready generalisation.

Focus on State Law

Finally it should be noted that the writers in this volume have chosen to focus on the operations and doctrines of state law, or national, 'official' law. The field has been implicitly defined as concerned only with the culture defence in state law. It is not proposed to depart from this, but it is suggested that we should be aware of the limitation. It is likely that there are non-state, customary and religious laws, or 'living laws',[18] which sometimes recognise other laws and so may contain culture defences. We exclude these from the discussion for convenience, not because we do not regard these other laws as 'laws'.

It is open to debate whether we conceive of state law as, in Roscoe Pound's terms, the law in the books or the law in action, or as a form of living law in the sense used by Ehrlich.[19] Renteln sees it as the law in action, and places emphasis on the elucidation of what happens in the courtroom.[20] From the viewpoint of the social observer, as distinct from the legal

[17] GR Woodman, 'Non-State, Unbounded, Unsystematic, Non-Western Law' in M Chiba (ed), *Sociology of Law in Non-Western Countries*, Oñati Proceedings 15 (Oñati International Institute for the Sociology of Law, 1993); GR Woodman, 'Why there Can be No Map of Law' in R Pradhan (ed), *Legal Pluralism and Unofficial Law in Social, Economic and Political Development*, Papers of the XIIIth International Congress, 7–10 April, Chiang Mai, Thailand (Kathmandu, ICNEC, 2003).

[18] E Ehrlich, *Fundamental Principles of the Sociology of Law* (WL Moll (trans), Cambridge, MA, Harvard University Press, 1936)

[19] D Nelken, 'Law in Action or Living Law? Back to the Beginning in Sociology of Law' (1984) 4 *Legal Studies* 157; Ehrlich, above n 18.

[20] Renteln, above n 3.

practitioner, this may be too narrow. On the other hand, in a discussion limited to state criminal law, it is often sufficient to focus on happenings in the courtroom.

The following definition of a culture defence is therefore proposed for the present purpose:

> A culture defence is a rule of state law which constitutes a complete or partial defence to a crime or mitigation which reduces the punishment, and which takes effect where the defendant would not have committed the criminal act had they not belonged to a particular culture.

CURRENT STATE OF THE CULTURE DEFENCE IN ENGLISH COMMON LAW

Much discussion of the culture defence, such as that of Renteln, ranges across many jurisdictions, even when, as in her work, it concentrates primarily on one. It may appear unduly insular to examine English law alone, especially as there are considerable similarities between the various systems of common law in the world. However, a concentration on one jurisdiction may facilitate more rigorous argument and enable comparative studies to be better conducted. Moreover, a distinctive version of common law is applied in England, and so developments in the field of the culture defence should not be assumed to be much the same in that country as those elsewhere.

Historical Recognition of Cultural Diversity

There are grounds for holding that English law has historically displayed a readiness to adopt bodies of non-state law observed by sections of the population. We may briefly summarise this argument.[21]

The rules and principles of English law emerged from the work of the royal courts in the early medieval period. These courts were seen as institutions established by the Crown to perform the function of applying pre-existing laws and customs. Generally it was accepted that there existed within the population a wide variety of personal laws with fields of application defined by groups of persons as well as by territorial areas. The royal courts established judicial customs or precedents specifying the rules applicable throughout the realm as 'common law', but did not discard the principle that the customary laws of particular communities within the

---

[21] The following paragraphs are a summary of arguments developed in GR Woodman, 'The One True Law, or One Among Others? The Self-Image of English Common Law', paper delivered at XIVth International Congress of the Commission on Folk Law and Legal Pluralism, Fredericton, Canada, 26–29 August 2004, to be published in revised form.

jurisdiction were to be recognised and enforced. Thus they recognised the customary laws of the Jewish community, as well as the customary laws of groups inhabiting particular localities provided that they met requirements of antiquity and reasonableness. The principle of recognition of personal law was continued subsequently through the colonial period. English law was exported to govern British citizens in colonial territories as settlers or officials, but the religious and customary laws observed by indigenous populations were also seen as valid laws. Colonial courts either declined jurisdiction when such local laws were applicable, or themselves endeavoured to apply these laws in appropriate cases. The courts of England continued to recognise and enforce customary laws, and increasingly gave recognition to newly emerging customary laws such as those of transnational commercial communities. It was only in criminal law, significantly for the present purpose, that there was generally an insistence on a near-exclusive enforcement of English state law.

Some of the issues of the culture defence which are acute in other jurisdictions do not arise in England. Questions as to the rights of an indigenous people to the use of natural resources have elsewhere in the world given rise to critical debate when indigenous peoples have been prosecuted for breaches of laws designed to control the use of natural resources such as forests and game. These have not arisen in England for a very long time.

English law is also distinctive in that it has until recently provided almost no room for explicit reliance on constitutional rules conferring rights to engage in practices derived from a specific culture, and which could override other laws, including primary legislation creating crimes. There were no such rights in English law. The law of the European Union, and the Human Rights Act 1998 (taking effect in 2000) which makes the European Convention on Human Rights enforceable in certain ways and to a certain extent in English law, have begun to move this law away from the doctrine of parliamentary sovereignty. However, EU law has at present little bearing on the issues of culture considered here. The Human Rights Act 1998 contrives to maintain parliamentary sovereignty: it requires laws to be interpreted to accord with the European Convention on Human Rights insofar as this is possible, but it does not invalidate laws which are incompatible with Convention rights. The particular arguments for a culture defence based upon, for example, the Bill of Rights in the Constitution of the United States cannot be embarked upon in England.

There have been certain recent general trends in criminal law which affect the question. One of the most obvious is the increase in the legal regulation of life, often in respect of relatively minor activities such as the driving of motor vehicles and the maintenance of health and safety at work, supported by criminal sanctions. Because there are more prohibitory rules in the law today, there are more possibilities of conflicts with the prescriptive or permissive norms of cultures, and so more circumstances in which there is likely to be debate over whether a culture defence should be available.

It is also noteworthy that law-makers in the common law world have historically been more reluctant to adjust the criminal law to allow for cultural diversity than they have been for most branches of law. The British colonial policy of recognising 'native law and custom' being generally rejected in the field of criminal law, in the latter half of the nineteenth century criminal and penal codes were enacted for most common law territories in the Commonwealth, except England. These codes made almost no explicit provision for concessions to particular cultures. Colonial legal policy in this respect reflected the policy of English law.

All suggestions that there might be a general defence based overtly on the culture of the defendant have been rejected. An oft-cited illustration is the case *R v Barronet and Allain*,[22] where the two accused, political exiles from France, had been seconds in a duel fought in England between two Frenchmen which had ended with the death of one of the duellists. They were charged with murder. They admitted the facts, but argued that within their culture these would not amount to murder if the duel was properly and fairly conducted, as it was in this case. The reported case concerned only their application for bail pending the trial, but for this purpose the probability of their conviction was relevant. The court held that there was no doubt that the admitted facts amounted to wilful murder. The accused were in exactly the same position as native born subjects, and would be dealt with at trial in exactly the same way. Bail would have been refused to English accused in such circumstances, and therefore it must be refused to them.

If culture defences can be found in English law, they are likely to arise from the implications of other, general defences, not from express provision. In the following discussion, therefore, the next, brief section considers exemptions which refer to culture, and the other, longer parts consider the possibility that culture defences may arise by implication.

'Exemptions' on the Ground of Culture

This is concerned with what have been called 'offence modification defences'.[23] Any such defence is a rule which modifies the definition of an offence by creating an exception so that, if specified circumstances are present, an act which would, in the absence of these circumstances, constitute the offence, is outside the definition. If the special circumstances are that the defendant had a certain culture, and did the act as a result of this, a

---

[22] (1852) 169 ER 633.
[23] Robinson, above n 8 at 12.

version of the culture defence could be involved. In English law there are few such cases. Those which exist are related to the increase in regulatory law just mentioned.

These exemption cases have been listed by Poulter.[24] Three apply especially to Sikhs. A requirement of the Sikh religion is that men should wear a turban at all times. The primary provision of the Motor-Cycle Crash Helmets (Religious Exemption) Act 1976 (since re-enacted in the Road Traffic Act 1988, s 16(2)) is to the effect that legal regulations requiring the rider of a motorcycle to wear a crash helmet 'shall not apply to any follower of the Sikh religion while he is wearing a turban'. The Employment Act 1989, s 11 provides that the legal requirements to wear safety helmets on construction sites shall not apply to a Sikh 'when he is wearing a turban'. The third provision does not mention Sikhs specifically but it was enacted with reference to the requirement of Sikh religion that men carry a *kirpan* (a small sword) with them at all times. The Criminal Justice Act 1988, s 139, creates the offence of having an article with a blade or a point in a public place. Section 139(5)(b) provides:

> it shall be a defence for a person charged with an offence under this section to prove that he had the article with him ... (b) for religious reasons.

This subsection is not restricted to Sikhs, although it is likely that they will be the main, if not the sole beneficiaries of the quoted paragraph.[25] However, the next paragraph exempts a person who has the article 'as part of any national costume', which could have a wider cultural implication.

The Slaughterhouses Act 1974, s 36(4), continuing in force earlier provisions, and the Slaughter of Poultry Act 1967, s 1, provide that animals must be slaughtered instantaneously, or rendered insensible to pain instantaneously until death intervenes. This excludes the forms of slaughter enjoined by the Jewish and Muslim religions; exemptions are provided from the criminal offences of breach of the Acts where a mode of slaughter is followed in pursuance of the requirements of those religions.[26]

Thus the list of such cases is short. Numbers of proposals to introduce other exemptions, for example, as to the use of prohibited drugs for religious purposes, have been rejected.[27]

---

[24] Poulter, above n 6 at ch 8, giving an account of the historical background to these provisions and the debates at the time of their enactment. See also A Samuels, 'Legal Recognition and Protection of Minority Customs in a Plural Society in England' (1981) *Anglo-American Law Review* (now *Common Law World Review*) 241, 244.

[25] Poulter, above n 6 at 50.

[26] The issues are examined, primarily with reference to the Jewish religion, in Poulter, above n 6 at 130–46. The issue is considered, in discussion of broader issues concerning the treatment of animals, in Renteln, above n 3 at ch 6, and especially the notes thereto at 268–9.

[27] On the use of cannabis by Rastafarians, see Poulter, above n 6 at 355–69. The legal position has not changed significantly since Poulter wrote.

Defences which may Include Cases of a Culture Defence

Thus there is no general culture defence in English common law, and the criminal law has been developed, largely through case law, on the basis that it should be uniformly applicable to all. Nevertheless, it is necessary to consider a number of general defences which operate when certain broad categories of facts are present, since some instances of these could conceivably form subcategories which would amount to a culture defence. As a hypothetical example (for the sake of illustration, although it is not an account of current English law) we could suppose a defence of duress which allowed a defendant to avoid conviction on the ground that they were compelled to do the criminal act. It is possible that a law could include within this defence some instances where the source of the compulsion was a prescriptive norm of a minority culture. The opening up of this possibility through general principles may be easier to achieve in fields subject to general common law than in those controlled by detailed regulatory law. Four such general principles are considered here, those of mistake, duress, self-defence and provocation.

The possibilities of the application of culture defences are limited. English law has identified some instances of offences attributable to culture where it is considered that overriding principles of justice require no concession to be made. Thus it is considered that honour killings, and presumably all forms of honour-related violence, are to be prevented by deterrence and by any other means which assert that these acts are not to be regarded as less culpable on the ground of the offenders' cultures.[28] Further, some practices such as female 'circumcision' (female genital mutilation), said to be required or encouraged by some cultures, but regarded as especially reprehensible, have been the subject of specific criminal provisions, notwithstanding that they were already criminal offences.[29]

There have been very few cases in England where there has been discussion of the possibility of applying these four defences as culture defences. The following exploration is in terms of potential, not actual development. The four defences to be considered have a common feature. It was said in *R v Graham (Paul)*:

> As a matter of public policy, it seems to us essential to limit the defence of duress by means of an objective criterion formulated in the terms of reasonableness ...

---

[28] A recent European exploration of this issue is B Björling *et al*, *European Conference Report, Honour Related Violence within a Global Perspective: Mitigation and Prevention in Europe* (Stockholm, 2004). The media in the United Kingdom indicate that this problem is increasing, but significantly there is no literature which discusses it in terms of a possible culture defence.

[29] Eg Prohibition of Female Circumcision Act 1985.

Provocation and duress are analogous. In provocation the words or actions of one person break the self-control of another. In duress the words or actions of one person break the will of another. The law requires a defendant to have the self-control reasonably to be expected of the ordinary citizen in his situation. It should likewise require him to have the steadfastness reasonably to be expected of the ordinary citizen in his situation. So too with self-defence, in which the law permits the use of no more force than is reasonable in the circumstances. And, in general, if a mistake is to excuse what would otherwise be criminal, the mistake must be a reasonable one.[30]

This reference in all four defences to the notions of 'reasonableness' held by 'the ordinary citizen' gives rise to the question whether the latter phrase means exclusively a person who belongs to the dominant culture. If that were the case, the possibility of defences based on specific elements of minority cultures would be excluded. The courts have sometimes recognised that that which is regarded as 'reasonable' may vary with the characteristics of the persons concerned. Thus in *R v Blaue*, a case where the victim of a stabbing had died, but would almost certainly have survived had she not refused on religious grounds to receive a blood transfusion (being a Jehovah's Witness), it was argued that her refusal was unreasonable.[31] The court held that whether it was unreasonable or not had no bearing on the liability of the attacker under the law of murder. However, on the question of reasonableness the court said:

> At once the question arises—reasonable by whose standards? Those of Jehovah's Witnesses? Humanists? Roman Catholics? Protestants of Anglo-Saxon descent? The man on the Clapham omnibus? But he might well be an admirer of Eleazar who suffered death rather than eat the flesh of swine (2 Maccabees. ch. 6, vv. 18–31) or of Sir Thomas More who, unlike nearly all his contemporaries, was unwilling to accept Henry VIII as Head of the Church in England ...

> [T]wo cases, each raising the same issue of reasonableness because of religious beliefs, could produce different verdicts depending on where the cases were tried. A jury drawn from Preston, sometimes said to be the most Catholic town in England, might have different views about martyrdom to one drawn from the inner suburbs of London. [Counsel for the defendant] accepted that this might be so: it was, he said, inherent in trial by jury. It is not inherent in the common law.

Thus in this case the uncertainty about the criterion of reasonableness was said to be a ground for not applying a rule which turned on that criterion. However, in the defences under consideration here the law seems to be committed to its use.

---

[30] *R v Graham (Paul)* [1982] 1 WLR 294, 300, approved by the House of Lords in *R v Howe* [1987] AC 417.
[31] *R v Blaue* (1975) 61 Cr App R 271.

These four defences are considered below. In the following section, there is consideration of the possibility of a culture defence operating not to prevent conviction but as a mitigating factor in relation to sentencing the accused after a conviction. Finally, in each instance where a culture defence may be available the practical question arises as to how the judge, who will not usually have much or any knowledge of the culture in question, is to be informed of the relevant aspects of that culture.

Mistake

The general rule of the common law is that, if a person does a criminal act as a result of holding a mistaken belief, they are not guilty if, had the belief been true, the act would not have been a crime. If, for example, a person shoots dead another person, in the belief that they are shooting an animal, they are not guilty of homicide. Strictly the mistake in this type of case does not found a defence but rather constitutes the absence of an essential element of the crime, *mens rea*, a guilty mind.[32] However, it is commonly referred to as a defence, sometimes called an 'absent element' defence.[33]

It was long held that, for a mistaken belief to provide a defence, it must be a belief which it was reasonable to hold in the circumstances, as stated in the passage quoted above from *R v Graham (Paul)*.[34] That rule could have been a significant restriction on a potential culture defence, since there could have been a tendency to categorise as unreasonable beliefs prevalent in other cultures but not held in the culture which was dominant in English law. The rule was decisively rejected by the House of Lords in 1976 in *R v Morgan*.[35] Today, while it is accepted that the defendant who claims to have held a highly unreasonable belief may not be believed, it is held that any belief if truly held can be the basis for the defence of mistake. The current law is stated in *R v Williams*, where it was said:

> The reasonableness or unreasonableness of the defendant's belief is material to the question of whether the belief was held by the defendant at all. If the belief was in fact held, its unreasonableness, so far as guilt or innocence is concerned, is neither here nor there.[36]

---

[32] *R v Morgan* [1976] AC 182, esp at 360, discussed AP Simester and GR Sullivan, *Criminal Law: Theory and Doctrine* (2nd edn, Oxford, Hart Publishing, 2003) 548–9.

[33] Robinson, above n 8 at 11–12.

[34] See also *The Queen v Tolson* (1889) 23 QBD 168, where a defence of mistake was upheld by a majority of the court, and it was assumed throughout the judgments that, if a mistake was to be a defence, it must be a reasonable mistake.

[35] *R v Morgan* [1976] AC 182.

[36] *R v Williams* [1987] 3 All ER 411, 415. A similar view was taken earlier in *Wilson v Inyang* [1951] 2 KB 799, where the lack of an 'honest belief' was held to be an element of the offence of 'wilfully and falsely [using] the title of physician', under the Medical Act 1858. It

A mistake as to the provisions of the law is not within this defence: 'ignorance of the law is no excuse'. This follows from the principle that the basis of the defence is an absence of one of the elements of a crime. It is not generally an element of a crime that the perpetrator should know that the act is contrary to law. Thus an early case established that a foreigner who entered England might be liable for an act which was a criminal offence in England, even though it was not an offence in their home country and they were unaware that it was an offence in England.[37] As in that case, it would seem that this rule may affect a disproportionate number of immigrants from non-European cultures, who would wish to use the defence of mistake as a form of culture defence. It can also affect European immigrants, as was shown in *R v Barronet and Allain*.[38] The claim there that the accused may not have known the English law on duelling was said to be immaterial.

It is arguable that there are minor exceptions to this rule on mistakes of law. A statutory provision which creates a crime may expressly or impliedly limit the offence to require knowledge of some element of the illegality. Thus the Theft Act 1968, s 1 provides:

(1) A person is guilty of theft if he dishonestly appropriates property belonging to another with the intention of permanently depriving the other of it.

and s. 2 then provides:

(1) A person's appropriation of property belonging to another is not to be regarded as dishonest:
(a) if he appropriates the property in the belief that he has in law the right to deprive the other of it.

Such a claim of lack of the element of dishonesty might be especially credible if advanced by a defendant accustomed to a quite different system of property law from the English state system.[39]

Another possible exception may be provided by Articles 6 and 7 of the European Convention on Human Rights guaranteeing the right to a

---

was held that, while it would not have been reasonable for a European in the position of the accused to believe that he was qualified to practise medicine, and so a claim to have honestly believed he was entitled to practice would not have been believed, the accused in this case having arrived from Africa only two years previously, the trial court could have reasonably concluded that he had an honest belief.

[37] *R v Esop* (1836) 173 ER 203. In that particular case there was no conviction, but only because the evidence was held not to be sufficient.

[38] Above n 22.

[39] See also *Wilson v Inyang*, above n 36, where the mistake was also in part a mistake of law.

fair trial and prohibiting retroactive criminal laws. Either of these might perhaps protect a defendant who could not have known of a newly enacted criminal statute.[40]

The defence of mistake commonly operates in conjunction with other defences. Thus if a case is adjudged on the basis that the facts were in reality as the defendant mistakenly believed them to be, the defendant may succeed in arguing the defence of duress, self-defence or provocation. Further consideration of mistake will be deferred until these defences are considered. Cases in which a mistake of fact, without more, is relied upon do not appear to be common in England, and none are known in which the mistake arose from the defendant's membership of a particular culture. We may note the possibility but it is not useful to pursue it further.

Duress and Coercion

Two types of the defence of duress have been established. First, duress by threat means that the defendant did a criminal act as a result of someone threatening to inflict death or serious bodily harm on the defendant or another person unless the criminal act was done, and there was no other means of avoiding the threatened attack. This defence applies:

> if the will of the accused has been overborne by threats of death or serious personal injury so that the commission of the alleged offence was no longer the voluntary act of the accused.[41]

Secondly, a defence of duress of circumstances appears to be available where there is a threat of death or serious bodily harm, but where the criminal act in response is not demanded by the person issuing the threat, and may indeed be done in order to escape from him. Thus in *R v Conway*[42] it was held that this defence could be advanced to a charge of reckless driving of a motor vehicle where the act was done in an attempt to escape from men who were believed to be attempting to kill the car's passenger. This defence is sometimes referred to as the defence of necessity, although some writers insist that the term should be reserved to a different defence, mentioned

---

[40] However, the recent decision in *Christian and others v The Queen*, unreported, Pitcairn Court of Appeal, 2 March 2006, holds that, if a criminal statute is 'accessible' to the general public, and it is generally known or assumed that the conduct is criminal, a defence based specifically on the Human Rights Act 1998 or generally on the principles proclaimed therein will not succeed. An appeal in this case to the Privy Council is pending at the time of writing.

[41] *R v Hudson* [1971] 2 QB 202, 206 (where the offence was perjury in giving false evidence at another criminal trial). The subsequent case *R v Graham (Paul)*, above n 30, has now been established as the leading authority on this rule for duress.

[42] *R v Conway* [1989] 1 QB 290.

below. The defence is not available in either case where the crime is murder or attempted murder.[43]

A defendant from a culture in which persons in their situation were expected to show a lesser degree of steadfastness in the face of threats, or of threats from certain classes of persons, might argue that they were deprived by their culture of the ability to act voluntarily even though a person from the dominant culture in a similar situation might have been able to resist. However, the quotation given above from *R v Graham (Paul)*[44] shows that 'the law requires a defendant to have ... the steadfastness reasonably to be expected of the ordinary citizen in his situation'. Thus an 'objective criterion formulated in terms of reasonableness' must be applied. The cases speak of the test as being that of 'an ordinary person sharing the characteristics of the defendant', but in which the only characteristics to be considered are those such as:

> age, where a young person may not be so robust as a mature one; possibly sex, though many women would doubtless consider they had as much moral courage to resist pressure as men; pregnancy, where there is added fear for the unborn child; serious physical disability, which may inhibit self-protection; recognised mental illness or psychiatric condition, such as post-traumatic stress disorder leading to learnt helplessness.[45]

This view has been criticised,[46] but it stands at present. It is not easy to envisage a culture defence succeeding as a special instance of a simple case of duress.

Of more potential for a culture defence are cases where the defence of duress is combined with a claim of mistake. A possible instance arises where a defendant has been threatened with death or serious injury, to be brought about by means such as sorcery, which are not believed in by members of the dominant culture. A court would presumably regard a belief in the efficacy of sorcery as mistaken, but might accept that it could be genuinely held. As has been seen, as a general rule the defence of mistake is subjective, not objective, so that a belief regarded as unreasonable can afford a defence. However, a difficulty arises. The decision in *R v Graham (Paul)* asserts that the approach in all respects to a defence of duress must be objective. In that case it was said that the judge should have directed the jury to consider whether the defendant had acted 'as a result of what he *reasonably* believed' had been said or done.[47] On the other hand, it was

---

[43] *R v Howe* [1987] AC 417; *R v Gotts* [1992] 2 AC 412.
[44] Above n 30.
[45] *R v Bowen* [1997] 1 WLR 372.
[46] KJM Smith, 'Duress and Steadfastness: in Pursuit of the Unintelligible' (1999) *Criminal Law Review* 363.
[47] Above n 30 at 300 (emphasis added).

held in *R v Martin (David)* that a subjective test should be applied, and if the defendant honestly believed that the threats would be carried out he was not liable, even if his holding the belief was shown by medical evidence to be attributable to his suffering from a schizoid-affective disorder, indicating that the threats would not have been credible to an 'ordinary' person.[48]

If the requirement of a reasonable belief is sustained, there may still be room for argument. To hold a mistaken belief of the type in question in a particular case may well be reasonable on the part of 'ordinary persons' within the defendant's culture, but not for ordinary persons within others. This may be a case where it will become necessary to decide whether the 'ordinary person' is only the person belonging to the dominant culture, or to adopt a wider, variable view of ordinariness.[49]

The similar defence of 'coercion' is referred to by statute in the following terms:

> on a charge against a wife for any offence other than treason or murder, it shall be a good defence to prove that the offence was committed in the presence of, and under the coercion of, the husband.[50]

The coercion need not amount to the physical force or threats of physical force which are requisite for the defence of duress.[51] It has been suggested that the defence is excluded if the defendant's marriage is polygamous, on the ground that this type of marriage was not recognised in English law at the time when the defence was developed.[52] It has been argued to the contrary that in modern circumstances this would be anomalous.[53] If this were the rule, the defence would generally be unavailable to those who belonged to cultures in which marriages are potentially polygamous.[54] It was held in one case that the defence was not available to a defendant who was not in law married to the instigator of the offence, even if she reasonably believed that she was,[55] although it has been argued that she should in principle be able to rely on the defence of mistake in such a case.[56] The entire defence of coercion as defined has been criticised and its abolition has been recommended.[57]

---

[48] *R v Martin (David)* (2000) 2 Cr App R 42.
[49] See Seidman, above n 13; RB Seidman, 'The Inarticulate Premiss' (1965) 3 *Journal of Modern African Studies* 567.
[50] Criminal Justice Act 1925, s 47.
[51] *R v Shortland* (1996) 1 Cr App R 116.
[52] *R v Ditta, Hussain and Kara* [1988] Crim LR 42.
[53] Simester and Sullivan, above n 32 at 602–3; JC Smith, *Smith and Hogan on Criminal Law* (10th edn), London, LexisNexis Butterworths, 2002 266.
[54] See generally Smith, *ibid* at 264–6.
[55] *R v Ditta, Hussain and Kara* [1988] Crim LR 42.
[56] Simester and Sullivan, above n 32 at 602.
[57] Simester and Sullivan, above n 32 at 603; Smith, above n 53 at 266.

Self-Defence and the Prevention of Crime

English common law, in the sense of law consolidated in judicial precedent, exempts a person from criminal liability for using force to defend themselves against an attack. An attack is itself usually a criminal offence, and English common law also has long exempted a person from criminal liability for using force to prevent the commission of a crime. This latter rule has been clarified and arguably extended by the Criminal Law Act 1967, s 3(1), which provides: '(1) A person may use such force as is reasonable in the circumstances in the prevention of crime'. It is generally assumed that this provision applies to all cases of self-defence, even when the attack is not a crime, as where the attacker lacks *mens rea* by reason of insanity, or the defendant acted on the mistaken belief that they were about to be attacked.[58]

It has been settled that the questions, whether it was necessary to use force, and whether the amount of force used was proportionate to the lawful objective, are questions of fact. However, the courts have stated in some detail what will be regarded as an appropriate reaction to an attack, indicating that certain normative standards will be employed. Thus it was said in *R v Julien*:

> It is not, as we understand it, the law that a person threatened must take to his heels and run...; but what is necessary is that he should demonstrate by his actions that he does not want to fight. He must demonstrate that he is prepared to temporise and disengage and perhaps to make some physical withdrawal. [59]

An argument could be made for claiming that such standards could justifiably be applied with varying results according to the culture of the accused. To persons from, for example, a culture which regards any affront to the physical integrity of a man as very serious and requiring to be resisted to the utmost, and which proclaims that a person should never 'withdraw', the amount of force which it is 'reasonable' to use in resistance may be greater than in other cultures. There seems to have been no mention of this possibility hitherto.

Again the greatest possibility of defences based upon the cultures of defendants would seem to lie in cases where the defendant has mistakenly believed in facts which, if they had existed, might have founded one of the forms of this defence. Again it is necessary to consider whether a mistake in these cases needs to be based on grounds which are reasonable in the view of the judge or jury. The case *R v Williams* quoted above was a case of prevention of crime, and it emphatically declares that the mistake need not be 'reasonable'. This approach appears different from that adopted in

---

[58] Simester and Sullivan, above n 32 at 603; Smith, above n 53 at 266.
[59] *R v Julien* [1969] 1 WLR 839, 843.

R v Martin (Anthony).[60] There it was held that, although the defendant's own belief as to the situation in which he was placed must be accepted, in deciding whether he had used excessive force no account should be taken of evidence that he may have been suffering from some psychiatric condition. The distinction has been criticised as 'spurious'.[61]

The grounds for doubt may be seen if we suppose the case of a defendant who, in accordance with his culture, believes that a certain person is liable to kill him or a member of his household by witchcraft, and reacts with violence against that person.[62] To determine whether the defendant has a defence, three questions must be negotiated. First, assuming that the court must categorise the belief as mistaken, it is necessary to decide whether it must nevertheless proceed on the basis of the view that the victim was a dangerous witch. If the answer is in the affirmative, the second question arises: is the defendant's estimate of the danger presented by the victim, if genuinely held, to be accepted, or must the court ask whether it was reasonable in the circumstances? This question can hardly be separated from the first. But thirdly, if it must be taken that the victim was threatening an imminent danger to the defendant or someone else, it is still necessary to ask whether the use of force by the defendant in the degree with which it was used, was reasonable in the circumstances. To answer this it would be simpler to ask whether the defendant's act would be regarded as reasonable within the defendant's community of culture than to ask whether the dominant culture would take that view on the counter-factual assumption that it believed in the supernatural danger. It would be difficult for a judge or juror of the dominant culture to apply their own cultural perspectives to determine whether, for example, a more appropriate reaction to a threat of harm by witchcraft would be to hire another sorcerer to produce an antidote 'medicine'.

In English law a defence of necessity has been debated in recent years.[63] Its rationale and scope are unclear, and it would seem premature to consider whether it could exist in a form which would amount to a culture defence.

Provocation

This is possibly the defence most commonly mentioned as having the potential to be used as a culture defence.[64] However, it is in other respects of

---

[60] *R v Martin (Anthony)* [2003] QB 1.

[61] Simester and Sullivan, above n 32 at 552.

[62] See Seidman, above n 13.

[63] Smith, above n 53 at 266–75; Simester and Sullivan, above n 32 at 631–9.

[64] Seidman, above n 13; AJ Ashworth, 'The Doctrine of Provocation' (1976) *Cambridge Law Journal* 292; T Macklem and J Gardner, 'Provocation and Pluralism' (2001) 64 *Modern Law Review* 815.

more limited scope than the other defences. It is a defence only to the crime of murder. Moreover, it is no more than a partial defence, since it does not, when established, result in an outright acquittal but merely reduces what would have been murder to the lesser homicide offence of manslaughter. However, a successful plea of provocation can have a significant effect on the sentence. For murder there is a mandatory sentence of life imprisonment. On a conviction for manslaughter the court has wide discretionary powers in the determination of the sentence, and it is not unknown for no custodial sentence to be imposed.

It might be generally agreed that the law of provocation is 'disputatious and unstable'.[65] If an attempt is made to state its relevant elements in outline, it may be said that it contains 'subjective' and 'objective' elements.

The 'subjective' element requires that the accused should have been provoked 'by something done or said'[66] to lose their self-control. It has been argued that, for something done or said to provoke it must be 'provocative', and this can only be determined by the social milieu of the accused:

> In deciding whether the defendant was provoked, the jurors need to adjust their horizons to accommodate different social milieus, with their different indigenous forms of insult.[67]

In this respect the defence will sometimes depend on the culture of the accused. There is evidence that this has been accepted.[68]

The 'objective' elements are derived from the words of the Homicide Act 1957, s 3, which amended the common law rules defining the scope of the defence. The section provides that the jury is to consider:

> whether the provocation was enough to make a reasonable man do as [the accused] did...; and in determining that question the jury shall take into account everything both done and said according to the effect which, in their opinion, it would have on a reasonable man.

Thus the objective elements are, first, that the provocation was so serious that it would have caused a reasonable person to have lost control of themselves (the gravity requirement), and, secondly, that the provocation would have caused a reasonable person, having lost their self-control, to do as much as the accused did (the proportionality requirement).

---

[65] Simester and Sullivan, above n 32 at 343.

[66] The words are taken from the Homicide Act 1957; see below.

[67] Macklem and Gardner, above n 64. That article focuses on provocation by insult, but the authors suggest that the arguments they present could be developed for other forms of provocative conduct such as goading, nagging or hassling: *ibid*

[68] R Ballard, 'Common Law and Uncommon Sense: the Assessment of "Reasonable Behaviour" in a Plural Society' www.art.man.ac.uk/CASAS/pdfpapers/commonsense.pdf

This was interpreted by the House of Lords in *R v Smith (Morgan)*,[69] where the majority view was that the question regarding the accused was 'whether in all the circumstances people with his characteristics would reasonably be expected to exercise more self-control than he did'. To take account of the 'characteristics' of the accused, which included in that case a mental condition which reduced his power of self-control, would seem to open extensive possibilities of taking account of the cultural background of an accused. However, that decision was disapproved in *Attorney General for Jersey v Holley*, a decision which represents the current authoritative view in English law.[70] This held that, in assessing the gravity of the provocation (ie, applying the gravity requirement), regard was to be given to the particular characteristics of the defendant. However, in then judging whether what he did was what a reasonable person might have done (applying the proportionality requirement), it was necessary to use an 'external standard'. This was the standard of self-control to be expected from an ordinary person of the age and sex of the accused, even if the accused had particular characteristics, such as the disease of alcoholism, as in that case, which made him less likely to achieve this standard of self-control. In neither of these cases was there any mention of the accused who had the particular characteristic of coming from a minority culture. It remains possible that, when this instance arises, the courts may hold that the accused must be judged against the standard of a person from that culture. However, this seems unlikely, given the stress placed in *Attorney General for Jersey v Holley* on the necessity of a uniform standard.

It has been noted that in the United States '[i]n many homicide cases defendants invoke cultural arguments, many of which turn on the question of provocation'.[71] That may well be the case for some other common law countries, but it cannot be said of England. [72] Consequently it is not possible to predict whether a culture defence will be permitted through the law of provocation, although the relatively restrictive form which has been given to the law of provocation in England seems to make it less likely to happen there than in other countries.

---

[69] *R v Smith (Morgan)* [2001] 1 AC 146.

[70] *Attorney General for Jersey v Holley* [2005] 2 AC 29. While the case concerned the law of Jersey it was stated at the outset of the main judgment that that law was on this subject the same as English law. It was a decision of the Judicial Committee of the Privy Council, composed in this case of Law Lords. It was recently held by the English Court of Appeal that *Attorney General for Jersey v Holley* must be regarded as having established the relevant principle of English law in place of that stated in *R v Smith (Morgan)*: *R v James* [2006] 2 WLR 887. For a study of the earlier law of provocation in relation to different cultures in England and some other common law countries, see B Brown, 'The "Ordinary Man" in Provocation: Anglo-Saxon Attitudes and "Unreasonable Non-Englishmen"' (1964) 13 *International and Comparative Law Quarterly* 203.

[71] Renteln, above n 12 at 475, repeated in Renteln, above n 3 at 32.

[72] Thus, Renteln, above n 3, cites a number of cases from Australia on provocation, but none from England.

Provocation may be combined with mistake, as where the accused mistakenly but genuinely believed that the victim had acted towards him in a certain manner which, if it had happened, would have been provocative. As has been seen, it is established that in such circumstances it is not necessary for the mistake to be reasonable. Again, therefore, a belief which accords with the culture of the defendant should suffice to support the defence even if it would not be a reasonable belief for members of the main culture.

Mitigation in Sentencing

The law formally gives considerable discretion to judges in determining the sentence to be imposed on a person found guilty. Among serious crimes, only murder attracts a mandatory sentence, in that case of life imprisonment. There are indications in the case law of the rules which are required to govern this exercise of discretion in English law.[73] In many individual cases there is lengthy consideration of the sentence to be imposed, and a wide range of factors may be considered, including many of which evidence was not admissible at the earlier stage of the trial when guilt or innocence was in issue. Especially important for the present purpose are the factors which may be considered in mitigation, that is, as tending to result in a lesser sentence than would otherwise have been imposed. Provocation is recognised as such a factor in non-homicide cases, and it is said that for sentencing purposes the concept is 'more loosely interpreted by courts' than when it is advanced as a partial defence to a charge of murder.[74]

Consequently there may be opportunities to secure a reduction in the punishment imposed on someone found guilty, by showing that their culture was a causal factor in the commission of the offence. This is a possibility in cases where the law offers no room for argument that a culture defence could be raised in relation to the issue of guilt. It may also be possible where one of the arguments considered in the previous subsections is rejected by a court on the ground that the law, properly interpreted, does not allow for it, or where a necessary element of an available culture defence has not been satisfied even though the culture of the defendant was shown to be a factor in the commission of the offence.

In some cases where pleas of exemption defences have been rejected, the courts have considered that reduced sentences should be given. This was not directly possible in *R v Barronet and Allain*,[75] because at that time the death sentence was mandatory for murder. But even here the judgments, while necessarily assuming that a sentence of death would be pronounced,

---

[73] M Wasik, *Emmins on Sentencing* (4th edn, London, Blackstone Press, 2001).
[74] *Ibid* at 60–1.
[75] Above n 22.

contain broad hints that in the circumstances a pardon would follow, and that it might not be conditional on a sentence of imprisonment. In many other cases where there has been no serious attempt to secure an acquittal on the ground of culture, because it was considered not arguable, this factor has played a part in the determination of the sentence. In *R v Singh and Singh*[76] the accused had been found guilty of making false claims for allowances for non-existent children over a period of 10 years. The sentence on the principal actor was reduced from two and a half years to one year three months after the court had heard that he was illiterate, and considered that he had a religious obligation to support his brother's children.

Many of the cases which illustrate this show also a restrictive feature of the judicial attitude towards cultural factors as mitigating circumstances. There emerges a general assumption that immigrants from other cultures will and must in the course of time become integrated into the dominant culture. Thus in *R v Rapier*[77] the appellate court, reversing a recommendation that the accused be deported after serving a prison sentence, and so effectively reducing the severity of the sentence, said that the accused had not had sufficient time to 'settle down' in England. In two cases young men recently arrived from the Caribbean had had sexual relations with girls aged 12 and 14, who had 'thrown themselves at' the accused. It was claimed in each case that the accused had not known that what they did was unlawful. In the first of these, *R v Bailey*,[78] it was said on appeal that the accused had received such a shock on finding that what he had done was unlawful that he was unlikely to repeat the offence. A sentence of nine months' imprisonment was reduced to a fine of £50. In the second case, *R v Byfield*,[79] the appellate court, having heard it claimed that social customs in the Caribbean were different, allowed an immediate discharge of the accused, who had then served three and a half months of an 18-month sentence, but warned him that whatever the social customs might be in the West Indies, he must in future comply with English law. These may be compared with *R v Finlay*,[80] where a 40-year-old Caribbean man had had sexual relations with a 12-year-old girl who was the daughter of his partner. It was argued that the moral code in the West Indies differed from that in England, but the appellate court responded that the moral code in England would not tolerate such conduct, and held that the trial court sentence of three years' imprisonment was 'not a day too long'. The insistence that immigrants should learn about and accept the requirements of the dominant culture is illustrated in *R v Derriviere*,[81] where a Caribbean man was charged with injuring his son through excessively

[76] [1967] Crim LR 247.
[77] [1963] Crim LR 212.
[78] [1964] Crim LR 671.
[79] [1967] Crim LR 378.
[80] [1963] Crim LR 299.
[81] (1969) 53 Cr App R 637.

violent chastisement. A few months earlier he had been convicted of a similar charge in respect of his daughter. On the previous occasion he had received a suspended prison sentence of six months. On this occasion he was ordered to serve the six months previously imposed, and sentenced to a further six months, to run consecutively. The appellate court upheld this sentence. It stated that English standards in the treatment of children must be observed, although West Indian notions were probably different. It noted that the sentence in the first case had been relatively light, and that the accused had then received a warning that he must in future observe English standards. It continued:

> [H]ad there been some real reason for thinking that the appellant either did not understand what the standards in this country were or was having difficulty in adjusting himself, the Court would no doubt have taken that into account and given it such consideration as it could.

Thus mitigation based on the defendant's ignorance of English law is likely not to prove a far-reaching form of culture defence, because immigrant individuals and groups become steadily less able to plead this persuasively the longer they have been in England.

Other anecdotal evidence suggests that courts may take a defendant's culture into account as a mitigating factor.[82] This appears to have been the basis of the decision in *R v Adesanya*,[83] where a Yoruba (Nigerian) woman cut facial marks on her two sons, following a practice which is common in Yoruba culture (although there were grounds for concluding that the acts in this case were not entirely in accord with the customary practice)[84]. She was convicted of assault occasioning actual bodily harm, but given an absolute discharge on the ground that she had been unaware that she was breaking English law.[85] However, such textbook literature as there is on sentencing law does not expressly allude to this.[86] As yet the considerable research in

---

[82] See, eg, Poulter, above n 6 at 63–4; Samuels, above n 24 at 242; also reports of cases in which expert evidence of culture was offered, referred to in the next section.

[83] Unreported but noted at *The Times*, 16 and 17 July 1974; (1974) 4 *RAIN (Royal Anthropological Institute Newsletter)* 2; S Poulter, 'Foreign Customs and English Criminal Law' (1975) 24 *International and Comparative Law Quarterly* 136.

[84] (1974) 4 *RAIN* 2, comment by P Lloyd, an anthropologist who had studied Yoruba culture and customary law.

[85] It is not entirely clear whether the element of culture affected the sentence in *R v Dad and Shafi* [1968] Crim LR 46. There, in the course of a family feud within an immigrant community a woman was kidnapped and held for about a week, but otherwise not ill-treated. The appeal court stated strongly that this conduct could not be tolerated, suggesting that the cultural aspect would not be considered a mitigating factor. However, the court also substituted, for consecutive sentences of two years' imprisonment each for kidnapping and false imprisonment, 'in all the circumstances' and 'as an act of mercy' an order for the sentences to run concurrently.

[86] Wasik, above n 73 at 60–9; DA Thomas, *Principles of Sentencing: the Sentencing Policy of the Court of Appeal Criminal Division* (2nd edn, London, Heinemann, 1979) ch 8; A Ashworth, *Sentencing and Criminal Justice* (3rd edn, London, Butterworths, 2000).

this field done in the United States by Renteln has not been replicated in the United Kingdom, and insufficient information has been published to support further conclusions.[87]

Proof of Facts About Cultures

Whenever a culture defence is seriously considered, the court being normally composed of members of the dominant culture is likely to require to be informed about the relevant aspects of the minority culture in question. For effective functioning of a culture defence, it is necessary that reliable information is given to and used by the judges and jurors who apply the rules. The information will usually have to be provided by expert evidence given to the court in oral or written form. In any case in which a culture defence is legally possible, on any of the grounds considered in the previous sections, such evidence is admissible.

There are, however, theoretical and practical difficulties in conveying information about a culture to persons outside that culture, especially in a formal court setting. There are also considerable problems in converting cultural facts and norms, assuming that they have been accurately communicated, into forms which can be applied or taken into account in deciding cases in state courts. For English law these questions remain largely unexplored.[88] There is some information on the processes in English courts for the taking of expert evidence on minority and foreign cultures, in the form of reports and reflections by those who have acted as expert witnesses.[89] Most of these cases have been civil cases, so have not involved the culture defence in the sense used here, and have been unreported. A recurring comment seems to be that the evidence is not used sufficiently or at all. If there is indeed a judicial reluctance to have regard to the features of minority

---

[87] Thomas, above n 86 at xiii, reports that an index of more than 10,000 judgments had been compiled and was relied upon in that work. As far as is known, this is not publicly accessible. In recent years there has been more frequent reporting of cases on sentencing law, but it is possible that cases involving issues about minority cultures have not been noticed in the selection of cases for report.

[88] Aspects of this problem in other jurisdictions, where customary law is enforced in state courts, are considered in GR Woodman, 'Some Realism about Customary Law: the West African Experience' (1969) *Wisconsin Law Review* 128; GR Woodman, 'Judicial Development of Customary Law: the Case of Marriage Law in Ghana and Nigeria' (1977) 14 *University of Ghana Law Journal* 115; GR Woodman, 'How State Courts Create Customary Law in Ghana and Nigeria' in BW Morse and GR Woodman (eds), *Indigenous Law and the State* (Dordrecht, Foris, 1988).

[89] Ballard, above n 68; WF Menski, 'Immigration and Multiculturalism in Britain: New Issues in Research and Policy' www.art.man.ac.uk/CASAS/pdfpapers/osakalecture.pdf; P Shah, *Legal Pluralism in Conflict: Coping with Cultural Diversity in Law* (London, Cavendish Publishing, 2005). The most voluminous collection of information is contained in Renteln, above n 3, but insofar as this is concerned with court activity, it is primarily concerned with this in the United States.

cultures, it may be inferred that the possibilities of developing a culture defence in the instances set out above are unlikely to be realised.

CONCLUSIONS: FUTURE POSSIBILITIES FOR THE DEFENCE IN ENGLAND

This has been a survey of the current state law of England regarding the use of the culture defence, with a view to assessing the potential for future development. This chapter does not consider evaluative questions of the desirability of extending or restricting the use of the defence, although it may be suggested that these questions can be better explored if the practical possibilities of development are clearly seen.

It has been shown that, unless there is a radical legislative intervention, it is most unlikely that the common law of England will develop a culture defence as a distinct general exemption defence. Even if that were to be considered, there could be difficulties arising from the implications of the Human Rights Act 1998 and the possibility of incompatibility between the Act and a statute introducing a general culture defence if it gave effect to aspects of cultures which were inimical to the observance of human rights.

It would seem that there is unlikely to be a significant increase in the enactment of particular exemptions from criminal provisions on the ground of cultural practices, such as those which have enabled Sikh men to continue to wear turbans when riding motorcycles and working on construction sites. A few more could be introduced if the need became apparent in particular instances, but they are likely to be rigid and narrow in scope.

The type of developments most likely are those which involve the expansion of the use of the general defences of mistake, duress, self-defence and provocation. However, a study of the current law and recent developments here suggests that significant expansion is dependent on a general acceptance by those who conduct the criminal justice system that England is and will remain a multicultural society. At present the frequent references to 'English values' suggest that there is still a widespread belief in the desirability, and perhaps in the inevitability of the assimilation of minorities into the dominant culture.

If a policy favouring development of a culture defence is adopted, difficult issues of implementation will arise, arising from factors mentioned above in respect of the 'Types of cultures in question'. It will be necessary to consider which cultures are to be taken into account. This chapter has referred primarily to ethnic and religious cultures, and the cases cited have considered these forms of cultures of immigrant communities. Many more cultures could be considered. Furthermore, it will be necessary to grapple with the implications of the observable facts that the normative content of most cultures is changing rapidly, especially among immigrant groups; and that the boundaries of cultures, defining who belongs to a given culture, and whether for all purposes or only for some are often unclear, even to the individuals who are (or may perhaps be) members. These issues have not been discussed here, because as yet the culture defence in English law is so underdeveloped that they hardly arise.

2

Culture, Crime and Culpability: Perspectives on the Defence of Provocation

KUMARALINGAM AMIRTHALINGAM

INTRODUCTION

CULTURAL CONSIDERATIONS ASSUME particular significance when an accused is from a minority culture, as it is the moral values of the majority that are relied on to determine the accused's criminal culpability. Occasionally, the accused is in a position of disadvantage as there may be a disjunct between the cultural values he or she is operating under and the cultural values relied on by the court in judging the accused. There is a question of fairness that is raised: is it justifiable to punish a member of a minority culture under laws or norms reflecting those of the majority culture? This question was tested in a series of cases in US courts, where defendants from immigrant communities in the United States introduced cultural evidence to argue against criminal liability on the ground that the conduct of the accused was not wrong, indeed in some cases that it was even mandated, according to the cultural norms of the accused's community.[1]

---

[1] Some of the classic examples include *People v Kimura* (case of the Japanese mother who drowned her children in a ritual parent-child suicide); *People v Moua* (case of the Hmong man who abducted a woman in accordance with traditional Hmong 'marriage by capture'); *People v Chen* (case of the Chinese man who murdered his adulterous wife). An extensive collection and analysis of 'cultural defence' cases may be found in AD Renteln, *The Cultural Defense* (New York, Oxford University Press, 2004). Academic commentators soon joined the debate and by the 1990s, there was an established body of literature on the subject. See especially AD Renteln, 'A Justification of the Cultural Defense as Partial Excuse' (1993) 2 *Southern California Review of Law and Women's Studies* 437; L Volpp, '(Mis)identifying Culture: Asian Women and the "Cultural Defence"' (1994) 17 *Harvard Women's Law Journal* 57; DL Coleman, 'Individualizing Justice through Multiculturalism: the Liberal's Dilemma' (1996) 96 *Columbia Law Review* 1093; VL Sacks, 'An Indefensible Defense: On the Misuse of Culture in Criminal Law' (1996) 13 *Arizona Journal of International and Comparative Law* 523; M Fischer, 'The Human Rights Implications of a "Cultural Defense"' (1998) 6 *Southern California Interdisciplinary Law Journal* 663; JV Broeck, 'Cultural Defence and Culturally Motivated Crimes (Cultural Offences)' (2001) 9 *European Journal of Crime, Criminal Law and Criminal Justice* 1.

The judicial and academic responses have covered a wide range of options, from the creation of a separate 'cultural defence' through the modification of existing defences to accommodate different cultural values, to the use of cultural evidence as mitigating factors in sentencing, to the rejection of cultural arguments. The debate is often emotional as there are political consequences; mainstream or majority cultural groups fear that the established legal order is threatened while minority cultural groups object to having their norms and value systems marginalised. There is the added complication that culture is seen as pertinent only to immigrants and 'coloured' racial minorities, connoting an inferior standard that has to be accommodated by the grace of the majority:

> [B]ehaviour that we might find troubling is more often causally attributed to a group-defined culture when the actor is perceived to 'have' culture. Because we tend to perceive white Americans as 'people without culture', when white people engage in certain practices we do not associate their behaviour with a racialized conception of culture, but rather construct other non-cultural explanations ... Under this schema, white people are individual actors; people of color are members of groups.[2]

This raises the question of whether a cultural defence should be available to the mainstream or majority culture in a society.[3] On 11 December 2005, thousands of white Australians were mobilised by text messages to gather on Cronulla Beach, Sydney and attack members of the Lebanese community. The mob violence was triggered by an assault by some youth of Lebanese origin on two white Australian lifeguards at the beach. There have been suggestions that one of the reasons for this violent reaction by young, white Australians against the Lebanese community was the 'Australian beach culture'. Young, white Australians felt that their traditional cultural space (the beach) was being threatened; as one media correspondent put it, the attack on the lifeguards who patrolled the beach was 'to threaten the very fabric of modern Australia and its strongly held traditions'.[4] One of the Australian youths involved in the violence referred to the beach and said, 'This is what we're fighting for, ... Like our fathers, our grandfathers, fought for these beaches and now it's our turn'.[5]

---

[2] L Volpp, 'Blaming Culture for Bad Behaviour' (2000) 12 *Yale Journal of Law and Human Rights* 89, 89–90.

[3] Cf S De Pasquale, 'Provocation and the Homosexual Advance Defence: the Deployment of Culture as a Defence Strategy' (2002) 26 *Melbourne University Law Review* 110, who argues that provocation itself is a cultural defence deployed by the majority culture.

[4] R Maynard, 'Racial Anger on the Brew', *The Straits Times*, 13 December 2005, 18.

[5] S Kearnley and C Overington, 'Digging in at the Beach', *The Australian*, 14 December 2005 (www.theaustralian.news.com.au/common/story_page/0,5744,17563468%255E601,00. html).

There is a real danger of overplaying the culture card in criminal law.[6] It may be more productive to simply reform and enhance the scope of existing defences by adopting a more culturally inclusive approach to criminal law. This chapter divides itself into two parts; the first provides some general theoretical background and context, the second studies a specific area, namely the defence of provocation. It is suggested that much can be gained by focusing on the distinction between justification and excuse to develop a politically acceptable and theoretically defensible approach to the accommodation of cultural arguments within the existing framework for criminal defences. The focus of analysis is the law of provocation, which relies on an objective assessment of culpability based on the reactions of an 'ordinary' or 'reasonable' person.[7] The problem is that the persona of this ordinary person is generally drawn from the dominant culture and potentially discriminates against minorities. Case studies from Australia and India will be used to illustrate some of the arguments and challenges.

CRIMINAL LAW AND MORAL BLAMEWORTHINESS

Criminal law discourse is deeply rooted in the tension between retributivism and utilitarianism.[8] Reacting against the utilitarian theory of crime and punishment, which had dominated criminal law discourse for over a century, criminal law scholars and philosophers in the later part of the twentieth century argued strongly for moral justification of punishment in order to protect the autonomy of individuals against the power of states. George Fletcher, one of the leading figures in this movement, argued that the utilitarian goal of prioritising social interest had 'overshadowed the more basic inquiry whether the punishment of the accused [was] morally justified'.[9] This is a concern that is now all the more acute in this age of fear, following the September 11 terrorist attacks. Common sense is sometimes ignored and the danger of punishing innocent individuals is high.[10]

---

[6] See below text at nn 42–48.

[7] The concepts 'reasonable person' and 'ordinary person' are used interchangeably here because the focus is on the objective dimensions of the test. The two concepts are in theory distinguishable, as 'reasonable' connotes a higher standard than 'ordinariness'.

[8] See J Feinberg, 'The Classic Debate' in J Feinberg and J Coleman, *Philosophy of Law* (6th edn, Belmont, CA, Wadsworth, 2000) 727.

[9] GP Fletcher, *Rethinking Criminal Law* (Boston, Little, Brown & Co, 1978).

[10] A recent, although not directly relevant, example of this 'prosecute first, think later' mentality is seen in the English case of *R v Goldstein* [2005] UKHL 63. Goldstein was an ultra-orthodox Jewish supplier of kosher foods in Manchester, who owed his business friend, also a Jew, some money, payment of which was overdue. Goldstein sent his friend a cheque and, as a joke, included in it some salt to acknowledge the age of the debt, as salt was used as a preservative in kosher foods. The envelope never reached the intended recipient, as some of the salt leaked out at the post office during sorting. This caused a scare, as the postal workers feared the envelope contained anthrax. The post office was evacuated, resulting in some delay

Fletcher's call to balance state power against personal liberty, made over a quarter of a century ago, is all the more important today in an era where states, even traditionally liberal ones, driven by fear of terrorism and threats to established order, are enacting increasingly repressive laws and dismantling many civil liberty safeguards.[11] Members of minority groups bear the worst of these changes, as they are often targeted under racial profiling policies.[12] Fletcher advocated an approach that embedded political and moral philosophy in the doctrinal analysis of criminal law:

> Criminal law is a species of political and moral philosophy. Its central question is justifying the use of the state's coercive power against free and autonomous persons. The link with moral philosophy derives from one's answer to the problem of justifying the use of state power. If the rationale or a limiting condition of criminal punishment is personal desert, then legal theory invariably interweaves with philosophical claims about wrongdoing, culpability, justifying circumstances and excuses.[13]

Many scholars share this preference for a moral justification for punishment based on the retributive theory;[14] academics supporting a cultural defence are particularly staunch supporters.[15] Utilitarianism and retributivism both have much to offer criminal law jurisprudence, but in different spheres. It is suggested that utilitarianism should be concerned with theories of criminalisation, while retributivism should be concerned with theories of punishment. Utilitarianism, with its instrumentalist outlook, provides sound reasons and justification for criminalisation of certain conduct or activities. It justifies restricting the freedom of the individual to engage in certain conduct because of its potential harm to others or to public order.

Where punishment is imposed for violation of a restriction, then such punishment can only be justified if it is deserved, ie, if the individual is

---

of some of the mail for that day. Goldstein was charged and convicted of public nuisance even though he never intended any harm and his friend gave evidence that had he received the envelope he would have understood the joke in its context. Goldstein's conviction was upheld on appeal to the Court of Appeal but, happily for him and for common sense, the House of Lords quashed the conviction. The fact that such a prosecution was even commenced is a cause for concern. One can imagine situations where particular cultural practices of some communities may put the individual on a collision course with the law.

[11] Detention without trial, denial of access to legal representation and intrusive surveillance are increasingly being sanctioned by legislation and practised by authorities in traditionally liberal countries including the United States, the United Kingdom and Australia.

[12] See, eg, M Woolf, 'Anti-terror Police Told to Target Asians', *The Independent Online Edition*, 13 September 2005 (http://news.independent.co.uk/uk/politics/article312202.ece).

[13] GP Fletcher, *Rethinking Criminal Law* (Boston, Little, Brown & Co, 1978) xix.

[14] R Dworkin, *Taking Rights Seriously* (4th edn, London, Duckworth, 1978); H Gross, *A Theory of Criminal Justice* (New York, Oxford University Press, 1979); W Sadurski, *Giving Desert its Due: Social Justice and Legal Theory* (Boston, D Reidel, 1985); A Von Hirsch, *Past or Future Crimes* (New Brunswick, NJ, Rutgers University Press, 1985); D Husak, *Philosophy of Criminal Law* (Totowa NJ, Rowman & Littlefield, 1987).

[15] See, eg, AD Renteln, *The Cultural Defense* (New York, Oxford University Press, 2004) 442.

morally blameworthy. A distinction should be drawn between justifying the institution of punishment, which is relevant to the process of criminalisation, and the justification of punishment in individual cases, which raises more poignant questions of individual rights and liberties.[16] Utilitarianism remains relevant to the former; retributivism focuses on the latter. The utilitarian argument that punishment of individuals is justified because it has a deterrent value may be challenged on both philosophical and empirical grounds. If one subscribes to the Kantian philosophy of human dignity as a categorical imperative,[17] the instrumentalist approach of utilitarianism becomes unacceptable. Empirically, it has been argued that punishment may be less of a deterrent than the belief of people that crime is wrong;[18] hence, even under an instrumentalist approach, the utilitarian justification of punishment flounders. Further, if a person is punished when he or she is not morally blameworthy, respect for law is weakened and individuals are less likely to abide by laws that they believe to be unjust.[19]

Modern retributivism is based on the just deserts theory of punishment, of which there are two aspects. The first looks at moral blame, ie, whether punishment is warranted at all. The second looks at the degree of harm and thence the degree of punishment that is required. This second aspect—the *lex taliones* principle—has overshadowed the first and has undermined the retributive theory.[20] It is important that the two aspects be kept separate, as each raises different questions.[21] The question: 'Is punishment justified?' is quite separate from the question: 'How much punishment is justified?' The first question is relevant to the imposition of punishment, the second, to the quantum of punishment.[22] The imposition of punishment can only

---

[16] HLA Hart, *Punishment and Responsibility* (New York , Oxford University Press, 1968) 4–9.

[17] In *Groundwork of the Metaphysic of Morals* (1785) Kant stated, 'Act so that you treat humanity, whether in your own person or in that of another, always as an end and never as a means only' (cited in J Rachels, *The Elements of Moral Philosophy* (4th edn, New York, McGraw-Hill, 2003) 131. See generally I Kant, *Groundwork of the Metaphysic of Morals* (HJ Paton (trans), New York, Harper & Row, 1964).

[18] See J Braithwaite, *Crime, Shame and Reintegration* (New York, Cambridge University Press, 1989).

[19] T Tyler, *Why People Obey the Law* (New Haven, Yale University Press, 1990).

[20] See M Bagaric, 'In Defence of a Utilitarian Theory of Punishment: Punishing the Innocent and the Compatibility of Utilitarianism' (1999) 24 *Australian Journal of Legal Philosophy* 95, 99.

[21] HLA Hart, *Punishment and Responsibility* (New York, Oxford University Press, 1968), 3: 'What we should look for are answers to a number of different questions such as: What justifies the general practice of punishment? To whom may punishment be applied? How severely may we punish?'

[22] The quantum of punishment is determined not only by the accused's moral blameworthiness but also by the harm that is caused. Take, eg, three accused who intend to kill their respective victims. One succeeds, the other causes grievous injury and the third causes minor injury. While the moral blameworthiness of each is the same, the harm is different and consequently the punishment is different; the first accused should be punished most severely and the third should receive the least punishment.

be justified if the individual deserves it, ie, if the individual is morally blameworthy. As the positivist philosopher, Hart put it:

> If a person whose action, judged *ab extra*, has offended against moral rules or principles, succeeds in establishing that he did this unintentionally and in spite of every precaution that it was possible for him to take, he is excused from moral responsibility, and to blame him in these circumstances would itself be considered morally objectionable ... A legal system would be open to serious moral condemnation if this were not so.[23]

CULTURE AND CRIMINAL LAW

The analysis of culture and criminal culpability may be divided into two categories. One concerns the legitimacy of the creation of a cultural offence by the dominant legal culture. The other focuses on the use of culture in the presentation of criminal defences by an individual from a minority culture.[24]

Cultural Offence

A useful description of a cultural offence is:

> an act by a member of a minority culture, which is considered an offence by the legal system of the dominant culture. That same act is nevertheless, within the cultural group of the offender, condoned, accepted as normal behaviour and approved or even endorsed and promoted in the given situation.[25]

The classic example is the wearing of the scarf by Muslim women and the banning of it in schools in certain non-Muslim countries, thus creating a cultural offence.[26] The situation is not limited to immigrants; in many cases, indigenous populations have become minorities in their own homelands. When their cultural norms clash with the dominant cultural norms of the legal system, their customary practices become crimes.[27] A third, and more complex, situation concerns former colonies where the dominant cultural values of the legal system reflect those of the erstwhile colonial masters. The local

---

[23] HLA Hart, *The Concept of Law* (Oxford, Clarendon Press, 1961) 173–4.

[24] See Broeck, above n 1, who argues that common lawyers tend to focus on the cultural defence while continental lawyers tend to focus on the cultural offence.

[25] *Ibid* at 5.

[26] See Li-ann Thio, 'Recent Constitutional Developments: Of Shadows and Whips, Race, Rifts and Rights, Terror and *Tudungs*, Women and Wrongs' (2002) *Singapore Journal of Legal Studies* 328, 355–7 and references therein.

[27] For example, traditional hunting and fishing practices by aboriginal groups. See discussion below at text to nn 29–39.

ruling elite in many cases retained these cultural values in the legal system even though these values were not shared by the majority of the population.[28]

An Australian example of a cultural offence, which found both judicial and political solutions, is seen in the context of traditional hunting and fishing rights of indigenous communities. In *Walden v Hensler*,[29] the accused was an Aboriginal elder who, with the permission of the landowner, went hunting and killed a bush turkey for food. His son captured a turkey chick and took it home as a pet. The accused was charged under the Fauna Conservation Act 1974 (Qld), s 54(1), which made it an offence to take or keep protected fauna, which included bush turkey. The accused argued that he was acting according to Aboriginal customary hunting practices. He did not know that bush turkeys were now protected fauna and that it was illegal to take or keep such fauna.[30] His defence was based on s 22 of the Criminal Code 1899 (Qld), which provided for the claim of right defence with respect to any property offence. By a three to two majority, the High Court of Australia rejected the accused's claim of right defence on the narrow and technical ground that the offence in question was not a 'property offence' and therefore did not attract the claim of right defence. Nevertheless, the High Court of Australia was unanimous in holding that the accused should be given a complete discharge.[31] Brennan made this pertinent observation:

> Nevertheless, the appellant was convicted, fined $100 and ordered to pay $260 by way of royalty, $30.50 court costs and $529 professional costs. It was ordered

---

[28] Some illustrations are provided in Broeck, above n 1 at 6. A striking example of the imposition of colonial cultural values is the view expressed by the English drafters of the Indian Penal Code who were of the opinion that Englishmen were far more robust and aggressive than their Indian counterparts, and instead of drafting the laws on self-defence to reflect the 'Indian culture' they took it upon themselves to use the English standard of manliness as the appropriate baseline: 'It may be thought that we have allowed too great a latitude to the exercise of this right; and we are ourselves of opinion that if we had been framing laws for a bold and high-spirited people, accustomed to take the law into their own hands, and to go beyond the line of moderation in repelling injury, it would have been fit to provide additional restrictions. In this country the danger is on the other side; the people are too little disposed to help themselves; the patience with which they submit to the cruel depredations of gang-robbers and to trespass and mischief committed in the most outrageous manner by bands of ruffians, is one of the most remarkable, and at the same time one of the most discouraging symptoms which the state of society of India presents to us. Under these circumstances we are desirous rather to rouse and encourage a manly spirit among the people than to multiply restrictions on the exercise of the right of self-defence'. Macaulay, *The Works of Lord Macaulay* (1898) vol II, 55–6.

[29] (1987) 163 CLR 561.

[30] One of the general principles of criminal law, derived from an ancient maxim, *ignorantia juris non excusat*, is that ignorance or mistake of law is not a defence. This is a rule that operates especially harshly on recent immigrants and disadvantaged groups. Interestingly, the only jurisdiction which abolished this rule was South Africa (*S v de Blom* 1977 (3) SA 513 (A)), which takes a liberal approach to the defence of mistake, quite possibly due to the fact that for a long time, the vast majority of South Africans were blacks living under white rule, with little access to the law and an enormous gulf in cultural norms and practices.

[31] This was permissible under the Criminal Code, s 657A, which allowed a court to impose nominal punishment or grant an absolute discharge if the court was of the view that it would be unjust to impose punishment.

that, in default of payment, he be imprisoned for one month. All this for gathering food from his own country for his own family—as he and his people had been entitled to do and had done since before white settlement, and as he had never been stopped from doing and they had sometimes been encouraged to do by white authority. A comparison between the moral innocence of the appellant's conduct in gathering food for his family and the heavy financial burden of $919.50 which was imposed on him for doing so makes a mockery of justice. When that occurs, either the law or its application, or both, must be at fault. Justice cannot be mocked by a just law, justly applied. It would not have been surprising if a question had been raised by the appellant as to whether and how it came about in law that Aboriginal people had their traditional entitlement to gather food from their own country taken away, but that question was not raised.[32]

The question alluded to by Brennan J was answered five years later when the High Court of Australia decided *Mabo and others v Queensland (No 2),*[33] where it rejected the *terra nullius* doctrine and held that native title had survived European settlement.[34] One consequence of this has been that traditional fishing rights have been relegitimised. In *Yanner v Eaton,*[35] the accused, a member of an Aboriginal community in Queensland, had killed two crocodiles according to traditional custom. He was charged under the same Act used against Walden, the Fauna Conservation Act 1974 (Qld), s 54(1). The High Court held that, following the *Mabo* decision and the subsequent Native Title Act 1993, the traditional hunting and fishing rights of Aboriginal people was recognised.[36] The Fauna Conservation Act 1974 (Qld) did not extinguish that right and therefore the charges against the accused could not stand, as he had not done anything wrong; he had merely been exercising his legally recognised cultural rights.

The recognition of native title rights has been pivotal in providing greater sensitivity to aboriginal cultural rights and practices. This is seen in the hunting and fishing cases and in the ongoing reform activity in this area, with various recommendations for greater recognition of traditional or customary practices in legislation relating to management of fisheries

---

[32] (1987) 163 CLR 561, 564–5.

[33] (1992) 175 CLR 1.

[34] *Terra nullius* (land belonging to nobody) was a concept developed in the seventeenth century, which distinguished territories that had inhabitants and were conquered from territories that were empty and settled by the English. In the latter, the laws of England were automatically transplanted to the new colony: *Craw v Ramsay* (1670) Vaughan 274; 124 ER 1072; *Blankard v Galdy* (1693) 2 Salk 411. See generally AC Castles, *An Australian Legal History* (Sydney, The Law Book Company, 1982) 7–14. The British application of *terra nullius* to Australia was a fiction, as Aboriginal communities had long inhabited the island.

[35] (1999) 201 CLR 351.

[36] Cf the earlier New South Wales decision of *Mason v Tritton* [1996] 1 AILR 19 where the court, by two to one majority, rejected the native title right to fishing. J Kirby, in dissent, held that such a right did exist.

and fauna in Australia.[37] Generally however, the Australian Law Reform Commission has considered and rejected the creation of a separate cultural (for migrants) or customary (for indigenous Australians) defence.[38] The Commission recommended that cultural factors be taken into account in sentencing to determine if any mitigation was appropriate.[39]

Culture and Criminal Defences

The creation, and elimination, of cultural offences is a matter that is politically sensitive and often requires a political solution. A cultural defence, on the other hand, can be developed judicially. However, there are several obstacles to the development of a cultural defence. It risks fragmenting the law and resulting in unequal treatment of individuals. As Coleman warns:

> While the cultural defense is consistent with 'progressive' criminal defense philosophy which advocates that justice should be as individualized as possible, it must be balanced against the risks of dangerous balkanization of criminal law, where non-immigrant Americans are subject to one set of laws and immigrant Americans to another.[40]

Too much emphasis on a cultural defence threatens the emotional security of members of both the dominant and minority culture by accentuating differences and creating greater alienation and disharmony within society.[41] There is also a risk that it may legitimise discriminatory practices against women

---

[37] See B Fraser, 'Aboriginal Fishing Strategy in Western Australia' (2004) *Indigenous Law Bulletin* 5; S Hawkins, 'Caught, Hook, Line and Sinker: Summary of the AJAC Report into Aboriginal Fishing Rights in NSW' (2004) *Indigenous Law Journal* 4. Two recommendations that are particularly important include making compulsory cultural awareness initiatives for employees involved in the management of fisheries and creating a separate class of fishing activity for customary fishing.

[38] Australian Law Reform Commission, *Multiculturalism and the Law*, ALRC 57 (1992) [8.11]; Australian Law Reform Commission, *The Recognition of Aboriginal Customary Law*, ALRC 31 (1986).

[39] Australian Law Reform Commission, *Multiculturalism and the Law*, ALRC 57 (1992) [8.14]–[8.15]; Australian Law Reform Commission, *The Recognition of Aboriginal Customary Law*, ALRC 31 (1986) [5.17]. Another inquiry is currently underway on sentencing in Australia: Australian Law Reform Commission, *Sentencing of Federal Offenders*, ALRC Issues Paper 29 (2005).

[40] DL Coleman, 'Individualizing Justice through Multiculturalism: the Liberal's Dilemma' (1996) 96 *Columbia Law Review* 1093, 1098. Cf J McHugh's statement for a contrary view, below text at n 93.

[41] Although written in a slightly different context, the view expressed here is illuminating: 'When my parochialism is threatened, then I am wholly, radically parochial: a Serb, a Pole, a Jew and nothing else ... Under the conditions of security I will acquire a more complex identity than the idea of tribalism suggests. I will identify myself with more than one tribe: I will be an American, a Jew, an Easterner, an intellectual, a professor'. M Walzer, 'New Tribalism' (1992) *Dissent* (Spring) 164, 171.

and children,[42] who often do not have a say in determining cultural norms.[43] Culture is a dynamic concept, which evolves over time and adapts to different influences from within and without. However, immigrants or diasporic communities, when asserting their cultural identity, tend to have a point of reference that is fixed to the time of the first wave of emigration or dispersion:

> The public/private split in Indian diasporic communities has resulted in a version of Indian (often Hindu) culture being maintained that is static and rigid. As Shamita Das Dasgupta has argued, the attitudes of Indians long settled in the US have frozen in time, even as India has changed. They tend to stick to the older picture of India.[44]

While cultural norms and practices evolve as part of the natural process of modernisation in the country of origin, migrant and diasporic communities strategically adopt or reject different aspects of their cultural identity. Practices that are no longer condoned, or have been outlawed in their original homelands, risk being championed in their adoptive countries under the guise of a cultural defence.

Proponents of the cultural defence have argued that it may be used as a 'mitigating defence' or partial excuse. This suggests a kind of compromise position, which, while superficially attractive, is not altogether desirable. The mitigating factor in partial excuses is generally a type of character weakness or flaw, as seen in partial excuses like provocation and diminished responsibility. The former is based on loss of control, generally due to emotions of anger or passion; it is recognition of 'human frailty'.[45] The latter is based on a deficient mental state and is recognition that the accused is not 'normal' or fully capable of being held personally responsible. It has been referred to as the 'half bad, half mad'[46] defence. To treat the cultural defence as a partial defence risks degrading the culture of the accused; it

---

[42] One problem that has received considerable attention is honour killing of women. Amnesty International, *Pakistan, Violence Against Women in the Name of Honour*, AI Index: ASA 33/17/99 (1999); Amnesty International, *Pakistan, Insufficient Protection of Women*, AI Index ASA 33/006/2002 (2002). The Government of Pakistan has condemned honour killings and vowed to treat it as murder.

[43] Since these matters will be addressed by other chapters in this volume, I will refrain from elaborating. Some of my views on this can be found in K Amirthalingam, 'Women's Rights, International Norms and Domestic Violence: Asian Perspectives' (2005) 27 *Human Rights Quarterly* 683; K Amirthalingam, 'Negotiating Law, Culture and Justice', *The Drawing Board*, 2 July 2004 (www.econ.usyd.edu.au/drawingboard/digest/0407/amirthalingam.html); see also S Mullally, 'Feminism and Multicultural Dilemmas in India: Revisiting the Shah Bano Case' (2004) 24 *Oxford Journal of Legal Studies* 671.

[44] K Visweswaran, 'Family in the US India Diaspora', *South Asian Women's Forum*, 19 March 2001 (www.sawf.org/newedit/edit03192001/womensociety.asp).

[45] Lord Bingham of Cornhill CJ in *R v Campbell* (1997) 1 Cr App R 199, 207, said: 'It is in recognition of human frailty that the scope of the defence of provocation has, to a very limited extent, been enlarged'.

[46] See S Yeo, *Criminal Defences in Malaysia and Singapore* (Malaysia, LexisNexis Malayan Law Journal, 2005) 234.

likens the culture to a human weakness or deficiency, suggesting that the culture of the accused is inferior to the culture of the majority.

A preferable approach is to encourage a culturally sensitive interpretation and application of existing defences. The experience with the development of the 'battered woman syndrome' defence by feminist scholars provides some valuable lessons.[47] Historically, women who killed their abusive partners and claimed self-defence rarely succeeded in their defence. One of the reasons was because the law required the killing in self-defence to be a reasonable response and in most cases involving abused women who killed their partners, courts found the response to be unreasonable. Feminist scholars argued that courts were using a male standard of reasonableness for aggression, which did not encompass a battered woman's response. When evidence of 'battered woman syndrome' was admitted, judges and juries were able to evaluate the response from an alternative perspective and in some cases were able to hold that such response was reasonable.[48] 'Battered woman syndrome' (BWS) was not proffered as a separate defence, but was instead used to educate judges and juries of alternative realities in order to allow the existing doctrines to be applied fairly to battered women who kill.[49] As leading Australian scholars in the area explained:

> BWS, and other expert evidence concerning battering and its effects, were origi-
> nally developed in order to extend traditional legal doctrine to the kinds of life
> experiences likely to be faced by women. It was not, as we have indicated above,
> intended to develop a special defence or pleading for battered women. It is to be
> hoped that there will come a time when community and judicial understandings

---

[47] See generally L Walker, *The Battered Woman Syndrome* (New York, Springer, 1984); E Sheehy, J Stubbs and J Tolmie, 'Defending Battered Women on Trial: the Battered Woman Syndrome and its Limitations' (1992) 16 *Criminal Law Journal* 369.

[48] See, eg, *State of Washington v Wanrow*, 88 Wash 2d 221; 559 P 2d 548 (1977); *R v Lavallee* [1990] 1 SCR 852; *R v Kontinnen* (unreported, Supreme Court of South Australia, J Legoe, 30 March 1992).

[49] See *Osland v R* (1998) 197 CLR 316 per Kirby J: 'In her reasons in [*R v Malott* (1998) 155 DLR (4th) 513], J L'Heureux-Dubé expressly stated, correctly in my view, that BWS was not "a legal defence in itself". It seems unthinkable that the Supreme Court of Canada, if it had been minded to create an entirely new "defence" or ground of exculpation (assuming that to be possible), would not have done so in language more explicit and with more elaborate reasoning. What that Court, and courts in other jurisdictions have been at pains to emphasise is that any expert evidence of BWS, or an analogous condition, must be related to the facts of the particular case. Specifically, whilst such expert evidence could not be tendered to usurp the decisions reserved by law to the jury, it might be offered as relevant to questions such as (1) why a person subjected to prolonged and repeated abuse would remain in such a relationship; (2) the nature and extent of the violence that may exist in such a relationship before producing a response; (3) the accused's ability, in such a relationship, to perceive danger from the abuser; and (4) whether, in the evidence, the particular accused believed on reasonable grounds that there was no other way to preserve herself or himself from death or grievous bodily harm than by resorting to the conduct giving rise to the charge. These considerations, accepted in *Malott*, are equally applicable in Australia where expert evidence is received to describe common features of the conduct of people in abusive relationships and where provocation or self-defence are put in issue'. (footnotes omitted)

46 *Kumaralingam Amirthalingam*

of domestic violence as a phenomenon are sufficiently informed and sophisticated that expert testimony is not necessary for the finder of fact to realistically understand the context in which women's defensive force might take place.[50]

THEORISING ABOUT CRIMINAL DEFENCES AND CULTURE

The dominant theoretical framework for the analysis of criminal defences is found in the distinction between justification and excuse. While this distinction was critical even two centuries ago,[51] it is in the last 30 years that it has come to the forefront of criminal law discourse.[52] This distinction provides a principled method of accommodating cultural contexts in criminal defences, without distorting general norms or threatening established legal and political order. A separate issue that warrants some theoretical discussion relates to the 'reasonable person' test. This is often the benchmark for judging the criminal culpability, and even civil liability, of individuals as it sets an objective standard that society expects of individuals. The problem is that what is objective and what is reasonable are largely determined by our cultural filters, and therefore it is critical that the reasonable person be sufficiently attuned to different cultural perspectives and norms.

Justification and Excuse

A justificatory defence arises where the conduct of the accused is sanctioned by society and the legal system. The classic example is self-defence. A person who kills another in self-defence is justified in doing so. The killing in self-defence is not viewed as a wrongdoing by society; a justificatory defence

---

[50] J Stubbs and J Tolmie, 'Falling Short of the Challenge? A Comparative Assessment of the Australian Use of Expert Evidence on the Battered Woman Syndrome' (1999) 23 *Melbourne University Law Review* 709, 739.

[51] CMV Clarkson and HM Keating, *Criminal Law: Text and Materials* (5th edn, London, Sweet & Maxwell, 2003) 271.

[52] See, eg, PH Robinson, 'A Theory of Justification: Societal Harm as a Prerequisite for Criminal Liability' (1975) 23 *UCLA Law Review* 266; GP Fletcher, 'The Right Deed for the Wrong Reason: a Reply to Mr Robinson' (1975) 23 *UCLA Law Review* 293; GP Fletcher, *Rethinking Criminal Law* (Boston, Little, Brown & Co, 1978); J Dressler, 'New Thoughts about the Concept of Justification in the Criminal Law: a Critique of Fletcher's Thinking and Rethinking' (1984) 32 *UCLA Law Review* 61; K Greenawalt, 'The Perplexing Borders of Justification and Excuse' (1984) 84 *Columbia Law Review* 1897; DL Horowitz, 'Justification and Excuse in the Program of the Criminal Law' (1986) 49 *Law and Contemporary Problems* 109; J Dressler, 'Justifications and Excuses: a Brief Overview of the Concepts in the Literature' (1987) 33 *Wayne Law Review* 1155; DN Husak, *Philosophy of Criminal Law* (Totowa, NJ, Rowman & Littlefield, 1987); LA Alexander, 'Justification and Innocent Aggressors' (1987) 33 *Wayne Law Review* 1177; S Kadish, 'Excusing Crime' (1987) 75 *California Law Review* 257; ML Corrado, *Justification and Excuse in Criminal Law: a Collection of Essays* (New York, Garland Publishing, 1994); J Horder, 'Criminal Law and Legal Positivism' (2002) 8 *Legal Theory* 221; M Berman, 'Justification and Excuse, Law and Morality' (2003) 53 *Duke Law Journal* 1.

thus negatives wrongdoing. The accused escapes liability because he or she has done no wrong. An excusatory defence arises where the accused has committed a wrongdoing, but under such circumstances that no blameworthiness can fairly be attributed to the accused. The classic example is mistake. A person who mistakenly believes he or she is shooting at an animal, but instead kills a human, is not guilty of murder.[53] The killing is viewed as a wrongdoing by society, but the accused escapes criminal liability because no blameworthiness can fairly be attributed.

There are several theories of excuse, variously based on character,[54] capacity,[55] choice,[56] motive;[57] common to all is the underpinning of the retributive theory. The question should be whether or not the cultural factors paint a picture of the accused, vis-à-vis the wrongdoing, that shows a person with a character that deserves punishment, or a person who did not freely choose to commit a crime or whose motive explained his or her conduct. By placing cultural defences within excuses, a balance can be maintained between preserving the established norms of society and treating individuals from different cultures fairly.

It avoids the pitfalls of the 'balkanisation'[58] of the criminal law, as excuses do not modify existing norms nor create precedents, in the sense that justificatory defences do.[59] It shows respect for individuals and other cultural norms by recognising that adherence to or guidance by one's cultural values is not a stain on one's character. By dealing with the justification of punishment within the criminal law itself, rather than outsourcing it to sentencing discretion, it also enhances the moral standing of the criminal justice system by being true to itself:

> To blame a person is to express a moral criticism, and if the person's action does not deserve criticism, blaming him is a kind of falsehood and is, to the extent the person is injured by being blamed, unjust to him. It is this feature of our everyday

[53] Depending on the jurisdiction, the mistake may or may not have to be reasonable. Under English and Australian criminal law, where the mistake may negative mens rea, it need not be reasonable. See S Bronitt and B McSherry, *Principles of Criminal Law* (2001) 337; under the Penal Codes of India, Singapore and Malaysia, the mistake has to be in good faith: Penal Code, s 79.

[54] See GP Fletcher, *Rethinking Criminal Law* (Boston, Little, Brown & Co, 1978) 802–7.

[55] See, eg, HLA Hart, *Punishment and Responsibility* (New York, Oxford University Press, 1968) 22–4.

[56] See, eg, DL Horowitz, 'Justification and Excuse in the Program of the Criminal Law' (1986) 49 *Law and Contemporary Problems* 109.

[57] See, eg, AD Renteln, *The Cultural Defense* (New York, Oxford University Press, 2004).

[58] See above n 40.

[59] 'Thus in the field of excuses, precedents have an inverse effect on the excusability of similar conduct in the future ... This inverse correlation brings out the radical difference between claims of justification, which do create precedents that others may rely on in the future, and claims of excuse, which do not. Decisions on justifying circumstances modify the applicable legal norm. Decisions on excuses, in contrast, leave the norm intact, but irreversibly modify the factual background of succeeding claims of excuse'. GP Fletcher, *Rethinking Criminal Law* (Boston, Little, Brown & Co, 1978) 812.

moral practices that lies behind the law's excuses. Excuses, then, ... represent no sentimental compromise with the demands of a moral code; they are, on the contrary, of the essence of a moral code.[60]

Reasonable Person

The ultimate determination of criminal and civil liability often turns on an objective standard based on the reasonable person.[61] The reasonable person is based on the notional reasonable person in society, classically described as 'the man on the Clapham omnibus'.[62] This phrase was originally used at the turn of the nineteenth century when Clapham was a locality populated by the working class, thus making the reasonable person of the law a white, working class, English, Christian male. Even under a more normative approach, where the reasonable person is meant to reflect the community's expectation,[63] it is inevitably the judge's or jury's own perception of what constitutes reasonableness that applies.[64] The judge's own cultural background and value assumptions become the default benchmark for the law's standard of reasonableness.

A major problem with using the reasonable person standard is that too much emphasis is put on 'person' rather than 'reasonable'.[65] So debate goes

---

[60] SH Kadish, 'Excusing Crime' (1987) 75 *California Law Review* 257, 264.

[61] The cornerstone of the tort of negligence is the reasonable person. One of the earliest references to the objective standard is found in *Vanguan v Menlove* (1837) 3 Benj NC 468, 475 per Tindall CJ: 'Instead, therefore, of saying that the liability for negligence should be co-extensive with the judgment of each individual, which would be as variable as the length of the foot of each individual, we ought rather to adhere to the rule which requires in all cases a regard to caution such as a man of ordinary prudence would observe'. Most criminal law defences, including provocation, self-defence, duress, necessity and to an extent, mistake, rely on some version of an objective test embodied in the reasonable or ordinary person.

[62] The phrase was first used in a negligence case to refer to the standard of care in *Hall v Brooklands Auto Racing Club* [1933] 1 KB 205, 224 per Greer LJ. The coining of the phrase is credited to Lord Bowen, as noted in *McQuire v Western Morning New Company Ltd* [1903] 2 KB 100, 109 per Collins MR.

[63] See, for recent perspectives on the reasonable person, M Moran, *Rethinking the Reasonable Person: an Egalitarian Reconstruction of the Objective Standard* (Oxford, Oxford University Press, 2003); C Lee, *Murder and the Reasonable Man* (New York, New York University Press, 2003); M Saltman, *The Demise of the Reasonable Man: a Cross-Cultural Study of a Legal Concept* (Edison, NJ, Transaction Publishers, 1991).

[64] 'If an English judge holds that the defendant has not used reasonable care, he means that "the defendant has not used as much care as I hold that he ought". The "reasonable man" is not the man activated by reason, or most men, or the usual or average man, but the man whom the judge takes as a standard'. Quoted in AS Diamond, 'Review of *The Law of Primitive Men: A Study in Comparative Legal Dynamics* by EA Hoebel, and *The Judicial Process among the Barotse of Northern Rhodesia* by M Gluckman' (1956) *International and Comparative Law Quarterly* 624, 627–8.

[65] Moran, above n 63 at 301–7. 'When the phrase "reasonable man" (coming from 19th century cases such as *R v Welsh* (1869) 11 Cox CC 336) is used ... the common lawyer immediately tries to visualise and define some physical human being with identified characteristics (apparently both reasonable and unreasonable) whereas what the phrase is doing is identifying a concept, a standard of self-control'. *R v Smith* [2001] 1 AC 146, 188 per Lord Hobhouse of Woodborough.

on as to whether the reasonable person should be male or female, culturally neutral or culturally specific, young or old, intelligent or mentally impaired. The man on the Clapham omnibus is one day the young girl on the DTC bus,[66] then the old man on the Yishun MRT,[67] and then the middle aged woman on the Nonthaburi tuk tuk.[68] This focus on the actual make-up of the person—the 'anthropomorphism'[69] of the reasonable person—generates unnecessary conflict and tension, diverting attention away from the real question of moral blameworthiness or accountability. This fictitious creature, arbitrarily attributed with some, all or none of the characteristics peculiar to the actual individual on trial, then becomes the 'ideal' by which the actual individual is judged. A comparison with this reasonable person is made; if the accused measures up to this reasonable person, he or she is blameless.

Instead, it is suggested that the reasonableness of the actual individual's behaviour be directly investigated. Has the individual, taking into account personal characteristics, including culture, behaved reasonably? Is his character vis-à-vis the wrongdoing such that moral blameworthiness can fairly be attributed? This is a judgment that has to be made normatively, with justice to the individual being the focus. Here, sensitivity to the cultural practices and norms of the individual is critical and judges should not be captured by the political or mainstream mood of the moment. Cynthia Lee provides a compelling illustration by demonstrating how Americans at one time believed slavery to be reasonable; now, they generally agree that it is unreasonable.[70] Americans in the 1940s thought it was reasonable to arbitrarily intern Japanese Americans; now most do not share that belief. Justice and fairness are ideals that should rise higher than the temporal interests of the majority culture or community.

A poignant question put by Lee is whether or not future generations will disagree with the current generation's apathy towards the indiscriminate incarceration and human rights violations of Asians and Middle-Easterners following the terrorist attacks of September 11.[71] If we lack cultural sensitivity in our construction of reasonable behaviour in matters of criminal liability, it is equally likely that history will judge us poorly.

PROVOCATION

Provocation operates as a partial defence to murder, reducing the charge to manslaughter (Australia) or culpable homicide not amounting to murder

---

[66] Delhi Transport Corporation, local bus service in New Delhi, India.

[67] Mass Rapid Transportation, the train system in Singapore; Yishun being a working class suburb.

[68] Three-wheeled mini taxi in a Thai province.

[69] See *R v Smith* [2001] 1 AC 146, 172 per Lord Hoffmann, at 188 per Lord Hobhouse of Woodborough.

[70] Lee, above n 63 at 236.

[71] *Ibid*.

(India).[72] Its practical effect is to reduce the punishment imposed on the accused. The rationale behind the defence is that a person who kills as a result of provocation is not as morally blameworthy as a person who kills in cold blood and therefore should not be labelled a murderer nor be subject to the higher penalties for murder.[73] The defence is less significant in jurisdictions where discretionary sentencing is available for murder, but remains highly relevant in jurisdictions where there is a mandatory penalty for murder, including death.[74]

The law on provocation is roughly the same in the two jurisdictions under discussion. The essential elements are that the accused must have lost control as a result of the deceased's provocation and the provocation must have been so grave that an ordinary person in the position of the accused could also have lost control and killed. The defence thus requires examination of loss of control at two levels: one subjective, questioning whether the accused actually lost control; and one objective, determining whether the ordinary person, similarly provoked, could have lost control. The problem is in constructing the ordinary (or reasonable) person for the objective test: how much of the personal characteristics, including the cultural background, of the accused should be attributed to the ordinary person? Since provocation is meant to be a concession to human frailty, too rigid an adherence to a purely objective test defeats the purpose of the defence.[75]

Australia

There is a tension between maintaining a purely objective test at the expense of including personal traits of the accused and diluting the objective test to the point of it becoming a subjective test by incorporating all of the personal characteristics of the accused. The compromise that courts arrived at was to draw a distinction between the gravity of the provocation and the level of control in determining whether the ordinary person could

---

[72] Provocation is also a defence to certain non-fatal offences under the Indian Penal Code and some Australian jurisdictions: Western Australia (Criminal Code, s 246); Queensland (Criminal Code 1899, s 269); Northern Territory (Criminal Code Act 1983, s 34); Indian Penal Code, ss 334, 335 (reduced penalties for assault caused by provocation).

[73] See Macaulay and Other Indian Law Commissioners, *A Penal Code Prepared by the Indian Law Commissioners* (Union NJ, The Lawbook Exchange Ltd, 2002) note M at 107–8. See also *R v Smith* [2001] 1 AC 146, 15961 per Lord Hoffmann. See generally J Horder, *Provocation and Responsibility* (Oxford/New York, Oxford University Press, 1992).

[74] Jurisdictions that have a mandatory death penalty for murder include Singapore, Malaysia and The Philippines. The Caribbean countries of Trinidad and Tobago and Jamaica had mandatory death penalties for murder until this was ruled unconstitutional by the Privy Council. *Reyes v The Queen* [2002] 2 AC 235; cf *Boyce v R (Barbados)* [2004] UKPC 32.

[75] This was recently recognised by the House of Lords in *R v Smith* [2001] 1 AC 146. See the strong criticism of this case in JC Smith, 'Case and Comment: Homicide – *R v Smith*' (2000) *Criminal Law Review* 1005.

have lost control.[76] Any individual peculiarity of the accused relevant to the sting or gravity of the provocation may be attributed to the ordinary person to determine whether or not the ordinary person could have been severely provoked. This would include the cultural make-up of the accused. For example, if the provocative conduct was a racial slur, then the racial background of the accused would be attributed to the ordinary person in order to assess the true sting of the provocation. However, in assessing the level of self-control expected of the ordinary person, the only characteristic of the accused to be attributed to the ordinary person is age,[77] as it would be unfair to expect the maturity of an adult in a child.[78] While this split approach allows for some contextualisation of the accused's cultural background,[79] it ignores the fact that culture is relevant not only to the sting of the provocation but also to the emotional response of an individual.

Aboriginal Offenders

Australian courts until the 1990s adopted an inclusive approach to the objective test when dealing with Aboriginal offenders and considered cultural factors in determining the level of self-control expected of the accused. For example, in *R v Muddarubba*,[80] the accused was a member of the Pitjintjara tribe who had been provoked by another tribe member and ended up killing him with a spear. Kriewaldt J said in that case, 'I shall continue to tell juries that the members of the Pitjintjara tribe are to be considered as a separate community for the purposes of the rules relating to provocation'.[81] Courts in the northern part of Australia are more attuned to Aboriginal sensitivities than courts in the south and south-east, due to the larger proportion of Aborigines living in the northern regions.[82] Even

---

[76] The argument was made by A Ashworth, 'The Doctrine of Provocation' (1976) 35 *Cambridge Law Journal* 292, 300 and subsequently adopted by the House of Lords. *DPP v Camplin* [1978] AC 705; *R v Morhall* [1996] 1 AC 90; *Luc Thiet Thuan v R* [1997] AC 131 (PC). The earlier approach was to insist on a purely objective test: *Bedder v DPP* [1954] 1 WLR 1119. For Australia, see *Masciantonio v R* (1995) 183 CLR 58; *Stingel v R* (1990) 171 CLR 312.

[77] *Stingel v R* (1990) 171 CLR 312.

[78] Similar sentiments are seen in the civil law of torts, where the reasonable person standard is modified to take into account the age of the defendant: *Mullin v Richards* [1998] 1 WLR 1304; *McHale v Watson* (1966) 115 CLR 199.

[79] The distinction is far too subtle to be applied in practice. To consider culture in determining gravity but to exclude it in assessing self-control requires extraordinary mental agility on the part of the judge or jury.

[80] [1951–76] NTJ 317. See also *R v MacDonald* [1953] NTJ 186; *R v Patipatu* [1951–76] NTJ 18; *R v Jimmy BalirBalir* [1951–76] NTJ 633; *R v Nelson* [1951–76] NTJ 327.

[81] [1951–76] NTJ 317, 322.

[82] 'In the exercise of its criminal jurisdiction the Supreme Court of the Northern Territory concerns itself with many aboriginal people. Of these, a number live under tribal culture and tradition and come from areas remote from the court. The court has for many years now considered it should, if practicable, inform itself of the attitude of the aboriginal communities

after the High Court of Australia held that an accused's culture should not be attributed to the ordinary person in determining the level of self-control to be expected,[83] some courts have continued to test ordinary levels of self-control with respect to provocation in murder cases by taking into account the accused's Aboriginal culture.[84]

Provocation is also a defence to assault in several Australian jurisdictions,[85] but in the assault cases, there is a slightly different approach to culture and the objective test. Because provocation operates as a complete defence to assault, resulting in an acquittal rather than merely a partial defence, it suggests that the accused was justified, as opposed to merely being excused. Not surprisingly, courts are less sanguine about taking into account cultural factors:

> Where provocation has a role merely in reducing the crime of murder to one of manslaughter, it may be arguable that taking account of characteristics of these kinds is merely a concession to the 'human frailty' of those who hold views which may be unacceptable to a majority in the community. Where, however, the defence results in a complete acquittal, if the law takes account of characteristics of this kind and merely asks what the gravity of the provocation is from the viewpoint of the accused, it sends an unambiguous message to, among others, undutiful wives or assertive daughters who may not share the accused's beliefs, that they must nevertheless conform to those beliefs or suffer violence which the law may not punish.[86]

This reinforces the significance of the distinction between justification and excuse when it comes to taking into account culture as an extenuating factor. Because an excuse does not modify the norm, attention can be focused solely on whether or not the accused is deserving of criminal sanction, without the distractions as to whether or not allowing a defence in the particular case will send a wrong signal to the community that such conduct is condoned.

---

involved, not only on questions of payback and community attitudes to the crime, but at times to better inform itself as to the significance of words, gestures or situations which may give rise to sudden violence or which may explain situations which are otherwise incomprehensible. The information may be made available to the court in a somewhat informal and hearsay style. This is unavoidable as it will often depend on consultation with aboriginal communities in remote areas'. *Re: The Queen and William Davey No NTG 14 of 1980* (1980) 50 FLR 57, 60–1.

[83]   *Stingel v R* (1990) 171 CLR 312.

[84]   *R v Mungatopi* (1991) 57 A Crim R 341; *Jabarula v Poore* (1990) 68 NTR 25. But, cf *R v Thorpe* [1999] VSCA 172, where an Aboriginal accused was charged with murder and the Court of Appeal applied the *Masciantonio* test, although emphasising the importance of the relevance of the accused's culture to the gravity of provocation.

[85]   Western Australia: Criminal Code, s 246; Queensland: Criminal Code 1899, s 269; Northern Territory: Criminal Code Act, s 34.

[86]   *Verhoeven v The Queen* (1998) 101 Australian Criminal Reports 24, 36 per Wheeler J.

Migrant Offenders

Courts have generally treated migrant communities slightly differently from Aboriginal communities when considering the cultural background of the accused. Some of the earlier decisions took into account the accused's culture in assessing the level of self-control to be expected of the ordinary person. In the Victorian case of *R v Dincer*,[87] the accused, described as a conservative Muslim of Turkish origin, had stabbed and killed his teenage daughter because she had left home against her parents' will and taken up with a young man. The court heard evidence that the accused came from a culture where the man was the head of the household and disobedience by children was not tolerated. In particular, loss of virginity in an unmarried daughter was a matter of great shame and dishonour to the family.

In explaining to the jury the objective test of loss of control in provocation, Lush J referred with approval to earlier Australian authorities,[88] which held that the ordinary person should be imbued with all permanent characteristics of the accused, and stated:

> The first question here is, who is an ordinary man for this purpose? Well, the answer is that ordinary men come in all shapes and sizes with enormous variety of backgrounds of race, religion, colour. It would be very hard to draw any satisfactory limit to the factors. All people, despite the vast differences within the scope of the few things I have mentioned, they are all people who could be classed as ordinary men, and, when a jury is considering whether what an accused man did was within the range of what an ordinary man might have done under the same provocation, the jury must consider an ordinary man who has the same characteristics as the man in the dock. In this case it has been put to you from the outset that you have to take into consideration the fact that Dincer is Turkish by birth, the fact that he is Muslim by religion, the fact that he is one whom some of the witnesses were prepared to describe as a traditionalist, the picture painted of him that he was a conservative Muslim, and as part of the consequences of those characteristics that he carries about with him as part of his own personality there are the social practices which are assessed by him as desirable or undesirable, permissible or not permissible, by reference to those essential background aspects of his character.[89]

This culturally accommodative approach was controversial and was halted in the 1990s, in a series of High Court of Australia decisions, beginning with the *Stingel v R*,[90] where the High Court affirmed the dualistic approach to

---

[87] [1983] 1 VR 460.
[88] *R v Croft* [1981] 1 NSWLR 126; *R v Dutton* (1979) 21 SASR 356. See also *Moffa v R* (1977) 138 CLR 601; *R v Webb* (1977) 16 SASR 309; *R v Romano* (1984) 36 SASR 283; *R v Saliba* (1986) 10 *Criminal Law Journal* 420; *R v Shea* (1988) 33 Australian Criminal Reports 394; *R v Voukelatos* [1990] VR 1.
[89] [1983] 1 VR 460, 466–7.
[90] (1990) 171 CLR 312.

the ordinary person test, distinguishing between gravity of provocation and level of self-control. The court held that the objective test with respect to the ordinary level of self-control could not be modified by the accused's characteristics, apart from immaturity due to age.[91] A few years later the High Court decided *Masciantonio v R*,[92] which involved an Italian immigrant who had murdered his son-in-law because the latter had ill-treated his wife, the accused's daughter. A majority reaffirmed the view in *Stingel*, but McHugh J rejected the *Stingel* view and made a powerful argument in favour of taking into account the accused's cultural background:

> In a multicultural society such as Australia, the notion of an ordinary person is pure fiction. Worse still, its invocation in cases heard by juries of predominantly Anglo-Saxon-Celtic origin almost certainly results in the accused being judged by the standard of self-control attributed to a middle class Australian of Anglo-Saxon-Celtic heritage, that being the stereotype of the ordinary person with which the jurors are most familiar … [U]nless the ethnic or cultural background of the accused is attributed to the ordinary person, the objective test of self-control results in inequality before the law. Real equality before the law cannot exist when ethnic or cultural minorities are convicted or acquitted of murder according to a standard that reflects the values of the dominant class but does not reflect the values of those minorities.[93]

McHugh J's emphasis on real equality pinpoints the critical issue in these cases. Understanding that there is a paradigm for 'ordinary standards' that differs from that of the majority culture does not diminish the strength of the law, nor does it necessarily result in negative stereotyping,[94] as long as the cultural accommodation is done sensibly and sensitively.[95] As an excuse,

---

[91] See also *Green v R* (1997) 191 CLR 334; *Masciantonio v R* (1995) 183 CLR 58.

[92] (1995) 183 CLR 58.

[93] *Ibid* at 74.

[94] The fear of negative stereotypes compelled one academic to change his view from supporting the use of cultural evidence to modify the ordinary person to restricting such evidence to the gravity of provocation only: S Yeo, 'Sex, Ethnicity, Power of Self-Control and Provocation' (1996) 18 *Sydney Law Review* 304, 316: 'Doubtless, the judges who delivered these decisions [concerning Aboriginal offenders] had fairness and justice as their paramount aims. However their decisions had the effect of promoting a greater evil, namely a negative stereotype of Aborigines being at a lower order of the evolutionary scale than other ethnic groups'. Earlier, S Yeo had argued for the inclusion of culture in the objective test: S Yeo, 'Power of Self-Control in Provocation and Automatism' (1992) 14 *Sydney Law Review* 3, 12-13. See also I Leader-Elliott, 'Sex, Race and Provocation: in Defence of *Stingel*' (1996) 20 *Criminal Law Journal* 72.

[95] *R v Kumar* [2002] VSCA 139 is a good illustration of an opportunistic attempt to introduce cultural factors in a desperate bid to bolster the provocation defence. The facts were that the accused, a 20-year-old Fiji-Indian, living in Australia, killed his estranged wife, a 36-year-old Fiji-Indian, some time after the couple separated, largely due to ongoing domestic violence inflicted on the deceased by the accused. The deceased moved from Ipswich, Queensland to Melbourne, Victoria to be away from the accused. He went looking for her in Melbourne and spent a few months there trying to reconcile the relationship. On the day of the killing, the accused went to the deceased's house but she refused to let him in and shouted at him, calling

the general norm is not affected; the court is not legitimising any particular cultural practice that may be viewed as incompatible with modern notions of equality and human rights. All the court is doing is focusing on the moral blameworthiness of the accused and making a context specific judgment as to whether or to what extent the accused deserves criminal punishment.

Despite McHugh J's strident comments,[96] which he restated in *R v Green*,[97] the law in Australia is that stated in *Stingel* and by the majority in *Masciantonio*: in determining the gravity of the provocation, the ordinary person is vested with all relevant characteristics of the accused, including cultural factors, but the assessment of the level of self-control of the ordinary person is purely objective and does not take into account ethnicity or culture. Recent cases from Victoria affirm this approach.

In *R v Yasso*,[98] the accused was a member of the Chaldean Christian community from Iraq who had migrated to Australia some years before the incident. The accused was charged with the murder of his wife and on appeal it was argued that the defence of provocation, including his cultural background, should have been left to the jury. It was argued that the deceased had been having an affair with another man and on the day of the killing had spat at the accused. According to the community, spitting at one's husband was considered the worst type of insult and infidelity was not tolerated. By a two to one majority, the Court of Appeal held that the defence of provocation should have been put to the jury, based on the *Masciantonio* test. At his retrial, the defence of provocation failed and the accused was found guilty of murder and sentenced to 20 years' imprisonment.[99]

In *R v Tuncay*,[100] the accused was a Turkish Muslim who killed his wife after she threatened to take the children and leave him because of his drinking. He pleaded with her to stay and she said '*gebher*', which according to the interpreter was a Turkish expression used when someone wanted to be free of another or if they want the other dead. The accused lost control and killed his wife. The defence of provocation failed at trial and, on appeal, the court held that the defence should not have been put to the jury on the

him a bastard and insulted his parents for belonging to a low caste of Hindus. The accused broke into the house and stabbed her. Defence counsel tried to argue that the accused's culture was relevant to provocation based solely on the evidence given by a Hindi language translator who simply said that the Hindi words were offensive and in her opinion would have been hurtful to a Hindu. The Court of Appeal correctly agreed with the trial judge that provocation was not open on the facts.

[96] An appeal by the accused in *R v Mankotia* [2001] NSWCCA 52 (unreported, 28 February 2001) to the New South Wales Court of Criminal Appeal to apply McHugh J's approach in *Masciantonio* was rejected.

[97] (1997) 191 CLR 334.

[98] *R v Yasso* [2004] VSCA 127.

[99] *R v Yasso* [2005] VSC 75.

[100] [1998] 2 VR 19.

ground that no reasonable jury could have concluded that the deceased's conduct was sufficiently provocative to cause an ordinary person to lose control and kill. The accused was sentenced to 18 years' imprisonment.

In *R v Abebe*,[101] the accused was an Ethiopian who murdered his ex-wife's lover. The accused relied on provocation and gave evidence that the behaviour of his ex-wife was against the norms of his community and extremely humiliating to him. Just before the murder, his ex-wife and deceased told him they were lovers and were going to live together. The deceased smiled at the accused in a provocative manner. The accused was convicted and on appeal it was held that the trial judge had misdirected the jury by failing to explain to them that, in the consideration of the gravity of the allegedly provocative conduct, the accused was entitled to have brought into consideration his ethnicity, that is, the fact that he and all the others involved were Ethiopian or Eritrean, the evidence of what was occurring between the accused's ex-wife and the deceased, the rumours in the Ethiopian community as to their relationship, and the accused's shame and humiliation. The accused was convicted of manslaughter and sentenced to eight years' imprisonment.[102]

In *R v Leonboyer*,[103] the accused was from Chile and had murdered his fiancée, who was from Colombia. The provocation consisted of the deceased's confession of infidelity and a taunt about the accused's sexual prowess. In rejecting the defence, Charles JA held that the cultural evidence did not add to any special understanding of the gravity of the provocation and made this observation on multicultural societies:

> He had, as I have said, lived most of his life in Australia. Having regard to the multi-cultural nature of present Australian society, there are strong reasons in public policy militating against acceptance of the view that the fact that a man comes from a particular cultural background puts him in any special or different position with respect to provocation.[104]

Charles JA's view is in contrast to that of McHugh J in *Masciantonio*; the latter reflects a more sensitive and just approach to criminal culpability, but the former reflects the current law and practice in Australia. Leave to appeal *Leonboyer* to the High Court of Australia was refused.[105] While it is speculative to draw any conclusions from these cases, one pattern that emerges is that courts tend to be less sympathetic to accused who murder their wives or fiancées as compared to those who murder the alleged paramour.

---

[101] [2000] 1 VR 429.
[102] *R v Abebe* [2000] VSC 562.
[103] [2001] VSCA 149.
[104] *Ibid* at para [147].
[105] *Leonboyer v The Queen* [2005] HCATrans 306 (www.austlii.edu.au/cgi-bin/disp.pl/au/other/HCATrans/2005/306.html?query=%5e+leonboyer).

India

Exception 1 to s 300 of the Indian Penal code provides the defence of provocation in the context of murder and it reads:

> Culpable homicide is not murder if the offender whilst deprived of the power of self-control by grave and sudden provocation, causes the death of the person who gave the provocation, or causes the death of any other person by mistake or accident.

The provision itself makes no mention of an objective test based on an ordinary person's response, but the Indian courts inexplicably read in an objective test, following English developments. Nevertheless, the Indian approach may be slightly broader than the Anglo-Australian approach with respect to culture and the ordinary person's level of self-control. In the seminal case of *Nanavati v State of Maharashtra*,[106] the accused was an Indian naval officer who was married to an English woman. On learning that she was having an affair with another man, the accused became enraged, armed himself with a gun and went to the lover's house where he confronted him and then shot him.[107] His defence of provocation failed because of the interval between the provocation and the killing as well as the fact that he had deliberately set out to kill the deceased. Nevertheless, the court made this crucial observation on the test for the ordinary person:

> Is there any standard of a reasonable man for the application of the doctrine of 'grave and sudden' provocation? No abstract standard of reasonableness can be laid down. What a reasonable man will do in certain circumstances depends upon the customs, manners, way of life, traditional values etc; in short, the cultural, social and emotional background of the society to which the accused belongs. In our vast country there are social groups ranging from the lowest to the highest state of civilization. It is neither possible nor desirable to lay down any standard with precision: it is for the court to decide in each case, having regard to the relevant circumstances.[108]

One reason why the Indian courts have had little trouble taking ethnicity into account is the fact that India is such a diverse country that there is an innate appreciation and respect for cultural difference. This has not been the

---

[106] [1962] AIR SC 605.

[107] Nanavati was eventually pardoned. The case attracted unprecedented media attention in India and even resulted in a Bollywood movie, *Yeh raste hain pyar ke* (*These are the Paths of Love*), starring the late Sunil Dutt who passed away on 25 May 2005 after serving as India's Minister for Sports. In true Bollywood style, the story was reworked so that the wife was depicted as have been seduced by the deceased and Nanavati's killing was treated as accidental.

[108] *Ibid* at 629–30 per Subba Rao J.

case in countries such as the United States, England and Australia, which traditionally were relatively homogenous and are now facing the challenges of multiculturalism following massive immigration.[109] As multiculturalism becomes internalised, reaching beyond political rhetoric and residing in the social conscience of the people, the debate on whether ethnicity should be recognised will resolve itself as naturally as it did in *Nanavati*.

In the earlier decision of *Ghulam Mustafa Gahno v Emperor*,[110] the accused had killed his wife who had made a rude gesture (*booja*)[111] which had provoked him. The accused and his wife were members of the Baluchi community in India. In considering the provocation defence, the court held that the ordinary person was 'the ordinary normal Baluchi, when dealing with Baluchis and the ordinary normal Englishman when dealing with the English'.[112] The question was whether the power of self-control of an ordinary Baluchi would have been affected to such an extent by this provocation that an ordinary Baluchi could have killed the provoker. An elder in the community testified that showing the *booja* was a terrible insult, but that it would not provoke an ordinary Baluchi to kill. The defence thus failed.

It may be argued that there was an element of cultural superiority in operation as the judge was an Englishman and may have taken a condescending view of the Baluch as a 'less sophisticated culture'. One should also question whether it is safe to rely, as the court did in *Ghulam Mustafo Gano*, on the testimony of one tribal elder, who in that case also happened to be the uncle of the accused. Should there have been broader consultation within the community or the appointment of an expert?

Taking account of cultural perspectives in determining reasonable or ordinary responses is not to give individuals from cultural minority groups a licence to break the law; it is simply to recognise that there are different standards of ordinariness or reasonableness. The standard is not based on the individual alone, but on the standards accepted by the cultural group as a whole. The danger is that there may be some 'cultural' standards

---

[109] 'The Australian legal system is a product of the society in which it has evolved over the past two centuries and, to a lesser extent, the society (England) from which it was transplanted 200 years ago. Since European settlement, the non-Aboriginal society has been predominantly Anglo-Celtic and has largely excluded the original inhabitants and ignored their cultures, at least until recently. As a result of the post-war immigration of large numbers of people from continental Europe and later from the Middle East, Asia and South America, the ethnic composition of Australian society has dramatically and irrevocably changed. While cultural diversity is now an accepted part of Australian society, the consequences of this for the legal system have not yet been fully considered'. Australian Law Reform Commission, *Multiculturalism and the Law*, ALRC 57 (1992) [1.16].

[110] (1939) 40 *Criminal Law Journal* 778.

[111] A '*booja*' was the showing of an outwardly turned palm of the left hand and is considered to be one of the most insulting gestures according to Baluch custom.

[112] (1939) 40 *Criminal Law Journal* 778, 780.

that are unacceptable because those standards themselves are inherently discriminatory to certain subgroups (usually women and children) within that cultural group itself. For example, in *Atma Ram v State*,[113] the accused killed his wife because she refused to have sex with him and swore at him. In taking into account his cultural background, the court said:

> It is important to emphasise that the impact of provocation on human frailty is to be judged in the context of the social position and environments of the person concerned. The restraint which is generally shown by sophisticated persons used to modern living is hardly to be expected in the case of a villager who still regards a wife as his personal property and chattel amenable at all times to his desire for sexual intercourse.[114]

Provocation and Multiculturalism: Moving Forward

It is important to recall that provocation is only an excuse and does not operate as a complete defence. Therefore, insisting on a standard that may not fairly represent that of the cultural group of the accused may be unjust. Where provocation operates as a complete defence, in the sense of a justification, the more stringent approach may be necessary, as seen in the Australian assault case, mentioned earlier.[115] The ordinary or reasonable person should not be determined solely by the dominant culture. The New South Wales Law Reform Commission has considered three options for the objective test with respect to self-control: expand the ordinary person test to permit consideration of culture and/or gender; abolish the ordinary person test in favour of a purely subjective test; or replace the ordinary person test with a subjective test together with the application of community standards. It favoured the last option on the ground that:

> it avoids the complexities of the ordinary person test while still allowing the jury to make a value judgment about whether or not a particular accused should be convicted of murder or manslaughter, in light of the particular mitigating circumstances of the provocation and the accused's blameworthiness.[116]

This is a sensible approach that places the focus on what is reasonable according to community standards. Full consideration of all relevant factors, including culture, should result in a sensitive and just determination of criminal culpability.

[113] (1967) *Criminal Law Journal* 1697.
[114] *Ibid* at 1698.
[115] *Verhoeven and others v Ninyette and another* [1998] WASCA 73.
[116] New South Wales Law Reform Commission, *Partial Defences to Murder: Provocation and Infanticide* [1997] NSWLR Rep 83 at [2.80].

CONCLUSION

We live in an increasingly multicultural world, which calls for more cultural accommodation by legislators, regulators and policy-makers. Criminal law, with penal sanctions that deprive or diminish an individual's life or liberty, is a prime candidate for greater acculturation to this new world. Whether this should be achieved by developing a separate cultural defence for certain cultural groups or by refining existing criminal law doctrines is a matter that merits ongoing debate. The view expressed in this chapter is that the latter strategy is preferable for the reasons given. Nevertheless, focusing the debate on the cultural defence compels legislators and courts to confront the issue and be more receptive to cultural concerns, as the feminist debate has shown.

While the battered woman syndrome problem did not result in a special 'woman's defence' (cf cultural defence) for abused women who reacted violently, it did catalyse reform of existing criminal law doctrine by internalising women's perspectives.[117] It also compelled judges, prosecutors and policy-makers to accept that there was an alternative, and equally legitimate, paradigm of standards and behaviour that deserved to be reflected in the law and legal process. Instead of treating abused women as 'different' and requiring 'special' treatment, their experience and perspectives were internalised into the law; fairness operated not as a matter of exception but as part of the general rule.[118]

Similarly, cultural minorities risk being treated unfairly as their experiences and perspectives are not always reflected in the law. Rather than entrenching a 'them and us' dichotomy, it is suggested that the fundamental principles of criminal culpability be refined in order to accommodate this diversity of norms and values. The theory of justification and excuse provides a rational strategy for maintaining the balance between individualising criminal justice while preserving a uniform criminal law that applies equally to all its citizens. Cultural accommodation has to be a two-way street: minority cultures need to recognise that they have an obligation to respect and obey the general laws of the nation-state to which they belong, whether by birth or choice; the majority have to accept that a global human culture is slowly evolving, which will be shaped by a diversity of norms.

---

[117] For example, the Government of New South Wales, Australia, established a Task Force on Domestic Violence in 1981, which made several recommendations for law reform. Among the reforms that were adopted were changes to the law of provocation to give women a fairer opportunity at pleading the defence. See D Brown *et al, Criminal Law: Materials and Commentary on Criminal Law and Process of New South Wales* (Sydney, The Federation Press, 1990) 725.

[118] For a sceptical reflection on this view, see J Stubbs and J Tolmie, 'Falling Short of the Challenge? A Comparative Assessment of the Australian Use of Expert Evidence on the Battered Woman Syndrome' (1999) 23 *Melbourne University Law Review* 709.

3

*The Use and Abuse of the Cultural Defense**

ALISON DUNDES RENTELN

INTRODUCTION

WHEN INDIVIDUALS COMMIT culturally motivated acts that clash with the law, they may ask courts to consider the cultural imperatives that inspired the actions in question. When they advance arguments of this sort, they usually wish to introduce expert testimony into court to underscore the validity of their claims. Unfortunately, judges are often disinclined to allow the introduction of such evidence and exclude it as 'irrelevant'. Their refusal to allow cultural evidence is unfortunate because it can result in a miscarriage of justice. My view is that the cultural defense should be established as official public policy as long as safeguards are put in place to prevent its misuse.

In this chapter I begin with a brief rationale for the adoption of this policy, analyze cases in which culture was improperly excluded from the proceedings, and then turn to a consideration of potential misuses of the defense in the context of a few examples. It is crucial to think carefully about possible difficulties that may arise with the implementation of the cultural defense, as it is only in legal systems that guard against the abuse of the cultural defense that this strategy has a chance of becoming a viable policy option.[1]

---

* This essay was originally published in (2005) 20(1) *Canadian Journal of Law and Society* 47. It is reprinted with permission.

[1] The debate over the cultural defence is taking place in countries across the globe such as Australia, Belgium, Canada, England, the Netherlands, South Africa and the United States. See, eg, J Van Broeck, 'Cultural Defence and Culturally Motivated Crimes (Cultural Offences)' (2001) 9 *European Journal of Crime, Criminal Law and Criminal Justice* 1; S Bronitt and K Amirthalingam, 'Cultural Blindness: Criminal Law in Multicultural Australia' (1996) 21(2) *Alternative Law Journal* 58; S Poulter, *Ethnicity, Law, and Human Rights: the English Experience* (Oxford, Oxford University Press, 1998); A Phillips, 'When Culture Means Gender: Issues of Cultural Defence in English Courts' (2003) 66 *Modern Law Review* 510; CM Wong, 'Good Intentions, Troublesome Applications: the Cultural Defence and Other

RATIONALE FOR THE CULTURAL DEFENSE

Cultural differences deserve to be considered in litigation because encul-turation shapes individuals' perceptions and influences their actions. The acquisition of cultural categories is largely an unconscious process, so individuals are usually unaware of having internalized them. The premise of the cultural defense argument is that culture exerts a strong influence on individuals, predisposing them to act in ways consistent with their upbring-ing. The theoretical basis for a cultural defense hinges on the idea that individuals will think and act in accordance with patterns of culture.

Legal systems must acknowledge the influence of cultural imperatives as part of individualized justice, and this cross-cultural jurisprudence does not represent a radical departure from existing policies in most criminal justice systems. Taking a person's cultural background into account is fundamen-tally no different from judges' taking into consideration other social attri-butes such as gender, age and mental state. Insofar as individualized justice is an accepted part of legal systems, the cultural difference is simply another factor to review in the context of meting out condign punishment.[2]

Well-established principles of law support the use of the cultural defense. These principles include the right to a fair trial, religious liberty and equal protection of the law. If individuals who come from other societies are entitled to these rights, it is incumbent on legal actors to take cultural dif-ferences into account.[3]

Another normative principle supports the use of the cultural defense. Under international human rights law, virtually all states have an obliga-tion to protect the right to culture. The right to culture is found in various international instruments, with the most important formulation in Article 27 of the International Covenant on Civil and Political Rights (ICCPR):

> In those States in which ethnic, religious or linguistic minorities exist, persons belonging to such minorities shall not be denied the right, in community with the

---

Uses of Cultural Evidence in Canada' (1999) 42(2), (3) *Criminal Law Quarterly* 367; D Woo, 'Cultural "Anomalies" and Cultural Defenses: Towards an Integrated Theory of Homicide and Suicide' (2004) 32 *International Journal of the Sociology of Law* 279; PA Carstens, *The Cultural Defence in Criminal Law: South African Perspectives* (2004) 2 *De Jure* 312. See also the essays on 'Folk Law in Conflict' in AD Renteln and A Dundes (eds), *Folk Law: Essays in the Theory and Practice of Lex Non Scripta* (Madison, University of Wisconsin Press, 1995).

[2] The challenge is to persuade courts to consider cultural motives. For a comprehensive treatment of culture in the context of criminal defenses, see AD Renteln, 'A Justification of the Cultural Defense as Partial Excuse' (1993) 2 *Southern California Review of Law and Women's Studies* 437.

[3] For a more complete argument, see AD Renteln, *The Cultural Defense* (New York, Oxford University Press, 2004). See also AD Renteln, 'Visual Religious Symbols and the Law' (2004) 47 *American Behavioral Scientist* 1573.

other members of their group, to enjoy their own culture, to profess and practice their own religion, or to use their own language.

The Human Rights Committee has construed the right as involving an obligation on the part of states to take affirmative steps to protect the right to culture.[4] As I have argued elsewhere, this right should mean, at the very least, that individuals who migrate to other countries have the opportunity to tell a court of law what motivated the actions that apparently clash with the law of the new country.[5] If construed in this way, the right to culture should authorize use of the cultural defense.

The main benefit of an official cultural defense is that it would ensure the consideration of cultural evidence in a court of law. Rather than leaving the decision about the appropriateness of admitting evidence to the whims of particular judges, a formal policy would guarantee that the courtroom door is open to data of this kind.[6] Of course, this does not mean that the information would necessarily affect the disposition of the case. What effect the cultural evidence should have is a separate question. Judges and juries would have to decide to what extent, if at all, cultural differences should mitigate punishment, make an ethnic group exempt from a policy or increase the size of a damage award.

SCOPE OF THE CULTURAL DEFENSE

Although many regard the cultural defense as a strategy for reducing punishment in criminal cases, it is, in fact, used in a much wider range of court cases and also affects pre-trial legal processes. In family court, the question may be whether or not to terminate parental rights. In civil cases, judges are asked to increase the size of a damage award because the particular action, eg, an unauthorized autopsy, affected a family more than one from the dominant culture because of the family's religious background. In the asylum context, immigration judges must analyze traditions to determine, for instance, if women have a well-founded fear that they will be forced to submit to an oppressive tradition if returned to their countries of origin, ie, the cultural argument is sometimes the basis of a request for political asylum.

---

[4] The Human Rights Committee issues policy statements clarifying the scope of rights in the form of general comments. For its interpretation of Article 27, see General Comment 23.
    [5] AD Renteln, *Cultural Rights: International Encyclopedia of Social and Behavioral Sciences* (Paul Baltes and Neil Smelser (eds), Elsevier, 2002); AD Renteln, 'In Defense of Culture in the Courtroom' in R Shweder, M Minow and HR Markus (eds), *Engaging Cultural Differences: the Multicultural Challenge in Liberal Democracies* (New York, Russell Sage, 2002) 194–215.
    [6] One of the earlier articles on this subject emphasized how crucial it is to ensure consideration of evidence. BL Diamond, 'Social and Cultural Factors as a Diminished Capacity Defense in Criminal Law' (1978) 6 *Bulletin of the American Academy of Psychiatry and the Law* 195, 203.

In *The Cultural Defense* I document the ubiquity of culture conflict cases and contend that this widespread phenomenon deserves greater attention. I advanced an argument in favour of a cultural defense, even though there are bound to be difficulties associated with the implementation of this policy. If courts are authorized to evaluate evidence concerning the cultural traditions of ethnic groups and indigenous peoples, there is no question that judges must verify the authenticity of claims put forward.

To minimize potential misuse of the defense, were it to be put into practice, I have proposed a cultural defense test that courts could use to help avoid abuse. Courts applying it would have to consider three basic queries:

(1) Is the litigant a member of the ethnic group?
(2) Does the group have such a tradition?
(3) Was the litigant influenced by the tradition when he or she acted?[7]

If courts are careful to insist upon answers to the questions posed here, this should help reduce the number of false claims and discourage illegitimate use of the defense.

To demonstrate how the test might be applied in the context of cases that invoke ostensibly legitimate cultural defenses, I will discuss a few examples. Following the consideration of these cases, I will turn to others in which the failure to investigate cultural claims risks undermining support for this policy.

Because there is widespread concern about the possible misuse of the cultural defense, I would like to draw attention to several examples of what I regard as unjustified attempts to raise cultural defenses. As we shall see, in some cases litigants fail to meet more than one of the requirements in the test.

This chapter focuses primarily on the question of how litigants should go about establishing their claims. I wish to note, at the outset, however, that even if they can authenticate their claims, courts might still wish to reject the cultural defense. Where cultural traditions involve irreparable harm to vulnerable groups, the defense should not influence the disposition of cases. To prevent improper use of the cultural defense, one must ask first whether the claim is factually accurate as an empirical matter, but then go on to determine whether accepting the claim that the right to culture should permit the custom, risks undermining other important human rights, such as the rights of women and children.

PROPER USE OF THE CULTURAL DEFENSE

Although there is a widespread perception that use of the cultural defense is improper, in many cases cultural information is crucial for understanding

---

[7] Renteln, *The Cultural Defense*, above n 4 at 207.

the context of actions. For example, numerous cases involve adults who touch children in the genital area and are subsequently prosecuted for child sexual abuse. Because those observing the conduct automatically assume that the action is sexual in nature rather than merely a way of showing affection, families have been broken up and even destroyed.[8] In the *Krasniqi* case, an Albanian Muslim father touched his four-year-old daughter in a public gymnasium. The prosecutor assumed that the touching was for the purpose of sexual gratification, and he had to establish the motive here because child sexual abuse is a special intent crime.[9]

When Sam Krasniqi was prosecuted in a Texas criminal court, an expert witness on Albanian culture testified that the touching was a way of showing affection, and the father was subsequently acquitted.[10] It appears that the court was satisfied that all three parts of the cultural defense were met: the father was Albanian, Albanians had a custom of touching children that was not erotic, and the father was motivated by the custom when he touched his daughter. Unfortunately, however, even though the criminal court exonerated the father, this had no effect on the earlier decision of the family court that had terminated his parental rights.[11]

Culture should also be taken into consideration in cases involving the defense of provocation.[12] In these cases, individuals claim that an insult or gesture provoked them to commit violent acts. There are two 'prongs' to the test for provocation: the subjective part, ie, whether the defendant was actually provoked, and the objective part, ie, whether the objective reasonable person would have been provoked. Although defendants may be able to prove the first, they have considerable difficulty with the second. Consider the unpublished decision of *Trujillo-Garcia v Rowland* in which two Mexican Americans were playing poker. After Jose Padilla lost US$140 to Trujillo-Garcia, he went home but then returned four days later demanding his money back. When Trujillo-Garcia refused, the man said '*chinga tu*

---

[8] See, eg, *State v Kargar*, 679 A2d 81 (Me 1996). See also NA Wanderer and CR Connors, 'Culture and Crime: Kargar and the Existing Framework for a Cultural Defense' (1999) 47 *Buffalo Law Review* 829.

[9] Most crimes require only mens rea (intent) and actus reus (act). Specific intent crimes also require proof of the motive or reason for the action. To be guilty of child sexual abuse, a parent must intend to touch the child, must touch the child, *and* must do so for sexual gratification. Otherwise parents would be unable to bathe their children or change their diapers.

[10] For an account of this case, see H Downs and B Walters, *We Want Our Children Back*, 18 August 1995, 20/20 (ABC 9:00 pm EST), transcript #1533, available on Nexis.

[11] Renteln, *The Cultural Defense*, above n 4 at 59. Touching children in the genital area should probably be discouraged not only because parents will encounter difficulty with the law, but also because children caught between two cultures may feel uncomfortable if they realize it is considered inappropriate conduct in the larger society. But incarcerating parents or breaking up families are illegitimate means of inculcating new values.

[12] It is a partial excuse that reduces a charge of murder to one of manslaughter.

madre', an extremely offensive phrase in Spanish.[13] Trujillo-Garcia drew a gun from his waistband and shot him dead.

The defense tried unsuccessfully to introduce evidence to show that the average reasonable Mexican would have been provoked by the phrase. The state courts agreed that the evidence was irrelevant. In federal court, Trujillo-Garcia argued that the court's failure to take into consideration the cultural context of his action violated his right to equal protection.[14] Whereas the nature of an act constituting a provocation is usually understandable to a jury, in the instant case, without the contextual information concerning the provocation that affected him, namely the verbal insult in Spanish, the jury could not comprehend the offensiveness of the insult. The federal courts insisted on adhering to the 'objective' reasonable person test and assumed that even if the court had allowed him to invoke a culturally relative standard and argue that the phrase would offend the average Mexican, this would not have constituted adequate provocation.

Had the court used the cultural defense test, it would have found that Trujillo-Garcia was indeed Mexican American, that this verbal insult was considered extremely offensive by members of his ethnic group, and that he was motivated by the insult when he killed the individual who uttered it. By excluding the cultural evidence, the court effectively made it impossible for him to raise the provocation defense.[15]

Provocation, even if successful, merely reduces murder to manslaughter; it does not result in an acquittal. Some may resist the suggestion that Trujillo-Garcia should have been entitled to avail himself of a culturally relative provocation defense because the defense is predicated on acceptance of the notion that individuals lose self-control in some circumstances, ordinarily when a jealous husband kills his wife or lover or both. If one thinks this premise is wrong, then the provocation defense should be discarded altogether. The philosophical difficulty here is that a criminal defense, theoretically available to all, in reality cannot be used by individuals from other cultures because they are provoked by insults different from those that would offend the objective reasonable person.

---

[13] For analysis of the term '*chingar*', see O Paz, 'The Sons of La Malinche' in O Paz, *The Labyrinth of Solitude: Life and Thought in Mexico* (Lysander Kemp (trans), New York, Grove Press, 1961) 65–89. See also Renteln, *The Cultural Defense*, above n 4 at 34–5.

[14] *Trujillo-Garcia v Rowland*, 1992 US Dist LEXIS 6199 (28 April 1992) US District Court, Northern District of California, 1993 US App LEXIS 30441 (10 November 1993), US Court of Appeals for the 9th Circuit; 114 S Ct 2145; 1994 US LEXIS 4219; 128 L Ed 873; 62 USLW 3793 (31 May 1994, cert denied).

[15] For a thoughtful treatment of the dilemma of a defendant from another culture seeking to use the provocation defense, see SMH Yeo, 'Recent Australian Pronouncements on the Ordinary Person Test in Provocation and Automatism' (1990–91) 33 *Criminal Law Quarterly* 280 and 'Provoking the "Ordinary" Ethnic Person: a Juror's Predicament' (1987) 11 *Criminal Law Journal* 96.

In some homicide cases, the question is whether cultural evidence must be presented during the sentencing phase, rather than the guilt phase, in an attempt to mitigate the punishment.[16] Failure of the attorney to present mitigating evidence concerning a defendant's cultural background arguably constitutes a violation of the constitutional right to effective assistance of counsel guaranteed by the Sixth Amendment. This was the contention in *Siripongs v Calderon*.[17] Jaturun 'Jay' Siripongs, a Thai national, was convicted of two murders with special circumstances for participating in the robbery of a convenience store during which two were killed. Siripongs admitted being present during the commission of the crimes but denied that he had pulled the trigger.[18] During the sentencing phase of the trial, he did not display any emotion and would not name the individual responsible for the actual killing; the jury sentenced him to death. His attorney failed to explain the cultural aspects of his behaviour, and this was subsequently the basis of an appeal of his death sentence. Despite a precedent in the same jurisdiction supporting the argument that failure to introduce cultural evidence may constitute a violation of the Sixth Amendment right to effective assistance of counsel, the Court of Appeals for the Ninth Circuit rejected his appeal. There was an enormous outpouring of support for Siripongs from members of the victims' families and the warden of San Quentin himself. Nevertheless, after two governors denied clemency petitions, Siripongs was executed.

Had the cultural evidence been admitted, it would have shown that in Thai culture, individuals are socialized not to display any emotion, even when they are under extreme stress. His stoic demeanour did not mean he lacked remorse, something which US juries often require if they are to spare a defendant's life. Moreover, the Thai notion of '*boon*' and '*baap*' might have helped the jury understand why Siripongs was unwilling to enlarge the circle of shame by identifying the individual responsible for the killing, even when his own life was at stake.[19] If the jury had had the benefit of the cultural information, they would have seen that Siripongs was from Thailand, that the Thai worldview includes the different notions of responsibility, and

---

[16] See, eg, M Winkelman, 'Cultural Factors in Criminal Defense Proceedings' (1996) 55 *Human Organization* 154; OL Clinton, 'Cultural Differences and Sentencing Departures' (1993) 5 *Federal Sentencing Reporter* 348; KL Holmquist, 'Cultural Defense or False Stereotype? What Happens when Latina Defendants Collide with the Federal Sentencing Guidelines' (1997) 12 *Berkeley Women's Law Journal* 45; YM Murray, 'The Battered Woman Syndrome and the Cultural Defense' (1995) 7 *Federal Sentencing Reporter* 197.

[17] *Siripongs v Calderon*, 35 F3d 1308 (9th Cir 1994), cert denied 512 US 1183 (1995); 133 F3d 732 (1998).

[18] As he was present during the commission of the crime, he was technically eligible to receive the death penalty under the felony murder rule whether or not he pulled the trigger. Nevertheless, a jury might have seen fit to spare his life had they believed someone else had actually committed the murder.

[19] For more on this case, see Renteln, *The Cultural Defense*, above n 4 at 43.

requires a stoic demeanour when in traumatic circumstances, and that these precepts affected his conduct. It is not clear whether he would have avoided the death penalty, but at least the trial would have been more fair. In the absence of cultural evidence during the sentencing phase of a trial, there is a serious risk that a defendant will receive a disproportionately harsh sentence.

In civil litigation, the cultural defense test can also be useful, as one can see in the case of *Friedman v. State*.[20] A 16-year-old woman, Ruth Friedman, went up the mountain to have a picnic with a male friend. Because the ski-lift company negligently posted the notice indicating the lift would stop early that day, the two did not see it and found themselves stranded halfway down the hill in a ski-lift chair late in the afternoon. When it became dark, Friedman became hysterical about violating religious law by remaining alone with a man after dark, and she threw herself off the ski-lift. In the lawsuit against the ski-lift company, she had to establish that she belonged to the Orthodox Jewish community, that a possible interpretation of Jewish law includes a belief that a young girl should not be left unchaperoned with a male because this would ruin her reputation, and that she was motivated by this belief when she jumped off the ski-lift chair. In this case the court, relying on expert testimony proffered by a rabbi, ruled in her favour, awarding her damages of nearly US$40,000.

The cases here show the importance of taking cultural information into account to prevent a serious miscarriage of justice. Judges unfamiliar with the folkways of various groups frequently exclude the evidence because they consider it irrelevant. If they were to use the cultural defense test, they could prove the accuracy of the cultural claims to their satisfaction. Because they may have an intuition that over-zealous attorneys will raise absurd cultural defenses, judges may be inclined to reject the defense altogether. This is unfortunate because there are legitimate cases in which courts cannot comprehend what has transpired without the benefit of evidence about the cultural context in which the acts occurred.

MISUSE OF THE CULTURAL DEFENSE

Critics of the cultural defense sometimes try to render it a ridiculous strategy by pointing to cases whose use of culture is so objectionable that even advocates of the cultural defense would reject it. For example, some refer to a case in which an African-American male prosecuted for assault wanted

20 *Friedman v State*, 282 N.Y.S. 2d 858 (1967), 54 Misc2d 448.

to introduce testimony to show a 'cultural difference' associated with 'black people'.[21] The defendant, arguing *pro se*, wanted to explain that when he invited the victim to his apartment, he spoke loudly. He claimed this had relevance for determining whether he had a reasonable belief the victim was consenting to sexual intercourse:

> He argues that he could have convinced the jury that she thought nothing of his loud voice because it is a common characteristic of black people to talk loudly to each other, and thus he reasonably thought she attached no significance to it because she was accustomed to such loud speech.

Not only does the defendant conflate culture with race, but he makes an even more egregious error, putting forward a bizarre generalization about African-Americans. Had he not been representing himself in court, he might not have sought to make such a patently absurd argument.

Another spurious use of the cultural defense case featured an Iranian Jewish husband who combined a battered husband defense with the 'cultural' argument that his wife henpecked him, made him sleep on the floor, and forced him to beg for money for cigarettes.[22] Media coverage described his 'cultural defense' as follows:

> Moosa Hanoukai, 55, admitted beating his 45-year-old wife Manijeh to death ... but claimed that she had abused him throughout their 25-year marriage. Testifying in Farsi and sobbing frequently, Hanoukai said that after the couple came to the United States in 1982 and opened a woman's clothing store, his wife forced him to sleep on the floor, prohibited him from spending any money, and persistently derided him as 'stupid' and 'garbage' in front of relatives.[23]

The lawyer also claimed that leaving the marriage was not an option in his community: 'Due to cultural and religious grounds, they were unable to get a divorce'.[24] Even members of the community expressed scepticism about the argument that denigrating her husband's virility violates 'the norms of Persian Jewish culture in which the male is dominant'.[25] Despite the

---

[21] *People v Rhines*, 131 Cal. App. 3d 298 (1982). For another case involving racism, see also P Fournier, 'The Ghettoisation of Differences in Canada: "Rape by Culture" and the Danger of a "Cultural Defense" in Criminal Law Trials' (2002) 8 *Manitoba Law Journal* 88.

[22] T Mrozek, 'Accused Wife Killer to Claim Mental Abuse', *Los Angles Times* (valley ed), 7 May 1993, B1.

[23] T Tugend, '"Cultural Defense" Plea Gets Sentence Lowered', *Jerusalem Post*, 29 March 1994, 3.

[24] T Mrozek, 'Cultural Defense in Wife's Death', *Los Angeles Times*, 4 March 1994, B3.

[25] One said: 'I think it's a stupid lawyer's trick', *ibid*.

questionable nature of the argument, the jury found the husband guilty of manslaughter instead of murder.[26]

If cultural defenses were raised in cases of only this sort, it would come as no surprise if everyone were to dismiss the cultural defense as an unreasonable proposal. To guard against the abuse of the defense, it is worthwhile evaluating some specific types of false claims that may be advanced.

In cases in which there is a *prima facie* legitimate cultural argument, the first question is whether the individual raising the cultural claim is actually a member of the group with the tradition in question. It is, of course, possible that an individual will pretend to be member of a group in order to be allowed privileges accorded that group. For example, students unfamiliar with the *kirpan*, the religious dagger that baptized Sikhs are required to wear, sometimes imagine that non-Sikhs might disguise themselves as Sikhs in order to wear knives in public. While it is conceivable that non-Sikhs might falsely claim to follow the Sikh religion in order to wear knives in public, it seems highly unlikely. Moreover, baptized Sikhs must also wear other religious symbols, which further calls into question the likelihood that someone will go to the trouble of masquerading as a Sikh in order to wear a dagger in public.

This question of whether the defendant is actually a member of the group has arisen. For instance, in *State v Bauer*, Rastafarians were not allowed to raise a religious defense when they were prosecuted for possession of marijuana and conspiracy to run a multimillion dollar marijuana farm.[27] While Rastafarians are known to use '*ganja*' in religious ceremonies, the federal judges in this case wondered if there were any Rastafarians in Montana.[28] The court explicitly stated that just because the defendants want to 'claim the name of a religion as a protective cloak', neither the prosecutors nor the court had to accept 'the defendants' mere say-so'.[29] Assuming the defendants really were members of the religion, the judges ruled that they should be permitted to raise a religious defense as to simple possession but not as to the conspiracy to distribute, possession with intent to distribute, or money-laundering charges.[30]

---

[26] T Mrozek, 'Prosecutor Says Accused Killer Lied', *Los Angeles Times*, 18 March 1994, B4. Despite accepting manslaughter, some jurors told the press they were 'not swayed by the cultural defense'; A Burke, 'Man who Said Wife Abused Him Guilty in Killing', *Daily News*, 26 March 1994.

[27] *United States v Bauer*, 84 F.3d 1549 (9th Cir. 1996). The judges thought they should be entitled to raise the religious defence with respect to the possession claims, but were doubtful as to whether the Rastafarian faith required the multimillion dollar farm.

[28] The appellate court said that when retried the defendants would have 'the obligation of showing that they are in fact Rastafarians and that the use of marijuana is a part of the religious practice of Rastafarians' (*ibid* at 1559).

[29] *Ibid*.

[30] 'As to the counts relating to conspiracy to distribute, possession with intent to distribute, and money laundering, the religious freedom of the defendants was not invaded. Nothing before us suggests that Rastafarianism would require this conduct'. *Ibid* at 1559.

In some cases, litigants fail to meet more than one part of the cultural defense test. For example, if a person is not a member of the group, then even if the group has the custom in question, he or she cannot claim to have been influenced by the cultural imperative. Hence the individual will not meet requirements (1) and (3). Likewise, if the person is a bona fide member of the group, but the group does not have the tradition, again the person will be unable to show he or she acted under the cultural imperative. So, while in theory, failure to prove one part would be sufficient to make the use of the cultural defense inappropriate, it happens that individuals attempting to raise the defense improperly will fail on more than one ground. I turn now to what I consider to be examples of egregious misuse of the cultural defense.

Adelaide Abankwah and her Gender Asylum Claim

In a case that received tremendous media coverage, Adelaide Abankwah, a woman from Ghana, sought political asylum in the United States to avoid the custom known as 'female genital mutilation' (FGM). She told immigration authorities that she was eldest daughter of the Queen of the Nkummsa people and that her mother had just died. Because she was next in line to assume the throne and because she was not a virgin, she had to be circumcised to avoid detection of her lack of purity. So as not to be forcibly subjected to FGM, she fled to the United States where she sought political asylum. She attracted considerable political support. Prominent feminists like Gloria Steinem and Hillary Clinton, the leading organization Equality Now, actresses Julia Roberts and Vanessa Redgrave, and legislators rallied around her, seeing her as a victim of a cruel cultural tradition.[31] The magazine *Marie Claire* had T-shirts printed with the phrase 'Free Adelaide'. Her gender asylum claim seemed promising as it followed a successful decision for a woman from Togo, Fausiya Kasinga, who won asylum in the United States to escape from precisely this custom.[32]

At first the Immigration and Naturalization Service (INS) denied Abankwah's asylum petition because she had not proved she had a reasonable fear she would be harmed if returned to Ghana.[33] During the course of the appeals, she was detained for two years at a detention centre in Queens,

---

[31] For a detailed account of the proceedings, see DA Martin's thoughtful essay 'Adelaide Abankwah, Fauziya Kasinga, and the Dilemmas of Political Asylum' in DA Martin and PH Schuck (eds), *Immigration Stories* (New York, Foundation Press, 2005).

[32] Kasinga proved that she had a well-founded fear of persecution and her fears were on account of membership in a social group. *In re Fauziya Kasinga*, 1996 BIA LEXIS 15. See also F Kassindja and LM Bashir, *Do They Hear You When You Cry?* (New York, Delta, 1998).

[33] She also requested withholding of deportation which is subject to different standards.

New York. Eventually, the US Court of Appeals for the Second Circuit accepted her account, rejecting the judgment of the Board of Immigration Appeals (BIA). The appellate court remanded the matter, ordering the BIA to grant her petition for asylum.[34] Judge Sweet was persuaded that Abankwah was a member of the Nkumssa tribe in central Ghana and accepted her story:

> Nkumssa tradition requires that the girl or woman next in line for the Queen Mother position must remain a virgin until she is 'enstooled'. During the ceremony to enstool a new Queen Mother, the designated Queen Mother must cup her hands and hold water in them. According to tribal legend, if the woman has disobeyed tribal taboos—including the one against engaging in premarital sex—she will be unable to hold the water in her hands, and it will spill out onto the ground. Even if the woman successfully holds the water, however, after her enthronement, the village elders select a husband for her who will inevitably discover whether she is a virgin or not. In either case, if the woman is believed not to be a virgin, she will be forced to undergo FGM.[35]

The federal appellate court discounted doubts expressed by the immigration authorities in the case.[36] The INS had noted that FGM was not practised in central Ghana, the area from which Abankwah came, although it was in Northern Ghana, and that Abankwah admitted that FGM 'is not regularly practised by the Nkumssa tribe'. The outcome was grounds for celebration among women's rights advocates.

Shortly after the Court of Appeals handed down its decision granting her request for political asylum, information came to light that Abankwah's claim was false. Adelaide Abankwah 'allegedly fabricated details of her background to portray herself as a human rights victim'.[37] An in-depth INS investigation and an article in the *Washington Post* confirmed that indeed Abankwah was an imposter.[38] Her real name was Regina Norman Danson, and she was not a member of the royal family: she was a former hotel worker, and she had stolen the identity of Adelaide Abankwah.[39] Moreover, her mother was still alive, and it was unclear from media coverage whether

---

[34] A Waldman, 'Woman Fearful of Mutilation Wins Long Battle for Asylum', *New York Times*, 18 August 1999, B3; W Hu, 'Woman Fleeing Mutilation Savors Freedom', *New York Times*, 20 August 1999, B4.

[35] *Abankwah v INS*, 183 F.3d 18; 1999 US App LEXIS 15545.

[36] The immigration judge apparently rejected her claim because Ghana outlawed FGM in 1994 and because there were no reports of the practice in the region from which she came. *Abankwah v INS*, 185 F. 3d 18, 20 (2d Cir. 1999).

[37] J Marzulli, 'Her Mutilation Tale is a Fake, Say Feds', *Daily News*, 10 September 2002, 10.

[38] DE Murphy, 'I.N.S. Says African Woman Used Fraud in Bid for Asylum', *New York Times*, 21 December 2000, B3; W Branigin and D Farah, 'Asylum Seeker is Impostor, INS Says', *Washington Post*, 20 December 2000, A1.

[39] AM DeStefano, 'Fraud Charge in Genital Mutilation Asylum Case', *Newsday*, 10 September 2002, A13. Her name Regina was the only regal dimension of her identity.

she and her mother were members of the Nkumssa tribe.[40] The people in Ghana had no such custom of circumcising adult women about to become queen, nor did they circumcise women as a form of punishment. In short, Regina Danson had assumed a false identity[41] and fraudulently claimed to be at risk of being forced to undergo FGM if returned to Ghana. According to a media report, a leader denied her claim: 'The tribal chief, Nan Kwa Bonko, testified that Danson was not part of the tribe's royal family, and that mutilation was not practised in his region of Ghana'.[42] Government officials in Ghana were amazed that the claims had been accepted without question:

> The government of Ghana was furious about Abankwah's claims. Ghana's Commissioner of Human Rights and Administrative Justice, Emile Short, cautioned foreign governments to be circumspect in accepting claims by illegal immigrants in their bid to regularise their entry. 'We had our grave misgivings about these allegations when they were made and we were surprised at how the political authorities and women's groups in the US rallied to her cause with such passion without conducting proper investigations in Ghana to verify the truth of the story'.[43]

A grand jury subsequently indicted her on nine counts, including perjury, passport fraud and making false statements to an immigration judge.[44] The INS filed charges just before the statute of limitations would have expired. In January 2003, Danson was convicted of several offences in federal court.[45] On 13 August 2003, she was sentenced to time served and two years of supervised release and received a fine (special assessment fee) of 900 dollars.[46]

It is remarkable that this hoax was not discovered during the course of the litigation. One possible explanation for this is that judges may not want to question the veracity of claims for fear they will appear culturally insensitive or even racist. Yet court failure to investigate the cultural claims thoroughly can lead to fraud of this kind. Those involved in the case should have verified her claim to being Adelaide Abankwah and assessed

---

[40] M Malkin, 'Mutilating the Truth', *Washington Times*, 20 September 2002.

[41] Evidently the victim of identity theft, the real Adelaide Abankwah, did not report her stolen passport for fear she would be deported. By cooperating with the INS she hoped to legalize her status.

[42] 'Sexual Mutilation Horror, or Hoax?', *Channel 2 CBS Los Angeles*, 23 January 2003 (Associated Press).

[43] TC Odediran, 'The Adelaide Abankwah Immigration Furore', *TransSahara News* (on file with the author).

[44] *United States v Danson*, indictment, F#2002R01952, available on FindLaw; 'Federal Court Convicts Phony African "Princess" of Falsehoods', (2003) 9 *International Law Update* 1. Available on Lexis/Nexis.

[45] W Glaberson, 'Perjury Conviction in Asylum Case', *New York Times*, 16 January 2003, B4.

[46] David Martin, Clerk's office, District Court of Brooklyn, personal communication, 4 October 2004, 20.

her characterization of female genital cutting in Ghana.[47] It is noteworthy that other Ghanaians living in the United States must have heard about the highly publicized case, could have exposed the false claims, and apparently chose not to do so.[48]

This case had negative repercussions for well-intentioned feminists and for women with valid asylum claims.[49] Not only did this single case permit ridicule of women's rights advocacy, but it also called into question the validity of allowing courts to evaluate arguments concerning cultural differences. Perhaps most worrisome is the possibility that legitimate petitions for asylum might be rejected because authorities will be fearful of being bamboozled by fraudulent claims. One scholar expresses concern that the media attention to the case generated 'public distrust' and says: 'that the public scrutiny after the INS follow-up investigation has cast a shadow on courts' presumption that applicants' testimony will be credible'.[50] Inadequate research threatens to undermine accurate cross-cultural jurisprudence, with dire consequences for many individuals whose human rights are in peril.

In this case Abankwah's claim was flawed in multiple respects. First, the group did not have the custom alleged in her asylum petition, secondly, it is unclear whether she is even a member of that group, and thirdly, her decision to flee from Ghana was evidently not motivated by the custom. The most outrageous aspect of the case was that she was not even the individual she purported to be, as she had stolen the identity of another woman! Surely this case demonstrates the potential risks of allowing cultural arguments to figure into legal proceedings without taking necessary steps to verify the factual basis of the claims.[51]

The *Reddy* Case and Sex Smuggling

Another misrepresentation of 'culture' in court involves the presentation of a social practice as though it were an accepted and normal cultural tradition,

---

[47] This custom takes various forms. For a careful consideration of different types, see E Gruenbaum, *The Female Circumcision Controversy: an Anthropological Perspective* (Philadelphia, University of Pennsylvania Press, 2001).

[48] I am indebted to Gordon Woodman, Professor of Law at Birmingham University and an expert on Ghana, for this observation.

[49] 'Her exposure as a fraud has brought a warm glow to America's conservatives and professional Hillary-haters'. M Kettle, 'Feminist Cause was Fraud', *The Guardian*, 21 December 2000; see also Malkin, above n 41.

[50] BJ Chisholm, 'Credible Definitions: a Critique of U.S. Asylum Law's Treatment of Gender-Related Claims' (2001) 44 *Howard Law Journal* (Spring) 427.

[51] Clerk's office, District Court of Brooklyn, personal communication, 4 October 2004. See also Martin, above n 32.

when it is instead the unfortunate consequence of economic necessity. A widely publicized case that illustrates this type of dubious characterization occurred in the case of Lakireddy Bali Reddy, who was criminally prosecuted and sued for bringing young girls to the United States from India for the illicit purposes of forced labour and sexual exploitation.[52]

Reddy was an extraordinarily wealthy businessman in Berkeley, California, who brought young girls to the United States to work in his family's vast commercial enterprises, estimated to be worth approximately US$70 million. The illegal activities came to light in 2001 when one of the young girls, 17-year-old Chanti Prattipati, died tragically of carbon monoxide poisoning caused by a defective heater in a rental property Reddy owned. The accidental death was discovered because a Berkeley resident, Marcia Poole, observed four Indian men carrying a green rug out the side-door of a dilapidated apartment building. She recalled: 'Then I saw this leg descend from it ... I realized they were carrying a body, and then they just threw it in the van'.[53] When the authorities arrived, firefighters told Poole she would be arrested if she did not leave the scene of the crime:

> The cops kept telling Poole that the girl's father said nothing bad was happening. He later turned out to be a fraudulent father for fake visa purposes only. "I knew instinctively he wasn't the father, says Poole. He wasn't crying. Only the sister was."[54]

Lakireddy Bali Reddy and his relatives were criminally prosecuted in federal court and after that were sued in a civil suit alleging slave labour practices.[55] Although none of the cases went to trial, as the criminal cases ended with plea negotiations and the civil cases settled out of court, cultural arguments were part of the legal proceedings. They were under discussion and appeared in the pre-sentencing memo in the criminal case.[56] Ultimately,

---

[52] IC Lee and M Lewis, 'Human Trafficking from a Legal Advocate's Perspective: History, Legal Framework and Current Anti-Trafficking Efforts' (2003) (10) *University of California Davis Journal of International Law and Policy* 169; A Wang, 'Beyond Black and White: Crime and Foreignness in the News' (2001) 8 *Asian Law Journal* 187. Wang compares the *Reddy* case with the *OJ Simpson* case, noting that race was explicitly addressed in the former but downplayed in the latter.

[53] A Chabria, 'His Own Private Berkeley', *Los Angeles Times Magazine*, 25 November 2001, 22–3, 40. Reddy had Sitha's body cremated in accordance with Hindu rites even though her parents were Christian.

[54] R Morse, 'Whistle-blower Ready for Justice', *San Francisco Chronicle*, 27 January 2002, A2.

[55] *United States v Reddy*, Indictment, 25 October 2000.

[56] S Kronland, personal communication, 29 July 29 2004. The main issues were the extent to which sexual abuse of minors is acceptable in India and how caste relationships affected the parties. See V Griffey, 'Reddy to be Sentenced Today: Lawyer's Defense Utilizes Cultural Context', *Daily Californian*, 19 June 2001.

Reddy was sentenced to more than eight years in prison and ordered to pay US$2 million in restitution to three victims of sexual abuse and the parents of the young woman who died.[57] The civil suit resulted in a nearly US$9 million settlement.[58]

The story that emerged was that Reddy used 'fraudulent visas, sham marriages, and fake identities to bring at least 33 men, women, and children into the United States'.[59] Many of the young girls brought to the United States were dalits or 'untouchables', a social group that historically undertook work deemed to be beneath Hindus, eg, cleaning latrines.[60] Because the chance to move to the United States was regarded as a golden opportunity, some considered Reddy's actions to be kinder than might first appear: 'Even American investigators admit that many of the alleged victims view Reddy as a savior rather than a trafficker in human lives'.[61] The parents who sold their daughters 'had a hard time feeding their daughters'.[62] In general, the defense relied on a notion that people in India were desperate to move to the United States.[63]

The cultural defense in the *Reddy* case incorporated two different claims. One contention was that sex with girls considered 'under-age' in the United States 'is not necessarily immoral if the age of consent is younger in other countries'.[64] The gist of the other argument was that in India it is common

[57] R Marech, 'Slavery Abounds in U.S., Rights Group Says', *San Francisco Chronicle*, 24 September 2004, A3; Human Rights Center, *Hidden Slaves: Forced Labor in the United States* (Berkeley, Human Rights Center, 2004). Initially Reddy expected a five-year sentence, but the judge increased it to eight years. See M Yi, 'Guilty Plea in Smuggling of Girls: Landlord Gets 5 Years in Prison', *San Francisco Chronicle*, 8 March 2001, A21; M Yi, 'Berkeley Landlord Jailed for 8 Years', *San Francisco Chronicle*, 21 June 2001, A15. One son, Vijay Lakireddy, received a two-year prison sentence for visa fraud and had to pay a US$40,000 fine. His uncle, Jayapakash Lakireddy, received 366 days for the same conviction. S Holstege, 'Berkeley Sex-Slave Civil Suit Settled. Victim's Family Claimed Wrongful Death, Sister Alleged Emotional Suffering', *Tribune*, 8 April 2004. Another son, Prasad Lakireddy, received only one year's house arrest and a US$20,000 fine. J Berton, 'But He was Just Taking Orders', *East Bay Express*, 16 June 2004. Some have questioned whether the Reddy family was sufficiently punished, eg K Kim and K Hreshchyshyn, 'Human Trafficking Private Right of Action: Civil Rights for Trafficked Persons in the United States' (2004) 16 *Hastings Women's Law Journal* 23. The interesting article by Kim and Hreshchyshyn discusses human rights lawsuits filed against Reddy under the Alien Tort Claims Act and the possible use of the Trafficking Victims Protection Reauthorization Act of 2003 (TVPRA) which created a private right of action for individuals trafficked to the United States.

[58] E Kurhi, 'Civil Suits Against Lakireddy are Settled', *Berkeley Voice*, 9 April 2004, A1, A9.

[59] Chabria, above n 54 at 22.

[60] A Dundes, *Two Tales of Crow and Sparrow: a Freudian Folkloristic Essay on Caste and Untouchability* (Lanham, Rowman & Littlefield, 1997).

[61] Chabria, above n 54 at 23.

[62] S Corrigan, US Attorney, personal communication, 29 July 2004.

[63] D Russell discusses how Chanti Prattipati and her sister were given by their 'poverty-stricken' parents to Reddy and had worked cleaning his properties in India before moving to California. D Russell, 'Why Did Chanti Die?' (2000) 30 *Off Our Backs* (Nov) 10.

[64] This argument is attributed to defence attorneys in HK Lee, 'Guilty Plea Seen in Sex Smuggling Case in Berkeley', *San Francisco Chronicle*, 22 June 2002, A15.

for dalits or 'untouchables' to be given menial employment for nominal pay. The idea seems to have been that because the girls were from such a low tier of the social hierarchy, the sex slavery arrangement would be acceptable in India. Furthermore, the Reddy family was said to wield tremendous economic control in the village from which the girls came, such that their families and the community as a whole had no realistic way of objecting to the way in which they were treated.

While it may be true that girls are victimized in India and in other countries, this social practice is not widely regarded as desirable. It is more accurately seen as a reflection of harsh economic conditions. Moreover, although caste differences persist in India, despite attempts to abolish this system of social categories, the claim that those belonging to higher castes are allowed to victimize those in lower ones would hardly be accepted in India.

Some have suggested that Reddy's so-called cultural defense was extremely weak and explains why Reddy and his accomplices agreed to plead guilty and to settle the civil matter out of court. The defendants realized that their cultural arguments would not be well received. Public reaction to the potential use of the 'cultural defense' in this case was entirely critical.[65] Almost a dozen citizens wrote to the judge in the criminal case, asking that Reddy receive the maximum possible sentence of 38 years.

If the defense arguments were so tenuous, one wonders why the prosecution did not insist on taking the cases to court. It is possible that the victims were already so traumatized by the molestation and other forms of abuse that they were unwilling to testify in court.[66] Another difficulty was the misconduct of the interpreter, who ostensibly told the victims to embellish their stories.[67] Her motivation for advising them to exaggerate the threats they faced is unknown but there was conjecture that it was to make the story credible to the 'Western ear'.[68]

In the end, what does one make of the so-called cultural arguments advanced in this case? One scholar, Gerald Berreman, professor of anthropology at the University of California, Berkeley, questioned the 'cultural' aspect of the defense, saying the issue is more properly viewed as one of economic circumstances and not Indian culture.[69] While one might wish to dismiss the cultural defense argument in the *Reddy* case as 'economic' rather than 'cultural', it does not make sense to deny that commerce is part of culture. The

---

[65] See, eg, C Johnson, 'Crimes Usual in India, Reddy Says', *San Francisco Chronicle*, 16 June 2001.

[66] Chabria, above n 54 at 40.

[67] J Chorney, 'Investigation into Interpreter in Landlord Sex Case; Translator may have Encouraged Alleged Victims to Exaggerate Testimony', *Oakland Tribune*, 7 November 2001.

[68] Chabria, above n 54 at 40.

[69] C Johnson, 'Crimes Usual in India, Reddy Says', *San Francisco Chronicle*, 16 June 2001.

problem with the cultural defense raised in this context is that the existence of a social hierarchy does not mean victimization of untouchables is accepted in India. The fact that laws have been enacted to try to stop discrimination demonstrates a desire on the part of Indian society to change this practice. Most important is that even if dalits are subject to maltreatment in India, smuggling of girls for sex slavery is hardly part of Indian culture.

In the *Reddy* case, the question is whether the cultural defense test could be met. As Reddy originally came from India, he is part of the community. The next question is whether in India selling young girls into slavery and enslaving untouchables are accepted cultural traditions. Although violations of the rights of the girl child and of the rights of dalits are phenomena which are known to occur, their existence reflects calamitous economic circumstances of families. The particular practices at issue in the *Reddy* case, sex slavery and forced labour, are not valued cultural traditions, but reflect desperation on the part of families. If one accepts the argument that India lacks these specific traditions, then Reddy could not allege that his actions were motivated by cultural imperatives.

Even if one were to accept the factual allegations about social practices in India, one could still reject the use of the cultural defense on normative grounds. If recognizing a cultural tradition would undermine the human rights of vulnerable groups, it should be rejected. There is no question that condoning sexual smuggling of girls violates the rights of women and children; and it should be condemned more harshly when it results in death. Under these circumstances, even though the right to culture is a human right which requires allowing defendants to explain the cultural context for their actions as they perceive them, other human rights clearly supersede the right to culture.

Normative Argument

Although courts should permit litigants to raise whatever cultural defenses they wish, individuals invoking the defense should have the burden of proving the authenticity of the claims. If we assume, for the sake of argument, that an individual can demonstrate that the practice is part of his or her way of life, that does not settle the question of whether the defense is used properly or improperly. Even if sex smuggling were completely accepted in other countries, individuals who migrate to new lands should be able to escape from customs that involve irreparable harm to them. There is no question that FGM is truly mutilation to women who do not wish to undergo the surgery. There is no question that being sold into sexual slavery causes irreparable harm to young girls. Consequently, it would be a misuse of the cultural defense, in my judgment, if judges exonerate defendants who raise the cultural defense in cases of this sort.

OTHER CONSIDERATIONS

A common criticism of the cultural defense is that it leads to 'essentializing' culture. The core idea is that the legal system is ill-equipped to interpret traditions and because of this judges will misinterpret what constitutes 'the culture'. This is a real danger, as can be observed in the English decision *R. v Adesanya*.[70] In this case, a Yoruba woman made tribal markings on her sons' faces to ensure the maintenance of their cultural identity. The judge rejected her position saying the 'Nigerian custom' was no defense to the charge of assault occasioning bodily harm. It is odd that he should refer to a 'Nigerian' custom when Mrs Adesanya was Yoruba, one of hundreds of peoples in Nigeria. The judge's reference to a 'Nigerian' custom gives the impression that he was unable to distinguish among the vast number of traditions of the many peoples in Nigeria. Despite explicitly rejecting her argument and ordering the jury to convict her, he imposed a suspended sentence, which makes one wonder about whether the cultural defense had an effect after all.

As there was a pretence of ignoring a cultural imperative, the judge may not have felt compelled to consider ritual scarification more carefully. Scholars who wrote about the case afterwards noted that the manner in which Mrs Adesanya made the marks differed from tradition in two respects: she did it at New Year, which was not the custom, and she did it when her sons were much older than is the usual practice.[71] This raises the question of whether for a cultural defense to be valid, a defendant must follow a tradition precisely as it was performed in the past. As no culture is static and traditions often evolve, it would be unfair to insist that traditions be carried out precisely as occurred in the country of origin.

A difficulty for Adesanya was that ritual scarification was said to be 'dying out' in Nigeria. So although it would be wrong to insist that the custom be performed in a 'traditional manner', if the custom has ceased to exist in the country of origin, there is a serious question as to whether a legal system should accept a cultural defense based on a discarded tradition.

Another matter of concern is how to handle a cultural defense involving a tradition which, although not yet extinct, is under attack in the country of origin. Oftentimes commentators contend that culture is 'contested'. It is worth clarifying the nature of this remark. Even if there is disagreement within the community as to whether it is necessary to wear the kirpan to be an observant Sikh, or for girls to have surgery in order to marry, members

---

[70] For more background and citations, see Renteln, *The Cultural Defense*, above n 4 at 49–51.
[71] P Lloyd, 'The Case of Mrs. Adesanya' (1974) 4 *RAIN: Royal Anthropological Institute News* (Sept/Oct) 2.

of the group will not deny that there is such a cultural tradition.[72] The point of disagreement is whether or not the custom should continue to be part of the way of life. It may well be that a cultural imperative will be less compelling if there is less support for it, but it does not render the argument invalid just because there is internal dissension over its use.

A serious objection to the cultural defense is the worry it will reinforce stereotypes about groups. It is important that the cultural question be handled with sensitivity, so that the case does not convey the erroneous impression that just because one individual followed a tradition everyone within a particular cultural community behaves in a way that violates the law. The risk is that some will fail to recognize that there are patterns of culture from which individuals inevitably deviate. Ways of acting do not correspond to specific social identities. Hence, those involved in cultural defense cases should make clear that the tradition is followed by some, but not all, members of the group. If this is not emphasized, it is conceivable that the public perception may be that the group as a whole engages in criminal behaviour, when, in fact, one defendant has acted in accordance with one tradition.

Improper generalization becomes an issue when the cultural practice central to a case seems bizarre. For instance, when Cambodians killed a dog to eat it, there was concern that this would generate anti-Asian sentiment.[73] Because there was genuine fear about this perception, a Cambodian organization denied that Cambodians ever ate dogs, even though this is historically inaccurate. To the extent that media coverage of a cultural defense case reinforces the notion that members of the ethnic group are 'the other', there will be legitimate concern about stereotyping. This suggests that reporters should take care in describing the issues at stake in a case.[74]

Most cultural defense cases involve a specific custom which means it is improper to interpret a cultural defense as placing the entire culture under siege. It is only the specific tradition on trial that is at the centre of the litigation that is at issue, which must be understood as only one aspect of the way of life. Failure to emphasize that the custom is but one part of the culture risks having outsiders miss positive dimensions of the culture.

Toward an Accurate Cross-Cultural Jurisprudence

Increasingly courts are confronted with issues of cross-cultural jurisprudence, so that their capacity for interpreting the facts in the context of

---

[72] For discussion about the significance of the kirpan for Sikh communities in the United States and Canada, see V Lal, 'Sikh Kirpans in California Schools: the Social Construction of Symbols, Legal Pluralism, and the Politics of Diversity' (1996) 22 *Amerasia Journal* 57. See also SV Wayland, 'Religious Expression in Public Schools: Kirpans in Canada, Hijab in France' (1997) 20 *Ethnic and Racial Studies* 545.

[73] Renteln, *The Cultural Defense*, above n 4 at 104–5.

[74] Wang's analysis of the *Reddy* case emphasizes the role of the media in disseminating racist stereotypes.

existing legal frameworks is challenged. It is clear that those who participate in legal proceedings need to be better prepared to evaluate cultural arguments. To ascertain the validity of cultural claims, professional associations should establish lists of members who have specialized in the study of particular ethnic and religious communities. It would be relatively easy for groups such as American Anthropological Association, the Society for Asian Studies, Latin American Studies Assocation, and other professional organizations to compile lists of experts. Those willing to be contacted could have their credentials and addresses posted on the websites of these organizations. In many urban areas, ethnic community centres, religious institutions and universities have resources that could assist courts with the analysis of cultural traditions.

There may be concern that when expert witnesses are 'hired guns', they may be pressured to find ways to reinterpret or distort ethnographic knowledge, in order to help the client. To prevent this sort of abuse, it would be desirable to establish a code of ethics for expert witnesses. This would not only help ensure that the information presented to a court is accurate, but it would also protect the scholarly reputation of the expert witness. Safeguards must be put in place to protect the integrity of the legal system and of scholarship.

Another objection to the use of experts who are 'outsiders' is that members of the group are the real experts on their ways of life. The tendency of courts to rely on experts rather than members of cultural communities may be considered insulting. Of course, there is no reason why courts could not hear testimony from both outsiders and insiders.

While it may be more politically appealing to request cultural information from members of the group whose traditions are in question, these individuals might also succumb to pressure to misrepresent a tradition to save a relative or friend. In addition, members of the group may also be prohibited from divulging sacred knowledge, eg, the precise boundaries of sacred sites. Another difficulty is that there may be divergent views about the custom within the group, so that the court cannot assume that the interpretation presented reflects the views of everyone in the group. There is also the possibility that the court may be more inclined to listen to the expert who has the requisite academic credentials. In the final analysis, it may matter less who presents the cultural evidence in court than that the information is available.

Often there are large populations of particular cultural communities in circumscribed geographical areas. Lawyers and judges can anticipate some culture conflicts and should at least be conversant with the cultures of groups located in their jurisdictions. Courses in cross-cultural jurisprudence should be taught at law schools. Tools for cultural analysis should also be a part of bar examinations. In addition, judges should have seminars in culture and study other languages to ensure that they are familiar with populous groups in their respective communities. Manuals outlining traditions of groups should be available. One model is the *Handbook on Ethnic Minority Issues* published by the Judicial Studies Board in London.[75]

CONCLUSION

It is imperative that the cultural defense be established as official policy. In order for this to be possible, policies must be formulated which ensure careful review of cultural claims. Not only is it crucial that the factual basis of claims be verified, it is also important to guarantee the protection of the rights of vulnerable groups from irreparable harm. The right to culture is an important human right, but it should be protected only so long as it does not undermine other human rights.

[75] Judicial Studies Board, *Handbook on Ethnic Minority Issues* (London, 1994).

II

Overview of Countries

4

The Cultural Defence in Spain

BARBARA TRUFFIN AND CÉSAR ARJONA

INTRODUCTION

Historical and Geographical Context

The Franco Dictatorial Regime

WHEN DEALING WITH any topic in the field of human sciences, it seems advisable to start with an historical overview of the matter. With respect to the question of the ways in which Spanish courts deal with cultural defence, and multicultural issues generally, the historical approach is particularly required. The Spanish experience is of great interest to those interested in the state responses to cultural pluralism.

Spain is the result of a union between different political units, of varying territorial sizes and culturally diverse. This union dates from 1469, when Isabel, Queen of Castile, married Fernando, King of Aragon. At that time both kingdoms comprised most of the territory of the Iberian Peninsula. In spite of the union between the Crowns, initially Castile and Aragon remained relatively independent, both in cultural and political terms. The strongest unifying force was religion (indeed, Isabel and Fernando are known in the history of Spain as the 'Catholic Kings'). This is most significant since the newly unified nation was pursuing the war against the Muslims. The war came to an end with the conquest of the Kingdom of Granada in 1492, the very same year in which the Jews, who had lived together with Muslims and Christians, were expelled from the country. It is a commonly repeated statement that from that point on, and for the next five centuries, Spain was unaffected by any significant cultural or religious influences from abroad. As for the internal situation, the degree of autonomy of the different parts of the country underwent significant changes over the years, with the dominant tendency being towards centralist absolutism and a corresponding resistance in peripheral regions. Legal traditions played an important role in that resistance. It is still the case, at the present day, that many regions have their own rules of civil law, an echo of the *fueros*, or local laws that were a privilege which such regions asserted against the Crown.

To understand the present condition of multiculturalism in Spain, it must be emphasised that the country in the late twentieth century experienced a period of extreme social and political change which had important consequences for relations between culture and the legal system. Two big transformations in Spain during the twentieth century influenced the way law approaches cultural diversity: (1) the Fascist dictatorship that ruled the country after the Civil War, and (2) the Constitution of 1978 and subsequent integration of Spain into the European Union.

After the end of the Spanish Civil War, in 1939, the Fascist dictatorial regime of General Francisco Franco ruled the country. This was a military regime, as Franco was a military man who led the 1936 insurrection against the Spanish Republic. It was also a confessional regime, in which the separation between the Catholic Church and the political power was anything but clear. And it was certainly an authoritarian regime, in which individual freedoms and liberties were not recognised. The dictatorship lasted until the death of Franco in 1975. A short period of intense political activity followed, the so-called *transición* (transition), which resulted in the Spanish people approving the 1978 Constitution which establishes the principles for the democratic government and constitutional monarchy that Spain now enjoys.

Spain is One

The official motto of the regime consisted of three features that were attributed to the Spanish nation: '*una, grande, libre*'. This means: Spain is one, great and free. From a cultural point of view, the philosophy of the regime is best defined by the first of those three points: *España es una* or Spain is one. State and nation were supposed to be one and the same thing. Only one Spanish people, speaking one single language, and working together for the same cause: the progress of the Homeland.[1]

This emphasis on the part of the regime must be understood in relation to the existence within the territory of Spain of several regions that can be clearly distinguished on cultural grounds. Differences include many folkloric matters, such as popular music, cuisine or ways of celebrating, but they cannot be reduced to them. Moreover, several of those regions have their own language and historical political institutions. Some of them want their national character to be recognised and there exists a serious claim (although not necessarily a majority claim) for independent sovereignty.

---

[1] Here we are focusing on the cultural dimension of this 'unity' principle. But, of course, it had more aspects. The fact that there was no freedom of association, or the fact that there was only one official political party and one trade union, were different instances of that same principle.

The Republican Government defeated by Franco had been sensitive to the existence of different peoples within the Spanish state. Consider the example of Catalonia, with its traditional institution for autonomous government, the Generalitat, which had been officially recognised during the Republic and had important powers in the Catalan territory. However, the dictatorship abolished the Generalitat, together with any political institution of any region different from the central state.[2] At the same time, any culturally distinctive feature was neglected. Significantly, no other language apart from Spanish could be officially used. Thus, to take the same example, the Catalan language became a clandestine language, and all other forms of identity (flags, festivities, typical dances, etc) were also forbidden. In short, multiculturalism was completely outlawed at the internal national level.

The 1978 Constitution: Many Nations within One Nation

The recognition of cultural identities within Spain was one of the biggest issues to be discussed during the design of the institutional system in the 1978 Constitution. The complexity of this whole question is reflected in the current political debate in Spain, which to a great extent centres on the interpretation of those constitutional precepts that deal with the question of cultural identity and with the distribution of powers between the state and the different regions.

The 1978 Constitution offers a clear contrast with the philosophy of the dictatorship in this particular issue. If, during Franco's regime, Spain was a model of a centralist unified country, the new constitutional state presents itself as a model of decentralisation. Although Spain is not a federal country as such (it is not, in fact, a federation of independent states), it recognises, together with the central state, the existence of the so-called *comunidades autónomas* (autonomous communities). The autonomous communities are real political entities that are democratically organised and enjoy a wide range of powers. They amount to much more than mere functional units for administrative decentralisation. The autonomy of these communities is dynamic, as they seek new rights and powers.

This new organisation established the basis for the political existence of those regions whose national distinctive features had been previously neglected. Traditional political institutions existing prior to the Franco years were restored, as for example is the case with the Catalan Generalitat, once again the official institution for the autonomous government. As a

---

[2] Once the Civil War was over, the Generalitat, although no longer official, still kept its institutional identity while in exile (as the Spanish Republican Government did). During the years of the dictatorship, it became a symbol, if not of resistance, at least of hope for the restoration of a regime of rights and freedoms in Spain where cultural diversity among Spanish peoples would be recognised.

result, Spain is now made up of 17 autonomous communities which share the government of their territory with the central state. They are not equal as regards their claims for cultural identity and it is a fact that some have a distinctive history that others are lacking. In any case, as many as eight political parties that claim to varying degrees to represent the cultural identity and political autonomy of their regions are currently in the central Parliament.[3] In short, internal multiculturalism is a defining feature of the Spanish state in the twenty-first century.

Emigrants and Immigrants

Besides this internal multiculturalism, society in Spain, as other European countries, is increasingly characterised by new forms of multiculturalism, mostly as a consequence of immigration.[4] Certainly, a historical misunderstanding would result from an analysis of multiculturalism as a new phenomenon, and this is also true in the Spanish case, as we showed in the previous section.

However, contemporary multiculturalism differs from older forms in at least two aspects. On the one hand, the questions of cultural differences and rights are more often related to the situations and demands of cultural minorities and migrants groups. On the other hand, there is an increasing tendency to conflate descriptive and normative questions when discussing multiculturalism and rights (de Lucas, 1998: 22–3). This normative slippage does not facilitate the dispassionate exchange of views, whether in the political arena or in scientific communities.

During the middle decades of the twentieth century, Spain was a relatively poor and undeveloped country as compared with other Western nations. The Civil War had devastating effects in many dimensions and consequently a whole generation of Spaniards grew up surrounded by extreme poverty. The isolated state-controlled economy imposed by the Fascist regime could not bring Spain up to the level of its neighbouring European countries, even though they were making a painful recovery from the Second World War. Under the circumstances, many Spanish workers decided they should

---

[3] Some constitutional law may help to illustrate the degree to which the constitutional situation tells a completely different story from the 'Spain is one' principle. Thus, the Preamble to the Constitution declares the will of the Spanish nation to: 'protect all the Spanish individuals and peoples of Spain in the exercise of their human rights, their cultures and traditions, languages and institutions'. Article 2 'recognises and guarantees the right to autonomy of the nationalities and regions' that constitute Spain. Article 3.2 declares languages different to Spanish official in their own autonomies and art 4.2 does the same in relation to flags and some other symbols. All 17 autonomies have their own *Estatuto de autonomía*, a foundational statute that occupies the second step on the normative hierarchy only below the Spanish Constitution.

[4] Many authors stress that the administration of justice in Spain faces an increase in the number of cases involving foreigners or cases where the status of foreigner is at the centre of the debate; see, eg, Azon (2002), Bernardi (2002).

emigrate to the richer countries of central and northern Europe.[5] In short, it is fair to say that Spain was for many years a country experiencing a great deal of emigration.

In comparison, the economic situation in Spain is flourishing in the twenty-first century. Two big factors explain the transformation. First, of course, is the end of Franco's regime accompanied by the establishment of a democratic form of government that put an end to the isolation of the Spanish economy, a tendency that had already been advanced during the final years of the dictatorship. The second relevant factor here was the entry of Spain into the European Union (at that time, European Economic Community) in 1986.

Both events occurred relatively close in time and brought about a complete change in the Spanish economy. Spain is no longer a source of emigration. On the contrary, its membership in the European Union, together with its new economic and industrial development, turned Spain into an attractive destination. Nowadays, immigrants coming from many other parts of the world (especially Africa and Latin America) constitute a significant proportion of the total population.[6] In a relatively short period of time, Spain experienced what most of the other European countries had been experiencing for many years: a massive influx of immigrants.

As a consequence, those who are currently attending primary school are the first Spanish generation to grow up in an intensely multicultural context. For most of the Spanish people, this is a new and strange phenomenon, with which it is difficult to cope. When immigrants raise cultural defences in Spanish courts, they are generally seen as an exotic and perplexing problem. Nevertheless, there seems to be a consensus among educated people and in particular among sensitive jurists that this will be a phenomenon of growing importance in the near future.

Restrictive Legal Standpoint on New Configurations of Rights

In the introductory section we offered an overview of the Spanish historical and geographical background relevant for approaching problems of

---

[5] This constitutes a second wave of emigration caused by the dictatorship, occurring in this case for economic reasons. The first wave was, of course, spurred by political events: many Republicans, including some of the most relevant Spanish artists and intellectuals of the century, had to emigrate to other European countries and to Latin America.

[6] According to the official information provided by the Spanish government, in 2004 there were almost 2 million immigrants with a residence card (*tarjeta o autorización de residencia*). This amounts to more than 4.5 per cent of the Spanish population. The percentage increases significantly in the most developed areas of the country. Thus, eg, in Madrid and Catalonia the percentage is around 7 per cent. These numbers neither take into account foreigners who are 'legally' in Spain for a period of time (eg, students) nor the so-called 'illegal' immigrants. Data taken from the 2004 *Immigration Yearbook* published by the Ministry of Social Affairs (*Ministerio de Trabajo y Asuntos Sociales*) is available at http://extranjeros.mtas.es/es/general/anuario_inmigracion_2004.pdf

multicultural jurisprudence. At the internal level, the dominant idea is that groups with different cultural identities exist within the framework of the Spanish nation, and they have their own language, political institutions and many kinds of culturally distinctive symbols. At the external level, the big issue is that Spain, which had been traditionally a country of emigrants, has experienced a large influx of immigrants attracted by its membership in the European Union.

These two points are closely related with the all-important fact of the democratic transformation of the country beginning in the late 1970s after the end of almost four decades of Fascist dictatorship. A great deal has happened very quickly in Spain since then. In both what we have called the internal and the external dimension, multiculturalism is the result of very recent transformations in the country. This point must be especially emphasised in the case of immigration. In managing the immigration issue, Spain is far behind many other European countries which had been taking in immigrants for many more years. The clash between the very slow administration of justice and the rapid developments taking place in the social arena provides an exciting subject for the study of the jurist and the anthropologist.

Faced with this sensitive problem, the Spanish legislature has not yet adopted a creative approach that would give judges effective tools to cope with particular changes in society. Spanish legislation has been passed to regulate some aspects of multiculturalism, but it has been done in a conservative manner (Marcos del Cano, 2004: 92).

This is especially the case for the Statute on the rights of foreigners adopted in 2000 (*ley de extranjería* 8/2000). Article 3.2 holds that 'foreigners' fundamental rights shall be interpreted in conformity with the Universal Declaration on Human Rights and with the international treaties and agreements in force in Spain. *Religious and cultural beliefs cannot be alleged to justify acts contradicting those norms*' (emphasis added).

The second paragraph prohibits submitting a cultural argument in a defence when the fundamental rights of foreigners are concerned. This is an awkward way to interpret the right of non-discrimination, the right to have a fair trial and the freedom of religious belief. The interpretation given by art 3.2 does not seem to produce a fair understanding of those fundamental rights.

In our view, this provision is highly restrictive. Taken to the limit, it would prevent the litigants presenting any argument about religious or cultural considerations and motivations when fundamental rights—life, property or freedom of expression among others—are at stake. To date, we have not found any Spanish judicial decision applying this interpretation on the basis of art 3.2 of the Foreigner's Statute.

We firmly believe that such a prohibition from raising cultural or religious arguments in a judicial setting, on the basis of a statute, should be treated as a violation of articles 14, 6 and 9 of the European Convention of Human Rights.[7]

There is an important distinction to stress. The discussions about the extent, the limits and the possibility of taking specific cultural and religious explanations into judicial consideration take place at a different analytical level than the legal prohibition against using such arguments in the construction of a defence. It is a completely different step to take. We believe that imposing, *a priori*, a restriction upon the kind of arguments to be used in the construction of a defence does not serve the proper administration of justice.

This legal provision indicates quite clearly that an explicit cultural defence is not regarded in official Spanish law as a relevant issue deserving reflection and elaboration. This legislative position and its aim at organising incompatibility instead of new configurations of rights and duties can hinder jurisprudential development from systematising sensitive issues and relationships between law and cultures.

At the present time, there is no Spanish legislation concerning how best to frame or treat cultural arguments raised in judicial settings. Cultural and religious arguments related to multiculturalism are treated by Spanish Statute as the negative facet of the protection of rights. This situation might affect the extent to which explicit arguments of cultural defence are being raised and settled in Spanish courts. We explore this influence below after a brief explanation of the methodology we used in our research.

Purpose and Methodology

Multiculturalism and Cultural Defence Illustrated with Judicial Decisions

Current legal provisions do not make room for a specific category of cultural defence. However, cultural considerations are not absent from

---

[7] Such a provision could be construed as an unjustified obstacle to freedom of thought, conscience and religion in the manifestation of religion or belief, in worship, teaching, practice and observance that are guaranteed by the ECHR. If freedom of religion has to be respected in worship and practice, on what basis might Spain justify a prohibition from mentioning such practices and beliefs in judicial discussions? We do not think that the conditions of admissible restrictions to the freedom of thought, conscience and religion are fulfilled by the Spanish Statute on the rights of foreigners. The protection of the rights of other persons is not afforded greater protection through restricting the scope of potential arguments advanced in the defence of the offender. Of course, it can be argued that limiting or regulating the *effect* of those arguments when dealing with violation of fundamental rights might offer greater protection to the victims. But the point here is the difference between the question of admissibility of the argument from the one of its judicial consequences. Moreover, this article also raises questions of non-discrimination in regard to the protection of Art 6 of the ECHR. Because this Statute strictly limits its scope to foreigner's fundamental rights, the potential offender will not be submitted to the same restriction in elaborating his or her defence (eg, an objection of conscience or other religious arguments) on the basis of the nationality of the victim. Such discrimination is not supported by specific motivation or made in regard to explicable criteria.

judicial processes and decisions in Spain. The analysis of empirical material could reveal interesting characteristics of Spanish law with regard to multiculturalism. But in order to do so, a good sample of cases and a coherent strategy of research are required.

There has been little empirical judicial research in Spain addressing issues raised by multiculturalism. This situation is probably related to a diffuse notion—the novelty of immigration—and also to a greater emphasis on internal issues, such as the constitutional debates on autonomy and 'nations' which remain very much at the centre of both legal and political debates. Because of the incipient nature of the debate regarding multicultural 'jurisprudence' in Spain, we have not limited our research of cases to explicit cultural defence figures. This approach should also reduce the risk of reproducing a restrictive definition of culture.

We have chosen to present our judicial material from two complementary standpoints. On the one hand, we have examined a judicial database for explicit claims of cultural expressions, conflicts and culturally motivated actions (the *hard cases* below); and on the other, we have additionally looked for cases where cultural or subcultural claims remain implicit in the judicial arguments and decisions (the *soft cases* below).

Collecting and Elaborating on Judicial Data

In both sections below, we deal with judicial materials and data. It is important to specify our strategy and techniques for selecting and analysing them.

Hard Cases

Starting from specific cultural conflicts involving rights should help us to understand how those conflicts are formulated and reformulated by Spanish law. But we rely on judicial decisions for our analysis of the way in which claims are framed and received. Therefore, we cannot study those conflicts outside of their constrained relationships with legal reasoning and the judicial setting. This direction of research is clearly not immune from the limitations inherent in making use of judicial sources. And it should not be assumed that all conflicts involving culturally opposing rights are found in the judicial setting. The examination of the cases we present only uncovers one facet of the multiple realities implicit in both laws and cultures.

To select this range of judicial cases, we have used a common legal database (Westlaw). We have searched for any judgment containing selected keywords. Through this technique we have selected cases where minorities and migrant groups are claiming or are accused of having committed culturally motivated acts.

First, we entered keywords referring to classically reported types of conflicts between state law and locally enforced norms (vengeance, honour, polygamy, genital mutilation). We also searched for the uses of the expression 'ethnic group' in the judicial texts as a potential indicator of cultural conflicts.[8]

The methods of investigation by 'keywords' disclosed a range of judicial cases from which we selected decisions involving either migrants or Romani (Gypsy) persons.[9] Through the analysis of those *hard cases*, it is possible to specify two main kinds of situations in which cultural considerations enter the judicial proceedings and reasoning. In some of them, the cultural context is considered in, or as arguments for, the defence; but in others, cultural considerations are used by prosecution, civil parties or refugee candidates in relation to legal 'aggravating' circumstances or as reprehensible behaviour by themselves.

It should be clear that our hard cases are not statistically representative either of the 'criminality' or deviance of any ethnic groups, or of the types of cases where explicit cultural arguments are to be found. First, this is because the words we entered in the database were directed at only certain types of conflict, and secondly, because the database does not contain the entire Spanish jurisprudence. It is built on a selection made for reasons of practical legal interest. It would be a methodological flaw to draw general conclusions from judicial material which is heavily constrained by such heterogeneous factors.

In order to compensate for this, we have chosen to extend our body of judicial data, and at the same time, we have slightly shifted the scope of our analysis. Because a consistent number of the hard cases we first review are related to Romani persons, we concentrate on this group and the use of cultural arguments. But here we try to present research material which

---

[8] The combination between 'ethnic group' and 'vengeance' resulted in 53 cases. Some of them concern Romani persons. 'Genital mutilation' gives a sample of 19 cases. Polygamy results in 20 cases. On this basis, we could investigate some of the legal categories associated with 'cultural arguments' raised by the defence. We then searched for 'ethnic group' combined with 'analogous', which alluded to a legal category of excuses used in the first decisions we found. This resulted in 51 cases. Not all of those cases included 'cultural defence', but they helped us to refine our criteria with regard to the types of conflicts and the ethnic groups our technique allowed us to study.

[9] The analysis of those decisions should ideally have been completed with interviews and observations of the unfolding of selected cases; a much more precise view of where and when conflicting cultural norms are expressed (outside a somehow biased written body of data) would then have been methodologically presented.

Unfortunately, we have not been able to follow such cases in the courts, nor to find anyone interested in responding to an interview on such an apparently sensitive subject. We have faced time limits and typical constraints associated with long-term involvements with focus groups. We hope that we might be able to continue our research in future to include this kind of material.

goes beyond the focus on criminal law and state reactions to perceived or denounced crimes.[10] We have searched in the legal database for other cultural demands of justice related to a similar cultural context. This overview gives a good idea of state law reactions to explicit cultural demands related to criminal, civil and social actions.

Moderated Cases

Explicit cultural arguments appeared to be unsuccessful defences in the decisions we have reviewed. It is then of special interest to determine the fortune of implicit ones. The cases we have selected in our range of *soft cases* are related to especially visible collectives in Spain, the *okupas* (squatters).[11] These collectives strongly contest state law in the Spanish urban landscape.

In our analysis of the squatters' cases, we basically relied on two types of legal materials, namely, judicial decisions and scientific/dogmatic literature in the relevant field. We also relied on non-academic materials (administrative reports and press releases) as well as on some original squatters' materials (brochures and underground publications). Although we did not have the opportunity to speak directly to squatters, we conducted interviews with lawyers who had themselves appeared in court defending the squatters.

Our research on the topic of squatters benefited from the necessarily limited scope of the field. As will be developed later, it is only very recently that peaceful occupation of empty buildings has become a criminal offence under Spanish criminal law. As a result, the number of judicial decisions by important courts is easily manageable. In spite of that, there is very little consistency in those decisions.

The inconsistency is the reason why we decided to analyse separately those arguments that judges used to condemn the squatters and those arguments that have justified their acquittal. With few exceptions, in neither of these groups is there a significant recognition of the squatters' cultural identity. Interestingly enough, the judicial strategy used in those cases does not explicitly involve 'culture' or beliefs, even though the involved actors

---

[10] Basically, we entered 'ethnic group' and '*gitano*' (Gypsy) to get a wider picture of possible conflicts involving Romani persons 'recorded' in judicial cases, and not only cases where culture was used to explain infringement of official right. It allowed us to displace a strictly criminal point of view to a more global vision of the use of arguments linked to a specific ethnic group. We came across some 71 cases, of which seven were relevant to our research.

[11] Among other reasons, we have selected the squatters' judicial material as soft cases on the basis of doctrinal work. They are used by the scholar Baucells to elaborate his concept of 'delinquency of conviction' (Baucells, 2000: 29). It is interesting to note that the definition of this doctrinal category (incompletely) echoes cultural or religious defence. It raises classical problems of compatibility between rights and the protection to be given to 'opinions' and 'beliefs' held to have 'motivated' the offence.

maintain in other settings strong cultural understandings of the conduct that made them subject to legal proceedings.

In order to enrich the analysis we speculate about other arguments we think might be useful in the defence of the squatters' legal positions. Those cases are integrated in a comparison in terms of scope and efficacy between the option of presenting or downplaying cultural claims in the Spanish legal setting.

General Purpose of this Chapter

If we treat the squatters' cases (soft cases) as *a priori* comparable with harder cases of cultural defence, it is to prevent our analysis from depicting a bias, namely the reification of cultures. The conflicts between norms and values are, as in the hard cases, truly cultural in the sense that they are entangled in differentiation processes and convey symbolic representations of collective values. Here, we rely on the dynamic conception of culture given by Sally Engle Merry (2001) following John and Jean Comaroff (1992). In such a perspective, culture is 'never a closed, entirely coherent system but contains within it polyvalent, contestable messages, images and actions' (Merry, 2001: 45).[12] The kinds of conflict entangled in the soft cases with which we are dealing are typically addressed by cultural studies (McRobbie, 2005). The theoretical and methodological commitments of those approaches have accurately questioned the exotic connotations attached to 'culture'. They contribute to an enlarged understanding of cultural processes.[13]

In the soft cases, culture is, as a matter of courtroom strategy, habitually played down by defence lawyers, whereas the conflicts that originated them have a (sub)cultural dimension. We shall also see that in these soft cases the use of state law seems more elaborate and efficient than in the hard ones. The judicial decisions concerning squatters integrate the assertions made by the squatters in terms of conflicts between different official rights. This is interesting to observe.

In the other types of case where cultural justifications are presented by the defence more explicitly, the conflicts and perspectives of the different

---

[12] 'To put it in other words, culture is a "semantic" space, the field of signs and practices, in which human beings construct and represent themselves and others, and hence their societies and histories. It is not merely an abstract order of signs, or relations among signs. Nor is it just the sum of habitual practices' (Comaroff and Comaroff, 1992: 27 as quoted by Merry, 2001:45).

[13] It is important to take into consideration that the definitions of culture used in judicial techniques are themselves 'cultural'. The classification of cultures, and conflicts between cultures they diffuse, can therefore not be taken for granted. In the cases of subcultural contestations, the problems of the definitions of culture can only be addressed if we displace its 'exotic' connotations. Our main interest lies in the analytical implications of such cultural displacement. When discussing those disputes, it is difficult to rely (even unconsciously) on an essentialist view of cultures as 'discrete, clearly bounded and internally homogenous, with relatively fixed meanings and values' (Cowan *et al*, 2001: 3).

actors are treated in a less developed manner. In these cases, where cultural arguments are explicitly raised, the judicial reasoning is more concerned with the question of compatibility than with dwelling on the structure of the conflicts. Wherever cultural arguments or motivations are in fact entangled in numerous conflicts, our jurisprudential material confirms that Spanish law does not consider whether there are any advantages in systematising a cultural defence. For this precise reason, it could be unfair for explicit cultural arguments to be excluded from adjudication.

We hope that a more general discussion of cultural defence could benefit from the double angle of approach we have adopted. This research strategy seems adequate to present the results of a very exploratory research without any pretension (not even in the format) to any kind of exhaustive or definitive knowledge on the subject.

This presentation should give the reader an overview of the Spanish judicial situation regarding cultural defences. The provisional conclusions resulting from this comparison of cases are intended to reflect the extent to which cultural considerations could succeed in the contemporary Spanish judicial system.

THE HARD CASES

Range of Cases

The types of case we have selected on the basis of our technique of research in the database concerned either Romani persons or migrants. What we tried to demonstrate is that in all those cases, references to culture are not very efficient as aids to defence strategy. In a system that does not have a legal provision or a legal principle of interpretation about cultural considerations, the mere mention of 'culture' in criminal cases seems to open the door to a serious debate concerning broad elusive jurisprudential questions. Under the current Spanish legal structure, courts cannot easily resolve such questions.

For Romani groups, the relationships with the state courts and legal system are anything but simple. This point is made for other European countries by Joke Kusters in Chapter 8 (see also Grönfors, 1997). It is also true in Spain, where important communities of Romani people are living. There are '200.000 to 400.000 Gitanos that are said to live in Spain' (Gay-Y-Blasco, 1997; San Román, 1994). Industrialisation, pauperisation and internationalisation processes had an impact on their ways of life and on the manner in which they relate to the rest of Spanish society (Ardévol, 1986; Calvo Buezas, 1990). However, the cultural emphasis on ethnic differences and the differentiated relations with non-Romani people, to whom Romani refer as *'Payos'*, remain especially important in maintaining and reproducing Romani identities.

In an overtly schematic attempt, one can conceive of the kind of 'legal consciousness' (Ewick and Silbey, 1998) entangled in Romani cultural identities as one being highly informed by repressive and negative representations about state law. It seems to be generally experienced as a type of domination and as an estranged culture. References to state law that until the end of the dictatorship criminalised the Gitano as 'vagabonds', are still vivid in the literature on Gitano rights (Calvo Buezas, 1990: 27; Presencia Gitana, 1991:10; Ramirez-Heredia, 2005). Most of the judicial cases involving Romani people selected through the database are thematically linked to a wide definition of 'family' matters. But interestingly enough, this emphasis on family is made explicit in the forms of criminal and social law and receives little response from civil law.

Through the use of the keywords, we also found interesting cases of invocation of cultural norms or practices concerning other groups. They are generally invoked in a negative sense, in procedures through which foreigners claim the legal status of being refugees. Most of these cases concern people fleeing from Africa, many of them from Nigeria.

Cultural Considerations Used to Mitigate Responsibility

The cultural considerations invoked in criminal cases are heavily shaped by the type of legal reasoning followed by the judges who have to examine criminal responsibility through the lens of legal provisions. Anticipating this reasoning, the defence against criminal charges would classically examine three possible strategies, as well as evidence for the material elements of the alleged offence. First of all, the defence can refer to causes of justification or non-imputability. In the Spanish Criminal Code, these references are assembled in the *eximentes category* (art 20). If an invincible error about a constitutive fact of the criminal offence can be established, the accused person's criminal responsibility is legally excluded (art 14). These causes are considered to negate the moral element of criminal responsibility.

Alternatively, the defence can establish the existence of mitigating circumstances *(circunstancias atenuantes)* (art 21). Among those mitigating circumstances, art 21.1 provides for the incomplete causes of justification found in art 20. Defences might also rely on some kind of non-defeasible legal error (art 14). Both non-defeasible error and mitigating circumstances are mechanisms that legally reduce the level of sanction, but not the commission of the offence itself.[14]

In Spanish law, none of these exceptions makes room for a specific cultural factor. It appears from the review of cases that cultural considerations

---

[14] Criminal Code, arts 66 and 68, establish the measure by which sanctions can be reduced depending upon the type of excuse accepted by the judges.

are most typically elaborated in the form of mitigating circumstances (art 21). We shall see that their extent varies on a case by case basis in the course of jurisprudential evolution.

Culture a Product of Passionate Emotions?

The excuse of '*pasión*' (state of passion) has been raised in the case of honour killings involving Romani people which we have reviewed. Article 21.3 allows a mitigation of responsibility if the offender had 'acted under causes or stimulus so powerful that they engendered an outburst of rage, obfuscation or other state of passion'.

In 1995, the argument was revised by the Supreme Court in a case of vengeance killing between Romani families.[15] The victim was the brother of a man considered by another family to have killed the brother of the offender. The victim was killed when opening the door of the family house, after having received constant threats during the previous month. The first murder had not given rise to judicial punishment, but the elements alluded to in the sentence do not permit us to deduce whether it was because the first murderer was not denounced or the trial had been abandoned for lack of evidence. In this case, the offender's defence lawyer based one of his cassation motives on a misevaluation of the mitigating circumstances of 'state of passion'.[16] The Supreme Court rejected the argument, stating that the passion invoked in art 21.3 always implies a very short period of time between the change of mental condition and the action.

The court ruled that 'the violent killing of the brother of the accused a month before could not be considered as a relevant factor for the unleashing of criminal passion under examination. It is so because rage and obfuscation can only operate in a very short time-span. As we said before, there has to be no time for reconsideration, rationalisation or meditation'.

Following this approach, cultural motivations are not to be apprehended as fulfilling a legal condition of passion. However, this ruling gives an ambiguous interpretation of an apparently cultural motivation. Vengeance is not considered to be a rational behaviour, but neither is it driven by passion because of the temporal sequencing of the action. It stands in between as it is neither strictly induced by 'passion' nor by 'reason'.

In another case, the excuse of passion was denied because of a 'lack of transcendence'. Two killings occurred in the house of a Romani family. It was the tragic conclusion of a meeting between families about the elopement of an adult daughter with her lover. The families met at the girl's father's home under the auspices of two mediators. The tensions between

---

[15] Sentencia Tribunal Supremo 3.2.1995.
[16] By 1995, the Criminal Code considered rage and blindness as attenuating circumstances in its art 9.

the families erupted when the father, alluding to the drug-addiction habits of the fiancé, declared he wanted to think further about the subject, during which time his daughter should wait at his house. The other family seems to have made a move to leave the house with the girl. At that moment, a brother and a sister of the girl shot at an uncle of the fiancé who entered the kitchen.

The defence attempted to establish the mitigating circumstance of 'state of passion'. This argument was denied by Sentencia Audiencia de Valladollid 30.3.2004. It stated: 'the article 21-3 mitigating circumstance is not established. The conflict about whether the daughter would stay or leave with the other family cannot be considered as sufficiently transcendent to have necessarily produced the rage, obfuscation or other state of passion that would have led them to behave as they did. Moreover, the daughter was adult and decided herself to leave her father's house on a voluntary basis'.

The Supreme Court followed the Audiencia of Valladollid on that point, but with much more qualified reasoning.[17] The defence pleaded cultural justification. What is 'usual in any family, is not in Gitano ethnic families. They have their own customs and norms of behaviour. In this affair, those norms had been clearly infringed. This is the reason why a meeting with mediators was held to regularise the situation of the daughter, even if she was by then an adult'. The defence described the end of the meeting at which 'the family of the victims provoked a very offensive and provocative situation in dragging the daughter from the paternal residence'.

The Supreme Court referred to 'various reasons to reject the motives. First of all, and with all the respect due to the customs of the ethnic Gitano families, it should be stressed that all of them are immersed in a society and a social climate where such situations are considered normal'. Then, the court made a reference to the primacy of the constitutional provision of non-discrimination over any behaviour or attitude rooted in ancestral customs.

Its main concern in rejecting the claims, the Supreme Court added, was respect for the proven facts in their integrity, order and meaning. Following the Supreme Court, 'it does not appear from those proven facts that there was any "state of passion" sufficient to have caused rage, obfuscation or other similar psychic results, with diminishing influence on the intelligence or will of the deeds' authors, which would have restricted their imputability'. It classified the atmosphere at the meeting as simple anger but denied any alteration in the consciousness which would have 'obsessed' the mind in such a way that the ability to understand the illicit character of the action or to control one's behaviour accordingly would have been reduced. The Supreme Court drew from the *modus operandi* the 'idea that they

---

[17] Sentencia Tribunal Supremo 8.3.2005.

were fully conscious of what they were doing as a result of their free and non-altered wills'.

The evaluation of cultural motivations and rationalities as equivalent to state of passion is unsatisfactory on various accounts. The 'passion' measure is in itself cultural and remains somehow insubstantial. Max Gluckman and Arnold Epstein have thoroughly demonstrated that standards of the 'reasonable' man or social roles' expectations are implicitly or explicitly used in conflict resolutions precisely because they are cultural. The contents of the standards vary from one group-situation to another. It follows that using one specific application of such standards as an analytical tool is not satisfactory. Arnold Epstein was quite clear on this point when he concluded that 'where the standard of reasonable expectation is found to play a part in the judicial process, it does not imply that the reasonable man so invoked will everywhere display the same profile ... the Lozi and Common Law systems appear to stress quite different attributes in their conception of the reasonable man' (Epstein, 1973: 663). In using a specific standard of 'passion', the court is making the analytical error decried by Arnold Epstein. Moreover, on a general level, to invoke a defence of passion in order to integrate cultural considerations into the reasoning of the judiciary is problematic. Indeed, it becomes very difficult to cope with the driving rationales (understood in a Webberian perspective) from a specific cultural context, if we have to translate them as 'losing one's minds'.[18] Those difficulties partly explain the circular character of such legal reasoning. But their insubstantiality makes quite clear that there are conflicts of 'legitimate' rationalities at stake in the judicial decisions.

The judicial manner of addressing this sensitive problem might in fact prevent a much more complete cultural understanding of specific offences. It is quite significant that the Supreme Court began its review of the case with a clear statement about non-discrimination and equality in order to respond to an explicit cultural defence. In a democratic state, it is clear that such a concern is more than merely fair. However, the primacy of this declaration in the decision somehow presupposes the irrelevance of other considerations. At one level, the decision may reveal a lack of an element which leads to understandings. The equality consideration is here unfortunately correlated with a quite monolithic view of culture. We believe that the principle of equality, and the level at which the court locates 'incompatibility', influence its understanding of the arguments and ultimately that of other cultures.

---

[18] The legal error would have equivalent consequences. Here, culture could only intervene if it affects the 'knowledge' of the offender about the legal prohibition. But cultural motivations can with difficulty be limited to informational data. Ethnicity always has a relational dimension and does not diminish, but on the contrary increases, with diffusion of knowledge that is inherently embedded in ethnic communications and configuration.

For instance, it would have been interesting to question the argument of the defence about the 'violation of ancestral rules'. Actually, if marriage by elopement is not the ideal form of marriage in Romani communities, anthropological and legal studies have well illustrated the fact that marriages by elopement are a ritualised alternative which have been used by many couples.

This is the case in Jarama, a neighbourhood of Madrid, according to Paloma Gay-Y-Blasco, where 'out of forty-nine Gitano women ... twenty-four had married with a wedding and twenty-five by elopement'(1997: 533):

> Like weddings, elopements follow a typical rite of passage sequence. The couple 'escape' and take refuge in the house of one of the boy's relatives: there they announce that they have married—that is, they have had intercourse. They remain for a few days at the relative's house until the boy's parents decide to bring them back home ... Although eloping is always considered a good alternative to the Payo life-style—approximately every second couple marries by elopement—it ranks much lower that a wedding in the Gitano's evaluation. (Gay-Y-Blasco, 1997: 528)

Marriage by elopement cannot be automatically defined as 'breaking an ancestral rule'. They do occur and constitute a 'regular' alternative to the ideal form of weddings. In a sense it is a rule of exception. The couples married by elopement might ultimately be recognised by their families as 'married'. This kind of consideration could have reduced the consequences attached to the infringement of 'ancestral rules' and should have helped jurists better understand how the crisis erupted. We cannot be sure that the findings about a specific group can be applied to the families concerned in our case. In any event, it would have been useful to examine what marriage by elopement meant with regard to ancestral rules and cultural considerations.

Cultural Motivations as an Ad Hoc Attenuating Factor

The same 'passion' argument was pleaded in another vengeance case. A Romani man took revenge on the men who had attacked his wife and son.[19] The Audiencia of Avila rejected its formulation but accepted an 'analogous' cause on the basis of art 21.8 and appreciated a reduction of the culpability of the accused.[20]

The judges found in the facts of the case some analogous mitigating circumstances in the combination of 'the weak educational level of the

---

[19] Here again, the previous offence was not judicially established.
[20] Sentencia Audiencia Provincial de Avila 27.1.2004.

accused linked to ethnical peculiarities of the group he belongs to'. These circumstances could, they hold, have implied a distorted appreciation of the socially admitted values and could have diminished, in some ways, his mechanisms of inhibition.

The Audiencia adamantly refused to accept 'that the simple fact of belonging to an ethnic group, a culture or a religion different from the majority would itself give rise to a circumstance authorising a differentiating treatment of someone who had committed a criminal offence'. The Audiencia referred to the legality and equality principles in criminal law and to the civic obligation to adapt to the common rules of cohabitation. But it added that 'the adaptation to the constitutional common values of the Spanish State can be facilitated not only through immersion in society but also by changes in the cultural and intellectual levels of the socialising person'.

The Audiencia said that:

> the accused, and generally every Romani person, is integrated in Spanish society. Consequently it is impossible to attach any relevance to their cultural peculiarities with regard to the basic norms of cohabitation which the accused inevitably should have known. Concretely, killing someone is not an admissible behaviour. The accused agreed to that in the hearing, because there are no reasons to justify it (and even without having deep knowledge on that matter, we have the feeling that for the Gitano culture the assassination of one member is inadmissible). But it is also true that this culture establishes the necessity to cleanse the dishonour that would result from aggression against a woman of the family by taking personal retaliations. Well, this has a name in Spanish, which is vengeance; a vengeance that could never justify the crime.

It added that, on the other hand, 'the weak intellectual and educational level of the accused has an effect on the interiorisation of the rules of cohabitation; they are less patent than for other individuals, as his basic cultural level treats retaliation almost as a social act'.

It is interesting to note that in this case, the judges decided to qualify a defence by taking account of broader cultural considerations, whereas the offender's defence lawyer had strategically diluted them by raising a variety of excuses. Although those developments are indeed interesting, they seem to affect the pronounced sentence only a little.[21] But the special attention given to cultural motivations, whatever their accuracy, offer a fairer evaluation than their denial.

---

[21] This decision was revoked by the Supreme Court because the Audiencia missed another attenuating circumstance. The defendant claimed to have been intoxicated when he acted. He stated that the Audiencia unduly refused him the right to establish this condition since intoxication was a legal cause of justification (art 20.2).

The language used by the judges seems to have been cautiously chosen. Here again, the mention of differences in culture is followed directly by the reaffirmation of the primacy of equality. This structure of reasoning treats incompatibility between cultures as some sort of premise for the discussion of the case. While the incompatibility question should not be understated as in purely relativistic approaches, it is equally problematic to depart from it. Here, the characteristics of criminal law and the principles of legality and equality are determinant in the judicial attitudes. But this determination might also be related to the type of crime (murder) and to the social awareness or symbolic status given to such issues.[22]

Cultural Considerations Treated as Aggravating Conditions or Circumstances

Vengeance and Treachery

In some cases, the cultural context is used in the establishment of the aggravating circumstance of 'treachery'. Article 22.1 of the Criminal Code defines treachery as an aggravating circumstance. When it applies to a murder, the offence becomes an assassination. Sentences contain some reviews of cultural considerations about treachery in cases of honour killings involving Romani peoples.

Article 22.1 of the Criminal Code states that there is treachery when an offence against the person is committed with means, forms or ways that directly or especially assure its perpetration, without having to personally face the risk of a reaction from the victim.

In 1995, the Supreme Court drew from the fact that the victim should have known that the brother of a man killed by his brother would look for revenge, that he was then especially unprotected when he opened his door to his murderer. In quite questionable reasoning, the Supreme Court considered that the victim would never have opened the door if he had suspected

---

[22] In another case, Romani culture is the object of a curious paragraph. A defence of a man convicted for domestic abuse made use of a report of a regional Department for Women. This stated that 'in Gitano culture, the woman does not have either voice nor vote; she only serves for domestic work, to give birth to the children and satisfy her man'. The court aptly replied that such argument could not justify domestic abuse, physical and psychological harm. The defence lawyer of the convicted man did not hesitate to use a gross and somewhat racist representation of Romani culture to justify an abuse. Using the report in an unexpected way, the defence tried to claim that the problems were due to the difficulty the woman found in 'adapting' to her spouse's family. This was a curious argument. In another part of the judgment, it appeared that the woman was herself 'Gitana' but from another city. In a highly instrumentalising attitude, the defence did not hesitate to obliterate the woman's cultural background. Such highly limited understandings of cultural dynamics are not likely to enhance a sensitive debate (see Sentencia Audiencia Provincial de Cadiz 27.12. 2002).

any trouble. The court considered that when the victim opened the door, he was in a state of mind of special confidence, an element which implied treacherous behaviour on the part of the offenders. Such an evaluation does not match the publicity surrounding the offender's intentions.

In 1999, the same court considered that because of the 'vindictive climates' in Gypsies' families, especially in affairs of adultery, treachery could not be established. The victim, a Romani man who seduced a married woman, should have known what the threats meant. Therefore, he was not caught by surprise. The deceived husband and his father tried several times to kill the seducer but were prevented by his vigilant family. In such a context it is difficult to claim that he was not aware of the offenders' determination and that the deceived husband acted treacherously.

This use of cultural dimensions has been confirmed in other cases by the Supreme Court.[23] This is an interesting evolution of the evaluation of a cultural 'vindictive climate'. The later decisions are much more meticulous in the review of the context.

Depending on where they stand in the criminal proceedings, Romani people involved in such cases might either try to prove treachery or deny it.[24] A vindictive background might well influence the invocation of legal arguments in order to dishonour the party that took revenge. Here again, the invocation of cultural 'norms' should not be taken for granted. Their examination necessitates cautious review and broad understanding of the rationales of vindictive processes (Verdier, 1980).

Demonisation of Cultures in Refugee Demands

In cases invoking refugee law, cultural references are sometimes minimised in a highly provocative manner, with the narrowly defined legal provisions conditioning the recognition of this status.[25] In the database we consulted, we found 13 recent cases where a supposed cultural rule or tradition was raised by the petitioner in order to benefit from the recognition of his or

---

[23] Sentencia Audiencia Provincial de Valladollid 30.3.2004.

[24] See Sentencia Supreme Court 30.9.1999.

[25] As in other European countries, the procedures to obtain such status are of a special kind. In Spain, it is the Spanish Asylum Office (Oficina de Asilo y Refugio) that in the first instance decides on the recognition of refugee status. The Delegate of the Government for Foreigners and Immigration determines the claims made by candidates presented on the basis of the Law of Asylum referring to the Geneva Convention. The participation of the UNHCR is guaranteed by the Law of Asylum at the resolution level. Negative resolutions can be reviewed through administrative control procedures. Until January 2004, the Audiencia Nacional was the jurisdiction competent for the examination of appeals. The Audiencia Nacional is a special High Court in the Spanish judicial organisation. At the present time, the jurisdiction in charge of this area of law are the Juzgados centrales de lo contencioso-administrativo, which have their seat in Madrid.

her condition as a persecuted person in the sense understood in the UN Convention relative to the Statue of Refugees.[26]

The sentences we examined were taken on appeal against denial decisions of the administration. Only one of them succeeded (Sentencia Audiencia Nacional 17.3.2004). A woman affirmed that while she was living with her family in Benin, she has been promised against her will to the 'Chief of the Village' by her father. 'She resisted and was then threatened to be sacrificed; she was also obliged to submit to a prenuptial circumcision'. Referring to a precedent sentence, the section of the Audiencia Nacional charged with the case admitted the appeal against the denial decision. The motivations of this review were the following:

> genital mutilation has to be considered as a personal and direct persecution in the sense of the Geneva Convention, because it stems from motives specified by the Convention, here belonging to a social group; State authorities do not offer protection to oppose it. This socio-political situation in Nigeria is attested by UNHCR.

It concludes that 'the woman is victim of a persecution derived from her belonging to the feminine social group because of an extended and rooted custom of this country of practising genital feminine mutilation'.[27]

However, in most of the cases where excisions are invoked, such arguments have been dismissed by the Audiencia. It either considers that the evidence of the petitioner lacks verisimilitude or it affirms that state authorities offered sufficient protection against the customs alluded to and insist that the petitioners should produce some evidence that they have denounced the offenders to their national authorities.[28]

---

[26] Geneva, 28 July 1951; entered into effect 22 April 1954.

[27] Compare with the following decisions: Auto Audiencia Provincial Zaragoza 13.5.2005; Auto Provincial Girona 11.2.2004 and Auto Provincial Girona 26.1.2004. Here, the courts admitted sufficient reality to threats of practising ablation in Gambia to deny the family of two young girls travel documents. They confirmed orders that the girls were not to leave the territory. It should be added that Spanish law had recently criminalised female genital mutilation (FGM) through a specific provision.

[28] In one of them, the fact that the woman presented the ablation she feared as financially motivated was treated as though it made this a dubious claim. The instructor of the case defined the ablation as practices maintained inside families and aimed to prevent prematrimonial relationships and adultery. It was also stressed that the plaintiff had not established that Nigerian state authorities would have allowed those practices if the woman had denounced them. Here, despite conflicting with past precedent, the tribunal used the reports of the UNHCR to establish that state authorities were indeed trying to fight the practices and therefore denied the application of the Geneva provisions to the claims. A woman explained that she fled because her family was chosen to offer her for genital ablation in a local ceremony; she said that she was opposed to this because her sister had died after enduring such a ritual two years previously; she claimed to have then been threatened by her family and decided to flee the country. Here, the first motivation of the denial revolved around the attitudes of state authorities and the possibility that the victim could have remained in her country (Sentencia Audiencia Nacional 17.2.2004). A Nigerian woman presented herself as fearing a circumcision imposed as a tribal punishment. She claimed to have been threatened with a forced marriage

There are other cases where human sacrifice and forced enrolment into secret societies were raised repeatedly. They were rejected in very similar terms by the Audiencia Nacional.[29]

In all those cases, cultural norms were used by petitioners in the attempt to establish their legal condition as persecuted victims. Here, some depicted, supposedly 'cultural', norms are used to establish the reality of a persecution for ethnic, religious or racial motives. It is exactly the same vision of cultures as being normatively incompatible with state law (here, international standards on persecution) that are used in the petitions.

These cases, nevertheless, did not receive any direct examination by the court. Generally, the claims were rejected because the petitioners were considered not to have sufficiently demonstrated the passivity or the participation of the state authorities. In some cases, the evaluation of cultural practices is not taken into account at all, because the entire testimony is said to lack the appearance of possibility or verisimilitude. The evaluation of those accounts is drawn from common knowledge and institutional informants, such as the United Nations High Commissioner for Refugees (UNHCR) or the US State Department.

The only 'expertise' in those procedures is to be found in the interventions of the UNHCR. The decisions are quite stereotyped, but the same can be said for the petitions. In this sample, the claims appeared to be structured along the same kind of arguments: sons of kings of a not specified tribe practising human sacrifice or excision and punishment against women resisting forced marriages. Such stereotypical stories clearly transcend national boundaries.[30] The peculiar proceedings of refugee law in regard to the high number

---

to an elderly man. Here, the Audiencia Nacional referred to US State Department report, *Nigeria: Report on FGM or FGC* to find that such practices were opposed by Nigerian federal state authorities and that FGM was punished by the criminal law in several states of Nigeria, among which was the one where the plaintiff lived (Sentencia Audiencia Nacional 7.4.2004). The same reasons led to the rejection of the claim of another Nigerian woman who stated that 'her mother died when she was an infant and her father was put in a psychiatric institution, which was the reason why she lived with her grandparents. She said that in her tribe, the Shekiri, it is compulsory to undergo ablation and that her sister died because of that. Here the custom described was contested by the Advocate of the State as not being credible because usually affecting pre-nubile girls. And the Audiencia added that even if it was a real motive, not lacking verisimilitude, it would not have originated in State authorities but in society; an origin that opens the possibility of receiving help from the authorities' (Sentencia Audiencia Nacional 9.2.2001).

In a recent case, the Audiencia Nacional refused to admit an asylum petition but gave a residence permit of one year for 'humanitarian reasons' to a woman who had suffered a clitoris ablation (*El País*, 12 April 2006, 41).

[29] See, among others, Sentencia Audiencia Nacional 17.9.2004; Sentencia Audiencia Nacional 20.2.2004; Sentencia Audiencia Nacional 18.2.2004; Sentencia Audiencia Nacional 24.2.2004; Sentencia Audiencia Nacional 30.12.2003; and as to a sacrifice punishing premarital relationships, see Sentencia Audiencia Nacional 20.4.2004.

[30] See Tribunal Administratif du Grand-Duché de Luxembourg, 4.7.2005, N. 19671, available at www.ja.etat.lu/19671.doc

of demands, time constraints, legal basis, human expertise and financial means might well produce stereotyped representations of cultures.

Common Characteristics of the Explicit Cultural Arguments under Scrutiny

Interestingly enough, the most explicit cases of cultural justification we found, were considered 'relevant' in criminal law or in refugee law.[31] Whatever the contents of the cultural conflicts and norms evoked, it is clear that their expression is highly determined by the legal categories, divisions and procedures that structured the legal reasoning and procedures. In criminal cases, evaluation of culture depends on other 'cultural' categories which are crucial in establishing criminal responsibility.

In the criminal cases we reviewed, explicit cultural considerations have a very limited influence on sentencing. The explicit cultural defence is most of the time presented by the accused party. But one of the most detailed discussions of such argument is found in a criminal case where the judges explicitly raised it.

Cultural Romani considerations are highly visible in honour killings. The vindictive climate tends to conflate the criminal representation of Romani identities. Without denying the problematic vigour of vindictive rationales, we should nevertheless be cautious about such material. By themselves, the judgments do not contain any definitive indications about Romani cultures. They speak rather about the nature of interactions between Romani identities and the penal process. Explicit cultural defences are used against the criminal law invoked by the families of the victims or by state representatives. They intervene in very difficult cases.

In contemporary refugee law, explicit cultural defences are even less likely to be taken into consideration and are obviously much more instrumentally stereotyped and easily overlooked in the petitions. In all those cases, incompatibilities between cultures are constructed in legal terms. The refugees' claims play heavily on such normative 'incompatibilities'. In an instrumental tactic, their structure tends to demonstrate that petitioners suffer from a cruel culture or custom. These documents display an unerring interpretation of who 'should' be a refugee: someone who can demonstrate having 'suffered' and fled a demonised culture.

Such peculiar representations of 'culture' completely underplay serious considerations about structural power which are at stake in the migration

---

[31] See the aforementioned decisions: Sentencia Tribunal Supremo 30.9.1999; Sentencia Tribunal Supremo 3.2.1995; Audiencia Provincial de Valladolid 30.3.2004; Sentencia del Tribunal Supremo 8.3.2005; Sentencia Audiencia Provincial Avila 27.1.2004; Sentencia Tribunal Supremo 8.3.2005; Sentencia Audiencia Provincial Cadiz 27.12. 2002.

movements. The same considerations are precisely excluded from the scope of restrictive legal categories of refugee and the status of 'non-UE' foreigner.

There are no traces of special expertise being brought into those cases. The judges' considerations about Gitano cultures seem to have been drawn from 'common knowledge'. The least we can say about those cases is that there are many difficulties in expressing cultural realities in contemporary Spanish legal settings, without great distortion. It is even more the case when the cultural picture is enlarged beyond the criminal and refugee scope. Because we do not want to reduce cultural concerns to explicitly made arguments, we will try to elaborate on another type of cultural justifications related to Romani identities in Spanish law.

What about Civil and Social Law in relation to Romani Cultures and Families?

For Romani people, the problem of how to articulate justice and culture goes far beyond the criminal domain. The problems of the effects of Romani marriages in the Spanish legal order are very sensitive. Marriage in Spanish civil law is either celebrated in official form, or in a religious one. The Romani marriage, as we shall see, is considered neither one nor the other.

Romani weddings are celebrated by families and revolve around the bride's '*honra*' which refers to the purity and feminine virginity. This ceremony has very strong social meanings for the communities involved. It has vivid implications of collective strength, family values and blessing of the alliances. However, they are not recognised as valid legal marriages and the social rights attached to the spouse or widowhood civil status are consequently denied to such couples.

There is one case where the civil effects of such a wedding were recognised. In a judgment of the Juzgado de lo Social de Madrid (Sentencia 217/2002 as quoted in Ramírez-Heredia 2005: 17), a Romani widow was recognised as being entitled to the pension paid by National Social Security Institute in case of widowhood.[32] The judgment states that:

> whilst celebrations corresponding to religious customs that were not long ago strange to our society are nowadays receiving legal consideration, gypsy marriage

[32] It should be noted that some effects of the 'Gitano marriage' have benefited in practice from the movement of legal recognition of 'factual union', as noted by Presencia Gitana (1991: 33). This also applies to the application of art 113 of the Criminal Code, establishing the extent of the concept of beneficiary for civil damages linked to a criminal offence as including 'persons linked by any kind of affection bond, including factual to the victim'. For a case applying this to a 'Gitana widow', see Sentencia Audiencia Provincial de Valencia 18.6.2002.

is still ignored in Spanish legislation in spite of the fact that this ethnic group is socioculturally deeply-grounded in our country. Besides the fact that it is not a religious question, we should deduce from this consideration an analogy permitting the recognition of gypsy marriage. Indeed, there is an identity of motives.[33]

This decision was appealed by the National Social Security Institute, and then overruled by the Tribunal Superior de Justicia de Madrid in 2002 (07.11.2002).[34] It clearly stated that:

> marriage, in order to produce civil effects, should be celebrated either in the civil or the religious forms in the terms already mentioned; the Gypsy matrimony does not conform, in the present state of our legal order, to the nature of one or the other; Art. 174 of LGSS [Law on the Social Security] requires the condition of 'spouse' of the beholder to benefit from the widow's pension; this term has been interpreted restrictively by a constitutional and ordinary jurisprudence in a repeated and well known way, even if it has been criticised; that in conformation of the jurisprudence *de facto* unions, and ultimately those who have not celebrated marriage in conformity with the applicable laws, have been excluded from the benefit of the widow's pension.[35]

The judgment accepts 'religious' marriages as the only 'other' forms of matrimony that the legal order can integrate on the basis of the Civil Code. The sentence explicitly rejects any cultural basis in order to avoid the possibility of discriminatory treatment and displaces the debate to a strictly defined religious arena.[36]

---

[33] The National Social Security Institute denied to the plaintiff the widow's pension because it did not consider the ceremony celebrated by the deceased and his widow a marriage; which indicates a discriminatory treatment for ethnic motives contrary to art 14 of the Spanish Constitution and to European Community Directive 2000/43 (Ramírez-Heredia, 2005: 17–18). Here, the non-discriminatory principle is introduced as a concluding point.

[34] See also Sentencia Tribunal Superior de Justicia de Cataluña 7.10.1999; Sentencia del Juzgado de lo Social 16 de Barcelona 11.10.2001; Sentencia Tribunal Superior de Justicia de Cataluña 12.12.2003; Sentencia Tribunal Superior de Justicia de Asturias 29.11.2002 and Castro Argüelles (1999).

[35] It is somewhat strange to conflate in the same category de facto unions (which contest to a certain extent the official forms of social control on the family) with unions that are the expression of social control. 'El matrimonio, pues, para que produzca efectos civiles, sólo podrá ser el contraído de forma civil o religiosa en los términos ya expresados, y el matrimonio Gitano no participa, en la actual conformación de nuestro ordenamiento jurídico, de la naturaleza de ninguno de ellos, exigiendo el art. 174 de la LGSS la condición de 'cónyuge' del causante al beneficiaro/a de la pensión de viudedad, término interpretado en sentido estricto por una jurisprudencia constitucional y ordinaria tan reiterada como conocida – a pesar de voces discrepantes – que, por ello, excusa su cita, y conforme a la cual han quedado excluidas de la prestación las parejas de hecho, y cuantos, en definitiva, no han contraído matrimonio conforme a la legalidad aplicable' (Ramírez-Heredía, 2005: 18–19).

[36] It is interesting to compare this solution with decisions about the civil effects attached to expressly prohibited forms of marriage, eg, bigamy and polygamy (Labaca Zabala, 2004). Here, we should distinguish between marriages celebrated under Spanish law (cases of undetected bigamy when the second spouse married in good faith, not knowing of the bigamy)

We do believe that the methodologically limited conclusions we draw from the criminal cases receive some confirmation from our brief review of related civil cases. Here again, while Spanish law does not make room for culture as such, Romani persons face difficulties in inserting important cultural meanings in the judicial setting. This is perhaps the reason why Romani organisations are encouraging the Spanish Parliament to legalise their forms of marriage through a modification of civil law.[37]

In civil and social law, strictly defined cultural defences are difficult to find because civil cases do not address actions requiring 'justification'. But cultural considerations also infuse the cases treated in those legal settings. Generally in Spanish law, whether criminal, social or civil, the procedures appear to be ill-fitted to take seriously into consideration specific cultural backgrounds.

At the risk of unduly simplifying complex processes, those cases give us an illustration of a quite problematic relationship between cultures and law. State law in those cases is symbolically acting as part of an 'external' control or appears as a denied help; it does not constitute a substantive part of the social capital for the Romani actors involved in those cases. When social protection is sought, it can be denied and opposed to other symbolic resources the actors are attached to, namely a collective identity with its own social values. But once again, it would be misleading to draw general conclusions from this preliminary investigation. The construction of legal consciousness of apparently problematic cultural groups should be more fully researched. Honour killings and the organisation of vindictive exchanges should be more precisely contextualised and evaluated on the basis of long-term observations. It is also absolutely necessary to research police control and its possible ethnic focus.

Whatever the limited scope of our enquiries, the analysis of the selected criminal and social cases clearly indicates that cultural considerations are

---

and marriages celebrated under other national laws. The two widows of a bigamous deceased received a divided pension in proportion to the time they had lived with the same Spaniard spouse (Sentencia Tribunal Superior de Justicia Asturias 30.11.2001; Sentencia Tribunal Superior de Justicia Madrid 26.12.2003). On the other hand, civil effects are also attached to polygamous marriages celebrated by foreigners: foreign couples who live in Spain but who were married under another law are allowed the application of international private law rules. The diminished exception of international public order applied by the courts gives a right to a pension divided between the widows. See Sentencia Juzgado de lo Social de Galicia 13.7.1998; confirmed by Sentencia Tribunal Superior de Justicia Galicia 2.4.2002; Sentencia Tribunal Superior de Justicia Madrid 29.7.2002; but Sentencia Tribunal de Justicia Cataluna 30.7.2003. Here again, the question of 'culture' is not integrated as such in the judicial reasoning, as the marriages are classified as 'foreign' and 'religious'. But the solution seem socially fairer than for Romani marriages.

[37] The Spanish Parliament has recently adopted a non-legislative text urging the government to take steps for the recognition of Gypsy people, promoting its culture, history, identity and idioms (Diario de sesiones del Congreso de los Diputados, Pleno y Diputacion permanente, No. 114, 27.9.2005, 5761–8). Adopting specific legal dispositions to legalise the Gitano marriage could have a much broader scope than the judicial recognition of its civil effects. The symbolic status of a Law could have an adverse impact on family politics and weaken more equally gendered perspectives of some Romani.

not receiving enough attention because of a lack of systematic integration and reflection about the analytical concept of culture in Spanish law. The absence of any specific categories or procedures might explain why cultural considerations are treated in a fragmented and not in a coherent manner. Generally, the mere mention of 'culture' elicits negative reactions in the decisions we reviewed. Because there is no special expertise, procedure or category, judicial reasoning seems always to centre on problems of normative compatibility. But the question of where the incompatibility review should operate is a complex one, and it should not hinder attempts to reach a more profound understanding of the unfolding of conflicts and practices.

We believe that cultural considerations deserve to be conceptualised in a more unified manner. The ill-informed cultural considerations those decisions reveal might be partly due to normative presuppositions about cultural 'compatibility' and legitimated differences. On the whole, this approach may be discriminatory. In the Spanish context, as perhaps is the case in other continental European legal cultures, the judiciary is poorly equipped to tackle sensitive issues of this sort. Consequently, there should be a concerted effort to develop specific tools governing expertise or procedures that will lead to a more coherent integration of cultures into state law.

THE SOFT CASES

Cultural Nature of the *Okupas* Phenomenon

Although *okupas*[38] (squatters), as defined below, appeared in Spain later than in other European countries (first occupations took place in the main urban areas during the mid-1980s), the movement has been active ever since. Their activities have attracted much attention since 1995, when a new Criminal Code was enacted that included as a criminal offence the peaceful occupation of empty buildings. Article 245-2 states:

> Those who occupy, without due permission, a land, a house or a building that do not constitute a home, or who remain in them against the will of the owner, will have imposed on them a term of imprisonment from three to six months.[39]

---

[38] Squatters are known in Spain under the name of *okupas*, a slang word derived from the Spanish *ocupación* or occupation. The term is normally spelled with a 'k' as a symbol of the anarchist roots of the movement. The right spelling in Spanish should be '*ocupas*' and indeed this second form is frequently used too, especially in legal writing.

[39] Under the old Criminal Code, *violent* occupation of buildings was a criminal offence, and so it remains according to art 245.1 of the new Code. However, *peaceful* occupation was considered irrelevant for criminal law. This option was consistent with historical tradition: only during two periods of time in the history of Spanish law has peaceful occupation been considered a crime, and this was so for very specific historical reasons.

Conflicting values and contesting cultural interpretations are at the core of the squatters' activities and claims and that is why they offer an interesting example of 'subcultural' formation.[40] The cultural dimension of the squatters phenomenon can be clearly ascertained in their daily actions. In spite of important differences among squatter groups, all of them use occupations as a form of contra-cultural expression. In many instances, the occupied buildings become real cultural centres housing a programme of conferences, debates, concerts, films, plays, etc. Squatters' groups publish underground materials covering a wide range of cultural expressions and try everything possible to make their voice heard in the neighbourhood.

Although there exists a material need at the core of the squatters phenomenon (the need for housing in cities where many young people cannot obtain decent and affordable housing), the significance of the movement transcends that particular economic need, as is shown by its evolution in Spain. Surprisingly enough, the 1995 Code which criminalised the activities of peaceful squatters gave the movement a boost. From that year on, there were more squatting actions and more people were involved in them. This was not the result of material or economic needs, since these had not changed substantially after 1995: there were no more people in need of housing after that particular year than before. However, criminalisation offered the movement a great opportunity to communicate its broader claims. Certainly, the squatters' demands are not limited to the housing culture and its corresponding legal framework; on the contrary, they extend the scope of their demands to many other questions related to the social and cultural life of the community and the world.

The individual life-stories of the squatters offer a parallel account. Although they typically approach the movement attracted by its claims in the specific field of housing, there are many other ways in which their experience in an occupied house has a dramatic influence on their lives. Their habits of consumption, leisure, labour, relation with the environment, involvement in politics and so on, change substantially, reflecting a new scale of cultural values both in their individual and social lives.

Criminalisation and Criticism

The legislature's decision to criminalise peaceful occupation has been criticised by most Spanish criminal law specialists. The dominant view is that the basic principles of criminal policy in a democratic society run counter to that particular legislative option.

---

[40] For a review of the development of subcultural studies, see, eg, Bennett and Kahn-Harris, 2004. For an intelligent discussion of disruption and subversion in subcultures, see Cohen, 1980.

On the one hand, there is the principle of minimum intervention. The squatters find actual support for their actions in very specific provisions of the Constitution (which we discuss below); and their actions acquire a certain recognition under the civil law, as is the case in the institution (of Roman origins) of the *usucapio* or acquisitive prescription.[41] For those reasons, the issue of proportionality of the criminal sanction is at stake.

On the other hand, the *ultima ratio* principle also advised against creating this new criminal offence. There is a general agreement that the Spanish system of civil actions offers effective and sufficient protection to the legitimate owner of a house or land against peaceful squatters. Moreover, many have suggested that the state should focus instead on the design and implementation of social policies in the fields of housing and youth. The lack of these policies is one of the most important arguments used by the squatters themselves to support their position.

Of course, all these arguments deserve to be discussed, and the counter-arguments should be carefully considered. However, the fact that the legislature did not offer any justification at all for the creation of the new criminal offence (not even in the Preamble to the Code) has led to further criticisms. Critics are not limited to the academics, and they include the Spanish Ombudsman (*Defensor del pueblo*) and one of the two main judicial unions in the country (*Jueces para la democracia*).[42]

Squatters in Court

Although some legal decisions expressly mention the existence of a controversy as regards the constitutionality of art 245.2,[43] the Constitutional Court has not yet had the opportunity to decide on the matter, nor is there a relevant Supreme Court decision dealing with the squatters issue. The only important decisions in relation to squatting come from trial judges (*juzgados de lo penal*) and courts of appeal (*audiencias provinciales*). Among these decisions there are different interpretations and subsequent applications of art 245.2.

---

[41] Spanish Civil Code, art 1979.

[42] The former sent an official brief to the Ministry of Justice reporting many opinions against the new precept and specifically recommending its repeal. The latter, *Jueces para la democracia*, made public their position against the newly introduced criminal offence, as did the Commission for Individual Rights of the Barcelona Bar. The General Attorney for Catalonia, Josep Maria Mena, declared that the squatters' conduct received only the 'slightest social rejection' (in Baucells, 1999: 70). In 1998, a minority political group in the national Parliament proposed the repeal of the article. The proposition was dismissed without any substantial debate (Herranz, 2000: 3–4; Baucels deals with this proposal, and some reactions to it, in Baucells, 1999: 72–3).

[43] Judge Vidal i Marsal, eg, does so in Sentencias Juzgado de lo Penal de Barcelona 31.05.2002, 6.10.2001, 6.3.2000.

When preparing their legal defence, squatters benefit much from a close relation with able lawyers willing to work for them. Indeed, the relationship between the squatters and their lawyers is not limited to the courtroom, and lawyers advise the squatters throughout the process of occupying a house. This is important in order to understand the legally sophisticated nature of the arguments advanced by squatters, who very rarely make explicit any kind of cultural confrontation, but who, on the contrary, use state law imaginatively in such a way that judges who are sympathetic to their cause can acquit them, according to strictly legal methods of interpretation.

The legal argument that has been most successful for the squatters is based on the right or interest protected through art 245.2: namely possession, that is, the actual and effective relation between a person and a thing that typically (but not necessarily) derives from ownership or other legitimate title.

As a rule, houses occupied by squatters are in a very poor condition, often falling into ruin. In most cases, the owner will have abandoned the building, typically awaiting for a change in the laws regulating the use of land or the like. Many courts conclude that in such cases there is no actual possession to protect. Since there is no attack on any right or interest that deserves criminal protection, there is no unlawful act either, even if a literal interpretation of the provision seems to indicate so.

Sentencia Audiencia Provincial de Barcelona 16.1.2003 is an important instance of this kind of reasoning. It decided one of the most famous squatting cases: the peaceful occupation of an old movie theatre in the very middle of the city of Barcelona, and subsequent violent ejection of occupants by the police.[44] The text of the decision includes the explanation of the police officer in charge of the ejection. The words of this officer make clear that, besides the possible resistance on the part of the squatters, the police were mainly concerned about the risk that the building would collapse during the operation, with the dramatic consequences this may have had for all individuals involved in the action. The fact that the building was, to use the officer's words, 'almost demolished', demonstrates that it was not possessed in any relevant sense deserving criminal protection. This is the main reason why the court acquitted the squatters.

Possession requires certain acts that may at least create public awareness that someone is actually possessing. For example, a holiday house that is empty during most of the time but occasionally occupied by its owners is possessed in a relevant sense, and there is a real interest to protect there.[45]

---

[44] Asens describes the facts in 1999: 77–80, emphasising the extraordinary use of force on the part of the police. This case had an important impact on public opinion.
[45] This should not cause squatters any problems since they never occupy buildings that are occasionally used by their owners (Herreros, 1999: 23).

However, criminal protection is not deserved when the building is completely abandoned.

Sentencia Audiencia Provincial de Girona 5.2.1999 decided the case of a young woman, ideologically close to the squatters movement, who entered a dilapidated house that had been abandoned for at least 11 years. With the help of other individuals, she was preparing the building in order to create a cultural centre when they were ejected and arrested. The court acquitted her because there was no possession to protect. The decision considered a very tentative list of general criteria that may be used to decide whether possession is relevant or not:

> The state of neglect of the house is the criterion that must determine whether it falls within the scope of 245.2. If we cannot establish definite categories of houses that are included in or excluded from 245.2—for example the fact that it is not used during a certain period of time, that it is dirty or in a certain state of abandonment, that it does not meet the basic conditions of habitability, or that it is falling into ruin—the evidence of one or more of these circumstances may lead in public awareness to the belief that the thing is abandoned, so as to lead to loss of possession under the Civil Code.

The court went a little further pointing out the ideological implications of the case. Although art 245.2 appears in the section of the Criminal Code dealing with attacks on the socio-economic order, the court considered that peaceful squatters were not attacking but on the contrary fighting for that very socio-economic order. The argument is based on three constitutional concepts: the social function of property, according to which property is not only something implying 'have' but also 'do', a duty to perform certain acts (Herranz, 2000: 7)[46]; the right to decent housing that squatters try to satisfy through occupation; and the prevention of property speculation.

In particular, it is the idea of speculation which more clearly embodies the confrontation between the squatters' values and the dominant housing culture. Article 47 of the Constitution, which recognises everybody's right to decent housing, urges public authorities to legislate on the use of land according to the general interest and to prevent property speculation. But speculation is the typical economic reason lying behind the phenomenon of abandoned houses. One of the central demands on the squatters' reasoning stems from the inability or lack of will on the part of the state to combat property

---

[46] Developing that concept, the Constitutional Court has declared that property does not only consist of faculties but also of 'duties and obligations established according to collective interests and values, that is, according to the end or social utility that every category of goods that are susceptible of ownership must fulfil' (Sentencia Tribunal Constitucional 26.3.1987). These duties are not observed by the owner who abandons a house, and this offers an answer to an argument typically used against squatters, namely, that they do not respect private property. They do so, indeed, when property fulfils a real social function (Vidal i Marsal, 1999: 51).

speculation. From their own point of view, the squatters are satisfying a constitutionally-protected interest when the state fails to do so. Sentencia Juzgado de lo Penal de Barcelona 6.3.2000 makes this contrast clear:

> It is difficult to accept that in the case of houses, stores, factories, that are abandoned and in a state of neglect or even threatening to collapse, that the requirement for prosecution can be fulfilled, since precisely what motivates those who peacefully occupy is ... to vindicate the underused space for collective activities.

But, as we said before, there is not a single dominant position of the judiciary, and squatters' legal arguments are not so successful when they confront judges who are less tolerant of the movement. However, as far as our research goes, there is not a single decision that clearly rejects the arguments that have been just advanced in favour of the squatters' legal position. On the contrary, those decisions that find the squatters guilty apply a typically legalistic line of reasoning that simply shuts the door on further discussion.

These decisions may recognise that there exists a debate on the constitutionality of art 245.2, but the courts consider it a purely legislative concern which they do not have authority to discuss.[47] In a strict application of the principle of legality, the judge must ignore any consideration that does not find literal support in the words of the written law. The main principle here is that since art 245.2 makes no reference to whether the building is or is not in a poor condition, there is nothing for the judge to consider.[48] Peaceful occupation by squatters is a crime, pure and simple. It does not matter if occupying the building actually performs an economic function or if it is falling into ruin. The social purpose of the rule, as well as its systematic interpretation within the framework of Spanish law, are equally silenced. Although the ideological motivation of squatters' activities is recognised, it is also deemed completely irrelevant.[49]

Certainly, this approach to judicial decision is better understood in a civil law country than in a common law jurisdiction. Still, this kind of attitude, which revives what the late Dean Roscoe Pound called 'mechanical jurisprudence' (Pound, 1908), cannot be easily adapted to the needs of a multicultural environment, as has been shown in some of the cases mentioned above. In a state that recognises pluralism as one of its defining constitutional principles and that has to cope with growing problems of cultural confrontation, it is appropriate to wonder whether this kind of judicial style is of any help at all.

---

[47] See, eg, Audiencia Provincial de Burgos, 17.1.2000.
[48] Sentencia Audiencia Provincial Barcelona, 8.3.2001.
[49] Sentencia Audiencia Provincial Barcelona 8.3.2001; Sentencia Audiencia Provincial de Madrid 2.11.2002.

Escaping Culture?

There are alternative legal procedures open to squatters that have been advocated both in the literature and in the courtroom. For example, they could directly challenge art 245.2 in the Constitutional Court, drawing on the many arguments that have been proposed against the constitutionality of the precept. They also could claim that art 245.2 does not condemn peaceful occupation (the word 'peaceful' does not appear on the text of the precept) but only violent occupation.[50] Furthermore, squatters could benefit from art 20 of the Criminal Code, which states that an individual who acts 'in the legitimate exercise of a right' (in this case, either a right to decent housing or freedom of conscience) is not to be held criminally responsible. Not as a justification, but as an excuse, squatters could raise the defence of legal error (*error de prohibición*), claiming that they did not know their action was a criminal offence, since they thought they were simply exercising their constitutional rights; indeed, as has been pointed out, 'the conditions of the illicit act are not adequately specified' (Barber, 1999: 20).

None of these constitute a form of cultural defence. Although squatters are willing to acknowledge their cultural distinctiveness, they do not make explicit cultural arguments in the courtroom. As a general rule, squatters do not like the legal system and do not trust its democratic foundations. However, instead of confronting the state law, they follow the principle asserted by the Spanish criminal law specialist, Professor García Arán, according to whom the main way for squatters to succeed is not to be hypercritical but to use the system for their own purposes, since 'the use of dogmatics grounded on the principles of a democratic criminal law may be more effective in the face of unreasonable or unsound legislative provisions than mere appeal to political and ideological criticism' (García Arán, 1997).

For the most part, this is the moderate way that squatters, advised by their lawyers, have chosen to proceed. They avoid cultural confrontation as well as radical ideological confrontation, since the Constitution seems capable of integrating different cultural groups and of creating a space for dialogue and negotiation. Although this may be imperfect, the fact that some judges actually recognise that squatters are defending the socio-economic values reflected in the Constitution demonstrates the movement's partial success.

Probably squatters would not benefit much from the creation of a formal cultural defence, if it existed. Let us insist once again: they find enough

---

[50] This argument has been advanced in Baucells, 1997 and followed at least in one judicial decision (Juzgado de Santa Coloma 7.10.1996).

support in the Constitution to construct strictly legal arguments that judges frequently accept, and do not explicitly resort to cultural arguments in order to defend their position. Furthermore, if there were a formal cultural defence, squatters would have to prove the cultural identity of the group as well as the authenticity of their claims. Although it is plausible to think that they could successfully do so, this is a dangerous step to take in a system which is not used to dealing with multiculturalism (as can be seen from the hard cases referred to above). And ultimately they do not need to do so, since their use of more conventional legal tools has proved successful.

Nevertheless, the fact that they can actually fight their battle in the courtroom using legal weapons is already a defining feature of the squatters' movement in comparison to other cultural and subcultural groups, such as the ones we reviewed above.

CONCLUSIONS

Traditionally, contemporary progressive thinking in the West has conceptualised the practice of equality in absolute terms; that is, treating everybody alike. However, the practical significance of a more sophisticated concept of equality, as defined by the Aristotelian formula of justice (treating like cases alike and different cases differently), becomes evident when dealing with situations of cultural pluralism. This creates apparent legal contradictions in democratic systems, such as the Spanish, in which both rights to culture and the principle of equality are constitutionally recognised. This tension brings us to the philosophical hard core of the problem: what does (legal) equality mean in a multicultural context? As de Lucas states, in relation to the Spanish experience, 'what we thought was definitely solved is frequently a provisional solution dependent on present conditions'. Now that the conditions are changing, the most pressing task is to determine the limits of the 'permissible' difference and the ways in which 'different' sorts of conduct should be treated 'differently'. In this chapter we have seen how judges are often reluctant even to confront the problem.

The special conditions of Spanish internal pluralistic cultural identity, as defined above, offer a significant framework in parallel with the problem of external multiculturalism. The tension between equality and cultural rights we have just referred to is at the forefront in the Spanish debate in relation to internal multiculturalism. Attempts on the part of some regions to obtain more political autonomy and specific rights is criticised as an attack on the value of equality symbolised by the national unity; the nation-state is supposed to secure the same rights for (and impose the same duties on) everybody, without privilege being recognised. However, those regions explicitly draw on arguments of equality to claim further autonomy. In this context, equality is understood as the recognition of the different nature of those who are different, which implies not forcing upon them schemes, rules of conduct or values that they do not necessarily share. With important differences as regards their factual conditions, very similar or even identical arguments are reproduced in relation to external multiculturalism.

The outcome of the comparison of our hard and soft cases, above, is that the lack of juridical instruments specifically to frame cultural claims has a strong impact in the construction of a good defence. Spanish law and jurisprudence have not made conceptual room for the different nature of explicit cultural claims, even if the right to assert culture is legally recognised. Paradoxically, neglecting differences might result in discrimination, especially with regard to the right to a fair trial.

The sample we have reviewed indicates that explicit cultural arguments are typically raised and addressed through stereotypes and shortcuts. To the contrary, playing-down cultural arguments may in fact advance the squatters' chances of a successful defence, if they rely on existing constitutional provision.

Generally, explicit cultural claims suffer from a lack of serious explanation and of thoughtful judicial evaluation. The courts have no power or expertise to verify if they are indeed facing 'an ancestral rule' or not. Moreover, the defendants are not encouraged to deepen the rationales of specific conflict. Their defences contribute to the reification of cultures and serve to cut the judges off from more specific understandings.

The lack of cultural expertise means that the possibility of raising this type of defence depends on the kind of cultural claims involved. It should be stressed that certain cultural claims are more easily integrated or disguised in the existent legal reasoning, whilst other more estranged cultural claims require an extended work of 'translation'. This effort of translation will not be possible unless a legal space for culture is explicitly created in Spanish law.

In the hard cases reviewed above, we identified a very general deficit in terms of reasoning. More specifically, as we mentioned, there are many instances of the reification of culture or of superficial reasoning and some striking examples of decisions completely lacking any kind of reasoning, which instead rely only on blatant stereotypes. This probably reflects a deep problem in the Spanish legal profession which has not directly addressed the question of cultural factors in legal processes. This is less crucial in cases where cultural considerations remain implicit but is of greater concern when they are explicit, since these cases normally require sophisticated and sensitive styles of reasoning. It would be interesting to establish whether this conclusion can also be applied to other countries, in particular to other jurisdictions in continental Europe.

Although the very nature of the squatters phenomenon is cultural, squatters' claims in the courtroom are not (or at least not overtly) cultural. Squatters are able to draw on the constitutional law in order to state their legal arguments. They conceal as much as possible their cultural identity when confronting the official legal system. However, outside the courtroom they are willing not only to acknowledge but to insist on such a cultural dimension. There are several reasons why they do not want to do so in the legal arena:

(1) they are able to base their claims on the text of the Constitution, as is positively acknowledged by an important number of judges;
(2) they work in close connection with lawyers, who play a significant role in the design of squatters' sophisticated legal strategies;
(3) in the present conditions of the Spanish legal system, expert ascertainment of the squatters as a culturally defined group would be highly problematic. Indeed, this is true in Spain as regards any cultural group in the widest sense of the term.

Thus, as a general rule, people are in a better position as regards the Spanish judicial system if they do not raise cultural questions in the courtroom. The point is clearly illustrated by the situation of the squatters in contrast to those instances of hard cases analysed above. As regards the latter, culture is such an apparent and obvious element that the affected individuals could not have concealed it even if they had thought it desirable to do so. Although a causal relation cannot be definitely established, the fact is that these groups have had worse results than the squatters in their confrontation with the law.

5

Visions of a Multicultural Criminal Law: an Australian Perspective

SIMON BRONITT[1]

TOWARDS A MULTICULTURAL CRIMINAL LAW IN AUSTRALIA

AUSTRALIA IS A multicultural society.[2] The distinctive aspect of multiculturalism is how it has been incorporated as a national strategy informing law reform in a wide range of areas. More than 15 years ago, the Federal Government proposed the adoption of *A National Agenda for a Multicultural Australia* (1989). This document promoted the value of cultural and social diversity. Its rationale, fundamentally, was related to protecting and promoting core liberal values and the rights of *individuals* rather than communities. The strategy focused heavily on the right not to be discriminated against on the basis of race, religion or culture. The centrality of equality to the idea of multiculturalism strongly resonates with the liberal philosophical foundations of law. As the *National Agenda for a Multicultural Australia* (1989) concluded:

> Fundamentally, multiculturalism is about the rights of the individual—the right to equality of treatment; to be able to express one's identity; to be accepted as an Australian without having to assimilate to some stereotyped model of behaviour.[3]

As a result of this political initiative, multiculturalism was placed on the national law reform agenda with the Australian Law Reform Commission

---

[1] This research is based, in part, on material published in S Bottomley and S Bronitt, *Law in Context*, 3rd edn (Federation Press, 2006). I am grateful to the publishers and particularly Chris Holt for permission to use some of this material in this chapter.

[2] See, eg, Department of Immigration and Multicultural and Indigenous Affairs, *The People of Australia: Statistics from the 2001 Census* (2003). The report provides statistical summaries and community profiles of ethnicity indicators based on data from the 1996 and 2001 Census of Population and Housing in Australia, available at www.immi.gov.au/research/publications/people_of_australia.pdf

[3] Commonwealth of Australia Office of Multicultural Affairs, *National Agenda for a Multicultural Australia* (AGPS, 1989) discussed in L McNamara, *Regulating Racism: Racial Vilification Laws in Australia*, Institute of Criminology Monograph Series no 16 (Sydney, 2002).

(ALRC) tasked with undertaking a major review of family law, civil and criminal law to determine whether the underlying principles of law and dispute resolution methods 'take adequate account of the cultural diversity present in the Australian community'.[4]

The challenge, as we shall explore below, is whether the liberal promise of equality before the law can in fact accommodate cultural and group-based difference. In this chapter, I explore this question through two case studies. The first considers whether the objective standards based on the 'ordinary' or 'reasonable person'—which are applied in various ways to determine criminal responsibility—can be developed in a more culturally sensitive fashion without violating the principle of equality before the law. The second case study examines the position of Aboriginal defendants, and whether there is scope, within our existing legal system, for further recognising Aboriginal law and customs within current sentencing law and practice. The final section explores the potential of the emerging concept and institutions of restorative justice, particularly conferencing, to provide the cultural context for the offence and to develop punishment which is both culturally appropriate and effective.

Case Study on Criminal Liability

The Reasonable 'Anglo-Saxon-Celtic' Person Test?

In many areas, legal doctrine resorts to objective standards against which the behaviour of individuals is judged. The 'reasonable man' first emerged in mid-nineteenth century common law.[5] It was later reconfigured in gender neutral terms during the twentieth century as the 'reasonable person'. It is a paradigm legal construct or legal fiction widely used both in the law of torts and criminal law: it lays down the standard against which the conduct or mental state of the accused is to be measured. It also provides the benchmark for determining the availability of defences, such as self-defence, provocation and duress, as well as determining whether conduct is criminally negligent.

The issue considered in this section is how ostensibly 'objective' standards, which seek to suppress the legal relevance of group-based differences,

---

[4] ALRC, *Multiculturalism and the Law*, Report no 57 (1992) xxii.
[5] The 'reasonable man' test emerged in the provocation defence in *R v Welsh* (1869) 11 Cox 336. In the law of negligence, the concept of the 'reasonable man' was originally encapsulated by the phrase 'the man on the Clapham omnibus', a term attributed to Bowen LJ and brought to prominence in the case of *McQuire v Western Morning News Co Ltd* [1903] 2 KB 100 (CA), 109 per Collins MR. In Australia the phrase was transformed by Justice Deane into 'the hypothetical person on a hypothetical Bondi tram' in *Papatonakis v Australian Telecommunications Commission* (1985) 156 CLR 7, 36.

may contribute to racial discrimination and injustice. The injustice in this context arises from the fact that these purportedly 'neutral' legal standards are constructed by judges and juries according to their own standards of 'reasonableness'. Where minority groups are not adequately represented in the legal system (in the judiciary or on juries), there is a danger that objective standards will simply default to Anglo-Saxon-Celtic values.[6] Upon closer scrutiny, the promise of consistency in the application of objective standards is illusory, as one leading English criminal law textbook concluded:

> Where 'reasonableness' tests are in play, doctrine veers between the application of an entirely 'objective' standard which fails to investigate who is the 'reasonable person', and modified 'objective' tests in which certain aspects of the defendant's particular characteristics are indeed taken into account. The operation of 'objective' tests in fact results in highly discretionary regulation. The tribunal here is effectively constructing the standard against which the defendant is judged: the legal process goes on to legitimise that standard as 'objective' and neutral.[7]

Although entrenched in the law since the nineteenth century, some judges have challenged the appropriateness of the reasonable person standard in the criminal law. In *Moffa v The Queen*,[8] Murphy J, dissenting, took the view that the defence of provocation (which reduces murder to manslaughter) needed substantial revision. The key element of the partial defence to murder was the objective test based on the reasonable or ordinary person. This provided the standard against which the self-control and responses of the accused were to be judged. In Murphy J's view:

> The objective test is not suitable even for a superficially homogeneous society, and the more heterogeneous our society becomes, the more inappropriate the test is. Behaviour is influenced by age, sex, ethnic origin, climatic and other living conditions, biorhythms, education, occupation and, above all, individual differences. It is impossible to construct a model of a reasonable or ordinary South Australian for the purpose of assessing emotional flashpoint, loss of self-control and capacity to kill under particular circumstances ... The same considerations apply to cultural sub-groups such as migrants. The objective test should not be modified by establishing different standards for different groups in society. This would result in unequal treatment ... The objective test should be discarded. It has no place in rational criminal jurisprudence.[9]

---

[6] ALRC, *Multiculturalism and the Law*, Report no 57 (1992) 183–4. See also S Bronitt and K Amirthalingam, 'Cultural Blindness: Criminal Law in Multicultural Australia' (1996) 21(2) *Alternative Law Journal* 58, 60.

[7] N Lacey, C Wells and O Quick, *Reconstructing Criminal Law*, 3rd edn (Butterworths, 2003) 56.

[8] (1977) 138 CLR 601.

[9] (1977) 138 CLR 601, 626 per Murphy J.

Murphy J's dissent went unheeded by other members of the High Court. For the purpose of provocation, the reasonable person—configured now as the 'ordinary person'—continues to govern the operation of provocation and many defences in Australia.[10]

Rather than abandon objective standards entirely, the approach of modern Australian courts is to contextualise the reasonable or ordinary person standard, attributing to the hypothetical legal subject the particular cultural background of the accused. Thus, in the Northern Territory, the courts imbued the ordinary and reasonable person with the accused's Aboriginal background: this modified standard was used to determine both the gravity of provocation and the standard of self-control.[11] However, Stanley Yeo has criticised the approach taken in the Northern Territory, pointing to the danger that this approach may condone offensive and negative stereotypes:

> Doubtless, the judges who delivered these decisions had fairness and justice as their paramount aims. However, their decisions had the effect of promoting a great evil, namely, a negative stereotype of Aborigines being at a lower order of the evolutionary scale than other ethnic groups.[12]

The current approach adopted by the High Court is best described as a modified objective standard. The High Court, in a series of cases in the 1990s, held that the cultural background of the accused was relevant, though only in a limited or partial sense, in determining the gravity of the provocation that caused the accused to lose self-control and to form an intent to kill: the jury had to consider whether an ordinary person, with the same cultural background as the accused, would have found the provocation grave or serious. In other words, cultural background can be used to contextualise the insults or threats that provoked the accused to violence. However, the standard of self-control against which the accused is judged is that of an ordinary person, devoid of such culture or background. According to the High Court in *Stingel* (1990), the rationale for applying this purely objective standard in relation to self-control was related to equality before the law:

> No doubt, there are classes or groups within the community whose average powers of self-control may be higher or lower than the community average. Indeed, it may be that the average power of self-control of the members of one sex is higher

---

[10] S Bronitt and B McSherry, *Principles of Criminal Law*, 2nd edn (LawBook Co, 2005) ch 5.
[11] *R v Patipatu* (1951–76) NTJ 18; *R v MacDonald* (1951–76) NTJ 186; *R v Muddarubba* (1951–76) NTJ 317; *R v Jimmy Balir* (1951–76) NTJ 633; *R v Nelson* (1951–76) NTJ 327; *Jabarula v Poore* (1989) 42 A Crim R 479; *Mungatopi v The Queen* (1992) 2 NTLR 1.
[12] S Yeo, 'Sex, Ethnicity, Power of Self-Control and Provocation Revisited' (1996) 18 *Sydney Law Review* 304, 316.

or lower than the average power of self-control of members of the other sex. The principle of equality before the law requires, however, that the differences between different classes or groups be reflected only in the limits within which a particular level of self-control can be characterized as ordinary.[13]

McHugh J had subscribed to this view, though he subsequently recanted in *Masciantonio* (1995), concluding that the notion of formal equality used above could be productive of injustice:

> I was a party to the joint judgment of the Court in *Stingel*. At the time, I thought that the principle of equality before the law, which is the rationale of the objective standard, justified rejecting any attribute of the accused to the 'ordinary person' except that of age. But after reading Mr Stanley Yeo's criticism of this aspect of *Stingel* and further reflection on the matter, I have concluded that, unless the ethnic or cultural background of the accused is attributed to the ordinary person, the objective test of self-control results in inequality before the law. Real equality before the law cannot exist when ethnic or cultural minorities are convicted or acquitted of murder according to a standard that reflects the values of the dominant class but does not reflect the values of those minorities.
>
> If it is objected that this will result in one law of provocation for one class of persons and another law for a different class, I would answer that that must be the natural consequence of true equality before the law in a multicultural society when the criterion of criminal liability is made to depend upon objective standards of personhood ... In any event, it would be much better to abolish the objective test of self-control in the law of provocation than to perpetuate the injustice of an 'ordinary person' test that did not take into account the ethnic or cultural background of the accused.[14]

Significantly, Yeo subsequently reassessed his own critique of objective standards. Persuaded by the work of another legal scholar, Ian Leader-Elliott,[15] Yeo recanted his earlier views, concluding that giving the ordinary person the accused's ethnic or cultural background may give rise to essentialist views of various cultures and thereupon give rise to racism.[16]

What does this discussion about provocation and multiculturalism reveal? Legal doctrine in Australia continues to struggle with competing and conflicting conceptions of equality. On the one hand, formal equality demands that all people, regardless of their sex and gender, should be treated the same. This is regarded as a fundamental legal value, finding

---

[13] *Stingel v The Queen* (1990) 171 CLR 312, 329 per Mason CJ, Brennan, Deane, Dawson, Toohey, Gaudron and McHugh JJ.

[14] *Masciantonio v The Queen* (1994) 183 CLR 58, 73–4.

[15] I Leader-Elliott, 'Sex, Race and Provocation: In Defence of Stingel' (1996) 20 *Criminal Law Journal* 72.

[16] S Yeo, 'Sex, Ethnicity, Power of Self-Control and Provocation Revisited' (1996) 18 *Sydney Law Review* 304.

expression both in the case law, constitutional doctrine and international human rights treaties to which Australia is a signatory.[17] On the other hand, to be treated *as an equal*, the accused's cultural background seems critical to contextualising their behaviour and responsibility, particularly in relation to determining whether a defence should be available. An equality standard that ruled out the relevance of significant group-based disadvantage would, as McHugh J noted above, simply perpetuate further injustice. The current law governing the defence of provocation, with its two-stage test, both subjective and objective, embodies this tension over the meanings of equality. A better approach, that avoids the inherent dangers of essentialising or negatively stereotyping different cultures, is to embrace a wider multicultural reference standard for the reasonable/ordinary person. Rather than embody this standard in doctrinal tests, which may be meaningless, a better strategy is to mandate cross-cultural training for judges and lawyers, and to ensure better representation of minorities on juries. This process of education could be aided by the wider use of expert evidence in appropriate cases.

Recognising the difficulties of accommodating cultural background in the defence of provocation, some have called for the abolition of the defence altogether. Indeed, Tasmania has recently taken this approach, influenced in part by feminist critique that the defence is gender biased and subject to abuse, and the belief that the presence of provocation should simply be considered at the sentencing phase as a factor relevant to mitigation.[18] The consideration of race and culture in the construction of standards of legal responsibility is clearly controversial. However, abolition of the defence simply means that these issues would be considered at sentencing, a relocation of the discussion about equality to the highly discretionary, less visible domain of sentencing adjudication. It also becomes an issue for the professional judge, rather than the lay jury.

Case Study on Criminal Punishment

Recognising Aboriginal Laws and Payback

Until 1992, the legal position relating to recognition of Aboriginal law was straightforward. Australia was a settled colony found to be *terra nullius*, a

---

[17] It should be noted that Australia, unlike most comparable common law systems including the United Kingdom, does not have an entrenched Bill of Rights: see G Williams, *Human Rights under the Australian Constitution* (Oxford, Oxford University Press, 1999).

[18] Criminal Code Amendment (Abolition of Defence of Provocation) Act 2003 (Tas). See R Bradfield, 'The Demise of Provocation in Tasmania' (2003) 27 *Criminal Law Journal* 322. The arguments for and against abolition are discussed in Bronitt and McSherry, above n 10 at ch 5.

land belonging to no one.[19] This was a convenient legal fiction that denied Aboriginal people their laws and their land, and persisted until it was finally overturned by the High Court in *Mabo v Queensland (No 2)* (1992).[20] The decision raised the prospect of argument for the wider recognition of Aboriginal law in the Australian legal system. As Deane and Gaudron JJ observed in *Mabo*:

> The common law so introduced was adjusted in accordance with the principle that, in settled colonies, only so much of it was introduced as was 'reasonably applicable to the circumstances of the colony'. This left room for the continued operation of some local laws or customs among the native people and even the incorporation of some of those laws and customs as part of the common law.[21]

The decision in *Mabo* did not raise issues about Aboriginal sovereignty or Aboriginal self-determination.[22] Rather, it raised the question of whether Australian common law, by analogy with native title, should recognise in some contexts the continued operation of Aboriginal laws, including customary defences. In the immediate aftermath of *Mabo*, Stanley Yeo, drawing the analogy with native title, argued that Aboriginal criminal jurisdiction survived unless expressly abrogated by Parliament or through Executive action.[23] Yeo suggested that even if Aboriginal criminal jurisdiction was held to have been abrogated by the adoption of general Acts dealing with criminal law,[24] *Mabo* provided a moral basis for its reinstatement as a gesture of reconciliation consistent with the trend toward recognition of Aboriginal

---

[19] A key decision affirming this was the Privy Council ruling in *Cooper v Stuart* (1889) 14 App Cas 286 that the colony of New South Wales was 'peacefully annexed' rather than conquered, because, at the time, it 'consisted of a tract of territory practically unoccupied': at 291. Until 1992, the High Court accepted this view, with some significant dissent from Murphy J who described it as a 'convenient falsehood': *Coe v Commonwealth of Australia* (1979) 24 ALR 118, 138. Gibbs J, for the majority in this case, continued to affirm the view that the 'settled colony' theory was 'fundamental': *ibid* at 129.

[20] (1991) 175 CLR 1 (*Mabo*). Until this legal fiction was ousted by *Mabo*, the law did not recognise native land rights, unless these rights were created by legislation.

[21] *Mabo* (1991) 175 CLR 1, 79.

[22] Although Aboriginal sovereignty is sometimes invoked in political debate, most representatives of Aboriginal groups in Australia conceptualise issues of governance in terms of a right to self-determination. Drawn from the international human rights treaties, the 'right to self-determination' suggests that colonised peoples are entitled to autonomy in a wide range of domains, and ultimately a right to liberation and independence.

[23] S Yeo, 'Native Criminal Jurisdiction after Mabo' (1994) 6 *Current Issues in Criminal Justice* 9; S Yeo, 'Editorial: Recognition of Aboriginal Criminal Jurisdiction' (1994) 18 *Criminal Law Journal* 193.

[24] Criminal law in Australia is split between Federal, State and Territory jurisdictions. While some jurisdictions have adopted comprehensive Codes that oust the common law, some jurisdictions continue to recognise common law, as well as statutory offences. See further Bronitt and McSherry, above n 10 at 70 *et seq*.

rights to self-determination or self-management.[25] This is an example of how debate about recognition of Aboriginal laws *within* the framework of Australian law slips into wider discussion of self-determination.

The challenge of recognising more than one system of law within the Australian legal system was considered in the High Court decision of *Walker v New South Wales* (1994).[26] This case concerned a claim, through the civil courts, that the Commonwealth and State Parliaments lacked the power to legislate over Aboriginal people without their consent. During the course of oral argument, the plaintiff introduced a further argument that Aboriginal criminal customary law had not been extinguished by British settlement. Refusing leave to appeal, Mason CJ noted that an argument framed in terms of indigenous sovereignty and rights of self-determination was doomed to failure, as it was in *Mabo*. The second argument also failed on the ground that the recognition of two concurrent, potentially overlapping, systems of criminal law was not only confusing to citizens; more fundamentally, it contradicted the principle of equality before the law:

> It is a basic principle that all people should stand equal before the law. A construction which results in different criminal sanctions applying to different persons for the same conduct offends that basic principle. The general rule is that an enactment applies to all persons and matters within the territory to which it extends, but not to any other persons and matters ... The presumption applies with added force in the case of the criminal law, which is inherently universal in its operation, and whose aims would otherwise be frustrated.[27]

Mason CJ continued that even if it was assumed that the customary criminal law of Aboriginal peoples had survived settlement, it had been extinguished by the passage of criminal statutes of general application, in this context the Crimes Act 1900 (NSW). No analogy could be drawn with native title:

> English criminal law did not, and Australian criminal law does not, accommodate an alternative body of law operating alongside it. There is nothing in *Mabo (No 2)* to provide any support at all for the proposition that criminal laws of general application do not apply to Aboriginal people.[28]

As the decision in *Walker* concluded, a main argument against recognition of Aboriginal law is that it would violate the principle of equality before the law. But must equality before the law be conceived in terms which deny a place for Aboriginal law and justice? Is this approach in *Walker* beyond

---

[25] S Yeo, 'Editorial: Recognition of Aboriginal Criminal Jurisdiction' (1994) 18 *Criminal Law Journal* 193, 196.
[26] (1994) 182 CLR 45 (*Walker*).
[27] *Walker* (1994) 182 CLR 45, 50.
[28] *Ibid*.

challenge? Is equality before the law really incompatible with recognition of another system of law? Are there any precedents for recognising parallel systems of justice?

Before *Mabo* agitated these questions, the ALRC had considered this issue in its report, *The Recognition of Aboriginal Customary Laws* (1988).[29] The ALRC took the view that any special laws or defences for Aboriginal people had to comply with the principle of equality before law. However, in the ALRC's view, the principle did not rule out different treatment for indigenous people where it was a necessary and reasonable response to the 'special needs' of Aboriginal persons.[30] Consequently, the ALRC rejected special offences and defences in favour of addressing the issue of Aboriginality and Aboriginal law, where appropriate, within existing substantive and procedural laws.

A different approach to this issue was taken in Canada. Rather than conceptualise equality as 'equal versus special treatment', the Law Reform Commission of Canada has recognised the limits of equality discourse, proposing instead the higher goal of 'ensuring equal access to justice, equitable treatment and respect' for Aboriginal peoples within the criminal justice system.[31] On this view, the principle of equality before the law would be consistent, rather than antagonistic, with the creation of parallel systems of indigenous criminal justice. Indeed, the Canadian Parliament has created a self-governing region, called the Nunavut, which grants a large measure of legal and political autonomy to the Inuit, who comprise 85 per cent of the population living in this territory in far North Canada.[32]

In debates about the recognition of Aboriginal law and jurisdiction, the question is whether equality before the law can be reconceptualised as requiring respect for difference, a reading which would admit, rather than deny, this system of parallel justice. Nielsen and Martin are highly critical of the High Court in *Walker* because of its use of formal equality to 'close down' arguments about native jurisdiction in the criminal law context:

> [T]his formal reading of the notion of equality is out of kilter with international jurisprudence, and so the continued denial of the Indigenous criminal justice system contravenes the cultural rights of Indigenous Australians.[33]

In addition to raising these concerns about equality before the law, the recognition of Aboriginal law also threatens the idea that laws, particularly those

---

[29] ALRC, *The Recognition of Aboriginal Customary Laws*, Report no 31 (1986).

[30] *Ibid* at paras [404]–[412].

[31] Law Reform Commission of Canada, *Aboriginal Peoples and Criminal Justice*, Report no 34 (1991) ch 3.

[32] The Nunavut was created as a self-governing territory in 1999: see www.gov.nu.ca/.

[33] J Nielsen and G Martin, 'Indigenous Australian Peoples and Human Rights' in D Kinley (ed), *Human Rights in Australian Law* (Federation Press, 1998) 111.

that interfere with liberty, must be clear and certain. A commonly heard objection levelled against Aboriginal systems of justice is that their legal norms are 'customary', that is, they are unwritten, determined by a caste of unelected elders. The objection that the law is not encoded into democratically derived posited rules seems equally applicable to the Australian common law system: a system in which appointed rather than elected judges are tasked with developing the law (through statutory interpretation or common law development) from the facts of particular disputes presented to them.[34] The difference between Aboriginal 'customary' law and Australian law is less stark if we reject the conventional positivist 'rule book' view of law in favour of definitions that emphasise the role of legal culture and professional norms in explaining legal conformity. The similarity between Aboriginal and common law systems is apparent if we adopt the definition of the common law offered by Brian Simpson: 'the common law is best understood as a system of customary law, that is a body of traditional ideas received within a caste of experts'.[35]

Another objection levelled against legal pluralism is that, unless confined to a particular geographical territory (as in the case of the Canadian Nunavut), jurisdiction in relation to Aboriginal law would be determined on the basis of one's *status* as a member of a particular race. The issue of Aboriginal identity and its recognition through law has been a matter of contention. 'Protection statutes' enacted in the early twentieth century adopted elaborate pseudo-scientific classifications based on *degrees* of Aboriginality. From a modern perspective, classifications based on the 'quantum of blood' are considered offensive and discriminatory. The current view, which is reflected in the jurisprudence of the High Court's interpretation of the 'race' power under s 51(xxvi) of the Constitution, is that the idea of race is not limited to biological markers. In *Commonwealth v Tasmania* (1983) the High Court held that Tasmanian Aboriginals fell within the race power, with Justice Brennan promoting a broad definition of race:

> Though the biological element is ... an essential element of membership of a race, it does not ordinarily exhaust the characteristics of a racial group. Physical similarities, and a common history, a common religion or spiritual beliefs and a common culture are factors that tend to create a sense of identity among members of a race and to which others have regard in identifying people as members of a race. As the people of a group identify themselves and are identified by others as

---

[34] It must be recalled that official authorised law reporting is a nineteenth century development. Much early colonial law survives through the private reporting of cases, by lawyers and newspaper reports. It is only in the late twentieth century, with the advent in the 1990s of searchable databases (such as www.austlii.edu.au) that legal decisions and legislation have become freely accessible to citizens.

[35] AWB Simpson, *Legal Theory and Legal History: Essays on the Common Law* (Hambledon Press, 1987) 362.

a race by reference to their common history, religion, spiritual beliefs or culture as well as by reference to their biological origins and physical similarities, an indication is given of the scope and purpose of the power granted by para (xxvi). The kinds of benefits that laws might properly confer upon people as members of a race are benefits which tend to protect or foster their common intangible heritage or their common sense of identity. Their genetic inheritance is fixed at birth; the historic, religious, spiritual and cultural heritage are acquired and are susceptible to influences for which a law may provide. The advancement of the people of any race in any of these aspects of their group life falls within the power.[36]

The court, perhaps mindful to avoid cultural essentialism, added no further indicators of Aboriginality. Indeed, this definitional approach was endorsed by the ALRC in its report, *The Recognition of Aboriginal Customary Laws* (1988):

95. The Commission's View.

Experience under Commonwealth and State legislation suggests that it is not necessary to spell out a detailed definition of who is an Aborigine, and that there are distinct advantages in leaving the application of the definition to be worked out, so far as is necessary, on a case by case basis. Constitutionally this presents no difficulties, as the High Court's decision in *Commonwealth v Tasmania* shows. On the other hand, it has sometimes been suggested that a special and more restrictive definition of 'traditional Aborigine' should be adopted for the purposes of this Report and its implementation. There are several reasons why such a special definition is both unnecessary and undesirable. Restrictive definitions of this kind have not been adopted in other related contexts. Experience so far does not suggest a need for more stringent definitions. The application of the Commission's recommendations in appropriate cases is to be achieved by the substantive requirements of the provision in question, and by related evidentiary requirements. Indeed, there may be cases where it is appropriate that provisions for the recognition of Aboriginal customary laws should apply to persons who are not Aborigines. These questions have to be considered on their merits, and cannot be resolved through the adoption of any more-or-less restrictive definition of 'traditional Aborigine'.[37]

In the ultimate analysis, it is important to recognise the political context of the law's attempt to construct 'identity'. The following passage forcefully puts the claim that issues of identity, Aboriginality and powerlessness are closely related:

Powerlessness means, among other things, having others say who you are, with the naming usually counting against you. Aborigines have been rendered largely

---

[36] *Commonwealth v Tasmania* (1983) 158 CLR 1, 244.
[37] ALRC, *The Recognition of Aboriginal Customary Laws*, Report no 31 (1986) 72–3 (footnotes omitted).

invisible and Aboriginal rights have been effectively denied throughout much of white Australian history. Who is 'really' Aboriginal, and what flows from that, has been laid down by governments, policemen, local officials and, more recently, anthropologists. Many Australians still make a distinction between 'real' Aborigines (usually presumed tribal/traditional/'full-blood') and 'part' and/or urban Aborigines—despite the discrediting of genetic determinism, and the fact that many 'urban' Aborigines know and have close links with country and kin. Such distinctions are not only personally and socially offensive and hurtful; they also have powerful political functions in challenging many Aborigines' right to speak for, or even about, Aboriginal claims.[38]

Definitional uncertainty in relation to Aboriginality presents problems, but these should not be overstated. Definition in law is often left hazy by the legislature and the courts. Yet systems of law continue to work tolerably well, and, in many instances, chronic indeterminacy over key definitions can be negotiated by the parties without even recourse to litigation.

Another objection is that recognition of Aboriginal law would promote and multiply conflicts of laws between overlapping and potentially contradictory systems of law vying for operation. In federal systems, which confront this type of conflict every day, such an objection is not persuasive. As Nielsen and Martin pointed out, the rejection of indigenous criminal law by the High Court in *Walker* ignored 'the pluralism already inherent within the Australian federation, which is comprised of three tiers of law-making authority, each of which is supposed to complement the others'.[39] As in the European Union and many European states, law within Australia is highly fragmented, divided between the nine jurisdictions of the Commonwealth, States and Territories. It is also overlaid by the military criminal jurisdiction, which provides an example *par excellence* of criminal laws being applied by virtue of 'status' (in this case, the accused's membership of the Australian Defence Force).[40]

With such complexity, legal and administrative mechanisms are developed to 'share' jurisdiction and to resolve potential conflicts. Indeed, Federal, State and Territory legislation could be developed to address the problem of potential conflict between Aboriginal and non-Aboriginal criminal jurisdiction: legislation could be adopted that clarifies the scope of and placed limits on Aboriginal laws, as in the case of native title claims. Indeed,

---

[38] J Pettman, 'Learning about Power and Powerlessness: Aborigines and White Australia's Bicentenary' (1988) 29(3) *Race and Class* 69, 75–6.

[39] J Nielsen and G Martin, 'Indigenous Australian Peoples and Human Rights' in D Kinley (ed), *Human Rights in Australian Law* (Federation Press, 1998) 111.

[40] It should be noted that the application of Australia's military laws, including criminal offences, is not confined to Australia's territorial borders: *Re Colonel Aird; Ex parte Alpert* (2004) 220 CLR 308.

the Northern Territory Law Reform Committee has recently recommended that general steps in this direction be taken:

> That upon application to the Attorney-General an Aboriginal community may apply for recognition, within the community, and by those who consent to it, of such Aboriginal customs and traditions as the community sees fit and which shall therefore be recognised as lawful and binding upon those who accept it, provided that such customs and traditions do not transgress the general laws of the Northern Territory or universal human rights and fundamental freedoms.[41]

The latter qualification foreshadows another objection against recognition of Aboriginal law, which arises from the administration of payback against offenders within Aboriginal communities.

'Payback' is an Aboriginal–English term used to describe the wide range of methods used to punish wrongdoers and to appease victims within some indigenous communities. It is not a form of revenge, but constitutes an admission of responsibility, typically involving some form of restitution or gift to the victim, or acceptance of punishment by the wrongdoer.[42] Forms of payback vary widely, ranging from death, spearing and duelling, through to shaming, education, compensation or exclusion.[43] In some communities, payback may be purely symbolic, involving no more than merely touching the accused on the thigh with a spear.[44] In its most serious form, it involves the repeated spearing of the offender in the upper inner thigh. While inflicting serious injury, payback is not typically intended to cause death. The type of payback varies according to the severity of the breach of indigenous law, the factors surrounding the offence, the parties involved and any other relevant matters. Once the type of payback is determined and carried out, that is regarded as the end of the matter and the potential for further violence between the clans is averted. Judges in the Northern Territory and Western Australia have a long history of recognising such indigenous 'customary law' in sentencing decisions.[45]

---

[41] Northern Territory Law Reform Committee, *Report on Aboriginal Customary Law* (2003) 19; the report is available at www.nt.gov.au/justice/docs/lawmake/ntlrc_final_report. pdf. See also New Law Reform Commission, *Sentencing Aboriginal Offenders*, Report no 96 (2000) and Western Australian Law Reform Commission, *Aboriginal Customary Law*, Final Report (2006).

[42] For a general review of the history and practices of payback, see M Finnane, '"Payback", Customary Law and Criminal Law in Colonised Australia' (2001) 29 *International Journal of the Sociology of Law* 293. *Jadurin v The Queen* (1982) 44 ALR 424, 427–8 contains a vivid description of a payback ceremony and its consequences for those involved.

[43] ALRC, *The Recognition of Aboriginal Customary Laws*, Report no 31 (1986) para [500].

[44] *R v Minor* (1992) 59 A Crim R 227, 229 per Asche CJ.

[45] *Ibid* at 237 per Mildren J. This was aided by legislation that permitted the court in murder cases to receive any evidence on native law or custom in mitigation of penalty: Criminal Law Amendment Ordinance 1939 (NT).

In many cases, recognition of Aboriginal law in sentencing decision-making is not problematic: courts routinely take judicial notice of laws, customs and practices within Aboriginal communities that shed light on the seriousness of the individual offender's wrongdoing. This may operate either to mitigate or aggravate the penalty, though sentencing courts are warned not to consider such matters without credible independent evidence on Aboriginal law and customs.[46] This reflects the general relevance of culture and cultural background to sentencing decisions, which has long been recognised under the common law and, until 2006 at least, was listed as a matter relevant to sentencing federal offenders.[47]

That said, Australian judges have approached the recognition of payback with some degree of ambivalence. It is, however, ambivalence tinged with pragmatism, reflecting the reality that Australian systems of punishment may not command respect within Aboriginal communities or be effective in terms of deterrence or rehabilitation. This lack of confidence is due to the high levels of over-representation of Aborigines in Australian gaols and high levels of Aboriginal deaths in custody.[48]

The ALRC has recognised the relevance of Aboriginal customary law to sentencing and recommended that *lawful* forms of traditional punishment could be incorporated into sentencing orders. However, the ALRC refused to sanction the incorporation of traditional punishment into sentencing orders that would involve a breach of the general law. Partial recognition of Aboriginal law was justified as being consistent with Art 27 of the International Covenant on Civil and Political Rights (ICCPR), which provides:

> In those states in which ethnic, religious or linguistic minorities exist, persons belonging to such minorities shall not be denied the right, in community with

[46] *R v Minor* (1992) 59 A Crim R 227, 237 per Mildren J.

[47] Following the recommendations of the ALRC in *Multiculturalism and the Law*, Report no 57 (1992), 'cultural background' was made a factor relevant to federal sentencing: inserted into Crimes Act 1914 (Cth), s 16A. The ALRC subsequently recommended that additionally legislation should endorse the practice of considering traditional laws and customs in sentencing Aboriginal offenders: *Same Crime, Same Time: Sentencing of Federal Offenders*, Report no 103 (2006). This was not implemented, and following a series of high profile cases in which culture was used to 'excuse' serious offending, the provision recognising the relevance of cultural background was repealed in 2006. This is discussed below.

[48] E Johnston, *Royal Commission into Aboriginal Deaths in Custody: National Report* (AGPS, 1991). Since 1991, the levels of Aboriginal deaths in custody have continued to rise, comprising nearly one-quarter of all deaths in 1999: V Dalton, 'Australian Deaths in Custody and Custody-Related Police Operations 1999' in *Trends and Issues in Crime and Criminal Justice*, No 153 (Australian Institute of Criminology, 2000). Latest data show a steady decline in prison deaths overall, though the rate of indigenous deaths in prison custody remains higher than the general prison population: in 2003 it was 2.1 per 1,000 indigenous prisoners, while the rate of non-indigenous deaths in prison custody was 1.6 per 1,000 non-indigenous prisoners: M McCall, *Deaths in Custody in Australia: 2003 National Deaths in Custody Program Annual Report* (Australian Institute of Criminology, 2004), available at www.aic.gov.au/publications.

others of the group to enjoy their own culture, to profess and practice their own religion or to use their own language.

While accepting the inevitability of payback involving the infliction of serious injury within some Aboriginal communities, the courts point out that payback is not retribution or vengeance and that the deliberate infliction of serious harm cannot be judicially condoned.[49] This position of judicial 'neutrality' allows the courts to factor payback into sentencing, while deftly avoiding judicial consideration of the question of its legality under either domestic or international law.[50] Yet, this position is difficult to maintain in cases of prospective payback where the courts impose punishment *conditional* upon payback. In *R v Walker*,[51] the sentencing court adopted a 'hands on' approach, requiring in the sentencing order that the Director of Correctional Services report back to the court as to whether payback occurred within a reasonable time. The judicial incorporation of payback into the sentencing order in *Walker* raises the question whether Australian law is sanctioning, perhaps even facilitating, 'cruel, inhuman or degrading treatment or punishment' prohibited by Art 7 of the ICCPR. This argument has not been raised before in either domestic or international courts, but distinguished international legal jurist, James Crawford, has suggested that nothing in the ICCPR prevents Australian courts from taking traditional spearing into account in sentencing decisions:

> The question, then, is whether the Covenant requires States Parties actively to suppress all treatment considered 'cruel' or 'degrading', even where the treatment occurs with the consent of the parties concerned, and as an aspect of the traditions

---

[49] *R v Jadurin* (1982) 7 A Crim R 182, 187 per St John, Toohey and Fisher JJ; *R v Minor* (1992) 59 A Crim R 227, 240 per Mildren J; *Re Anthony* (2004) 197 FLR 354, 358 per Martin CJ.

[50] It has been suggested, obiter, that payback may not constitute an assault: *R v Minor* (1992) 59 A Crim R 227. The Northern Territory Code provided that an assault is not illegal where it is authorised by the victim, and the person who commits the assault does not intend to kill or cause grievous bodily harm. According to Mildren J, a person who administered payback on behalf of the Aboriginal community does not intend to kill or cause grievous bodily harm. Neither does the person who administers the payback inflict grievous bodily harm. Mildren J pointed to authority which supported the view that mere spearing into the thigh muscle may not in fact cause any permanent injury to health so as to fall within the definition of grievous bodily harm. This aspect of the judgment in *Minor* represents a novel approach to offences against the person. Previously, severe forms of payback by spearing had been assumed to be unlawful even where the victim had consented. In a Western Australian case, the judge refused to grant bail to an accused to allow him to undergo payback on the grounds that the spearing would be 'unlawful': 'Judge Rejects Spear Justice' in *The Western Australian*, 4 October 1997, 3. This hostile approach to payback has been followed most recently in the Northern Territory in *Re Anthony* (2004) 142 A Crim R 440, casting doubt on *Minor*. In *Anthony*, bail was granted, but only on condition that the accused *not* attend the place where the traditional punishment was to be administered.

[51] *R v Walker* (unreported, SC NT, Martin CJ, SCC No 46 of 1993, 10 February 1994), discussed in (1994) 68(3) *Aboriginal Law Bulletin* 26.

and customs of the ethnic group within which it occurs, and no matter what other consequences such suppression, with its associated policing, would involve for the group in question. Quite apart from the question whether such punishment is 'cruel' or 'degrading', the answer must be that it does not. Nothing in the Covenant prevents the law enforcement authorities from adopting a policy of intervening in indigenous communities only upon complaint, in cases not involving threats of life or suppression of complaints.[52]

This approach again side-steps the issue of legality, hiding behind the prosecutorial discretion not to proceed in the absence of a complaint. From an international perspective, the toleration of payback by domestic law poses a significant challenge to the universality of human rights. International law, while accepting some 'margin of appreciation' in the application of human rights, is reluctant to dilute the universal quality of fundamental rights. This claim of universality is strongest in relation to rights that are not qualified, such as Art 7 of the ICCPR that prohibits torture, cruel, inhuman or degrading treatment or punishment. The ALRC has acknowledged in its Discussion Paper no 17, *Aboriginal Customary Law—Recognition* (1980), that it is impossible to escape the culturally determined nature of fundamental concepts:

> But by what standard are the notions of human rights to be measured? Obviously there is a wide gap in some areas between Western notions of human rights and those which apply in Aboriginal society. These issues pose questions of justice which have never been answered satisfactorily anywhere and which are probably unanswerable. There is a direct clash between the imperative of imposed law and indigenous custom, a clash between irreconcilable moral imperatives.[53]

As considered above, the clash requires the legal system—domestic and international—to choose between competing rights. After reviewing these issues, the ALRC concluded that the right to culture under Art 27 was 'qualified' by Art 7: 'Article 27 protects the right of a minority "to profess and practice" its religion. It does not in terms protect cruel or inhumane punishments connected with it'.[54] On balance, the ALRC was satisfied that prohibiting cruel punishment would not have a significant detrimental effect on Aboriginal culture since there were other means of preserving Aboriginal culture such as land rights and language.

---

[52] J Crawford, 'International Law and the Recognition of Aboriginal Customary Law' in B Hocking (ed), *International Law and Aboriginal Human Rights* (LawBook Co, 1988) 63; S Blay, 'The International Covenant on Civil and Political Rights and the Recognition of Customary Law Practices of Indigenous Tribes: the Case of Australian Aborigines' (1986) 19 *Comparative and International Law Journal of Southern Africa* 199, 203–7; ALRC, *Aboriginal Customary Law—Recognition*, Discussion Paper no 17 (1980) 53.
[53] ALRC, *Aboriginal Customary Law—Recognition*, Discussion Paper no 17 (1980) 52.
[54] *Ibid* at 53.

In Australia, debate over recognition of Aboriginal law in sentencing decisions unfortunately has fixated negatively upon 'payback spearing'.[55] This overlooks the restorative foundations of Aboriginal community-based punishment. Notwithstanding the typical construction of payback as a blood feud and vengeance, the promotion of community involvement in the punishment, victim restitution and offender restoration aligns it more closely to restorative rather than retributive justice.[56]

Payback involving spearing exposes the limits of equality and rights discourse and presents challenges which the criminal justice system has only just begun to address. The ALRC's solution is an example of the tendency of individual rights to trump collective rights. It also reveals the process by which laws and cultural practices of 'others' can be constructed as 'inhuman and degrading punishment', denying legal recognition to practices that play a vital role in sustaining individual and group identities.[57] While payback may be viewed as unlawful under domestic law, or inhuman or degrading treatment under international law, this overlooks the current legal approach to many forms of legitimate 'violence' within Anglo-Saxon-Celtic culture. One only has to consider how the current law of assault excludes from its ambit injuries inflicted, often deliberately, in the course of sport (such as boxing and rugby), or more generally through larrikinism or 'rough horseplay'.[58]

The legal space in which Aboriginal law and culture can be 'received' into Australian law seems to be diminishing. In 2006, the relevance of culture and cultural background as a legitimate factor in sentencing has been challenged in recent reforms in the federal jurisdiction. The Crimes Amendment (Bail and Sentencing) Act 2006 (Cth),[59] passed in December 2006, removed

[55] For a typical media depiction of payback, see *The Independent*, May 1994, where the front-page banner 'Bloody Justice' is pierced by a blood-splattered spear. On the importance of indigenous involvement in sentencing see N Löfgren, 'Aboriginal Community Participation in Sentencing' (1997) 21 *Criminal Law Journal* 127.

[56] It is common to misconstrue systems of punishment. For example, the *lex talonis* is usually traced to the Old Testament injunction 'an eye for an eye, a tooth for a tooth': *Exodus* 21:24. Paradoxically, this provision of Jewish law relates not to a measure of punishment, but rather a principle of just compensation in the civil law: M Lew, *The Humanity of Jewish Law* (Soncino Press, 1985) ch 1. The phenomenon of restorative concepts being hijacked by retributive discourse has also been found in the evolution of Greek and Anglo-Saxon laws: J Braithwaite, *Restorative Justice and Responsive Regulation* (Oxford, Oxford University Press, 2002). Braithwaite suggests (at 5) that restorative justice, rather than being a recent innovation, has been 'the dominant model of criminal justice throughout most of human history for perhaps all of the world's peoples'.

[57] See Editorial, 'A Defence of Consent to Indigenous Customary Punishment' (2003) 27 *Criminal Law Journal* 229; S Bielefeld, 'The Culture of Consent and Traditional Punishments under Customary Law' (2003) 7 *Southern Cross University Law Review* 142, 148–9.

[58] Sports such as boxing, wrestling, football and hockey involve body contact that may lead to serious harm. The general rule is that by engaging in sport, the participant accepts the inherent risks involved in that sport: *Billinghurst* [1978] *Criminal Law Review* 553. In relation to rough horseplay, the courts have held that assaults inflicted as part of military hazing rituals may be lawful on the basis of an 'implied' consent: see *R v Aitken* [1992] 1 WLR 1006.

[59] Crimes Amendment (Bail and Sentencing) Act 2006.

cultural background as one of the matters that a judge may consider when making sentencing and bail decisions. Crimes Act 1914 (Cth), s 16A(2A) states expressly:

the court must not take into account [in these decisions] any form of customary law or cultural practice as a reason for:
(a) excusing, justifying, authorising, requiring or lessening the seriousness of the criminal behaviour to which the offence relates; or
(b) aggravating the seriousness of the criminal behaviour to which the offence relates.

The political context for the reform relates to a moral panic about crime in indigenous communities, and how custom has been pleaded as mitigating factor, in one case significantly reducing the penalty for sexual offending against a minor.[60] In proposing the reform, the ideal of equality before the law loomed large in the parliamentary debates. As the government proponents of the Bill noted:

All Australians should be treated equally under the law ... Criminal behaviour cannot in any way be excused justified, authorised, required or rendered less serious because of customary law or cultural practice. The Australian Government rejects the idea that an offender's cultural background should automatically be considered, when a court is sentencing that offender, so as to mitigate the sentence imposed.[61]

As noted above, the value of this liberal conception of equality remains deeply contestable: not only does it suppress the relevance of salient difference but it also subtly signals that the cultural context may justify a more harsh penalty to deter 'primitive cultural practices'. This may have been avoided, at least in federal legislation, which adopted the Senate Committee's recommendation to state expressly that culture may never be taken into account to *aggravate* the penalty (see s 16A(2A)(b) above). The federal reform in 2007 contradicts the recommendations of the ALRC, and other law reform agencies that have examined the issue.[62] With the high level of Aboriginal over-representation in custody, these symbolic laws that deny cultural relevance will do little to address the structural disadvantage

---

[60] The most controversial case, attracting media attention, involved an Aboriginal man who anally raped his 14-year old wife. The Northern Territory Chief Justice Brian Martin sentenced him to one month's imprisonment, accepting the defendant's view that he was entitled to act as he did under customary law: *The Queen v GJ*, Supreme Court of the Northern Territory, SCC 20418849. The sentence was increased on appeal to three years' imprisonment: *The Queen v GJ* [2005] NTCCA 20. The High Court dismissed GJ's appeal against the harsher sentence on 19 May 2006. See further C Lorimer and S Harris-Rimmer, *Crimes Amendment (Bail and Sentencing) Bill 2006, Bills Digest*, 27 November 2006, no 56 (2006–07).

[61] Second Reading Speech, Senate *Debates*, 14 September 2006, 9.

[62] ALRC, *Same Crime, Same Time: Sentencing of Federal Offenders*, Report no 103 (2006) n 4.

and injustices experienced by Aboriginal offenders. Indeed, a more proportionate solution to the controversial case discussed above would have been to exclude cultural arguments in cases involving violence against women and children, a position which is consistent with international human rights treaties and an argument advanced by scholars elsewhere.[63]

TOWARDS A NEW MULTICULTURAL JURISPRUDENCE: RESTORATIVE JUSTICE

Much of the academic debate about multicultural jurisprudence thus far has focused on how the criminal law, particularly defences, is discriminatory and could be further developed to better respect cultural difference. My final concluding thoughts are whether our focus on criminal responsibility rather than punishment may be misplaced. In most criminal justice systems, including Australia, offenders accept responsibility for the harm caused, which explains the prevalence of pleas of guilty. Dissatisfied with the existing system, restorative justice has become a significant driving force for reform in Australia, and elsewhere. In this final section, I explore how restorative justice mechanisms have a greater potential for contextualising the offender's conduct and developing a criminal justice response that is culturally appropriate. Embracing restorative justice may also have additional 'payoffs' in terms of reducing recidivism and fostering community respect for the law and justice system—as it is an initiative being adopted across the criminal justice system, applicable to all offenders, it avoids the criticism that such initiatives constitute special or exceptional treatment for people from a different cultural background.

There is a growing international social movement in favour of reconstructing criminal justice to promote 'restorative justice', with a particularly strong uptake of this initiative in Australia, Canada and New Zealand. Under this influential model, the search for legitimacy is redirected away from the state and its power to punish, towards community-based initiatives that offer the prospect of reintegration and restoration for offenders, victims and communities affected by crime. There is a wealth of literature, from both practical and theoretical perspectives, exploring the emergence of restorative justice as an effective alternative to retributive forms of justice.[64]

---

[63] Article 4 of Declaration on the Elimination of Violence Against Women, which was proclaimed by the United Nations General Assembly on 20 December 1993, states that 'States should condemn violence against women and should not invoke any custom, tradition or religious consideration to avoid their obligations with respect to its elimination'. See further S Bronitt and K Amirthalingam, 'Cultural Blindness: Criminal Law in Multicultural Australia' (1996) 21(2) *Alternative Law Journal* 58, 60.

[64] There is extensive literature evaluating trials carried out in Australia, the United States, Canada and New Zealand: see H Strang, *Restorative Justice Programs in Australia: a Report to the Criminology Research Council* (2001), available at www.aic.gov.au/crc/reports/strang/report.pdf

It is difficult to offer a simple definition of restorative justice because it encompasses a range of methods and goals, partly as a result of its emergence as a 'unifying banner' under which informal traditions of justice were adopted.[65] It has been defined broadly as 'action that is primarily oriented towards doing justice by restoring the harm that has been caused by a crime'.[66] Restorative justice practices have a number of goals, including:

(a) that offenders confront and accept responsibility for their conduct and its consequences;

(b) that families and communities surrounding the protagonists play a role in both reintegration and support for both the victim and the offender; and

(c) to provide a resolution for disputes.[67]

In essence, restorative justice is about inclusive participation, reparation and resolution.

The centrepiece of restorative justice is the meeting that brings together those people affected by a particular offence in order to determine on a consensual basis how to deal with the aftermath of that offence. In Australia, this meeting is convened as a 'conference' where offenders are brought together with the victims of their crime, usually with their respective families and a facilitator, to discuss the impact of their actions on the victim and the community and ways to repair the harm done. There will be cases where the offender simply cannot be 'restored', in which case increasingly coercive controls become legitimate, but only when other more dialogic forms (using restorative justice or deterrence) have been tried but have failed to secure compliance with the law. Diversionary conferencing is now widely used for dealing with juvenile and increasingly adult offending in many jurisdictions, as well as informing an increasing array of pre-trial and post-conviction decision-making by police, prosecutors and the courts.[68]

---

and J Braithwaite, 'Restorative Justice' (1999) 25 *Crime and Justice: a Review of Research* 1 for extensive reviews. Generally, the literature reports extremely high levels of perceived procedural justice. Some record further benefits to the victims and the offenders, as well as the community. See, eg, H Strang and J Braithwaite (eds), *Restorative Justice: Philosophy to Practice* (London, Ashgate, 2000); D Roche, *Restorative Justice* (London, Ashgate, 2000); J Braithwaite, *Restorative Justice and Responsive Regulation* (Oxford, Oxford University Press, 2002).

[65] D Roche, *Accountability in Restorative Justice* (Oxford, Oxford University Press, 2003) 6.

[66] L Walgrave, 'Extending the Victim Perspective towards a Systemic Restorative Justice Alternative' in A Crawford and J Goodey (eds), *Integrating a Victim Perspective within Criminal Justice* (London, Ashgate, 2000) 260.

[67] K Daly and H Hayes, 'Restorative Justice in Conferencing in Australia' in *Trends and Issues in Crime and Criminal Justice*, no 186 (Australian Institute of Criminology, 2001), available at www.aic.gov.au/publications/tandi/ti186.pdf.

[68] For example, the Young Offenders Act 1997 (NSW) establishes a system of youth justice conferencing as a diversionary programme from the children's court, administered by the Department of Juvenile Justice.

Important preconditions to participation in such conferences apply. The New South Wales legislation, typically, requires the participant to admit guilt to an offence. In addition there must be consent by all parties. The stated aims of the Young Offenders Act 1997 (NSW) are to:

(a) emphasise restitution by the offender;
(b) ensure acceptance of responsibility by that person for his or her behaviour; and
(c) meet the needs of victims and offenders (s 3(ii), (iii)).[69]

Although restorative justice conferencing has been adopted in all Australian jurisdictions, thus far its use has been mainly confined to juvenile justice, though it is being gradually extended into all areas of the criminal justice system.[70]

There has been no research specifically on whether these new processes offer a more effective cultural context for offending and develop outcomes for offenders and victims that are more culturally sensitive. More specifically, in responding to Aboriginal offending, the various legal systems in Australia have been experimenting with new forms of justice. As noted above, in many rural areas with large Aboriginal populations, magistrates took account of local customary laws and practice in their decision-making process. A significant movement to recognise and legitimate the role of these systems of Aboriginal justice occurred in the 1990s, with the establishment of Aboriginal courts in urban as well as rural areas. Modelled on the 'circle sentencing' courts in Canada established in 1992, an increasing number of initiatives are being trialled around Australia with great success.[71] While sharing some of the objectives of restorative justice,[72] it has been suggested that indigenous courts and justice practices are not the same. Drawing on empirical fieldwork from around Australia, a recent paper suggests that

---

[69] An evaluation conducted 12 months after the introduction of the Act found that most of the conferences met the Act's objectives and aims. The report found high levels of satisfaction with the conference experience from all participants (ie, the victims, victims' supporters, offenders and offender supporters). More than 90 per cent of all parties felt that the conference was fair to both the victim and the offender; and over 90 per cent felt they had the opportunity to express their views, and 79 per cent said they were satisfied with the way their case had been dealt with by the justice system: L Trimboli, *An Evaluation of the NSW Youth Justice Conferencing Scheme* (NSW Bureau of Crime Statistics and Research, Attorney General's Department, 2000).

[70] See, eg, Crimes (Restorative Justice) Act 2004 (ACT).

[71] E Marchetti and K Daly, 'Indigenous Courts and Justice Practices in Australia' in *Trends and Issues in Crime and Criminal Justice*, no 277 (Australian Institute of Criminology, 2004).

[72] Indigenous justice institutions are commonly viewed as exemplifying therapeutic or restorative justice: A Freiberg, 'Problem-Oriented Courts: Innovative Solutions to Intractable Problems?' (2001) 11(1) *Journal of Judicial Administration* 7 and M Finnane '"Payback", Customary Law and Criminal Law in Colonised Australia' (2001) 29 *International Journal of the Sociology of Law* 293.

these developments should be viewed as *sui generis*, in a category of their own. The distinctiveness of such initiatives lies in the key role that indigenous communities played in 'correcting and modifying established criminal processes in ways that are less apparent to relevant "communities" in other specialized courts'.[73] The paper concludes that such developments have something to offer the wider system of justice: 'The core element of animating these courts—improved communication, citizen knowledge/control and appropriate penalties—could be applied to all court processes and all defendants'. Outside the Aboriginal context, restorative justice conferences have the clear potential to reveal the wider cultural context of offending and develop community-based punishments (though it may not be appropriate in every case to adopt distinctive cultural punishments that are recognised within specific ethnic communities). The ordinary application of restorative justice principles and process should be able to achieve consensus between the offender and affected communities as to the appropriate punishment in a particular context. As this discussion reveals, 'restorative justice is much more than just a new technology of disputing'.[74]

CONCLUDING REMARKS

This chapter has identified a number of areas in Australia where legal norms and processes are being adapted to better accommodate cultural difference. Many of these efforts have generated controversy because they conflict with the principle of equality before the law, a fundamental ideal and source of legitimacy for the criminal law.[75] The problem in law is that inequality is approached from the liberal standpoint of individualism. By conceiving discrimination as the different treatment of *individuals* on specified grounds such as race, culture, ethnicity or gender, etc, there is only limited scope for addressing and remedying group-based disadvantage. Indeed, this model of equality explains the recent reforms in 2006 which have sought to banish the relevance of culture from the federal sentencing arena entirely. A danger arises under this model that people from minorities in Australia will be judged by reference to legal standards set by and for the dominant (Anglo-Saxon-Celtic) culture. Moreover, any legal efforts to identify and accommodate cultural difference tend to be viewed as special treatment or exceptional derogations to the principle of equality before the law.

The scholarly challenge for theorists of discrimination, one which is shared by feminists, is to engage in the normative reconstruction of legal

---

[73] Marchetti and Daly, above n 71 at 4.

[74] J Braithwaite, *Restorative Justice and Responsive Regulation* (Oxford, Oxford University Press, 2002) 357.

[75] Bronitt and McSherry, above n 10 at ch 2.

doctrine in ways that expose rather than conceal the issue of disadvantage and subordination.[76] Rather than viewing equality narrowly as an *individual* right to be treated the same as others, it must be reconfigured more inclusively in terms of 'equality as acceptance' or 'equality as respect for difference'.[77] This new conception of equality, which is sensitive to issues of disadvantage and subordination, inheres within both individuals *and* communities. Unlike existing equality jurisprudence, it would require the criminal law to respect (rather than deny) the significance of culture in determining liability as well as punishment; although as argued above, it may be necessary to impose some restrictions on cultural norms and practices that harm or discriminate against women and children, a position that is required by our international human rights obligations. As this chapter reveals, the task of normative reconstruction has only just begun, and will continue to remain one of the key challenges facing the development of a multicultural criminal jurisprudence in Australia.

APPENDIX

Arguments For and Against Restorative Justice

SUPPORTING ARGUMENTS	OPPOSING ARGUMENTS
restorative justice practices may restore and satisfy victims, offenders and communities better than existing criminal justice practices	participation provides no benefits to unknowing victims (ie, the criminal justice system only applies in 10% of offences committed)
restorative justice practices may reduce some forms of crime more and rehabilitate offenders better	because more than 90% of crimes are untouched by state processes it may have no significant impact on the crime rate
conferences are structurally fairer due to the nature of participation	in some cases it may increase victim fears of revictimisation

[76] This may involve a radical reconstruction of discrimination in terms of subordination: see C MacKinnon, *Toward a Feminist Theory of the State* (Harvard University Press, 1989) ch 12; J Morgan and R Graycar, *The Hidden Gender of Law* (Federation Press, 2002) 28–31. Feminist lawyers have also proposed for adoption a gendered equality right for a Bill of Rights which specifically addresses women's subordination: J Morgan, 'Equality Rights in the Australian Context: a Feminist Perspective' in P Alston (ed), *Towards an Australian Bill of Rights* (CIPL and HREOC, 1994) 144.

[77] N Lacey, *Unspeakable Subjects: Feminist Essays in Legal and Social Theory* (Hart Publishing, 1998) 239–41, discussing the work of feminist theorists, Drucilla Cornell and Luce Irigaray.

greater procedural justice, which in turn communicates respect	it can make victims props for attempts towards offender rehabilitation
conferencing is more cost-effective	it can be a 'shaming machine' that worsens stigmatisation
restorative justice practices enrich freedom and democracy	it may widen nets of social control (though Braithwaite found this not to be the case in Australia or New Zealand)
	it fails to redress structural problems inherent in liberalism like unemployment and poverty
	it may disadvantage women, children, racial minorities
	it may 'trample rights because of impoverished articulation of procedural safeguards'

Extracted from S Bronitt and B McSherry, *Principles of Criminal Law*, 2nd edn (LawBook Co, 2005) 28. This table is based on John Braithwaite's key arguments for and against restorative justice process: 'Restorative Justice' (1999) 25 *Crime and Justice: a Review of Research* 1, 21–101.

6

The Paradox of Cultural Differences in Dutch Criminal Law

MIRJAM SIESLING AND JEROEN TEN VOORDE

INTRODUCTION

THE NETHERLANDS HAS become transformed from a religious pluralistic society into a multi-ethnic and multicultural society. In 2005, figures showed that approximately 16 per cent of the inhabitants were foreign-born or had parents who started a new life in the Netherlands.[1] As a consequence of ongoing immigration, Dutch society has become increasingly multicultural.[2] This raises the question of how a nation should deal with differences that originate from the cultural diversity of its population. The answer to this question was a rather simple one a few years ago. Cultural diversity was seen as a welcome supplement to the rather dull society the Netherlands once were. More recently, we have witnessed a development in thinking, in which we have realised that multiculturality in fact does not only have positive effects, but also some 'problematic implications'.[3] This means that some acts committed by immigrants (in Dutch generally called 'allochthonous people') cannot be accepted in Dutch society, because the conduct conflicts with ruling norms, and can result in criminal offences. One type of such acts are the so-called cultural offences.

A cultural offence is defined as 'an act by a member of a minority culture which is considered an offence by the legal system of the dominant culture. That same act is nevertheless, within the cultural group of the offender, condoned, accepted as normal behaviour and approved or even endorsed and promoted in the given situation'.[4] Examples are honour-related violence,

---

[1] See Garssen, Nicholaas, and Sprangers (2005). See for an historical account Entzinger (1994).

[2] Wetenschappelijke Raad voor het Regeringsbeleid (Scientific Council for Governmental Policy) (2001: 37).

[3] Sociaal en Cultureel Planbureau (Social and Cultural Planning Bureau) (1998: 263).

[4] Van Broeck (2001: 5).

female circumcision and elopement. In recent years these cultural offences have received considerable attention in Dutch criminal law. Judges, lawyers and prosecutors are exposed to an increasing number of cultural conflicts and increasingly experience offences which one professor of criminal law once rather patronisingly called foreign 'folklore'.[5] In recent years, journalists and politicians have also turned their attention to this subject. Interestingly, as a consequence of this expansion of interest, the fact that cultural offences occur in Dutch society is nowadays regarded not only as a legal problem, but is seen as a sign that allochthonous people are not sufficiently integrated into Dutch society. Cultural offences have therefore become a societal and political problem.

As a consequence of the attacks on 11 September 2001 and the rise and death of the right-wing politician Pim Fortuyn and the provocative film-maker Theo Van Gogh, who was killed by a Muslim fundamentalist, the political climate has changed.[6] This is most clearly visible in the way integration policy has changed. One aspect of this change is the increasing debate about cultural offences and the changing view on how to deal with these kinds of offences. One specific example is the way in which the Dutch deal with honour-related violence.[7] In our opinion, the way in which honour-related violence is approached nowadays has not brought about much innovation. Although the tone of the debate has changed radically, the terms used in this debate continue to provoke the same problems as the terms in the 'old' debate used to do. Ongoing uncertainty exists, for example, about the following issues: (a) what the relation is between criminal law and culture; (b) what is meant by culture and how this factor can be used in individual criminal cases; and (c) what limits can be imposed upon respect for cultural differences.

In this chapter, we will first provide a short introduction to the three topics. We will discuss the issue of conscientious objectors, the openness that exists to discuss cultural offences without sliding back into discussions about discrimination; and related to this openness, the criminal law's unique flexibility to take cultural differences into account. The core of this argument is that criminal law is insufficiently clear about how to take into consideration cultural differences. Thirdly, illustrated by the discussion surrounding honour-related violence, we will show how the debate on culture and criminal law is carried on at the present time. In our conclusion we will interpret the problems and offer a comparative analysis of comparable approaches.

---

[5] GE Mulder in comment on Supreme Court 2 July 1990, NJ (Nederlandse Jurisprudentie (Dutch Case Law)) 1991, 110. (This is a misuse of the term folklore which refers to a scholarly discipline including over 200 genres.)

[6] See Snel (2003).

[7] Honour-related violence is any form of mental or physical violence committed in reaction to a (threat of) defilement of a person's honour and through that, his or her family's honour, about which defilement the public knows or will find out (Ferwerda and Van Leiden, 2005: 25).

DEVELOPMENTS IN DUTCH CRIMINAL LAW RELATED
TO CULTURAL OFFENCES

Government Attention to 'Allochthonous Crime'

Connection between Crime and Culture

In criminological research and theory minorities have been a central concern for several decades. In the 1930s, research was carried on among Catholic communities; during the 1960s and 1970s, attention shifted to people from the Moluccan Islands; and since the 1980s and 1990s also towards migrants and their offspring (ie, allochthonous people). The research that was conducted in the 1980s was biased by the proposition that criminal justice institutions were discriminatory.[8] Allochthonous crime, as criminality amongst allochthonous people is called, could be sufficiently explained by social and economic deprivation.[9] From the beginning of the 1990s, a shift in criminological paradigm can be discerned. Social and economic deprivation do not explain all allochthonous crime. More specifically, deprivation does not explain differences in crime between various allochthonous groups.[10] Various studies for that reason opted for another theory, first introduced by Thorsten Sellin, in which culture and culture conflicts play a pivotal role.

The premise of this theoretical approach is that allochthonous crime can be explained by the defendant's cultural background insofar as it differs from the dominant culture. After some initial hesitation, Dutch criminal policy adopted these ideas at the beginning of the 1990s. In the government report *Criminality in Relation to the Integration of Ethnic Minorities* (CRIEM), the Ministry of the Interior and the Ministry of Justice adopted the assumption that allochthonous criminal behaviour could be explained by culture.[11] The disproportionate number of allochthonous people in crime statistics is caused by cultural approval for certain behaviour and by the failure of allochthonous people to integrate into Dutch society. The CRIEM report, which established Dutch governmental policy concerning allochthonous crime and remains the central starting point for every policy concerned with allochthonous crime, concluded that combating allochthonous crime would only be effective if insight was gained into allochthonous people's cultural background and if criminal law institutions became more culturally diverse themselves.

---

[8] See Junger-Tas and Van der Zee-Nefkens (1977).
[9] See Van der Hoeven (1985, 1986).
[10] See Bovenkerk (1992), Junger (1990).
[11] Kamerstukken Tweede Kamer (Proceedings of the Second Chamber of the States General (Dutch House of Representatives)) 1997–98, 25.726, no 1.

Multicuturalisation of criminal law institutions meant that staff members should increasingly be recruited from minority groups. This immediately raised questions such as whether members of the judiciary could be allowed to wear headscarves together with their legally proscribed gowns.[12] More important for our purposes is to what extent criminal law itself should be adapted to societal cultural diversity. At first glance, the answer to this question must be in the negative. Acknowledging cultural diversity in society does not necessarily mean accepting this diversity in criminal law. For instance, the CRIEM report stated that on a fundamental level, the principle of equality of all before the law overruled any formal cultural defence.[13] The report also stressed that it was the government's task to react as effectively as possible against criminal behaviour, whoever was the perpetrator.

The report also mentioned that categorical judgements must be prevented. If it is necessary to take into account the defendant's cultural background, then this can be done in no other way than on the individual level.[14] At this level, 'made-to-measure' approaches must be offered. As a consequence, general statements about combating allochthonous crimes cannot be offered. If, however, we trace the concrete effects of these policies, it is seen that made-to-measure approaches should only be offered where this results in effectiveness. In the CRIEM report, criminal justice's effectiveness is paramount. This *can* mean that the defendant's background is taken into account for mitigation. In general, this means that the defendant can make a claim for mitigation based on culture, if this is done on an individual basis. If the weighing of that background leads to effective punishment, in the sense that the defendant will be prevented from committing future offences, the defendant can indeed invoke her culture.

The report underscored the point that criminal law institutions need to take into account the defendant's culture, in the sense that in criminal law proceedings, an understanding of the defendant's culture must be shown. An example of this is the special boys' institute for Moroccan boys, which was opened in 1993 in Amsterdam. It was called Amal, meaning 'hope' in Moroccan. This institute was hotly debated, but began as an experiment. The boys would be treated within their own cultural background and also in relation to their experiences in Dutch society. The aim of the treatment would be the boys' integration into Dutch society. Moroccan norms and

---

[12] There has been considerable debate about members of the judiciary wearing headscarves. The Commission for Equal Treatment stated in an opinion in 2001 that members of the judiciary should be allowed to wear headscarves (Commissie Gelijke Behandeling no 2001-53). In a response, the Minister of Justice distanced himself from this opinion. To date, the Minister has not changed his opinion, having the support of the majority in and (most likely) outside Parliament. See also Van der Sloot (2004), Piret (2003).

[13] See Kamerstukken Tweede Kamer 1997–98, 25.726, no 1, 23.

[14] See also in general Sheybani (1987: 781), Kim (1997: 116 *et seq*).

values would be leading references. In 1993 and in the first half of 1994, it was made public that in Amal, boys were being beaten by staff members who were also of Moroccan descent. Five staff members were arrested for assault and Amal was closed.[15]

Some Remarks concerning the First Topic

At first glance, the CRIEM report offers room for cultural differences and appropriately, in our view, points to an individual approach (which prevents individuals from hiding behind their minority group). This approach takes into account the fact that individual problems *can* have a relation to culture. However, if we examine the details of the CRIEM report and the justification it provides for taking culture into account, a couple of questions arise. First, why is the connection between criminality and culture so easily made, and secondly, is the emphasis on effectiveness an unproblematic one?

To deal with the first question; the report states that the most important explanation for allochthonous criminality is culture. More specifically, the cultural distance between allochthonous and autochthonous people is stressed, as is allochthonous people's poor integration into Dutch society. The authors of the report do not mean it explicitly, but the question is to what extent culture is *criminalised* here. Culture is easily portrayed as synonymous with crime, without offering insight into the complexity of cultures, let alone the occurrence of criminal acts within a culture.[16] This development can be seen, for instance, in criminal policy against female genital mutilation[17] and honour-related violence. The latter will be dealt with extensively below.

The second question deals with the CRIEM report's clear emphasis on a criminal justice system that should operate as effectively as possible. Essentially, we do not deny that criminal law has a so-called *instrumental* side. This means that criminal law focuses not only on protecting the defendant's rights, but also on the protection of society against criminal offences.[18] The CRIEM report, however, states that the only reason to acknowledge cultural differences in criminal law is when this helps to bring down crime rates. The consequence of this approach is that those who think that a culturally sensitive criminal law reduces crime, wish to use culture in a way that benefits the defendant. On the other hand, those who believe that culture worsens crime seek to use culture in a way that is detrimental for the defendant. Examples of the latter are recent draft laws that aim to design

---

[15] See Van Vliet (1995).
[16] See for this point in general Nelson (2004).
[17] See Kool *et al* (2005).
[18] See 't Hart (1995). For an account of his legal theory in English, see 't Hart (1986).

separate criminalisation schemes providing for high maximum sentences for cultural offences.[19]

Conscientious Objectors in Dutch Criminal Law

Short Description

An example of Dutch multicultural jurisprudence can be found in the way in which Dutch courts in the past have dealt with so-called conscientious objectors. In Dutch criminal law religious minorities' conscientious objections have long since been acknowledged. Conscientious objections refer to the defendant's moral scruples against complying with a certain legal obligation.[20] The defendant claims a higher norm than the norm that is laid down in criminal law. Because of this expressed motivation, the courts seem reluctant to take into account conscientious objections: anarchy would prevail if we were forced to acknowledge all claims made to higher norms, especially if these claims lead to criminal behaviour.[21] There has been, however, since the end of the Second World War, case law in which conscientious objection has had a mitigating effect in legal trials.[22] Several scholars (mainly of Christian origin) claim that dealing with conscientious objectors so as to mitigate their sentences is the civilised approach, and represents one important reason why we at the present day are prepared to show in criminal law and criminal justice some consideration for different cultures.[23] The case law is related to draft resisters,[24] for example, but also to persons who for religious reasons refuse to insure themselves or to pay pension contributions.[25] In this connection, we would draw attention to three criminal law cases concerning a refusal to take a blood test (as prescribed in the Road and Traffic Act, art 163, para 6).[26] Lastly, there was an interesting case of a Muslim defendant who refused to have his daughter take part in obligatory swimming lessons. These lessons were co-educational, ie, boys and girls swimming together, and the defendant could not reconcile this with

---

[19] This is not stated as such in the CRIEM report, but may be inferred from the way in which culture and crime are connected. See Kool *et al* (2005); Adviescommissie Vreemdelingenzaken (Advisory Commission for Allochthonous Affairs)) (2005).

[20] See Holland (1989: 23).

[21] See Remmelink (1970: 189, 191).

[22] Supreme Court 20 June 1950, NJ 1951, 348.

[23] See Hirsch Ballin (1993).

[24] Supreme Court 14 September 1998, NJ 1999, 119, Supreme Court 19 March 1996, NJ 1996, 480, Supreme Court 18 April 1995, NJ 1995, 611.

[25] Supreme Court 13 April 1960, NJ 1960, 436.

[26] Supreme Court 3 March 1987, NJ 1988, 7, Supreme Court 9 June 1987, NJ 1988, 318, Supreme Court 18 October 1988, NJ 1989, 679.

his faith. He kept his daughter home from school, although she was of school age, which is considered a criminal offence in Dutch law. In court, the defendant pleaded his religious conviction, which he claimed was protected by Art 9 of the European Convention on Human Rights (freedom of thought, conscience and religion), as well as art 6 of the Dutch Constitution (freedom of religion).[27]

The Supreme Court rejected this claim on grounds that had been developed in earlier cases. First, the Supreme Court acknowledged that the defendant had a right plead his religious conviction and also that the lower courts had a legal obligation to give a reasoned response (Code of Criminal Procedure, art 358, para 3 jo 359, para 2). The district court had done so by examining the defence's substantive arguments. The court rejected this contention by referring to the Qu'ran, and stating that the Qu'ran does not contain a verse that explicitly forbids mixed swimming. Although the Supreme Court did not explicitly examine this striking reasoning, from the court's case law it can be inferred that such reasoning is not acceptable.[28] Since 1957, the Supreme Court has adhered to the so-called rule of 'interpretative restraint', [29] which means that lower courts are not allowed to discuss the accuracy of the interpretation of religious texts to which a defendant refers in a legal case. This rule of interpretative restraint has been designed at first instance for religious cases. Yet it can be applied to culture in criminal law cases, too, as the right to culture, connected with the state's reticence in cultural matters, is embodied in Art 27 of the International Covenant on Civil and Political Rights.[30]

This reticence, however, did not mean that the Muslim father was acquitted. According to existing case law, courts could only take into account someone's conviction where, first, the basis for such conviction was laid down in law and, secondly, the defendant used this legal rule to protect his belief. This was not the case with the Muslim father. He had simply kept his daughter at home, contravening compulsory education, had not searched for alternative resolutions and only pleaded his religious belief in court. The Supreme Court, referring to well-established case law, held that the defendant's claim could only be accepted if the relevant legal provision included a clause legitimising conscientious objections. In this case, Dutch education legislation had such a clause; but as the defendant had not negotiated his objections with his daughter's school, but simply kept her at home, he had not complied with the provisions of the legislation, and therefore his claim could not be accepted.

---

[27] Supreme Court 26 May 1992, NJ 1992, 568.
[28] See Galenkamp (2005).
[29] Supreme Court 15 January 1957, NJ 1957, 201.
[30] See Thornberry (1991: 163).

Some Remarks concerning the Second Topic

The doctrine of interpretative restraint, because of the room that is offered to citizens to live according to particular norms, appears to be developing so as to support respect for cultural diversity without the state's interference. Courts guarantee a certain amount of freedom by reasoning with restraint about the content of cultural norms and the meaning of these norms for the minority group in question.[31] Such caution seems to be a common good and has been applied in various cases. Furthermore, the doctrine of interpretative restraint has come to be read more extensively. It no longer merely applies to internal matters (for which the doctrine was primarily designed), but also to external matters, ie, conflicts with the outside world. The outside world, however, professes another religion, or is secular, or adheres to a clearly different set of norms and values. The interpretative restraint, therefore, is then useful in avoiding the need to deal with these matters too deeply, for if we do, it can open up serious conflicts, which can cause deep misunderstanding, mistrust or even violence among varied groups. What we see here is some sort of Hobbesian fear that man is prepared to fight for his religion, which can only be counter-balanced if we do not discuss the content of religion at all.

Notwithstanding these developments, we can raise a number of objections against conscientious objections and the rule of interpretative restraint.[32] First, this rule tends towards cultural relativism. If a judge is not able to take part in the discussion, he is not able to demarcate limits within which religious and cultural expressions can be accepted. Perhaps it is a bit too extreme to state with Barry[33] that this is a situation of 'moral anarchy', but he does indeed touch upon a sensitive subject by introducing this term. If the judge is not able to take part in it, the debate about the tenability of certain cultural norms is very much simplified. Eventually, nothing can really be discussed: not the harmful aspects of cultural offences, nor their neutral or beneficial aspects. The debate then concentrates on the problematic aspects (which is not surprisingly as the discussion takes part in a criminal law trial) without having to discuss the culture as a whole. From a culturally relativistic viewpoint, such a distinction as to the harmful, neutral and beneficial aspects of culture can hardly exist.[34]

Secondly, there is a risk that in cultural offence trials, the judge may rely excessively upon cultural experts' opinions. This is problematic because the forensic expert is not obliged to follow the principle of interpretative restraint in the same way that the judge is. Indirectly, the judge is offered

---

[31] Supreme Court 18 September 1989, NJ 1990, 291.
[32] Galenkamp (2005: 253–5); Ten Voorde (2007b: 155–61).
[33] Barry (2001: 71–3).
[34] See also Gutmann (1993).

all the information about a culture, without being able to ask for it himself. This calls into question the efficacy of the doctrine of interpretative restraint. Another problem is that the forensic expert is trusted by the judge in such a fundamental way that he is welcomed as a *deus ex machina* in cultural cases, a true messenger of truth. Certain criminal law cases, however, issue a warning that truth, including cultural truth, only has a relative meaning. An example can be offered by the so-called *Veghel* case,[35] which concerned a 17-year-old Turkish-Kurdish boy (Ali) who, provoked by his father, shot another Turkish boy for honour reasons. In this case, the boy's sister had run away with her boyfriend, staying in Turkey for a week. When discovered, the girl claimed that she had been abducted because the boy wanted to marry her. The girl's parents were outraged, accusing the boyfriend of having fouled their family's honour. Following the 'abduction', Ali was put under pressure by his father to 'solve' this honour matter. One afternoon, the ex-boyfriend turned up at Ali's school, although he was not a student. In great fury, Ali rushed back home and phoned his father to tell him he had been provoked in school. His father immediately came home, took a gun from his bedroom, drove Ali back to school and handed him the gun, saying that he should 'finish' the boyfriend or otherwise he would do it himself. During the proceedings, at least three forensic cultural experts were called, each of them presenting a differing view on the role of culture in this case.[36] The judge was then confronted with the difficult task of choosing which evidence to accept, inhibited by the doctrine of interpretative restraint. This would seem to be an impossible task, unless the judge decided to loosen the doctrine's constraints a little. The more complex a case is, the sooner the judge will urgently feel the need to call in an expert, but simultaneously, the judge introduces greater confusion by involving experts in the process. The judge is then caught in a *Catch 22* situation: if he does deal with culture in a case, he risks violating the doctrine of interpretative restraint. If he does not discuss culture, he reaches a half-hearted verdict that will leave everyone dissatisfied, because it is clear from the outset that in such a case, the cultural background is a paramount consideration.

Thirdly, there is a risk that in following the doctrine of interpretative restraint regarding conscientious objections, adherence to a certain cultural norm would permit the actor to engage in all kinds of conduct which are considered highly unacceptable by the rest of society. A telling example of this is the trial of the imam El Moumni, who stated in a television interview that homosexuality is a disease that can and should be cured. He was acquitted of criminal discrimination (arts 137c and 137d Dutch Criminal Code) by the district court and the court of appeals, because his religion

---

[35] Veghel is a small town in the south of the Netherlands, not far from the city of 's-Hertogenbosch. See for this case Strijbosch (2001); Van Eck (2002).
[36] District Court 's Hertogenbosch 13 February 2001, NJ 2001, 130.

justified these public opinions.[37] This outcome of this trial can be identified as one of the incidents that caused public debate to shift towards a more demanding integration policy.[38]

The consequence of all this is a paradoxical development. The doctrine of interpretative restraint is meant to express respect for minority groups *in iure*, by preventing the judge from interfering with the definition of religious and philosophical matters. This respect, however, is not found in court; rather, its opposite. First, culture is reduced from a complex interplay of rules and persons, who act according to this culture, to a singular framework of rules that do not conflict internally and give a clear direction for structuring life to a clearly defined group of people. Secondly, culture is reduced to a fundamental entity, which offers no room for renewal but rather rewards orthodox opinions and silences every debate within and among the groups that form part of it.[39]

Unique Flexibility in Dutch Criminal Law

Explanations for Unique Flexibility

As a consequence of the breakdown of the so-called pillar based society[40] from halfway through the 1960s, there was a growing critique of criminal law. Gradually, criminal law institutions experienced a legitimation crisis,[41] which was conquered only through great effort. A solution for this crisis was found in greater flexibility in the criminal law.[42] One means for this was the doctrine of 'functional interpretation'. It must be stressed that this was merely one possibility, but one that influenced criminal law theory for a long time. The core idea of this theory was the introduction of a new methodology, in which legal principles and norms are not fossilised dogmas, but are attributed meaning in legal practice, especially in court. Furthermore, this meaning is dependent on the way in which the legal proceedings are shaped.[43] The point of departure is that legal proceedings are not about neutral values, but hold a culturally embedded debate about the

---

[37] District Court Rotterdam 8 April 2002, LJN (Landelijk Jurisprudentienummer (National Case Law no)) AE 1154, Court of Appeals The Hague 18 November 2002, NJCM-bulletin 2003, 461. In favour of the verdict of the district court and Court of Appeal is Rozemond (2001). We must make clear that in these cases courts do not only refer to the freedom of religion, but also to the freedom of free speech (Art 10 of the ECHR and art 7 of the Dutch Constitution). See also Supreme Court 14 January 2003, NJ 203, 261.

[38] See Vlemminx (2002); Loenen (2003). See at an earlier stage De Winter (1996).

[39] See Tempelman (1999). This applies to religion and culture alike.

[40] See Lijphart (1975).

[41] Heijder (1970).

[42] 't Hart (1994) ch 1a; (1999: 161).

[43] Ter Heijde (1965).

meaning of legal norms. This vision was connected to the idea that, with the emergence of a multicultural society, legal debate was taking place in a changing culture.[44] Taking this methodology into account, this means that these perceptions (which in turn can be explained by cultural differences) must be included in the debate. This calls for a continuous debate about the legal norms[45] and for a thoughtful judge who actively creates room for these changing perceptions in court within the historical framework of the law.

An increasing number of academic contributions deal with the question to what extent in criminal law cultural differences can be taken into account.[46] One aspect of these contributions is that they do not search for a new legal defence based on culture, the 'cultural defence', but rather space for culture is sought in existing doctrine.[47] In the legal debate, this discussion is focused on two different defences, namely self-defence and duress. Self-defence (Criminal Code, art 41 para 1) is only possible if a person has to defend herself against an immediate and unlawful attack against her or another's body, virtue or goods. The defence of duress (Criminal Code, art 40) is only available if the defendant can claim that she was forced by an external power to act and commit a crime. This defence especially is seen as the Dutch variant of the cultural defence.[48] It can be argued that the external power includes the power of a group, or more abstractly, a culture. Case law has not rejected this view. However, committing a crime under duress requires that the external power be such that any reasonable person could not withstand the pressure placed on her. Reasonableness does not refer to a reasonable White Anglo-Saxon male Protestant, as is referred to in Anglo-Saxon oriented legal discussions about the cultural defence.[49] Reasonableness is explained in a way that expresses some compassion for the defendant.[50] If the defendant can claim that 'her culture made her act as she did', judges are not entirely unwilling to agree. However, judges also look at the type of solution the defendant uses to deal with the external power. If the defendant chooses to kill another, this solution will not be seen as the most appropriate one. If life is at stake, then, duress will not be accepted.[51]

---

[44] Habermas (1998: 217).
[45] See Hildebrandt (2001: 328–30).
[46] Wormhoudt (1986a, 1986b); Wiersinga (1993); Huisman (1995).
[47] See recently Wolswijk (2004).
[48] See Knoops (1998: 268–70).
[49] See Chiu (1994).
[50] See recently Dolman (2006: 173 *et seq*) and Kelk (2006). See more general 't Hart (1997).
[51] Court of Appeals Leeuwarden 19 June 2000, LJN AD 8362, Supreme Court 27 June 2000, NJ 2000, 605, District Court 's Hertogenbosch 13 February 2001, LJN AA 9954, District Court The Hague 2 October 2001, LJN AD 3929, District Court The Hague 25 February 2002, LJN 9565, District Court The Hague 25 February 2002, LJN 9567.

As a consequence, certain doctrines are clearly not so inflexible that they could not negotiate societal changes. Simultaneously, indirectly it is acknowledged that the formal cultural defence is an anomaly, which is not easily compatible with criminal law theory.[52] On the other hand, this means that legal norms at least *theoretically* can be changed because of the changing composition of society. The question then is not *if* but *how* cultural differences can be taken into account in criminal law proceedings. At the same time, the existing criminal law framework, including its dogmatic principles, is retained. This conservatism leads to the view that indeed, room can be made for cultural differences, but strictly limited to the extent that traditional principles are not elbowed aside completely.[53] Of paramount concern is that the criminal law framework must be preserved; culture can only be taken into account as far as possible within this existing legal framework.

This ambivalence towards cultural offences in Dutch legal theory is also expressed in case law. Dutch judges are all but unanimous in the way in which they deal with cultural differences. By the end of the 1970s, judges were committed to restraint,[54] whereas in the 1980s there was more possibility to take cultural differences into account for mitigation. One court of appeals, for instance, ruled that a defendant's claim on culture should lead to a lessening of sentence.[55] The Supreme Court also expressed itself in a similar positive way when it stated that in a case of self-defence, cultural differences should be taken into account, although it was unclear whether this would always be in a positive manner for the defendant. This verdict clearly shows the above-mentioned ambivalence. On the one hand, the Supreme Court acknowledged that the doctrine of self-defence was not so restricted that cultural differences could not be included. On the other hand, this room for culture could only be shaped in a way that left the doctrine of self-defence intact.[56] In the following, more case law will be analysed to corroborate the claims of judicial ambivalence.

Some Remarks concerning the Third Theme

Although judges' willingness to make room for cultural diversity is characterised by a certain ambivalence, it is significant that the law itself is open to this development to a certain extent. This can be explained by the fact that law is not merely looked upon as a 'manifested fact of social power'.[57] Law is also a purposeful enterprise—in other words, an action system.[58]

---

[52] See Magnarella (1991: 82–3).
[53] 't Hart (1997: 312).
[54] District Court Dordrecht 12 January 1979, NJ 1979, 214.
[55] See Court of Appeal Arnhem as cited in Supreme Court 15 April 1986, NJ 1986, 741.
[56] Supreme Court 18 September 1989, NJ 1990, 668.
[57] Fuller (1967: 145–51).
[58] Habermas (1996: 107; 1998).

In a democratic procedure, in which each citizen introduces her cultural background as the fundament for her contribution to the debate, legal norms have to be attributed meaning. This means that a legal norm is shaped by the acting together of citizens in a democratic procedure that is intended and designed to that end.[59] This idea of a democratic public debate is grounded on two assumptions: that (a) allochthonous citizens can take part in the debate as equal partners, and (b) allochthonous citizens are prepared to take part in this debate.

Let us consider point (a). This democratic model is one of the most persistently mentioned regarding culture and criminal law.[60] This does not mean, however, that the model is flawless. The first flaw is that allochthonous citizens are presumed to be equal partners in the debate. But is this truly the case? An important problem that has been pointed out by many scholars is that criminal law proceedings do not offer free communication, but rather must be perceived as a form of so-called 'coercive communication'.[61] This means that as a consequence of the way in which a trial is performed, the defendant is compelled to express himself or herself through a particular form of communication. This 'communication strait-jacket' can be explained in various ways. It leaves the defendant powerlessness to tell his or her own story.[62] An example of this is the way in which Turkish defendants interact in criminal court. Van Rossum has shown that judges expect a defendant to act in a specific way. This is a culturally embedded way, which means that the judge expects a defendant to behave in a specific manner. People with a different cultural background seem to have more problems behaving the way a judge expects them to behave than those from the dominant culture. These problems occur in the context of verbal issues (when the defendant cannot express himself properly in Dutch), but more especially in non-verbal aspects. Van Rossum gave various examples of allochthonous defendants who behaved normally, according to their culture, but abnormally in the opinion of the judge. The effect, in some cases, was that the defendant was punished more severely because she did not behave appropriately. If a defendant has to behave appropriately, this means that she has to adapt to the cultural norms used by the judge and is not able to behave according to her own traditions.[63]

---

[59] See Habermas (1996: 107–11, 118 *et seq*).

[60] 't Hart (1995, 1997, 1999, 2001); Hildebrandt (2001); Wiersinga (2002). See more critically also Ten Voorde (2007a) chs 3 and 4.

[61] Bal (1988: 254) (English translation).

[62] Van Walsum (1992).

[63] See Van Rossum (1998). See Vrij (1991) and compare the *Ventura* case where a Mexican suspect was sentenced to 40 years' imprisonment for murder. Ventura had not confessed, but the way he behaved made the police conclude he was guilty. He had lowered his eyes during police interrogation. See DeMuniz (1999).

Judges, as well as other parties to proceedings, take for granted certain stereotypes about allochthonous people's behaviour and often use these beliefs, consciously or not, as a frame of reference on the basis of which the trial is performed. This frame of reference is often stereotypical and insufficiently nuanced.[64] It is based upon an amateurish general feeling of 'we know the ins and outs of it'. This was, for instance, clear in a case where the judge decided herself whether the defendant acted on account of her culture, without consulting the defendant on the issue.[65] A consequence of this is that the defendant is not treated as capable of elaborating on her interpretation of the story. This is simply rendered unnecessary: the story is known to the judge, because of the constructions she has made of it herself. These constructions are supposed to be the only true ones; any deviation, for example introduced by the defendant, is ignored.[66]

Paradoxically, lawyers who are aware of this way of thinking use similar stereotypes because they know this strategy can sometimes offer short-term success. This means that the defendant receives a lower sentence or, in very rare cases, is acquitted. Famous examples are the US *Chen* case and the *Kimura* case.[67] The long-term consequences are not considered, however. This means that the defendant may burn her fingers: the next time she or a group member is standing accused, the same stereotypical approach will be applied. That approach may have been successful the first time, but, with the change in position, may subsequently work out rather negatively for this or another defendant.[68]

Potential respect for cultural differences is jeopardised here, for it is strongly determined by individual opinions which influence the extent to which cultural differences are taken into account. Recently, a changing trend in these opinions can be discerned. Culture is more and more often described as a social problem, although the possibility of taking culture into account remains, for criminal law is flexible and offers room for taking into account changing social circumstances. If, however, these circumstances lead to an aversion to other cultures, this increases the possibility that

---

[64] This should not be suprising as judges are trained in cultural matters through obligatory one-day courses. These courses take the form of cultural blueprints, recipes for cultural traditions, which judges are trained to apply to real cases. They are not trained, however, in matters of culture as changing objects or cultures as sources of many identities (constructivist vision on culture).

[65] District Court Den Bosch 13 February 2001, LJN AA 954.

[66] See, eg, Supreme Court 14 October 2003, LJN AJ 1457. In this case, the mother of a 16-year-old girl was convicted of being an accessory to murder. Her lawyer tried to convince the court that the mother was strongly influenced by her husband and was not able to distance herself from the murder, because of her cultural background. That background forbade her to disobey her husband. The court did not even mention this argument and stated that by not distancing herself, she was an accessory to murder.

[67] See Volpp (1994); Woo (1989).

[68] See Briggs and Mantini Briggs (2000); Holmquist (1997); Yen (2000). See also Siesling (2006).

culture will be used in court as a means to punish more severely. We can discern another paradox here: this time the criminal law's flexibility does not automatically mean that cultural differences are taken into account in a manner that helps the defendant. Culture can equally well serve as an argument for a more repressive criminal law. This paradox is dealt with below, in respect of policy on honour-related violence.

There is another problem related to the question of which cultural differences can be taken into account in court. Theo van Gogh's killer, for example, appeared to hold a strongly fundamentalist view of his religion. The district court[69] acknowledged that this religious background was the most important motive behind the crime. The perpetrator, however, was not willing to defend himself and invoked his right to remain silent. Should his religious motives still be taken into account as mitigatation in criminal proceedings? Answering this question affirmatively seems to go too far; in the first place, his deed disturbed society more than any other disaster that has hit the country in the past 50 years. In the second place, it appeared that the perpetrator did not wish to have anything to do with Dutch society or the constitutional state that is part of it. Our constitutional state was not his. This contention touches upon an important part of the discussion about cultural offences: can we be flexible towards cultural offences when the motive behind these offences is a deep aversion to the fundamental principles of society itself? The answer to this question in the case of Van Gogh's assassinator is quite evident. A constitutional state can only exist for as long as its members debate its content, but agree upon the necessity that it should be a constitutional state.[70] The problem, however, is that the question of whether one embraces the constitutional state finds its answer in one's actions. Similarly to violent acts based on Muslim fundamentalism, honour-related violence and female genital mutilation are a threat to the constitutional state and are a sign that the perpetrators wish in general to overthrow the constitutional state. The very existence of these offences shows, according to right-wing politicians such as Hirsi Ali and Wilders, the flaws in the idea of a multicultural society and justify a plea for acculturation or even assimilation.[71]

Conclusion

Judges using the doctrine of interpretative restraint, the government promoting openness towards allochthonous cultures in all layers of society, and the flexibility of criminal law norms—all this makes for the development

[69] District Court Amsterdam 26 July 2005, LJN AU 0025.
[70] Habermas (1998: 226); Ten Voorde (2007a: 295–6).
[71] For the meaning of and difference between these concepts see Bauböck (1998).

of a framework in which both fundamentally and pragmatically society's cultural diversity can be negotiated in criminal law. This negotiation takes place fundamentally by commencing from the standpoint that in a constitutional state, norms should never be interpreted in terms that are formulated beforehand, but must be determined in a debate in which culturally inspired opinions lead to a renewed interpretation of norms. Pragmatically, this negotiation is shaped by pointing out the greater effectiveness of criminal justice if cultural differences are taken into account. On the other hand, these themes appear also to carry negative consequences. The fundamental room required seems not always possible in practice and cannot be realised, or only with great difficulty.

DEVELOPMENTS IN RECENT YEARS:
HONOUR-RELATED VIOLENCE

Dutch judges, when dealing with cultural offences, are confronted mostly with honour-related violence cases. These cases often occur in Kurdish families, who come from countries such as Turkey (eastern part) and Iraq. Honour-related violence is also documented in Afghan families, Moroccan families and Surinamese families. Mostly these families live according to tradition. Women and girls are supposed to lead a chaste life. In the 1990s and the beginning of the new millennium, there were cases involving (mainly) Kurdish women and girls who were killed by their fathers or husbands because they were allegedly living in too liberal or were behaving in too 'Westernised' a fashion. On 12 March 2004, a Turkish woman named Gül, who was living anonymously in a women's shelter, was shot dead by her ex-husband. This assassination led to a political discussion about the safety of allochthonous women in refuge centres. Family members were trying to track down such women's addresses in order to force the women to return home.

Dutch Governmental Policy concerning Honour-Related Violence

There has been a debate about whether perpetrators of honour-related killings should be punished more harshly.[72] This happened in 1999, after a Turkish woman was shot by her ex-husband in the presence of her children, and in 2003, after an 18-year-old Turkish girl was shot dead by her father while on holiday in Turkey. In both cases, the perpetrators stated that the

---

[72] Albayrak, a former socialist Member of Parliament, raised questions about the legal position of Turkish women. She stated that this position was threatened by possible sentence reduction for their violent husbands.

women's behaviour was a disgrace to the family and killing them was the only remedy for restoring family honour.[73] In 1999, the time was politically not right for these discussions. In 1998, the Dutch Prime Minister stated for the first time in public that honour-related crime was a problem, but this statement did not lead to specific action.[74] The discussion about allochthonous crime still did not concentrate on this kind of offences, partly because of a mistaken notion that only a few cases occurred every year. Inspired by the discussion surrounding Gül's death in 2004 and under pressure from Members of Parliament,[75] the Ministers of Justice and of Immigration and Integration announced in April of that year that they wanted to investigate the possibility of registering the ethnic background of perpetrators and victims of domestic violence. From November 2004 on, in two police regions in the Netherlands a pilot research project was conducted investigating the occurrence of honour-related violence. The purpose was to ensure that police officers had the ability to recognise the characteristics of honour-related violence and as a consequence prevent future cases.[76] A preliminary investigation showed that in the period 1 October 2004 to 1 January 2005 about 150 men and women seem to have been the victim of honour-related violence in the region of the city of The Hague.[77] These figures resulted in an even fiercer appeal in Parliament to adopt legal strategies to punish perpetrators of honour-related violence more harshly.[78] By this time the debate about immigrants had changed, due to a different political situation. Integration of immigrants was the topic most discussed in Dutch politics and stringent measures were taken to integrate allochthonous people more quickly into Dutch society, without leaving very much room for cultural differences. The policy was mainly concerned with problems concerning integration and the appearance of cultural offences seemed to be clear evidence for the argument that integration of immigrants was failing.[79]

A second finding within the same research project that ran from April 2005 until September 2005 showed that perpetrators of honour-related violence were often in a relatively poor social and economic position: they were poorly educated and without any form of employment. For these reasons, such persons were very dependent on their social community.[80]

---

[73] 'The Invisible Frontier: Honour Killings', *Trouw*, 30 December 2003.
[74] Handelingen Eerste Kamer der Staten-Generaal (Proceedings Senate), 18 November 1998, EK 8-160.
[75] Honour-related violence needs separate, national registration. See Handelingen Tweede Kamer 2003–04, 29.203, no 6.
[76] Letter from the Minister of Immigration and Integration to Parliament (Kamerstukken Tweede Kamer 2004–05, 29.203, no 15).
[77] www.nu.nl (2 February 2005).
[78] Handelingen Tweede Kamer 10 February 2005.
[79] See Kamerstukken Tweede Kamer der Staten-Generaal 2005–06, 30.304, no 1-2, 35–6.
[80] Timmer *et al* (2005: 13). See also Janssen (2006).

This second part of the study mentioned that in the period October 2004 until June 2005, seven reports were filed with the public prosecutor regarding murder or manslaughter cases with a background in honour-related violence. These cases occurred all around the Netherlands and were, at the time the report was published, still pending. The Unit on multi-ethnic policing that ran the pilot drew several key conclusions from the cases regarding factors that may aid the police in reacting appropriately to honour-related violence cases:

(1) People (especially women and girls) who are reported missing should be registered more accurately.
(2) Tapping of suspects' telephones should be made easier.
(3) Children born out of wedlock must be kept away from hostile family members.[81]
(4) Early witness statements are very important as they are probably the most genuine ones. The longer a case takes, the greater the chance that the family will pull together again and try to silence a family member who has been communicating with the police. It is also crucial to work with qualified interpreters from the outset, so that witnesses and suspects cannot claim afterwards that they did not understand the questions properly.
(5) Asylum proceedings can be prolonged. During this time, especially male asylum-seekers can suffer from frustration because they are not able to work and have to live 'like women' at home. These men tend to cling to their daughters' and wife's chastity because it is the only source of honour that is left.[82]

Honour-Related Violence in Dutch Criminal Law

In the Netherlands, public debate about honour-related violence has changed dramatically from relative compassion for the offender in the 1970s and 1980s to quite harsh measures at the end of the 1990s and the early

---

[81] An 18-year-old Muslim woman gave birth to a child whose father was not Muslim. She was lured back to her family under the false pretence that they would accept the baby. This was not true, however, and in her aunt's home she was killed by her brother. The police suspected that the girl's family still intended to kill the baby, who was being cared for in a children's home. One family member who regularly visited the child had been warned by the police to act with extreme caution. The brother was sentenced to 12 years' imprisonment for premeditated murder. See District Court Arnhem 11 November 2005, LJN AU5991.

[82] There are several examples of Dutch criminal cases in which the suspect was an asylum-seeker who killed another for honour reasons. Sometimes judges takes the poor social circumstances of people living in asylum centres into account in a mitigating way, although with restraint. See, eg, District Court Leeuwarden 3 May 2005, LJN AT4973 District Court of Amsterdam 7 July 2004, LJN AP8622.

twenty-first century. There is not much case law during the early period, but we have managed to identify some decisions. These cases are not all about honour-related violence, however they show a fairly lenient attitude on behalf of judges towards cultural offences. One example is a decision of the Supreme Court concerning a man charged with fraud. He claimed to be a voodoo master, and thus able to cure diseases. The patients who consulted him, however, were never cured, although they paid a considerable amount of money. Standing before the Supreme Court, the defendant claimed that he had not acted fraudulently because he was in a trance during the rituals. In other words, he stated that he did not possess the necessary mens rea for fraud. The Supreme Court reasoned that the lower courts had not made it sufficiently clear why the defendant's claims had been dismissed. For that reason, the court of appeals' verdict was quashed.[83] In 1974, a defendant from the Moluccan Islands was sentenced to nine months' imprisonment for attempted murder. In the verdict, the court stated, on the one hand, that all defendants, irrespective of their cultural background should know that they have to adapt to Dutch social conventions. Furthermore, the defendant should have known that serious criminal behaviour, such as shooting at someone with sharp ammunition (which the defendant was accused of) cannot be tolerated at all in an ordered society. On the other hand, however, the judge took into account that people from the Moluccas often experience 'adaptation problems' when residing in the Netherlands.[84] These problems should have a mitigating effect, according to the court. The man received a nine-months sentence for attempted manslaughter.

The first Supreme Court decision concerning honour-related violence was the case against a 19-year-old man, suspected of killing another man. The defendant claimed that he had committed the crime to restore his honour. The district court was very lenient and stated that due to his age and because of his cultural background, he should not be punished severely. He was sentenced to six years' imprisonment, when he could have received a life sentence.[85] In 1979, a district court sentenced an under-age Turkish boy to six months in a community home because he killed his half-sister.[86] She had allegedly undermined the family's honour. Although the boy claimed he had acted under duress, the court held that there were other, less violent ways to deal with family problems. The sentence was nevertheless rather lenient.

Although we did not find any relevant decisions in the 1980s, we found one case that took place at the beginning of the 1990s involving a Turkish man who shot his son but received quite a light sentence. During the 1990s,

---

[83] Supreme Court 26 November 1968, NJ 1969, 361.
[84] District Court Arnhem 1 March 1974, NJ 1974, 259.
[85] Supreme Court 1 February 1977, NJ 1977, 563.
[86] District Court Dordrecht 12 January 1979, NJ 1979, 214.

there was a period of rather positive ideas about culture. Culture was not perceived as problematic, but rather as a means of alternative dispute resolution. This lenient attitude towards culture in criminal justice matters has changed since the end of the 1990s. As mentioned previously, in 1999 a Turkish woman was shot dead by her former husband while their two young children were present. She was hiding from him in a women's shelter, but he tracked her down and killed her. The defendant claimed that the victim was seeing another man, although they were still married. As a consequence, his honour was undermined, and he needed revenge. The defendant was sentenced to 15 years' imprisonment and detention under hospital order. The district court was quite clear in opposing honour-related violence:

> the Court reasons that such emotions [feelings of undermined honour that needs to be revenged] can in no way be an excuse in the Dutch legal order for the use of violence and/or taking someone's life. Such a motive for killing a person can never have any mitigating effect. In that sense, this sentence is meant to have a general preventive effect.[87]

Apart from this clearly expressed policy, the court stated that the defendant's personal 'system', ie, his family and social community, constitute part of the problem: they could trigger the defendant into using future violence again, for reasons of honour, because family honour is valued so greatly. This statement was upheld on appeal as well.

The court of appeals agreed that the appellant's background (his family and friends) pose a serious risk for future honour-related violence.[88] This tendency, attributing responsibility in court not only to the defendant but also to his family, is repeated in other cases. In 2004, six members of a Turkish family were prosecuted for attempted murder. A female family member, a 19-year-old girl, had confessed to a brother-in-law that she was secretly seeing a married Turkish man, although she had been 'given away' already to a future husband. By seeing another man secretly, she had defiled the family honour. Immediately after this confession, the girl was locked up in her parents' house. After a series of family meetings, the son-in-law bought a firearm (the money required for the weapon was provided by an aunt) and shot the lover, who barely escaped death. In court, four family members were convicted for taking part in the conspiracy. The son-in-law, who confessed to being the assailant, was sentenced to six years' imprisonment for attempted murder. The son-in-law's grandfather, who was perceived to be the conspiracy's mastermind, was, on appeal, sentenced to seven years' imprisonment. The girl's father, brother and sister were convicted of

---

[87] District Court Dordrecht 30 December 1999, LJN AA4019.
[88] Court of Appeals The Hague 21 April 2000, LJN AD9578.

unlawful detention and received relative short prison sentences. The court said it was shocked to see that the discovery of the girl's affair had led to such violent reactions. It was especially offended by the fact that these incidents occurred in a family that had been living for almost four decades in the Netherlands.[89]

Analysis

If this case law is analysed, it is clear that in criminal proceedings culture is the problem, and not the solution for honour-related violence. Overall, judges react quite dismissively towards these crimes. If a judge is willing to take mitigating circumstances into account, these are mostly framed as being a consequence of the defendant's 'primitive background' or 'archaic state of mind'. For instance, in 1994, a Turkish man was convicted for shooting his son to death. The boy had been provoking his father. The court reasoned that this case concerned a serious offence, but that it was nevertheless prepared to take into account the defendant's cultural background, especially the fact that the defendant was a man who 'lived and acted from an archaic state of mind'. For that reason, the defendant was sentenced to four years' imprisonment.[90] Lawyers admit to using this defence strategy based on 'primitiveness' in court, as it may have a mitigating effect in the sentencing phase. If they can paint a picture of a defendant as being a primitive person, who is not aware of societal developments, who is not able to think and act coherently, this might convince the judge to impose a lighter sentence: in murder or manslaughter cases, this means, for example, a sentence of 10 instead of 12 years' imprisonment.[91]

The overall dismissive stance judges take in cultural offence cases, especially in cases of honour-related violence, is evident in public debate as well.[92] As was mentioned earlier, in the Netherlands politicians on a regular basis launch proposals to enact a specific criminal law targeting individuals who commit honour-related violence. Also, legislative proposals

---

[89] District Court Dordrecht 24 June 2004, LJN AP4401, AP4470 and AP1791. Court of Appeals The Hague, 23 June 2005, LJN AU0180.

[90] District Court Almelo 31 May 1994 (not published).

[91] See, eg, District Court Amsterdam 7 July 2004, LJN AP8622 and Court of Appeals Amsterdam 21 March 2005 LJN AU0361 for the case against a Moroccan man who was sentenced to 12 years' imprisonment for slashing his wife's throat. He had stated that he acted out of frustration and shame because his wife had humiliated him and stated that she wanted a divorce. According to his lawyer, this man was from a primitive descent, ashamed to return to his country of origin as an unmarried and otherwise failed person.

[92] As one Member of Parliament for the Christian Party stated: 'Everybody [the representatives of all political parties] seems to agree that on honour related violence we need to take a strong line'. See Proceedings of the Second Chamber of the States General, 57th Meeting, 9 March 2005.

for higher sentences can be found for those who commit these offences or who can be considered accomplices (for instance, family members).[93] One extreme example in this context is the proposal to define honour-related violence as a terrorist act, which would make it possible to tap the phones of suspect families.[94] Allochthonous organisations also take part in the public debate about honour-related violence and take a strong negative stand against it.[95]

At the same time, the victims of honour-related violence are considered a high priority in the public debate.[96] These efforts do have positive effects, especially if measures are taken to ensure that minority women can live safely and without fear for their lives.[97] This emphasis on the victims' position is not surprising as the (inter)national debate about honour-related violence is promoted primarily by persons working in welfare institutions, who deal with victims of honour-related violence every day. They try to identify best practices and strive for the emancipation of women who often live in strongly patriarchal worlds. As a consequence, victims' rights are at the heart of the discussion and a strong policy against perpetrators of honour-related violence may prove successful in deterring future acts of violence. This policy depends on a belief in the oppressive and preventive effects of criminal law institutions in general. There is a subtle but persistent tendency in this debate to underscore victims' rights and to minimise defendant's rights: the perpetrator should not be left under any illusion that a cultural defence based on honour will have a mitigating effect in court. A much-used one-liner, not only in the Netherlands, but abroad as well, is: 'there

---

[93] Minister Verdonk of Immigration and Integration considered this after the murder of Theo Van Gogh. See *Het Parool* 5 November 2004: 'Verdonk wil eerwraak strafbaar stellen' ('Verdonk wants to penalise honour-related violence'). She repeated this statement in an interview in November 2006. See *NRC Handelsblad* 13 November 2006: 'Er zijn er die menen dat ik het beter zou doen' ('There are those who think that I will handle these problems better').. See also the motion proposed by two Members of Parliament that urged the Minister of Integration to examine the legal possibilities to detect, prosecute and try 'all those concerned with honour-related violence', TK 2003–04, 29.203, no 4 (Proceedings of the Second Chamber of States General).

[94] This proposal was made by Ayaan Hirsi Ali, a former Member of Parliament for the Liberal Party, but it was refused by the rest of the Party. See 'Plan Hirsi Ali van tafel' ('Hirsi Ali's Plan Brushed Aside)', *Parool*, 9 February 2005.

[95] Tukish and Kurdish organisations started a national petition that will last a year. The purpose of the petition is for allochthonous communities to take a public stand against honour-related violence and violence against women in general. See 'National Campaign Against Honour-related Violence', *Reformatorisch Dagblad*, 29 November 2005.

[96] One Member of Parliament pressed the Ministry of Social Affairs and Employment to present 'hard figures' about harmful physical and mental traditional practices to allochthonous women and girls, especially female genital mutilation and honour-related violence. Handelingen Tweede Kamer 2002–03, 28 600 XV, no 105.

[97] See, eg, two letters sent by the Minister of Justice in which he promised to ameliorate the position of women in shelter homes, Handelingen Tweede Kamer 2004–05, 29.203 and 28.345 no 17; Handelingen Tweede Kamer 2004–05, 28.345, no 34.

is nothing honourable in using deadly force'.[98] Implicit in this statement is that other human rights outweigh cultural rights, and claiming a cultural defence in court is no more than declining responsibility, which should rather be interpreted as an aggravating circumstance.[99] Furthermore, whoever commits an act of honour-related violence forfeits his right to a criminal trial in which mitigating circumstances (whatever the background) are taken into account as well as aggravating circumstances.[100]

What seems to be forgotten here is that this right to a fair and balanced trial is no cultural right, but a human right (as it is embodied in Art 6 of the European Charter for Human and Civil Rights) as much as the right to integrity of the body is, the right that is appealed to often and appropriately by opponents of a cultural defence. It is very significant indeed that the anti-cultural defence rhetoric mentioned here is not only expressed by politicians (votes are often easily gained by proclaiming to be 'tough on crime') or persons working with victims of honour-related violence on a daily basis, but also by people in academic positions and by legal professionals. A Swedish lawyer, having assisted many victims of honour-related violence, stated that according to her the Swedish Criminal Code is flawed because it does not stipulate an aggravating effect of honour-related violence. She is of the opinion that 'honour' should always be taken into account as an aggravating circumstance and should result in 'harsher' punishment.[101] A Dutch prosecutor, dealing with a case of a Turkish man who allegedly stabbed his wife to death, said that if he learned that the defendant was influenced by honour, he would immediately demand a higher sentence.[102] What we see here has been mentioned earlier by Kim in respect of US cultural defence cases: 'Under this theory [bestowing a cultural meaning on allochthonous

---

[98] See the report *Findings from the Multi-agency Domestic Violence Murder Reviews in London* (December 2005) 21, available www.met.police.uk/csu/pdfs/MurderreportACPO.pdf.

[99] Key note speaker Aisha Gill (Roehampton University, Surrey) said that we have to try to understand the cultural background, but that honour-related violence remains murder.

[100] See, eg, A Cryer, MP for the UK Labour Party: 'To try and treat such crimes as anything other than that—a heinous crime—serves only to accept the attempts by the perpetrators of such crimes to see them as different or excused by their interpretation of cultural values... Murder is murder and legislation—rather than being sensitive—needs to be clear beyond doubt', in *Honour Related Violence within a Global Perspective: Mitigation and Prevention in Europe,* European Conference Report, Stockholm, 7–8 October 2004 (available at www.kvinnoforum.se/english/ (September 2006)). See also *Honour Related Violence: European Resource Book and Good Practice* (Stockholm, Kvinnoforum, 2005): 'The acceptance of cultural defences as mitigating circumstances in cases relating to "honour crimes" in UK courts is in itself a violation of international and domestic UK and EU laws' (at 105).

[101] *Honour Related Violence within a Global Perspective: Mitigation and Prevention in Europe,* European Conference Report, Stockholm, 7–8 October, 2004, 53.

[102] The defendant would not state anything about the circumstances that led to the stabbing and otherwise nothing was revealed that would point towards honour so the prosecutor demanded eight years' imprisonment for manslaughter. This case was pending at the time of writing.

crime], a prosecutor could introduce evidence about a defendant's cultural background to prove that the defendant was more likely to have committed a crime because of his or her cultural background'.[103] What is problematic about these interpretations is that there is a substantial risk of not hearing the defendant's voice and giving no room in criminal proceedings for the defendant's story. His story is considered self-explanatory: any addition on behalf of the defendant is unnecessary or even unwanted.[104]

Apart from creating an out-of-balance equilibrium between defendant and victim, focusing on victims and their rights when discussing honour-related violence can have another negative effect, this time for the victims themselves. If they are, for instance, approached in too direct a manner about emancipation, this might be counter-productive. This was the main criticism of Ayaan Hirsi Ali who produced a short film together with the late Theo van Gogh, titled *Submission*. In this film, naked women were shown with Qu'ran texts printed on their bodies. A voice-over told about abusive relationships and how violence towards women is allegedly excused by Qu'ranic verses. Even highly educated women who claimed to take a progressive stance in religious matters dismissed the film, saying that this was the wrong way to try to help Muslim women out of their isolation, which was Hirsi Ali's main purpose. Hirsi Ali moved on to producing *Submission II*, which dealt with the position of gay people in Islam. One or two Muslims took her to court on the grounds that *Submission I* had been offensive, but the judge ruled the film could be produced.[105]

ANALYSIS

Relation between Law and Culture

Earlier, we saw in connection with the CRIEM report how culture is being related to crime and how the problem of allochthonous crime is being solved in criminal law. First, we made it clear that culture is rather easily linked with criminality. As a result, culture seems to be criminalised. One problem, however, is that culture cannot explain all criminal behaviour. It is just one of many explanations.[106] This insight is not accepted in the CRIEM report. Culture still remains one of the dominant explanations for

---

[103] Kim (1997: 113). See also Margulies (1998: 72).

[104] Compare Siesling (2002).

[105] 'Muslims Complain in Court about Submission II', *Elsevier*, 1 March 2005. In spring 2006 it was discovered that Hirsi Ali had lied in her asylum petition. As a consequence she resigned as a Member of Parliament and emigrated to the United States. Her work, however, continues to be appreciated by numerous (feminist) activists, both in the Netherlands and abroad. We do not know whether *Submission II* was produced.

[106] See Bovenkerk (2002).

allochthonous crime, and this provided for the introduction into public policy of typical cultural offences, such as honour-related crime.

This gives us a clear link to the problem we observed concerning the criminalisation of culture. At a time when the integration of allochthonous people is a controversial topic, when cases such as honour-related crime are used to plead for harsh mearures and a less voluntary integration policy, the connection of crime and culture is more than just a criminological explanation of crime. The connection has become political. Since virtually all means are acceptable to enforce integration, which at the present time means more and more acculturation to Dutch norms and values,[107] one can imagine that virtually all means are acceptable in the struggle against honour-related crime as well. Even if we do not question the acceptability of these measures in relation to the fundamentals of criminal law, the way in which honour-related crime is used as a synonym for Kurdish culture worries us. A culture cannot be reduced to one aspect, as if a culture is just as simple as that.[108] Every culture has a negative side, but that does not mean that this side is all there is.

This brings us to a second idea. The CRIEM report uses criminal law as a simple mechanism, in other words as an instrument to achieve certain goals. The effectiveness of criminal law is its primary goal. This is even more so concerning honour-related crime. First, Wiersinga has signalled that the fact that a murder was committed because of a slur on honour makes it easier to convict the defendant for murder instead of manslaughter.[109] This is problematic, in our opinion, because the question of whether or not a crime can be defined as an honour-related murder is then only focused on the most serious punishment possible (life imprisonment for murder, 15 years for manslaughter), instead of seeking to understand the background of the act and motives of the offender. Secondly, an instrumentalist vision of law is problematic, because the legislator is able to use honour-related motives as a very simple argument to plead for lengthening the sentence as well as broadening criminal liability. To claim that honour-related crime is a form of terrorism is an example of using the criminal law in an extremely instrumentalistic way. Analysing contemporary developments therefore shows that our earlier analysis is particularly relevant in the case of the policy concerning honour-related crime.

Use of Culture in the Criminal Law

In the section dealing with the rule of interpretative restraint, we discussed relativism—the almost blind trust judges have in expert witnesses and the

---

[107] See Galenkamp (2002).
[108] See Tempelman (1999); Baumann (1999). See also Brenda Oude Breuil in Chapter 12.
[109] Wiersinga (2001).

problem of accepting religious fundamentalism. When analysing the policy concerning honour-related crime we focus on the problem of the expert witness. We noticed that judges extensively rely on experts when dealing with cultural offences. This is also the case concerning honour-related violence. In our view, the pilot project is a perfect example of this view. A second example is the search for a simple, conclusive definition of honour-related violence that is sought by Members of Parliament. A difference between, on the one hand, judges in cases where they have to maintain the rule of interpretative restraint and, on the other hand, politicians and judges in cases of honour-related violence, is that in the first case judges need the expert to provide for order in the chaos, without judging that chaos and the order the expert makes of it. In these cases, the expert is an all-knowing narrator. In the second case, the expert is only a means to provide a scientifically-based definition, but is no longer the all-knowing narrator. An expert may heave a sigh in feeling that she is being used by judges and others seeking for information. The expert is placed in a strait-jacket. She is only useful if she gives plain answers, which are incontrovertible and solid enough to be used as evidence. One example in case law is the verdict of the district court in Haarlem that used expert evidence in a case of alleged honour-related violence. The expert claimed that the case was an honour-related crime. The district court rejected this opinion, stating that the expert had not used her own definition of honour-related crimes, which she had explained in a book.[110] The court, using the book, came to the conclusion that this case did not involve honour-related crime. The court therefore acted as an expert, as some sort of 'super anthropologist',[111] thinking that it could explain a difficult cultural phenomenon according to a given definition, without listening to either the expert or the defendant. The court therefore adopted rather simplistic opinions about culture, honour-related crime and the relation between the crime and culture. Interestingly, we noticed the same problem in relation to cases where the rule of interpretive restraint is used.

Different Flexibility

In relation to the third topic about the unique flexibility of Dutch criminal law, we made two remarks. The first was aimed at the problem of coercive communication, and the second on limiting the range of cultural offences which the criminal law system can allow. Coercive communication seems to be shifted from an empirical fact to a norm in the discussion about honour-related crimes. One interesting aspect of the discussion is that the position

[110] See Bovenkerk (2006).
[111] De Winter (1996: 2).

of the offender is not mentioned.[112] As a consequence, lawyers state that introducing culture in court leads to more severe punishments. This is not always the case, but it is a fact that culture in present day court decisions is frequently used as an argument for a longer sentence.[113] Judges and prosecutors seem to think that one should not and cannot communicate with a person who has committed an unacceptable crime. One example of this seems to be the verdicts of the Arnhem Court of Appeals concerning three brothers-in-law who were accused of stabbing their sister-in-law to death. She had to be killed because she was separated from her husband and lived with another man. This was unacceptable to the defendants because, by so doing, the victim had undermined family honour. The court stated that, should the defendant's cultural background be taken into consideration for mitigation in the first place, this was overruled by the principle of general deterrence which requires that defendants be punished severely.[114]

Our second remark was about the limits of flexibility. In the case of fundamentalist defendants, who refuse the constitutional state as such, we stated that all flexibility ends there. We still approve of this statement. A constitutional state can only function with a minimum acceptance of its principles. Rejection of violence against the constitutional state seems to us to be an important minimum principle.[115] But does the rejection of such violence encompass honour-related violence and other forms of cultural offences? We consider this as reaching too far. Someone who commits an act of honour-related violence does not do so to overthrow the constitutional state but rather to clear his honour and reputation. Whatever one may think of this, in our opinion, honour-related violence is a criminal act that should be prosecuted like any other criminal act. This does not mean that the person who commits an honour-related violent act should be totally silenced. As explained previously, this seems to have become the starting point of many public debates, not only in the Netherlands.[116] Aided by the unique flexibility of criminal law, there is a striking possibility of adapting criminal law to changing circumstances. It seems that every change in society has the effect

---

[112] See, eg, District Court Haarlem 9 May 2001, LJN AB 1503. Court of Appeals Arnhem 12 June 2002, LJN AE 4029; District Court Middelburg 15 October 2003, LJN AL 9045; District Court Dordrecht 24 June 2004, LJN AP 4470; Court of Appeals The Hague 23 June 2005, LJN AU 0180; District Court Arnhem 11 November 2005, LJN AU 5991.

[113] Ten Voorde (2004). See for a recent example District Court Utrecht 23 March 2006, LJN AV7352.

[114] See Court of Appeals Arnhem 5 September 2002, LJN AE 7332, *ibid*, LJN AE 7333, *ibid*, LJN AE 7334. We will not deal with the question of whether deterence or any other theory of punishment should be used in relation to cultural offences. Renteln has argued quite convincingly that the theory of deterrence does not solve the problems we have in dealing with cultural offences. See Renteln (1993).

[115] See 't Hart (1997).

[116] See Siesling (2005).

of undoing earlier adaptations. It appears that criminal law ought to be useful only to ensure a certain amount of order and is a legitimate instrument to guarantee this order in all circumstances. Recent opinions expressed by Members of Parliament do not reassure us that a change of views on the role of the criminal law is to be expected.

CONCLUDING REMARKS

Does this means that there is no light at the end of the tunnel? Will Dutch criminal law, when confronted with cultural offences, never be able to deal with cultural differences in a better way? In our opinion, this would be too simple a conclusion of our contribution. According to us, the main problem of present day criminal law concerned with cultural offences is an instrumentalistic vision of law, and a misuse of the concept of culture. This does not mean that criminal law is not capable of dealing with cultural offences. As Foblets states, in our view correctly: 'Everything depends on how we deploy the law'.[117] We have seen that the way the law is being used today is in need of change. In these concluding remarks we would like to offer some recommendations. For this, we can return to the three themes presented in this contribution. Each topic holds some interesting starting points on which to base the future analysis.

First, in the relation between law and culture, we think that the problem of instrumentalism can be counteracted if we begin to analyse the meaning of law in a multicultural society thoroughly. If law indeed has a social-ethical dimension that is embedded in a given history, then the question is what does this embeddedness tell us about the possibilities of the law to guarantee not only respect for the heterogeneity of society, but also the limits of this cultural diversity? We believe that this analysis will elucidate an idea that law in a culturally diverse society is always seeking to extend the limits of diversity, where it is able to cut itself off from the classical framework in which the law is seen as the result and reflection of an homogeneous society. The presumption that law can only function in a culturally homogeneous society is in our opinion one of the main causes of the ongoing instrumentalisation of law in a multicultural society.[118] The recognition that law can also function in a multicultural society and is able to limit the effects of the 'deep complexity' that results from it, must be a starting point for a new, more critical legal theory that can counteract instrumentalism.

Secondly, a more critical legal theory will need to develop an idea about culture that does not see culture as something people have or are part of, but

---

[117] Foblets (2005: 38).
[118] This is one of the main theses of Jeroen ten Voorde's PhD research. See Ten Voorde (2007a: ch 3).

recognises the importance of culture in action. We cannot 'forget' culture as an analytical tool that can be used to understand processes in society. Culture is seen by many as an important element of their lives and helps them to define themselves and make clear were they belong. The recognition of the importance of culture does not lead us to some sort of cultural relativism that does not recognise that in a multicultural society, several aspects of culture are not seen by others just as aspects of culture but as very problematic. The classical idea that to kill one's father is murder to one person, but just an important element of another person's culture and therefore not to be judged by others (Benedict), is too simplistic Especially when elements of culture condone harm to others, within or outside one's group, we think that the criminal law has a task to punish those who harm others.[119] This means that judges should not use the interpretative restraint in the most extensive way. In using the rule of interpretative restraint, judges rely too much on expert evidence, but only in such a way that provides them with the simplest story possible. Important nuances, whether introduced by the expert or the defendant, are in danger of not being recognised. We believe that every participant in a criminal trial has a specific task of searching for the truth,[120] in a way that takes account of the complexity of every case and therefore deals with diversity in a way that fully appreciates the difficulties we face when we try to answer questions about culture, diversity, and other considerations. In our view, the truth can only be found if we create a space for every relevant aspect in a criminal case. This means hearing the defendant, the victim (if present), experts (if necessary), and as many witnesses as possible. The judge can only give a considered judgment if she can refer to a plurality of visions,[121] and does not just use the perspective of one expert who offers the simplest vision of reality possible; or worse, where the judge decides on the basis of her own prejudices about culture.

Thirdly, an important principle of criminal law is that it guarantees every citizen the right to participate equally and freely in public debate, and express her culturally based ideas. First of all, this means we must try to resolve the problem of coercive communication in the criminal law. We have to create ways of raising questions about the defendant's cultural background or the act she committed. Secondly, legal norms should remain flexible. Without this type of flexibility, it is impossible to deal with cultural differences. One of the important aspects of present day criminal law is that it has shown at least a theoretical possibility of dealing with cultural differences. With this theoretical basis, in realising what went awry in the past, we have to restart our research. This will be one of the main issues in Dutch criminal law in the years to come.

---

[119] Renteln (2004: 217–18).

[120] This chapter is based on our knowledge of Dutch criminal law, one of the clearest examples of a civil law system.

[121] See Gutwirth and De Hert (2001: 1078).

7

The Cultural Defence in Criminal Law: South African Perspectives

PIETER A CARSTENS*

To strike a mean between the Batonka fisherman living his primitive life in some remote spot on the Zambesi, and the professor at the University College of Rhodesia, is to set a task even an arch-exponent of the 'reasonable man test' would shrink from attempting.

(*R v Nkomo* 1964 (3) SA 128 (SR) on 131 per Beadle CJ)

INTRODUCTION

T HIS CHAPTER CONSIDERS the nature, scope, application and extent of the so-called 'cultural defence' in South African criminal law. The role of cultural factors in establishing traditional criminal law defences in South African law is considered. Ultimately the question is evaluated whether an accused's/defendant's cultural background could entitle him/her to advance any defence that could negate the essential elements of criminal liability with specific reference to unlawfulness (in the case of command or obedience orders), criminal capacity, intent (lack of knowledge of unlawfulness, mistake of law or mistake of fact), or if convicted, advance cultural factors in mitigation of sentence. Although the cultural defence has been widely debated in US, English and continental systems of law,[1] it has/should have particular significance in a hybrid legal

---

* This chapter is an adaptation of the article 'The Cultural Defence in Criminal Law: South African Perspectives' (2004) 2 *De Jure* 312–30 and is reprinted with the permission of the editor.
[1] See in the US context, Harvard Law Review Editors, 'The Cultural Defense in Criminal Law' (1985–86) 99 *Harvard Law Review* 1293; AD Renteln, 'Women and the Courts: a Justification of the Cultural Defense as Partial Excuse' (1993) *Southern California Review of Law and Women's Studies* 437; V Sacks, 'An Indefensible Defense: on the Misuse of Culture in Criminal Law' (1996) *Arizona Journal of International and Comparative Law* 523; A Gross, 'Beyond Black and White: Cultural Approaches to Race and Slavery' (2001) *Columbia Law Review* 640; C Ly, 'The Conflict Between Law and Culture: the Case of Hmong in America' (2001) *Wisconsin Law Review* 471; NA Gordon, 'The Implications of Memetics for the Cultural Defence' (2001) *Duke Law Journal* 1809; KM Neff, 'Removing the Blinders in Federal Sentencing: Cultural Difference as a Proper Departure Point' (2003)

system such as South Africa where the new constitution[2] (as a value-driven legal dispensation in which human rights are entrenched) is often in conflict with principles of customary law. In this regard, two 'systems of law' impact on the lives of many South Africans: the national law and customary law. Many experience conflict between the values and norms of these two systems. In this regard, much has also been made in South Africa of the differences between Western and African systems of thought. This chapter offers a brief discussion of these differences and conflicts between African and Western cultures.

An assessment of the cultural defence in South African criminal law necessitates an understanding of cultural practices in South Africa. In traditional African context, cultural practices pertaining to belief in witchcraft, *muti* and *muti* killings (medicine murder) and necklacing are briefly assessed with particular reference to the impact thereof on the motivation for crime within the South African criminal justice system. It should be noted that other cultural practices also exist in South Africa, notably female genital mutilation and ritual male circumcision: these practices fall outside the present discussion.[3] It goes without saying that the impact of the cultural defence should be assessed within the framework for criminal liability as prescribed by the general principles of South African criminal law. In this regard it will be necessary to explain the applicable general principles.

Chicago-Kent Law Review 445; KL Levine, 'Negotiating the Boundaries of Crime and Culture: a Sociological Perspective on Cultural Defence Strategies' (2003) *Law and Social Inquiry* 39; for examples in English law see J Lewis, 'The Outlook for a Devil in the Colonies' (1958) *Criminal law Review* 666; C Howard, 'What Colour is the "Reasonable Man"?' (1961) *Criminal Law Review* 41; J Herring, 'Provocation and Ethnicity' (1996) *Criminal Law Review* 490.

[2] Act 108 of 1996. It should be noted that the South African Constitution (in terms of structural and interpretative framework) was influenced by the Canadian and German Constitutions; see Davis *et al*, *Fundamental Rights in the Constitution* (Cape Town, Juta, 1997) 6, with reference, eg, to the application of the leading Canadian case on the limitation of constitutional rights of *R v Oakes* (1986) 26 DLR (4th) 200; for debate on the cultural defence in South African law and South Africa see G Chavunduka, 'The Reality of Witchcraft' (2001) *African Legal Studies* 163; J Hund, 'African Witchcraft and Western Law: Ontological Denial and the Suppression of African Justice' (2001) *African Legal Studies* 22; J Hund, 'Witchcraft and Accusations of Witchcraft in South Africa: Ontological Denial and Suppression of African Justice' (2000) *CILSA* 366; JA Van den Heever and JMT Labuschagne, 'Geloof in towery en die dekonkretiseringsproses' (1996) *Obiter* 310; JMT Labuschagne, 'Geloof in towery, die regsbewussynsdraende persoonlikheid en die voorrasionele onderbou van die regsorde: 'n Regsantropologiese evaluasie' (1998) *SAJE* 78; JMT Labuschagne, 'Geloof in Toorkuns: 'n morele dilemma vir die strafreg' (1990) *SACJ* 246; see also E Du Toit, *Straf in Suid-Afrika* (Johannesburg, Juta and Kie, 1981) 31; PWW Coetzer, P Carstens and H Kloppe,r 'Some Medical Forensic Aspects of Cultural Practices' in PWW Coetzer, P Carstens, C Fosseus and CF Blok (eds), *Clinical Forensic Medicine and Medical Jurisprudence* (Megkon, Pretoria, 2001) 1–68.

[3] For a detailed discussion of these cultural practices see Coetzer, Carstens and Klopper, above n 2 at 16–33.

In conclusion, a brief assessment with recommendations/proposals are canvassed.

AN OVERVIEW OF CULTURAL PRACTICES IN SOUTH AFRICA

An assessment of the cultural defence in South African criminal law necessitates an understanding of the nature and scope of a variety of cultural practices in South Africa. This understanding is also important to sustain any argument for the rejection or recognition of the cultural defence in South African criminal law. Not only is the nature and scope of cultural practices important, but the whole context of a possible application of the cultural defence should also be canvassed with due consideration to medico-legal aspects, medical forensic aspects and epidemiology of cultural practices. In this regard, the overview serves as important background to the present discussion and is indicative of the cultural pluralism in South Africa. In the overview the focus will be on witchcraft, *muti*-killings and necklacing. In terms of presentation, each reviewed cultural practice is followed by a brief discussion of the legal aspects thereof. The overview is followed by an analysis of the possible application of the cultural defence in South African criminal law.

It should be noted that during the 1980s and 1990s in South Africa, there was a sharp increase in witch killings in a particular province (Northern Province, South Africa) which could directly be attributed to the wide political unrest preceding the advent of the constitutional democracy in South Africa in 1994. Alarmed by the scope and brutality of these killings, a provincial commission of enquiry, popularly known as the Ralushai Commission, was appointed in 1995. The final report of the Commission was published in 1996 and contains essential information for those interested in traditional law and forensic medicine.[4]

WITCHCRAFT

Concepts and Definitions[5]

Divining bones *Ditaola* (Sesotho); *Thangu* (Tshivenda); *Tihlolo* (Xitsonga) is a set of divining dices consisting of knuckle bones of animals, shells, pieces of wood and other articles.

---

[4] Most of the clinical information, unless otherwise stated, regarding witchcraft and *muti* killings in this overview is derived from the Ralushai report and is hereby formally acknowledged.

[5] It should be noted that in the analysis of definitions and concepts in this representation, reference will be made to an understanding of these in the context of the various indigenous people living in South Africa, eg, the Vendas, Sesothos, Xhosas, Zulus, etc. It should also be noted that there are 11 official languages in South Africa, indicative of the cultural pluralism.

Herbalist is a person who can treat a disease, based on her knowledge of roots and herbs. She claims no special relation to the spirits, but simply dispenses the drug without making use of divining bones.

Musika (Tshivenda); *Letšwa* (Sesotho); *Kusikela* (Xitsonga) is a drug or magic used to kill or harm people at a distance, employed against a thief by the aggrieved owner or by a bereaved family against the one held responsible for the death of a relative.

Seipone mirror (Sesotho); *Xivoni* (Xitsonga) is a traditional healer or a prophet who uses crushed and fermented leaves (roots) of certain plants. This fermentation has an intoxicating effect. A client is given this potion to drink and afterwards ordered to sit in the sun to hasten the process of intoxication. When she[6] is intoxicated, she is taken into a dark room in which there will be a white cloth pasted on the wall. The client is ordered to look at the cloth in which she will see images of people and animals, some of which will be known to her and some not. From this observation the traditional healer or prophet tells the client that the people she has seen on the screen are the ones who bewitched her. Later on the client is given a purgative to cleanse out the effect of the substance that causes hallucination. It is believed that if the effect of this hallucinating substance is not neutralised, the client becomes demented. This whole process is called the *mirror* or *television system*.

Tshiganame (Tshivenda); *Xiganama* (Xitsonga); *Sekanama* (Sesotho) is a reputed deadly poison prepared from crocodile's brain or liver and so-called because the victim falls on his or her back and dies instantly.

Witch: the English word witch is gender specific and confined to women only. The male equivalent is wizard. The Sesotho word *moloi* (pl *baloi*) is derived from the verb *loya*, which means to bewitch and is attributed to those people who, through sheer malice, either consciously or subconsciously, employ magical means to inflict all manner of evil on their fellow human beings. They destroy property, bring disease or misfortune and cause death, often entirely without provocation to satisfy their inherent craving for evil-doing. The Tsivenda word for witchcraft is *vhuloi*. The Nguni equivalent is *ukuthakatha* (verb) and *umthakathi* (noun). African terminology referring to witches or wizards is gender neutral.[7]

Witch purging[8] includes expelling (banishing) or killing a witch.

Zombi (Nguni); *setloutlwana* or *sethotsela* (Sesotho); *Xidadjani* (Xitsonga); *Matukwane* (Tshivenda) is a person who is believed to have died, but

---

[6] The client may be male or female.

[7] A Minnaar *et al*, 'Witch Killing with Specific Reference to the Northern Province in South Africa' in E Bornman, R Van Eeden and M Wentzel (eds), *Violence in South Africa: a Variety of Perspectives* (Pretoria, Human Sciences Research Center, 1998) 175–300.

[8] T Botha, '*South African Police Service: Special Investigations, Witchcraft and Related Crimes* (unpublished, 1999) 1–18.

because of the power of the witch, she[9] is resurrected, and made to work for the person who turned her into a zombi. To make it impossible for her to communicate with other people, the front part of her tongue is allegedly cut off so that she cannot speak. It is believed that she works at night only and that by the power of a witch, she can leave the rural areas and work in the urban areas, often far from her home. Whenever she meets people she knows, she vanishes or is believed just to be invisible for those who would recognise her.

Nature and Practice of Witchcraft

Cultural Perspectives and Belief Systems

Some cultures in the Northern Province believe that death, illness or misfortunes are caused either by the ancestors (as punishment) or by evil spirits (witches). If witches are suspected witchdoctors, diviners or traditional healers will point out the individual through the process of divination (smelling out).

The Commission of Inquiry into Witchcraft, Violence and Ritual Murders in the Northern Province of the Republic of South Africa has found that the overwhelming majority of people interviewed in the Northern Province, both rural and urban, and including some members of the South African Police Services (SAPS), believe in witchcraft and therefore the existence of witches (*baloi*).

Some people are born as witches. In some cultures it is believed that should a baby be thrown against a wall and that baby clings to the surface without falling, he or she will grow up to become a witch. Some people acquire witchcraft by medicine from a traditional healer or witchdoctor.

Many animals are associated with witchcraft such as owls, bats, baboons, pole-cats, hyenas, cats and snakes. Articles associated with witchcraft include razor blades, mirrors, brown bread, traditional dishes, whirlwinds, pot-lids, plates, saucers, spoons, traditional horns blown at night, ball pens, gramophone records and books.

Whites are not believed to practise witchcraft, nor can they become the victims of such craft.

Lightning is of two types. Lightning caused by the mythical thunder bird never damages crops, dwellings, animals or humans. It is perceived as good lightning. Humans, on the other hand, cause lightning which kills or destroys by putting *muti* (eg, person's urine) near the place where the lightning is required to strike. This is perceived as bad (evil) lightning (*tladi*).

---

[9] Zombis may be of either sex.

Sex Distribution

Women are more often accused than men of practising witchcraft, at a ratio of 2:1. Some of the reasons given for this sex distribution include the following:

(a) gender power struggles following the assumption of male roles by women whose husbands are away on migrant labour;
(b) women are supposedly more prone to sexual jealousy or envy of their neighbours who possess more material wealth than they do;
(c) female reproductive processes such as menstruation, pregnancy or child-birth are regarded as impure or the result of supernatural powers.[10]

Age Distribution

Witches are usually older than 20 years of age. Most are middle-aged females.

Incidence and Perpetrators

In the past witches were mostly expelled (banished) from their homes to isolated places where they formed small communities. Since the 1980s, however, witch killings started to increase in South Africa, notably in Venda, Lebowa and Gazankulu in the Northern Province (Minnaar *et al*, 1998). From January 1990 until April 1995, 455 cases related to witchcraft were reported to the SAPS in the Northern Province of South Africa.

Prior to the 1980s, most witches were killed by the community *en masse*. In later years, the killing was done by *comrades* (youths) ranging in age from 14 to 38 years. Some people believe that the youths were used by politicians or unscrupulous adults for their own purposes. The perception that many of these murders were politically instigated seems to be borne out by the statistics. In 1996, the number of witchcraft related cases dropped from 676 in the first semester to 417 in the last semester, a decrease of 38 per cent. In the first semester of 1998, not a single witchcraft related murder was reported in the Northern Province.

Witch killings tend to increase during times of violent turmoil.

Reasons for Killing Witches

Jealousy for material belongings is a common cause for witch killings. Especially in the past, witch killing was also resorted to in order to achieve

---

[10] Minaar *et al*, above n 7 at 175–300.

political aims.[11] Power struggles relating to gender roles also play an important part.

Methods of Killing

Witches are traditionally burnt because a belief exists that fire will destroy their souls and in so doing break all links with his or her ancestors. Killing at night is often effected by wiring the door shut while the victim is asleep, dousing the roof with petrol or paraffin and setting it alight.

Victims seized during the day or while fleeing from a mob are often killed by the necklace method or slowly roasted to death while held spread-eagled over the open fire. Some of them may also be strangled, hurled from a precipice, drowned or, as in the Eastern Cape, shot to death.

The possessions of the witch must be destroyed after the killing. Where burning is not employed as the manner of execution the bodies are often set alight afterwards.

Medico-Legal Aspects of Witchcraft

Legal Aspects of Witchcraft

It is illegal to accuse a person of witchcraft or sorcery, or to name a person as a witch or wizard or to injure or damage any person or thing on the advice of any witchdoctor, witch-finder or similar person.[12] The Witchcraft Suppression Act further determines that any person who:

(a) Imputes to any other person the causing, by supernatural means, of any disease in or injury to any other person or thing, or who names or indicates any other person as a wizard;

(b) Professes or pretends to use any supernatural power, witchcraft, sorcery, enchantment or conjuration, imputes the cause of death of, injury or grief to, disease in, damage to or disappearance of any person or thing to any other person;

(c) Employs or solicits any witchdoctor, witch-finder or any other person to name or indicate any person as a wizard;

(d) Professes a knowledge of witchcraft, or to use the charms, and advises any person how to bewitch, injure or damage any person or thing, or supplies any person with pretended means of witchcraft;

---

[11] Bornmann, Van Eeeden and Wentzel, above n 7.

[12] Witchcraft Suppression Act (3 of 1957), s 1, as amended by the Witchcraft Suppression Amendment Act (50 of 1970) and the Abolition of Corporal Punishment Act (33 of 1997). It should also be noted that over and above the Witchcraft Suppression Act, various provincial and local government Acts have been passed in the past to suppress acts of witchcraft.

(e) On the advice of any witchdoctor, witch-finder or any other person or on the ground of any pretended knowledge of witchcraft, uses or causes to be put into operation any means or process which, in accordance with such advice or his own belief, is calculated to injure or damage any person or thing;

(f) For gain pretends to exercise or use any supernatural power, witchcraft, sorcery, enchantment or conjuration, or undertakes to tell fortunes, or pretends from his skill in or knowledge of any occult science to discover where and in what manner anything supposed to have been stolen or lost may be found;

Shall be guilty of an offence and liable in conviction.

In the case of the so-called witchcraft-murder (witch-killing), the court may view a truly held belief in witches and witchcraft to be a mitigating factor in the sentencing of the accused. It has been accepted that although the reasonable person does not believe in witchcraft, a subjective belief therein may be factor which may, depending on the circumstances, have a material bearing on the accused's blameworthiness. This is of particular significance where the belief in witchcraft is the only explanation offered for the accused's killing of the deceased,[13] even though the Act denies the existence of witchcraft in recent years.

It is clear that certain offences pertaining to witchcraft under the Act are subject to severe punishment. It has, however, been argued[14] that in terms of criminal law the cultural aspects of cases involving witchcraft should be analysed and evaluated according to ethnological guidelines and the context of the social milieu in which they occurred. Cognisance should also be taken of s 15 of the Constitution of the Republic of South Africa (Act 108 of 1996). Section 15 states that everyone has the right to freedom of conscience, religion, thought, belief and opinion. The freedoms contain in this section are, however, not absolute and should be balanced with reference to the limitation clause (s 36) in the Constitution.[15] It would seem that the suppression of witchcraft is a limitation that is reasonable and justifiable in an open and democratic society based on human dignity, equality and freedom.

---

[13] See *S v Netshiuvhu* 1990 (1) SACR 331 (A); cf *R v Biyana* 1938 EDL 310; *R v Fundakabi* 1948 (3) SA 810 (A); *S v Ndhlovu* 1971 (1) SA 27 (RA); *S v Mokonto* 1971 (2) SA 319 (A) 320G-H; *S v Ngubane* 1980 (2) 741 (A) 745D; *S v Motsepa* 1991 (2) SACR 462 (A); *S v Phokela* 1995 (1) PH H22; *S v Phama* 1997 (1) SA 539 (E).

[14] A Minaar, 'Witchpurging and Muti Murder in South Africa' (2001) *African Legal Studies* 1.

[15] In particular the limitation clause (s 36) in the South African Constitution reads as follows: 'The rights in the Bill of Rights may be limited only in terms of law of general application to the extent that the limitation is reasonable and justifiable in a open and democratic society based on human dignity, equality and freedom, taking into account relevant factors, including (a) the nature of the right; (b) the importance of the purpose of the limitation; (c) the nature and extent of the limitation; (d) the relation between the limitation and its purpose; and (e) less restrictive means to achieve the purpose'.

In recent years, belief in African witchcraft, specifically when in conflict with the Western idea of law, has been construed as a *cultural defence*—more so from an anthropological and jurisprudential point of view.[16] To be convicted of murder in South Africa, the state has to prove all the elements of the crime beyond reasonable doubt. This implies that for the crime of murder the state has to prove beyond reasonable doubt an unlawful act/or omission by the accused who intentionally caused the death of the deceased. An element of intention (as a form of mens rea) is so-called *knowledge of unlawfulness*. The accused in his/her subjective mind (in South African criminal law the test for intention is purely subjective in terms of the psychological approach to fault as applied in South African criminal law) must thus be aware of his or her wrongdoing at the time of the commission of the crime. The argument is often advanced by perpetrators accused of witchcraft murders, that they, on account of their belief in witchcraft and the supernatural which formed part of ritual practices for centuries in a community, lacked knowledge of unlawfulness during the commission of the crime. Since South African criminal state courts do not, in principle, accept the defence of belief in witchcraft, the validity of the cultural defence remains a moot point open to debate.

The specific application of the cultural defence can be illustrated with reference to the controversial South African case of *R v Mbombela*.[17] The accused was found guilty of the murder of a nine-year-old child. The accused (between 18 and 20 years of age), lived in a rural area and was

---

[16] JTM Labuschagne, 'Geloof in Toorkuns: regsantropologiese perspektiewe' (1997) *SACJ* 202; V Faure, 'Notes on the Occult in the New South Africa' (2001) *African Legal Studies* 170; Hund, above n 2 at 22; D Kohnert, 'Magic and Witchcraft in the Democratisation of South Africa' (2001) *African Legal Studies* 177.

[17] 1933 AD 269; for a discussion of this case see J Burchell and J Milton, *Cases and Materials on Criminal Law* (Cape Town, Juta, 1997) 388; J Fedler and I Olckers, *Ideological Virgins and other Myths* (Pretoria, Justice College, 2001) 83; also cf *S v Sikunyana* 1961 (3) SA 549 (E) where four appellants were charged with assault with intent to cause grievous bodily harm. The evidence showed that they had caused the complainant to inhale fumes of medicine which was sprinkled over live coals. During the 'treatment' the complainant was badly burned. The appellant averred that the complainant had consented to this treatment as a legitimate method to exorcise an evil spirit. In dismissing the appeal, the court ruled that no person can be excused on a charge of assault where actual injury is done, merely upon proof that the victim consented to the infliction of the injury; see also *S v Netshiavha* 1990 (2) SACR 331 (A) at 333: 'Objectively speaking, the reasonable man does not believe in witchcraft. However, a subjective belief in witchcraft may be a factor which may, depending on the circumstances, have a material bearing upon the accused's blameworthiness ... as such it may be a relevant mitigating factor to be taken into account in the determination of an appropriate sentence'; see also *S v Mokonto* 1971 (2) SA 319 (A) where an appellant killed the deceased, an elderly woman who was practising witchcraft and who provoked him by telling him that he would not see the sun set that day. He was convicted of murder with extenuating circumstances; *see also* JTM Labuschagne, 'Geloof in Toorkuns as versagtende omstandigheid: *S v Phokela* 1995 1 PH H22' (1997) *TRW* 202; see also S Campbell, *Called to Heal: Traditional Healing Meets Modern Medicine in Southern Africa Today* (Johannesburg, Zebra Press, 1998) 17.

described by the court as of rather below normal intelligence. On the day in question, some children were outside a hut which they believed to be empty, and they saw something that had two small feet like those of a human being. They were frightened and called the accused. The accused apparently thought that the object was a *tokoloshe*, an evil spirit, which according to widespread superstitious belief, occasionally took the form of a little old man with small feet. According to this belief, which was shared by the accused, it would be fatal to look this spirit in the face. The accused fetched a hatchet and, in the half light, struck the form a number of blows with the hatchet. When he dragged the object out of the hut, he found that he killed his younger nephew. His defence was that he had genuinely believed that he was killing an evil spirit (*tokoloshe*) and not a human being. In the trial court his defence was dismissed and he was convicted of murder and sentenced to death. On appeal, his defence was also rejected, on the ground that to succeed the mistake pertaining to the object had to be reasonable. A conviction of culpable homicide was substituted since the accused's mistake was unreasonable with reference to the yardstick of the *reasonable man in the same circumstances* (thus the test for criminal negligence as the other form of mens rea). The correctness of this decision is open to debate as it is submitted that this is a scenario where the cultural defence could have succeeded, as the accused lacked knowledge of unlawfulness, thus excluding intention. It should also be noted that mistake in fact/law in South African criminal law will only be an excuse if the mistake is *material* as opposed to reasonable.[18]

The defence may call upon an anthropologist and/or a behavioural scientist, usually a social psychologist, to present expert evidence in mitigation of sentence based upon psychological phenomena such as conformity, (blind) obedience to authority, group polarisation, deindividuation, frustration-aggression, relative deprivation and bystander apathy. Where victims are killed by mobs, some members of the crowd who had not directly participated may still face trial as a result of the doctrine of common purpose. In this regard, crowd psychology is important in South African murder trials.[19] It is thus imperative that the accused/defendant makes proper use of cultural evidence to sustain any defence.

In the context of the possible recognition of the cultural defence, much has been made in South Africa of the differences between Western and African systems of thought, partly as a way for Africans to reclaim the beauty of their heritage in the wake of the brutalities, distortions and

---

[18] See CR Snyman, *Criminal Law* (Butterworth, SA, 2002) 189 *et seq*.
[19] *Ibid* at 261 for a discussion of the application of 'common purpose'; also see WD Hammond-Tooke, *Rituals and Medicines: Indigenous Healing in South Africa* (Johannesburg, Donker, 1989) 20.

diminishments of apartheid. In this regard it has been stated by Fedler and Olckers[20] that the basic unit in Western culture is the nuclear family, in which the independence of individuals is stressed. By contrast, the extended family with strong communal ties forms the basis of African culture. Whereas the Western value system endorses an individualist approach to law, in which individuals are regarded as rights bearers and separated from all other human beings, African values reflect a more communitarian juris-prudential approach, in which individuals are seen in relationship to others. This pivotal difference is captured in the adage of *ubuntu botho*. It means the essence of being human. You know when it is there and when it is absent. It speaks about humanness, gentleness, hospitality, putting yourself out on behalf of others, being vulnerable. It recognises that one's humanity is bound up in that of others—for we can only be human together. While Western orientation in the world tends to work towards the future, much of African tradition is about reverence for the ancestral spirits of the past. African tradition is deeply oral, while the West favours the written word. African culture honours the dream and intuition as repositories of wisdom, whereas in Western culture it is mostly acquired knowledge that commands respect.[21]

Criminal Investigation

Cases of witch burning are often not reported to the police for fear of victi-misation or, if chiefs or their families were involved, experience has taught complainants that perpetrators are never brought to justice.

The police investigation of witch burnings is complicated by the fact that few, if any, of the members of the community are willing to give testimony on attacks involving witches. Potential witnesses should be interviewed separately and *in camera* and only be allowed to communicate with other potential witnesses after all interrogations have been held.

Medical Forensic Aspects of Witchcraft

All deaths associated with burns are to be referred for autopsy under the South African Inquest Act (58 of 1959).

Penetrating burns confined to the buttocks, posterior thighs and lumbar region with a vague history, incompatible with the injuries, are suggestive of roasting. Healthcare staff belonging to the same community may neglect the patient. Death is therefore a common outcome. It is usually futile to

---

[20] Fedler and Olckers, above n 17 at 102.
[21] See *ibid* 102; these sentiments are also echoed by anthropologists such as Hammond-Tooke, above n 19 at 17 *et seq.*

attempt to obtain a true history. If roasting is a real possibility the police should be notified and a dying declaration may be obtained.

MUTI AND MUTI KILLINGS

Concepts and Definitions

Muti (Isizulu); *Mushonga* (Tshivenda); *Murhi* (Xitsonga); *Sehlare* (Sesotho). This literally means a tree or plants, but for the people's interpretation it means medicine or herb. Although *muti* is an isiZulu word meaning herb or medicine it has now been assimilated into South African English. The term '*muti* murders' is familiar to all. It includes medicinal potions made from a mixture of herbs, animal products or anorganic substances.[22] It is used by virtually all African cultures and when it does not contain any human body parts, carries no sinister significance. Unfortunately many of the substances, such as *imPila* (Zulu) (*Callilepis laureola*) are toxic and outbreaks of fatalities have occurred where the plant was applied as a leaf or root infusion or decoction.[23] It is used as an abortifacient, purgative, vermifuge or a cough remedy. It is a powerful liver and kidney toxin.

Muti murder[24] is a ritual during which a victim, who complies with particular requirements (eg, child or virgin) is selected in order to obtain specific body parts such as the eyes or genitalia used for medicinal purposes after having been mixed or boiled with other plant or animal constituents. The tongue, eyes, heart and genitalia are believed to make the most potent *muti*. The body parts must be removed while the victim is still alive. Victims therefore die during or after the procedure as a result of pain, haemorrhage and surgical shock. The consciousness of the victim is said to ensure the magical power of the medicine. *Muti* murders can only be inferred if a mutilated corpse is discovered (12 to 15 such corpses are received into Durban's morgues each year).[25] Some proportion of children who vanish without a trace are probably also the victims of *muti* murders, but this remains speculation only. The practice is therefore by no means all that rare. *Muti* murders tend to increase during times of hardship (eg, droughts) and political upheaval. Certain types of *muti* will increase the *isithunzi* (personality and status) of the person who uses it. Ordinary people approach *inyangas* for *muti* to overcome their personal problems, fulfil their ambitions or get the better of their

---

[22] J Evans, 'Muti Murders: Ritual Responses to Stress' (1991) *Indicator South Africa* 46.
[23] JM Watt and MG Breyer-Brandenwijk, *The Medicinal and Poisonous Plants of South Africa* (Edinburgh, Livingstone, 1932) 20.
[24] Evans, above n 22 at 46–48.
[25] *Ibid* at 46–48.

enemies. Only the minority of *inyangas*, however, will kill or contract to kill for human *muti*.

Igquirha (pl *Amagquirha*) (Xhosa). Priest, diviner, physician, pharmacist, psychologist, judge and controller of evil. He or she uses scarification, potions, fomentations, decoctions and enemas of plant or animal origin. Some plants administered are known to be poisonous.[26] Training takes about three years.

Sangoma. Traditional healer who makes a diagnosis by divination, eg, by throwing the bones. He or she usually provides treatment in the form of herbs, poultices, animal products or scarification. The true *sangoma* shuns all forms of witchcraft.

Traditional healers. This is an umbrella term for all practitioners of healing according to traditional African methods. In 1997 there were about 200,000 such practitioners in South Africa with about 60 per cent of all South Africans consulting them at one time or another.[27]

Belief Systems regarding the Uses of Human *Muti*

Body parts used as *muti* serve specific objectives:

(a) blood produces vitality;
(b) the eye will make an important business venture succeed or give far-sightedness to the consumer;
(c) the ear will make people listen to the views of the owner of the business;
(d) the breast will make customers dependent on the owner, as the infant is dependent upon the breast. It will also ensure fertility;
(e) whereas a young girl's vagina is said to bring productivity and wealth to a business venture, testicles are often used for enhancing sexual prowess and performance;
(f) a skull of a human being may, for instance, be built into the foundation of a new building to ensure good business;
(g) the hands of a victim or parts of the hand, eg fingers, are regarded as a method of attracting many clients. It is also believed that ritual murderers could hypnotise their victims by showing them a human hand.

According to the Ralushai Commission, people are killed ritually for financial gain, to make rain, to bring luck, and in the case of the politically

---

[26] J Broster and H Bourne, *Amagqirha: Religion, Magic and Medicine in Transkei* (Cape Town, Juta, 1981) 64.
[27] B Van Wyk, B Van Oudtshoorn and N Gericke, *Medicinal Plants in South Africa* (Pretoria, Briza Publications, 1997) 34.

powerful, to increase power and authority. Only powerful chiefs in Lesotho[28] or the King of Swaziland (in the early twentieth century) had the right to use this type of *muti*. Because the rulers were supposed to use the positive results of the *muti* for the benefit of the people they ruled, the practice was sanctioned by the particular society.

The Commission also discovered that in the past, especially amongst Venda people at the beginning of the ploughing season, royal seeds were mixed with those of the local subjects, and later sowed in the field. It was believed that this practice would yield a good harvest for the nation. This practice was called *Tshirenwarenwane*. Some people believed that if the royal seeds were mixed with human fat, especially if the fat was derived from a person of royal descent, the harvest would be even better. Ritual murder was therefore employed to obtain the fat.

It is also alleged that human fat was used by iron ore smelters. The purpose of using human fat was to make the embers glow in such a way that the iron ore would melt faster.

Various organs are believed to be used for various purposes. In the Northern Province, these organs have allegedly been utilised by businessmen, Zionist church members, *inyangas* and traditional healers.

Although traditional healers flatly deny that they use human parts for treating patients, at Ga-Lekalakala in the Northern Province, an old traditional healer told the Ralushai Commission that the bone of a person killed by a vehicle could be used to join the fractured bones of a patient. This would be done as follows: one portion of the bone is burnt to ashes while the other portion is ground into powder. The powder and the ashes are then mixed. The mixture is then rubbed into the injured area where some cuts have been made with a razor blade.

It seems that South African *inyangas* have learned the power of advertising. A cursory look at the classified sections of newspapers reveals a kaleidoscope of attention-grabbing advertisements aimed at the superstitious and the millions of dedicated *muti* users. The advertisements urge readers to spend money on dubious potions, herbal and chemical mixtures and powder purported to remove evil spirits, increase wages, enlarge penises, bring luck in finances, love, examinations, competitions, horse racing, and cure almost every disease imaginable.

The substantial risk involved in *muti* killings is offset by the profits to be made from making available human body parts. Only a few cases of whites killed by ritual murder have been documented. Some blacks maintain that organs derived from whites make more powerful medicine. Organs are also obtained from air crashes, mortuaries or even operating theatres. Traditional healers are often the original contractors for ritual killings.

---

[28] J Gunther, *Inside Africa* (New York, Harper, 1995) 61.

Usually the body parts are removed while the victim is still alive. Ears, nose, lips, eyelids, genitals and breasts may be removed. The dead body is not usually buried but is left in a secluded place, dropped from a cliff or thrown into a river.

Legal Aspects of *Muti* Killings

Muti murders are distinctly different from witchcraft murders and should accordingly be combatted and prosecuted in a different manner. The circumstances of a *muti* murder are different to those of a witch killing, which is usually carried out in a public manner by members of a community acting as a group. The so-called *muti* murder pertains to the killing of innocent victims in order to obtain certain body parts. Although controversial, the term 'ritual murder' or 'medicine murder' is often used to describe the *muti* murder.[29]

South African criminal law, however, makes no distinction in the prosecution of *muti* murders or witchcraft murders, and perpetrators are all prosecuted for the common law crime of murder. A *muti* murder is investigated in the normal way by police who are responsible for finding the perpetrators and bringing them to justice. If a body part, or body with parts missing, is found, a forensic autopsy is performed to ascertain the actual cause of death. The forensic evidence may point to a *muti* murder and the police investigation can then pursue this possibility.

The South African courts[30] have generally viewed *muti* murders as particularly heinous and calculated, the commission thereof motivated by greed for personal and/or financial gain, totally devoid of any real subjective belief in the supernatural or fear thereof.[31] In this regard, unlike witchcraft murders, perpetrators of *muti* murders could seldom rely on extenuating circumstances or mitigating factors.

It should be noted that in *muti* murders, individuals or small groups of perpetrators operate in secret. In this regard the whole group should be seen as participants to the crime of murder and should thus be convicted of murder on the basis of the doctrine of common purpose. In terms of the criminal law construction of participation, the supplier of *muti* (the traditional healer), the initiator (the client) and any other person (sharing in

---

[29] Minnaar *et al*, above n 7 at 175.

[30] *S v Modisadife* 1980 (2) PH H 109 (A); see also *S v Mavhungu* 1981 (1) SA 56 (A); *S v Malaza* 1990 (1) SACR 357 (A); see also the discussion by CJ Nel, T Verschoor, FJW Calitz and PHJJ Van Rensburg, 'Die belang van 'n Antropologiese perspektief by toepaslike verhore van oënskynlike motieflose moorde' (1992) *South African Journal of Ethnology* 85.

[31] Du Toit, above n 2 at 23.

the loot) for whatever motive, should all be treated as accessories after the fact to murder, and should be punished accordingly.[32] It is more difficult to combat and deal with *muti* murders than witch purging. It is also observed that *muti* murders are strongly tied to existing beliefs in the power and benefits of *muti* consisting of human parts.[33]

NECKLACING

Necklacing (*itayari*) originated in Angola but was employed in South Africa with devastating effect as an instrument of terror to bring about political change.[34] Victims are necklaced by placing a rubber tyre filled with petrol or paraffin around their necks and setting it alight. The hands are severed with a machete or tied behind the back with a rope or wire. The victim is sometimes doused with petrol. Alternatively, the tyre can be stuffed with cloth or paper soaked with petrol or paraffin. The victim is sometimes forced to imbibe petrol before being set alight.[35]

The first incident of necklacing occurred in Uitenhage, South Africa in 1985. Its initial purpose was to eliminate *impimpi* (informers or collaborators with the apartheid government)[36] but the practice was later extended to kill witches as well.[37] Victims were tried in 'kangaroo' courts by militant youths or comrades (freedom fighters, *amaqabane*). Comrades operated from a base, which was any facility or building from which they could conduct their activities. A base consisted of between 28 and 40 comrades.

From January 1984 to August 1986, 348 persons were killed by necklacing. A further 20 survived the ordeal, sustaining severe injuries (Bureau of Information, 1986). Between January 1985 and September 1988, 101 persons were sentenced to death for necklace murders (Minister of Justice, 1986). Between 1 September 1984 and April 1992, nearly 400 people were otherwise burnt to death as a result of politically motivated violence. The usual methods employed were dousing petrol

---

[32] Snyman, above n 18 at 189; see *S v Mavhungu* 1981 (1) SA 56 (A).

[33] Minnaar *et al*, above n 7 at 177.

[34] NC Nomoyi, *Necklacers Speak Out on Hunting Down and Demolishing Transgressors*, paper presented at the Research Internship Sala (Pretoria, Human Sciences Research Council, 1995).

[35] See J Mihalik and Y Cassim, 'Ritual Murder and Witchcraft: a Political Weapon' (1992) *South Africa Law Journal* 138.

[36] Mere social interaction with a police officer without divulging any information was enough to ensure the death penalty. Many people were executed for insignificant reasons or because of personal vendettas.

[37] A Minnaar, 'Desperate Justice: Necklacing Vigilantism and Peoples' Courts', paper presented at the South African Political Studies Association, Biennial Conference, University of Stellenbosch, 1995.

and setting the victim alight or wiring the doors and windows shut before setting the dwelling on fire with the hapless occupants trapped inside, usually in the dead of the night. Although the incidence of politically motivated killings has recently dropped dramatically, these bizarre methods of execution are still occasionally utilised today in witch killings, faction fights and kangaroo courts, especially following on child rape or murder.

Legal Aspects

The offences involved are those of murder or attempted murder (if the victim survives). Because of the additional elements of mindless cruelty and the resort to torture, one would expect the courts to impose the maximum sentence in every instance, but the following case illustrates how psychological factors operating in the group may drastically influence the severity of the sentence. In 1990, after a retrial,[38] the death sentences of six members of a mob that participated in the necklacing of 18-year-old Nosipho Zamela of Mlungisi, near Queenstown, South Africa in 1989, after being accused of being an *impimpi*,[39] were commuted to only 20 months' imprisonment. This dramatic turnaround was brought about after hearing expert evidence from a social psychologist, based in England, who testified that extenuating circumstances existed for all six of the accused as a result of conformity, obedience, group polarisation, deindividuation and bystander apathy. The trial judge accepted all of his testimony, which extended over three days.[40]

Because the crimes of witch killing and necklacing are usually carried out by mobs, some individuals may not be actively involved in the killing itself. The doctrine of common purpose, however, states that they may well be held criminally responsible.

AN ANALYSIS OF THE CULTURAL DEFENCE IN SOUTH AFRICAN CRIMINAL LAW

It should be noted that the 'cultural defence' has not been formalised in the South African criminal law: that is to say, that as a matter of principle an accused/defendant cannot rely on/or plead 'the cultural defence'.

---

[38] *S v Gqeba and others* 1990, Case no 53/89, Supreme Court of South Africa, Eastern Cape Local Division; for a further example of a necklacing case see *S v Motaung* 1990 (4) SA 485 (A).

[39] A police informer, the ultimate crime during the struggle.

[40] AM Colman, 'Crowd Psychology in South African Murder Trials' (1991) *American Psychologist* 1071.

Cultural factors/background as part of the formal evidence may, however, be advanced in support of any other recognised defence or in mitigation of sentence. An analysis leads one to conclude that this defence, if recognised as a defence, could potentially strike at various elements required for criminal liability, and in this sense the 'cultural defence' could clearly operate as a multiple defence (as is presently the case with intoxication, provocation and mental illness in South African criminal law).[41] The potential multiplicity of the cultural defence can be illustrated with reference to the following required elements for criminal liability.

Element of Unlawfulness

The cultural defence, if successfully and formally raised, could negate the unlawfulness of an accused's act or omission. This may conceivably be the case where an accused within a particular culture causes the death of a victim due to duress/compulsion or perceived obedience to orders (thus acting in a state of necessity which is regarded as a ground of justification excluding unlawfulness); for example, a headmen (*nkosi*) of a tribe may order/instruct one of his henchmen to assist in the killing of an elderly member of the tribe to obtain the perceived 'life-giving' parts of the body (the eyes and the genitals) to be buried near the site of an annual initiation ceremony to be held to ward of evil spirits and to please/appease the ancestral spirits. In terms of the hierarchy of power, a henchman cannot refuse the orders of a *nkosi* as disobedience (albeit to an objectively unlawful order) will give rise to severe punishment (even death). In South African criminal law, relative compulsion is regarded as a ground of justification negating unlawfulness, but is also recognised as an excuse excluding culpability—it may thus be a complete defence even to a charge of murder.[42] Cultural factors may clearly influence this element of criminal liability.

---

[41] It has been accepted that intoxication and provocation can either negate the voluntariness of an act/omission, or the criminal capacity of an accused, or the intention of an accused, or it may lead to diminished responsibility or mitigation of sentence; see J Burchell and J Milton, *Cases and Materials on Criminal Law* (Cape Town, Juta, 1997) 261–96; Snyman, above n 18 at 221–40; *S v Chretien* 1981 (1) SA 1097 (A); *S v Wiid* 1990 (1) SACR 561 (A); *S v Moses* 1996 (1) SACR 701 (C); *S v Eadie* 2002 (1) SACR 663 (SCA); mental illness may cause an accused to act involuntarily (insane automatism), alternatively to lack criminal capacity due to the inability to distinguish between right and wrong or to act in accordance with that appreciation; cf *S v Kavin* 1978 (2) SA 731 (A).

[42] See *S v Goliath* 1972 (3) SA 1 (A); *S v Bailey* 1982 (3) SA 772 (A); *S v Mandela* 2001 (1) SACR 156 (C). Obedience to orders is also regarded as a ground of justification excluding unlawfulness if the order was manifestly lawful and if there was a *duty* to obey the order (see *S v Banda* 1990 (3) SA 466 (B); *S v Mohale* 1999 (2) SACR 1 (W)). Obedience to a manifestly unlawful order due to duress or compulsion may, however, lead to a lack of culpability on the part of the accused.

Criminal Capacity

Cultural factors may also impact on an accused's criminal capacity. A person is endowed with capacity if he has the mental abilities required by law to be held responsible and liable for his unlawful conduct. The mental abilities which a person must have in order to have criminal capacity are (a) the ability to appreciate the wrongfulness of his conduct and (b) the ability to conduct himself in accordance with such an appreciation of the wrongfulness of his conduct.[43] It is quite conceivable that an accused in South Africa, on account of belief in witchcraft or the medicinal power or *muti*, may lack criminal capacity in respect of requirement (a) or (b). In this respect it may be equated to the already recognised and existing defence of *non-pathological incapacity* (in respect of provocation).[44] The defence of non-pathological incapacity is subject to judicial scrutiny and the formal proof thereof has been delineated by the courts: the state has to prove the capacity of the accused beyond reasonable doubt; as soon as the state has presented *prima facie* evidence, the onus shifts to the accused to rebut such evidence on a preponderance of probabilities, by laying a foundation for his defence by way of expert evidence. The courts view this defence with circumspection.[45] It is submitted that if the cultural defence is formally recognised and accepted (along the same lines as non-pathological incapacity) then this delineation could also find application.

Element of Fault (in the Form of Intention)

Even though capacity is one of the grounds for the blame inherent in culpability, it does not follow that capacity and fault are one and the same thing. They are two different concepts. In determining whether an accused had intention, one must ascertain what knowledge he had. In determining whether he had capacity, the question is not what knowledge he had, but what his mental abilities were. Awareness of unlawfulness deals with an accused's knowledge or awareness of the unlawfulness of his act.[46] It follows that certain cultural practices may influence the subjective mind of

---

[43] The concept of criminal capacity is unknown in Anglo-American legal systems. It hails from the European continent, mainly from German criminal law theory.

[44] See above n 17; it should be noted that provocation on account of belief in witchcraft as in *S v Mokonto*, above n 17, could have led to a defence of non-pathological incapacity but for the fact that this defence was not in existence in 1971 in South African criminal law when *Mokonto* was decided.

[45] Snyman, above n 18 and the cases referred to there.

[46] Snyman, above n 18 at 160–2.

an accused to the extent that there is no knowledge of unlawfulness and consequently no intention. A conviction on a charge of murder can therefore not be sustained in view of the maxim *nulla poena sine culpa*.[47]

Diminished Responsibility and Mitigation of Sentence

It is accepted in the positive South African criminal law that cultural factors (as advanced by expert evidence) can at least lead to diminished responsibility and mitigation of sentence.[48]

Constitution of the Republic of South Africa (Act 108 of 1996)

Pivotal to the possible formalisation of the cultural defence in South African law is the constitution as the supreme law of the land. Section 15 of the Constitution entrenches the right of everyone to freedom of religion, belief and opinion. Section 9 (the equality clause) outlaws any discrimination, *inter alia* on account of religion, conscience, belief and culture. Section 36 (the limitation clause) states that no right is absolute and may be limited if it is, *inter alia*, reasonable and justifiable in an open and democratic society based on human dignity, equality and freedom. The right to life in terms of s 11 also enters into the equation.[49] Constitutional interpretation by the country's onstitutional court also dictates that there is a duty on the courts in general to develop the South African common law with reference to the constitutional values.[50] It would therefore seem as though the Constitution could be seen as a motivating force for the formal recognition of a cultural defence, albeit in the context and balance of the limitation clause.

CONCLUDING SUBMISSIONS

It is submitted that the South African legal system (through the Constitution), in recognition of cultural pluralism, advances a strong argument for the formalisation of the cultural defence within the substantive criminal law. The formalisation of the defence should, however, be done along the accepted parameters of the limitation clause and formal requirements along the same lines as enunciated by the courts with the defence of non-pathological

---

[47] See the example of *S v Mbombela* 1933 AD 269 ('no punishment without fault').

[48] See reported South African case law above n 13.

[49] The acceptance of the cultural defence in limited circumstances would mean that the constitutional right to life could be infringed upon. This would be the case of a 'justifiable' homicide motivated by cultural factors/beliefs.

[50] See *Carmichele v Minister of Safety and Security* 2002 (1) SACR 79 (CC).

incapacity. In accepting/recognising/formalising the cultural defence in South African law, universalism is ousted in favour of cultural specificity, cultural pluralism, equality and individualised justice. It is notably with regard to the element of intention (more specifically *lack* of intention on account of absence of any knowledge of unlawfulness) that the cultural defence will in all probability find application, although the defence could be regarded as a multiple defence. It goes without saying that from a formal point of view, relevant expert evidence would be imperative to sustain the successful application of such a defence. The cultural defence should also be viewed with circumspection, and this calls for a categorisation of the defence: crimes committed which are induced by a genuine belief in witchcraft (and borne out by expert testimony) should be viewed on a different footing than, for instance, *muti* killings for greed and financial gain (where the defence should not find application) or necklacing (for political motives). It is submitted that the limitation clause in the Constitution will play an important role in balancing the effective application of the defence. A denial of the cultural defence erodes the notion of justice in the African cultural context. Too often, cultural pluralism is equated with being primitive and uncivilised.[51] The possible application of the cultural defence will no doubt offer new challenges to South African criminal courts, to balance justice and cultural pluralism. Ultimately, the effective application of the defence will be in the hands of the judiciary, objectively and free from preconceptions and prejudices (sentiments which will particularly be challenged by the cultural defence). In this respect, the following observation by Cameron AJ certainly rings true (specifically with reference to the judgment quoted at the beginning of this chapter):

> Judges do not enter public office as ideological virgins. They ascend the Bench with built-in and often strongly held sets of values, preconceptions, opinions and prejudices. These are invariably expressed in the decisions they give, constituting 'inarticulate premises' in the process of judicial reasoning.[52]

---

[51] In this regard one can support the views expressed in the Note in (1986) *Harvard Law Review* 1293 *et seq* as opposed to the views of Sacks, above n 1; see also KL Levine, 'Negotiating the Boundaries of Crime and Culture: a Sociological Perspective on Cultural Defence Strategies' (2003) *Law and Social Inquiry* 39, who maintains that where a defendant uses culture only to explain why he wanted to harm the victim and asks that the court be tolerant of such behaviour, considerations of culture should not be allowed, although culture may offer an alternative explanation of the defendant's intent.

[52] E Cameron, 'Judicial Accountability in South Africa' (1990) *South African Journal on Human Rights* 251.

III

Specific Issues

8

Criminalising Romani Culture through Law

JOKE KUSTERS

T HE MULTICULTURAL CHARACTER of contemporary society has given
rise to myriad political and philosophical questions, which are
related to new challenges in legal reasoning. In the criminal law, the
difficulties are manifest in discussions of cultural defence and/or offence.[1]
When considering the desirability of recognising 'culture' as a significant
factor in criminal courts, there is, however, more to the matter than merely
asking to what extent, and how, one can leave room for a specific cultural
trait in the final jurisprudential decision. Although they present themselves
as neutral, rules governing jurisdiction and legislation are in fact already
permeated with cultural presuppositions and of course in the final analysis
law itself is culture.[2] When dealing with a cultural defence/offence issue, it
might therefore be worthwhile also to consider the implicit processes that
occur prior to the adjudication of a criminal court case.

This chapter seeks to illustrate the above contentions in the light of the
situation of Romani people within state legal systems. Because of certain
cultural practices, Romani people, more often than others, live on the
margin of society. The most salient feature is that nomadism collides with
the assumption of state legislation that individuals remain in one location,
although other problematic cultural aspects will also be examined. I will,
however, deal with these issues mainly from the perspective of the right to
respect for the home and the right to appropriate housing. Besides having
particular relevance to their situation, the implementation of these rights
offers a good opportunity to illustrate how Romani cultural concepts could
be more appropriately integrated into the state legal order.

---

[1] For a conceptual clarification see, eg, J Van Den Broeck, 'Cultural Defence and Culturally
Motivated Crimes (Cultural Offences)' (2001) 9(1) *European Journal of Crime, Criminal Law
and Criminal Justice* 1.
[2] See, eg, P Fitzpatrick, *The Mythology of Modern Law* (London, Routledge, 1992);
G Binder, 'Twentieth-Century Legal Metaphors for Self and Society' in A Sarat *et al* (eds),
Looking Back at Law's Century (New York, Cornell University Press, 2002).

When discussing the situation of Romani people, various topics could be considered. As regards the relationship between Romani people and the criminal law, one could focus on Romani people as victims.[3] Generally though, they are perceived as being primarily perpetrators of crimes.[4] Even in this case, they might also be considered as victims of circumstances or forces beyond their control which have made them delinquent. Cause and effect are often mingled in this respect, but the central theme of this essay is based simply on the notion that Romani people can be regarded as outlaws because of a multiplicity of factors. Some of these factors can be found in the fact that residence, identification, nationality, etc, as ordering concepts of the state system, might not always have existed within the Romani cultural framework.[5] As there is no Romani homeland,[6] this scattered people is bound to occupy a minority position in the 'host country'. To date, certain mechanisms have resulted in the continued exclusion of this minority, whose framework of cultural references knows no principles of state adherence. Of course, both sides (host country/minority) have their own mechanisms of reinforcing their respective cultural values, but the host country is in the best position to win the power struggle.

This study focuses on institutionalised cultural preoccupations as one of the implicit means through which this exclusionary process takes place. Although most authorities are fully prepared to respect the Romani culture on the level of human and constitutional rights, another process can be observed in operation on a more basic level. Through the use of criminal law (public order) and for instance planning regulations, state legal systems still seem to aspire to acculturation. When the criminal law is used to this end, this is bound to lead to a process of criminalising Romani culture. Nevertheless and to some extent to set this straight, national legislation and its de facto application can be challenged by invoking the human and constitutional rights dimension. At the level of jurisprudence, then, the right to the Romani cultural identity might eventually be incorporated into legislation, or such legislation can simply be declared unconstitutional or contrary

---

[3] In the worst case, their victimhood is combined with a reluctance of the authority to protect their Romani citizens as they would do other citizens: see, eg, I Pogany, *The Roma Café: Human Rights and the Plight of the Romani People* (London, Pluto Press, 2004) and the highly documented website of the European Roma Rights Centre, www.arrc.org/Romarights_index. php. Romani can furthermore be straightforward victims of agents of the criminal system, see R Lee, 'The Rom-Vlach Gypsies and the Kris-Romani' in WO Weyrauch (ed), *Gypsy Law: Romani Legal Traditions and Culture* (Berkeley, University of California Press, 2001) 229.

[4] See, eg, I Durnescu, C Lazar and R Shaw, 'Incidence and Characteristics of Rroma Men in Romanian Prisons' (2002) 3 *Howard Journal* 237.

[5] See below.

[6] In Hancock's glossary of Romany terms, the word 'Rromanèstan' is, however, defined as 'the notional homeland of the Romani people': I Hancock, 'A Glossary of Romani Terms' in WO Weyrauch (ed), *Gypsy Law: Romani Legal Traditions and Culture* (Berkeley, University of California Press, 2001) 184.

to certain human rights. This study seeks to analyse some examples of this type of interaction between national legislation and jurisprudence, and makes reference to various legal and anthropological insights.[7]

My basic conjecture here is that a certain level of multicultural jurisprudence is desirable, both from an ideological as well as a policy viewpoint, and I make use of the Romani to support this hypothesis. What is more, I regard multicultural jurisprudence as the jurisprudential embodiment of a basic respect for cultural minorities that is not only based on considerations of desirability, but increasingly is considered to be a basic right. While it might still be open to debate as an autonomous basis for a legal claim,[8] its de facto incorporation into other rights can by and large not be disputed, as will be shown in the following sections. In these I will try to demonstrate this through an analysis of the ways in which a multicultural jurisprudence for Romani culture is being established.

I begin with a largely descriptive outline, after which I will evaluate the status quo from an anthropological point of view. The judicial conceptualisation of Romani culture can thus be confronted with a more emic perception to see whether the emergent aspirations are met with in reality. As will be illustrated further on, the anthropological approach can also help in solving some fundamental misunderstandings and in truly coming to a multicultural jurisprudence. In striving for such a multicultural jurisprudence, an anthropological approach is by no means equivalent to an absolute respect for any cultural manifestation whatsoever. In my opinion, it does help to establish support for a right to cultural identity. However, such an (independent) right to culture has to be weighed against other rights, such as the right to education and women's rights.

ROMANI CULTURE: TERMINOLOGY AND SOME GENERAL FEATURES

When trying to sketch certain general features of Romani culture within a limited frame, one risks over-generalising. First of all, there is great internal diversity. In-depth knowledge acquired through expertise with one subgroup is not necessarily representative of another.[9] Although Romani culture is considered to be a transnational culture, there is also great

---

[7] Cf M-C Foblets, 'Cultural Delicts: the Repercussion of Cultural Conflicts on Delinquent Behaviour: Reflections on the Contribution of Legal Anthropology to a Contemporary Debate' (1998) 3 *European Journal of Crime, Criminal Law and Criminal Justice* 187.

[8] See, eg, Y Donders, *Towards a Right to Cultural Identity?* (Antwerpen, Intersentia, 2002); A Renteln, *The Cultural Defense* (New York, Oxford University Press, 2004).

[9] Most of the knowledge is necessarily acquired through fieldwork given the essentially oral character of this culture. See also TA Acton, 'A Three Cornered Choice: Structural Consequences of Value-Priorities in Gypsy Law as a Model for a More General Understanding of Variations in the Administration of Justice' (2003) 3 *American Journal of Comparative Law* 639.

geographical diversity in the groups of people that are mainly associated with Romani culture. In Belgium, for instance, there are the autochthonous Voyageurs, in France there are the Manoeches, in Germany you have the Sinti, in England one speaks of 'Gypsies' and Travellers and in the United States there are the Vlax-Roma.[10] My point is not to try to make an inventory of all possible variations and certainly not to focus on internal differences. On the contrary, I aim to define some characteristics that these diverse groups have in common and to search for what exactly makes them a transnational, non-territorial minority. The delineation here takes place with reference to the initial point of departure for this analysis, ie, in light of some particular aspects of the conflicted relationship between certain Romani cultural practices and the state legal system.

TERMINOLOGY

I have chosen to focus on some 'Romani' cultural practices. By using the term 'Romani', at least some obstacles can be overcome. The term that was formerly used, 'Gypsies', could quite accurately embrace the matter here concerned. This term is, however, purely employed by non-'Gypsies' and has no meaning within the community.[11] It is, moreover, deemed to be highly derogatory, as is the German and Dutch translation thereof '*Zigeuner*'.[12]

It is also not ideal to take the name of one subgroup and consider it representative for the global community. Increasingly, the term 'Roma' has come to take the place of 'Gypsies'. Not only is this just one of the communities under study,[13] but voices from within this community have disputed this broadening of their identity. The association of the 'Roma' with a nomadic way of life is, according to them, neither desirable nor (always) accurate.[14]

Why then 'Romani'? As an adjectival form it can be considered to embrace all the self-ascribed ethnonyms,[15] as well as to capture some general features that the subgroupings have in common. It used to refer only

---

[10] Of course, all of these can be found in other countries as well.

[11] N Girasoli, 'Roma/Gypsies and Immigration Issues in the EU' (2000) 1(2) *Revue des affaires européennes (Law and European Affairs)* 128.

[12] WO Weyrauch (ed), *Gypsy Law: Romani Legal Traditions and Culture* (Berkeley, University of California Press, 2001) vii.

[13] T Machiels, *Keeping the Distance or Taking the Chances* (Brussels, ENAR, 2002) 17.

[14] R Rose, 'Sinti and Roma as National Minorities in the Countries of Europe', available at www.geocities.com/Paris/5121/sinti-roma.htm and M Eycken, 'De Roma afkomstig uit Slowakije plaatsen België en Europe voor hun verantwoordelijkheid' in M Eycken (ed), *Het recent Euro-nomadisme, Roma-zigeuners in een 'nieuwe beweging'?* (Brussel, Cultuur en Migratie, themanummer, 2001) 93.

[15] See I Hancock, 'A Glossary of Romani Terms' in WO Weyrauch (ed), *Gypsy Law: Romani Legal Traditions and Culture* (Berkeley, University of California Press, 2001) 175.

to the Romani language but is now used in a broader sense, in English as well as in Romani language (Rromani).[16] As a term with the fewest negative connotations and with at least some self-ascribed references, it seems to be the most appropriate and 'workable' concept to function as a collective term. Only when referring to the wordings of jurisprudence or quoted literature, 'Gypsies' and 'Roma' will still be used.

Some General Cultural Features

The characteristics, then, to which 'Romani' is supposed to refer are, among others, an adherence to Romanya law ('Gypsy' law),[17] a (semi-) nomadic lifestyle, a strong sense of collectivity, etc.[18] Only those that, in one way or another, impinge upon the state legal sphere will be examined here. As this characterisation is overly inclusive, those groups that in the strict sense cannot be called Romani, but because of some features do relate to the issue, will also be included in the scope of this study. The point of delineation is a cultural tradition important for the way of life, which will be discussed subsequently.

The main feature under consideration here is the *(semi-)nomadic lifestyle* of the Romani people. This might, as already said, come into conflict with the sedentary assumptions of the nation-states. The contemporary meaning of nomadism can range from a true itinerary lifestyle to permanent residence in a 'mobile' home. Either way, it does have considerable significance, as even for those people who now live in houses or flats, forced into this by circumstances[19] or out of their own choice, the reference to the nomadic way of life or the nomadic milieu may remain an important feature of their identity.[20] The *economic activities* of the Romani, too, are largely inspired by the nomadic way of life. Nowadays these activities mainly concern trade, in textiles and others.

Another issue related to this nomadism is a strong sense of *family* and *collectivism* within Romani communities.[21] Since living '*en famille*' is deemed

---

[16] *Ibid* at 185.

[17] Cf Acton, above n 9; Weyrauch, above n 12; WO Weyrauch (ed), 'Gypsy Law Symposium' (1997) 2 *American Journal of Comparative Law* 225; E Banach, 'The Roma and the Native Americans: Encapsulated Communities within Larger Constitutional Regimes' (2002) 3 *Florida Journal of International Law* 353.

[18] Weyrauch, above n 12; J Kanwar, 'Preserving Gypsy Culture through Romani Law in America' (2000) 4 *Vermont Law Review* 1265.

[19] The reverse might also be true in the sense that some people might be forced into continuous migration without this corresponding to any will of their own or cultural tradition, see Eycken, above n 14, where he states that, for the Roma, nomadism is rather a survival strategy in response to state policies.

[20] http://home2.pi.be/tmachiel/doelgroe.htm.

[21] R Lee, 'The Rom-Vlach Gypsies and the Kris-Romani' in WO Weyrauch (ed), *Gypsy Law: Romani Legal Traditions and Culture* (Berkeley, University of California Press, 2001) 197.

quintessential, one seldom travels alone. A relocation of caravans therefore implies the simultaneous need for several places. This collectivism manifests itself in specific concepts of honour and property as well. An example will show that even means of 'state identification' can be considered a collective good. State identification is a challenging issue on other levels also. Romani individuality tends to be defined through the person's place within the collectivity, and in ways that do not necessarily correspond to the state's system. As such there can be problems in relation to name-giving. One Romani name can easily correspond to 10 civil names. As a consequence, official identification can become very difficult. In addition to this, there exists a reluctance, or even fear, of identification and *registration,* a fear which appears not always to be unfounded even in modern times.[22] Besides these identification problems, there may also be a problem of *nationality* or statelessness in certain (East European) countries.[23]

The adherence to *Romanya law,* finally, manifests itself mainly in the sphere of family matters, personal relations and obligations. It is the Kris, the Romanya court, which settles these issues according to Romanya law. A recent publication, for instance, mentions elopement as one of the issues that the Kris has to consider the most.[24] In 2005, the elopement of a 15-year-old girl was reported in the Belgian newspapers.[25] It seemed it had been provoked by a marriage refusal.[26] To understand the possible state

---

[22] See, eg, I Pogany, *The Roma Café: Human Rights and the Plight of the Romani People* (London, Pluto Press, 2004) and the website of the European Roma Rights Centre, www.arrc.org/Romarights_index.php.

[23] See, eg, A Haun, 'The Long Road: the Roma of Eastern and Central Europe and the Freedom of Movement and Right to Choose a Residence' (2000) 1 *George Washington International Law Review* 155; MD Darden, 'The Czech Republic and the EU's Influence on its Treatment of Roma' (2004) 4 *Vanderbilt Journal of Transnational Law* 1188; J Siklova and M Miklusakova, 'Law as an Instrument of Discrimination: Denying Citizenship to the Czech Roma' (1998) 7 *East European Constitutional Review,* available at under 'On Citizenship', http://www.law.nyu.edu/eecr/vol7num2/special/denyingcitizenship.html.

[24] Lee, above n 21 at 221. Although it is said that marriage is not so much associated with a romantic concept of love and is rather to be considered as a family matter through which relations and linkages can be created and/or sealed, there nonetheless is the contracting of a marriage through *elopement,* see M Grönfors, 'Institutional Non-Marriage in the Finnish Roma Community and its Relationship to Rom Traditional Law' in WO Weyrauch (ed), *Gypsy Law:Romani Legal Traditions and Culture* (Berkeley, University of California Press, 2001) 149–69; A Renteln, *The Cultural Defense* (New York, Oxford University Press, 2004) 120–23; cf J Timmerman, 'When her Feet Touch the Ground: Conflict between the Roma Familistic Custom of Arranged Marriage and Enforcement of International Human Rights' (2004) 2 *Journal of Transnational Law and Policy* 475.

[25] 'Roma-meisje misschien ontvoerd omdat ze huwelijksaanzoek afwees', *De Morgen,* 7 June 2005 (author's translation: 'Roma-girl possibly kidnapped because of rejection of marriage proposal').

[26] 'Ontvoerd Roma-meisje teruggevonden', *De Standaard Online,* 9 June 2005 (www.destandaard.be) (author's translation: 'Kidnapped Roma-girl was found'). Although the case law under study in this article does not concern the legal qualification of this issue, it is highly interesting: see references above n 24.

legal qualification of these phenomena, the state legislation first has to be examined.

(INTER)NATIONAL LEGAL CONTEXTS

To analyse the matter on various levels, we will take different legal contexts into account. The Belgian situation will be the point of departure. In this context, I will set out the legislative framework, after which I will consider how two prominent cases were handled. As a more jurisprudential approach is utilised in the European context, I also examine cases that were judged by the European Commission/Court. I discuss all the cases which concern respect for the individual's 'private life, family life and home' in relation to Romani. I look for the ways in which particular traits of Romani culture are incorporated in, and guaranteed by, the human rights system. This also indirectly affects the internal legal orders of the different states involved. In order to restrict the scope of the study, the various internal legal systems are not fully discussed. Instead, I include them only to the extent necessary to understand the essential theoretical significance of the decisions involved. In this light, I hope to search for the possible implications of the human rights in the European Convention on Human Rights (ECHR) on internal state orders, independent of the state legal system. In conclusion, a most interesting US case (*United States v Nicholas*) is considered on its merits. Although this case deviates from both a geographical and thematic viewpoint, I include it in the study for it gives an apt illustration of the cultural misunderstandings that may arise during the course of legal proceedings. Furthermore, it is illustrative of the ways in which Romani culture may act as an impediment to legal comprehension, quite apart from the nomadic context.

Belgian Context

General: Romani Population in Belgium

Since the Romani population is rather reluctant about registering, it is hard to give an accurate estimate of this population. Moreover, the number depends to a high degree on the definition that one uses. Reference to those living in a mobile home is not as useful in practice as it might seem, because many people are forced into regular housing, on a temporary or permanent base. The VCW (Flemish Centre for social work among caravan dwellers) nevertheless estimates the number of Romani residing in Flanders at some 10,000 to 15,000 people. In addition to this, there are deemed to be some 1,000 people passing through every year. These figures include Voyageurs,

Rom and the Manoeches.[27] The distinct category of the Roma (20,000) is not included in this calculation.[28]

Legislation

General Framework

In Belgium/Flanders, the Decree concerning the Flemish policy towards the ethnic-cultural minorities is of special importance. As one of these ethnic-cultural minorities:

> 'caravan dwellers' are considered as 'persons with a nomadic culture, who reside legally in Belgium and who traditionally live, or have lived, in a caravan, in particular the autochthonous Voyageurs on the one hand and the 'Gypsies' on the other, and those who live together with these people or are descendants thereof in the first degree.[29]

This Decree thus forms the basis of a policy that addresses the issue of nomadic people. It first of all implies an identification of Romani as caravan dwellers. When working with this 'received' definition, one should be aware that, however practical a solution it may be, it includes certain categories of people while excluding other similar ones. For instance, as it includes only those who traditionally live a nomadic life, it excludes new entrant groups such as New Age Travellers. In contrast, people who are unwillingly forced into a static lifestyle might still be considered caravan dwellers if, in the wording of the Decree, they 'have lived' a nomadic lifestyle or if they are descendants in the first degree of people that do live nomadically.

Subsequently, a decision of the Flemish government of 2001 stated that a caravan should be acknowledged as having the status of a full habitat.[30] In order to comply with this decision, the Flemish Housing Code (Vlaamse Wooncode) incorporated this nomadic mode of habitat into its textual framework. It is thus fully covered by the protective measures concerning

---

[27] Vlaams Minderhedencentrum., *Voyageur, Manoesj, Rom: Cultuur, historiek, woonwagenwerk* (Brussels, Vlaams Minderhedencentrum, 2002) 3; T Machiels, *Keeping the Distance or Taking the Chances* (Brussels, ENAR, 2002) 17 and http://home2.pi.be/tmachiel/doelgroe.htm.

[28] Y Matras, *Problems Arising in connection with the International Mobility of the Roma in Europe* (CDMG, 1996), available at www.social.coe.int/en/cohesion/action/publi/roma/matras.htm.

[29] Article 2, 3rd Decreet 28 April 1998 inzake het Vlaamse beleid ten aanzien van etnisch-culturele minderheden, Belgisch Staatsblad 19 June 1996 (author's translation).

[30] Beslissing Vlaamse regering 11 mei 2001, as cited in *Jaarrapport 2001 inzake het Vlaamse beleid naar etnisch-culturele minderheden* (Brussel, ICEM/Ministerie van de Vlaamse Gemeenschap, 2002) 109, available at www.wvc.vlaanderen.be/minderheden/ICEM/jaarrapport2001/.

housing. What is more, guarantees relating to one's 'home', based on the Belgian Constitution, are now fully applicable.

Constitutional Rights

First of all, art 15 of the Constitution guarantees the inviolability of the home. Secondly, art 22 of the Constitution states that everybody is entitled to respect for his private and family life. As a partial reflection of Art 8 of the ECHR, it is especially this article that raises the question whether there could be a positive obligation for the Belgian state to provide a sufficient number of 'residing places' for caravans in order to meet the exigencies of this constitutional right. Article 22 does indeed comprise a positive obligation on the state to ensure the protection of respect for one's private and family life, which clause has direct effect.[31] But the exact extent of this positive obligation remains vague. One can only say that if the scope of this constitutional right is to be interpreted as fully analogous to the scope of Art 8, art 22 does hold an obligation for the Belgian state to provide for a sufficient number of dwelling places. Thirdly, art 23, which guarantees the right to 'proper' housing, is particularly relevant. Since the nomadic way of life is acknowledged full legal status, one would expect it to be treated equally with other forms of dwelling, such as living in a house or an apartment. For that population where the reference to a nomadic abode is a fundamental element of cultural identity, this right might be the ultimate means through which the right to one's own cultural identity can be implemented. Here, the question arises as to whether this right to proper housing also includes a right to reside in accordance with one's culture and lifestyle. The right to live in a caravan (the right to nomadism) would in this interpretation necessarily imply the right to stop and park the caravan.[32] Since this article does not have any direct effect, no subjective rights can be drawn from it. It therefore cannot serve as an independent ground for a claim. But it can nevertheless have important effects through its other working mechanisms: the duty incumbent on the judiciary to interpret norms in accordance with the Constitution, on the one hand, and the 'stand-still' effect,[33] on the other hand.

---

[31] E Brems, 'De nieuwe grondrechten in de Belgische Grondwet en hun verhouding tot het internationale, inzonderheid het Europese recht' (1995) 12 *Tijdschrift voor Bestuurswetenschappen en Publiek Recht* 625. Article 8 of the ECHR also holds the positive obligation for member states to ensure these rights, but it differs from the Belgian Constitution inso-far as this positive obligation was not deemed to be sufficiently precise and unconditional to have direct effect.

[32] P Delhez, 'Le droit au logement des gens du voyage: une revendication incongrue' (1997) 3 *Droit en Quart Monde* 10; L Tholomé, 'L'article 23 de la Constitution n'est pas un simple déclaration de principe' (2000) 4 *Echos du Logement* 121.

[33] The stand-still effect entails the principle that the degree of the safeguarding of constitutional rights may not decrease, once established: E Brems, 'De nieuwe grondrechten in de Belgische Grondwet en hun verhouding tot het internationale, inzonderheid het Europese recht' (1995) 12 *Tijdschrift voor Bestuurswetenschappen en Publiek Recht* 631.

Other Relevant Legislation

When considering the plight of Romani people, there are in addition a number of practical regulations with significant repercussions. As to urban planning, it is important to know that a permit is necessary for the stationing of a mobile home, except when placed near a permitted building.[34] This is precisely what I mean by criminalisation. Violations of town and country planning requirements, as well as breaches of traffic regulations, are policed by the municipality as being a public nuisance or a violation of the civil order.[35] The legal position of nomadic people is furthermore determined by the regulations governing one's domicile. This concept is the point of reference for a great many rights and duties, such as social security.[36] People who do not stay in one place for a period of more than six months, for whom it is legally impossible to have their domicile at their 'place of residence',[37] require what are termed 'reference addresses'. As such, the problem for actively itinerant people remains twofold. First, they must appeal to a natural person, who is willing to function as a referee.[38] Secondly, the use of a reference address makes it impossible to obtain a trading licence. However, trade is the profession par excellence for these itinerant people.[39] Here again, the mere existence of legislation can result in criminalisation.

[34] Article 99 s 5 Decreet Vl Gem 18 May 1999 houdende de organisatie van de ruimtelijke ordening, Belgisch Staatsblad 8 June 1999 in conjunction with art 3 Besluit van de Vlaamse regering 14 April 2000 tot bepaling van de vergunningsplichtige functiewijzigingen en van de werken, handelingen en wijzigingen waarvoor geen stedenbouwkundige vergunning nodig is, Belgisch Staatsblad 18 May 2000.

[35] For the sake of completeness we have to mention the possibility of depenalisation. The legislator made it possible for the municipalities to handle the illegal stationing of caravans in an administrative way. It is a matter of local policy whether do so in practice or not, cf Omzendbrief 3 January 2005 aangaande de uitvoering van de wetten van 13 May 1999 tot invoering van gemeentelijke administratieve sancties, van 7 May 2004 tot wijziging van de wet van 8 April 1965 betreffende de jeugdbescherming en de nieuwe gemeentewet en van 17 June 2004 tot wijziging van de nieuwe gemeentewet, Belgisch Staatsblad 20 January 2005.

[36] J Fierens, 'Logement familial et droit au logement' in P Delnoy, Y-H Leleu and E Vieujean (eds), *Le logement familial* (Diegem, Story-Scientia, 1999) 441; A Ottevaere, 'Le droit des tsiganes à la protection sociale. La culture du voyage au pays des sédentaires' (1996) 7 *Sociaalrechtelijke Kronieken* 315.

[37] Article 1 Wet Bevolkingsregisters.

[38] For the region of Antwerp it is even deemed as one of the most problematic issues, since around 400 people are all located at one reference address belonging to a couple who are 70 years old. The question of what will happen in the near future is a very urgent one (personal communication of a non-Romani fieldworker).

[39] Thus, whenever the local police hear that illegal trade has taken place, they confiscate any of the goods they can still find (personal communication of non-Romani fieldworker). This could be solved by opening up the possibility of placing one's referential address at the address of a 'legal entity'. In the process of putting into effect the Decree related to ethnic-cultural minorities, more than one official 'corporation' has been called into existence that could serve such a goal.

Jurisprudence

A good jurisprudential illustration of the overall issue can be found in a judgment of the Justice of the Peace of Verviers.[40] A few 'Gypsies' were to be evicted from an industrial site where they had parked themselves illegally. They claimed to be willing to leave this particular site voluntarily, but only when the local government would give them another site suitable for them to live on. The authorities at Verviers did not consider it their task to provide them with such a site and thus refused to do so. In court, the Justice of the Peace ruled that it was indeed the duty of the authorities to adopt specific measures in order to guarantee the right to proper housing. According to him, this obligation implied the duty to provide for appropriate housing when 'Gypsies' are to be evicted and the term 'appropriate' implies that the housing offered must accord with the cultural lifestyle. The government thus could not simply fulfil this duty by providing them with a social welfare house, if that did not correspond to their wishes or cultural traditions. By giving it this express interpretation, this ruling is an accurate illustration of what I mean by multicultural jurisprudence and a firm step in the right direction.

In a similar case, where some 300 caravan dwellers had illegally occupied a private site, the President of the Court of First Instance at Nivelles (Nijvel) had to decide whether an eviction order was to be given.[41] After a first judgment, the caravan dwellers tried to draw attention to the fact that, because there was an urgent lack of official sites, they were in practical terms forced to park illegally. In the second judgment, the President stated that there was indeed a positive obligation for the state to provide a sufficient number of sites. It could not be the task of the citizens to put their property at the disposal of the Romani community, so the local government, in the opinion of the President, had to provide the necessary infrastructure for caravan dwellers. This judgment thus supported the first in the sense that it favoured a multicultural jurisprudence.

European Context

General

In the European context there has already been quite a bit of attention focused on the Romani problems. First, the OSCE has recognised the fact

---

[40] Vred. Verviers 30 June 2000 (2000) 4 *Echos du Logement* 119, note L Tholomé. Although this is not the Flemish part of Belgium, it can nevertheless be used as an illustration here because of the similar legal framework.

[41] Vz.Rb Nijvel 15 October 2003, unpublished and Vz Rb Nijvel 17 October 2003, unpublished: as cited in J Kusters, 'Het recht op huisvesting voor woonwagenbewoners' (2004) 28 *Juristenkrant* 11.

that the majority of Romani lead a non-migratory lifestyle, but that this, more often than not, is a consequence of forced policies, especially in Central and Eastern Europe.[42] Their report thus (re)commends the regularisation of the plight of the Roma people and points out the importance of freedom of choice and the obligation to provide the possibility of leading a nomadic lifestyle.

Also, the Council of Europe has acknowledged the special position of the Romani people within Europe:[43] 'A special place among the minorities is reserved for 'Gypsies'. Living scattered all over Europe, not having a country to call their own, they are a true European minority, but one that does not fit into the definitions of national or linguistic minorities'.[44] This touches upon the essence of the problem, as people with a nomadic lifestyle, because of the absence of territorial commitment, are truly *outlaws* of a sedentary society.[45] The problems are manifold. The definitional capacity of law and the (lack of) conceptual correspondence between different cultural frameworks play a manifest role in the granting of some basic human rights. It, for instance, obscures the granting of the freedom of movement and the right to choose a residence for the Romani people, a right that could nevertheless be highly relevant and in a way even mirrors their nomadic culture.[46] In the framework of this analysis, I focus on Art 8 of the ECHR as this article deals with the same issues as those treated in the Belgian context. The reasoning of the Commission and the Court form a good illustration of a possible human rights approach toward this matter.

[42] See www.osce.org/hcnm/documents/recommendations/roma/index.php3.

[43] Parliamentary Assembly, Recommendation 563 (1969) 'On the situation of Gypsies and other travellers in Europe', as cited in M Danblaki, *On Gypsies: Texts Issued by International Institutions* (Midi-Pyrénées, Gypsy Research Centre CRDP, 1994) 54.

[44] Parliamentary Assembly, Recommendation 1203 (1993) 'On Gypsies in Europe', as cited in M Danblaki, *On Gypsies: Texts Issued by International Institutions* (Midi-Pyrénées, Gypsy Research Centre CRDP, 1994) 55. After recommendation 1203 there followed another: European Commission against Racism and Intolerance, General Policy Recommendation 3 on Combating Racism and Intolerance against Roma/Gypsies, available at www.social.coe.int/en/cohesion/action/publi/roma/append8.htm, as well as Parliamentary Assembly, Recommendation 1557 (2002) concerning the Plight of Roma in Europe, available at http://assembly.coe.int. See also European Committee on Migration, *Report on the Situation of Gypsies in Europe* (CDMG, 1995) 11 final. This implies a drastic U-turn in comparison with a former statement where the nomadic lifestyle itself is problematised by the Parliamentary Assembly (Recommendation 563 (1969) 'On the Situation of Gypsies and other Travellers in Europe', as cited in M Danblaki, *On Gypsies: Texts Issued by International Institutions* (Midi-Pyrénées, Gypsy Research Centre CRDP, 1994) 54: 'Considering that permanent residence for Gypsies and Travellers are almost necessary conditions to enable them to receive a proper education and to adapt to modern society'.

[45] Girasoli, above n 11 at 131.

[46] It is, however, obvious that it deals with another conception of nomadism: see especially Haun, above n 23; M Nys, 'Les Tsiganes: ces exclus de l'Europe' (1995) 6 *Droit en Quart Monde* 3.

European Convention on Human Rights

Within the framework of the ECHR, it is especially Art 8 of the ECHR that has proved to be a valuable instrument for cultural minorities. The guarantees of respect for one's private life, family life and home that this article secures have been interpreted so as to include the right for a minority group to enjoy respect for the particular lifestyle they have. The first time that this was stated as such was by the Commission in 1983 in the case of *G/Norway*. In this case, however, the facts involved the particular lifestyle of the Sami.[47] Later, some important cases defined the meaning of this basic principle for the Romani population. First, there were a few cases where no violation of Art 8, nor of Art 14, was deemed to have occurred. These cases raise some fundamental issues, some of which unfortunately as yet remain unanswered by the Commission/Court.

Jurisprudence: European Commission/Court of Human Rights

The first significant claim was made in *Powell v United Kingdom*,[48] where the applicants were a few non-travelling Roma who had been established on a municipal caravan site for 15 years. For five months a year, they travelled with one of the caravans looking for jobs as seasonal workers, while another caravan stayed at the site. At that time in England, the Caravan Sites Act 1968 was still in effect. On the basis of this particular Act, the applicants were evicted from the site. The same would not have been possible if the vehicles had fallen under the scope of the Mobile Homes Act 1983, which guaranteed better protection and was in force concurrently with the Caravan Sites Act but applied to other kinds of sites. Thus, apart from the eviction being a breach of their right to respect for their home, the legal situation was, according to the applicants, a breach of Art 14 on the basis of the fact that non-Roma people were better protected under the Mobile Homes Act 1983. The Commission did not find a breach of Art 8, although the existence of a limitation of this right was acknowledged. This limitation was, however, justified because it was needed for guaranteeing the rights of others. The government had the duty to provide adequate sites for all 'Gypsies'. This would become impossible if everyone, notwithstanding long absence, could claim a permanent residence. Furthermore, the different legal status of the inhabitants was based on the classification of the site and not on the status of the person residing there, thus no breach of Art 14 had occurred, according to the Commission.

---

[47] *G/Norway*, ECHR nos 9778/81 and 9415/81, 3 October 1983, European Commission of Human Rights, *Decision and Reports*, no 53, 30.
[48] *P/United Kingdom*, ECHR no 14751/89, 12 December 1990, European Commission of Human Rights, *Decision and Reports*, nos 67, 264.

In *Beckers v Netherlands*,[49] again the Commission stated that the particular limitation of Art 8, as practised by the government of the Netherlands through the Woonwagenwet, was deemed legitimate. The fact that only certain people could get a permit to reside in a caravan served a legitimate goal, in view of the over-population of the Netherlands. Moreover, the measures taken were not disproportionate in view of the fact that the applicant himself did not belong to a minority group that deserved special protection under Art 8. This is in itself a very significant ground because here the Commission acknowledged the special role for culture. If a Roma had filed a comparable complaint, the result might have been different.

In *van de Vin v Netherlands*,[50] another line of argument was followed by the applicants, but was not accepted by the Commission. The complaint was based on Art 2 of the Fourth Protocol, which guarantees a right to free movement and free choice of residence for whomever 'is legally on a territory'. This article, in the words of the Commission, could not imply a right to a specific abode if a person did not have a legal title to reside in a place.

In a subsequent case, a very important question was raised concerning the duty of states to provide a sufficient number of sites. The authorities had not provided a sufficient number of places, and people with a nomadic lifestyle were under the constant threat of evictions and fines, according to the applicants in *Smith v United Kingdom (No 1)*.[51] Although it was a matter of national discretion how to implement certain obligations through policy, the Commission was of the opinion that the specific circumstances made it clear that there were a sufficient number of sites. Article 8 furthermore does not imply an explicit right to accommodation.

In *Smith v United Kingdom (No 2)*,[52] the applicants went even further and stated that the UK legislation had led to the criminalising of the nomadic lifestyle, and that this legislation thus violated Art 8. The UK legislation made it a crime to camp in places which are not specifically designated for that purpose. Moreover, as this legislation was directed toward 'Gypsies', it was in violation of Art 14. An in-depth analysis of this statement was unfortunately not obtained, as the case foundered on a formal argument. The applicants did not prove to be a personal victim of the measures, since they camped on an authorised site and did not show that they wanted to move.

---

[49] *Beckers/Netherlands*, ECHR no 12344/86, 25 February 1991, available at http://hudoc. echr.coe.int/hudoc/.

[50] *Van de Vin/Netherlands*, ECHR no 13628/88, 8 April 1992, available at http://hudoc. echr.coe.int/hudoc/.

[51] *Smith/United Kingdom (No 1)*, ECHR no 1445/88 (), 4 September 1991, available at http://hudoc.echr.coe.int/hudoc/.

[52] *Smith/United Kingdom (No 2)*, ECHR no 18401/91, 6 May 1993, available at http:// hudoc.echr.coe.int/hudoc/.

In the next case, *Buckley v United Kingdom*,[53] the Commission determined that Art 8 had been violated. The case involved a single mother who had bought a plot of land with the object of placing a caravan on it. She was, however, not given a permit to do so and consequently received an enforcement notice after she put her caravan on the plot. She was then fined for not complying with the enforcement notice. She filed a complaint, stating that her rights under Art 8 as well as Art 14 had been violated. With respect to the alleged discrimination, the applicant claimed that 'the criminalisation of unauthorised camping discriminated against Gypsies by preventing them from pursuing their traditional lifestyle'. Unfortunately, the Commission did not express any opinion on this matter. Apparently, it could not examine this aspect because the applicant could not show that she had been directly and immediately affected by the legislation objected to in the way she claimed.

The applicant, however, also argued that a violation of her right to respect for her private and family life and home had occurred on the grounds that she could not place her caravan on her own land, unauthorised camping was a crime and the official sites were either full or dangerous because of the high concentration of criminal activities on such camping sites. In the first instance, the Commission did think that a violation of Art 8 had occurred. The measures taken by the authorities served a legitimate goal, but were not deemed to be proportionate. The disproportionate element furthermore made the limitation inconsistent with the requirement of necessity in a democratic society. Precisely because of the fact that, in this case, there were no real alternatives for accommodation for the applicant, the aims of the policy considerations (highway safety, the preservation of the environment and public health) were guaranteed through a disproportionately severe limitation of the right of the applicant. It is noteworthy that the Commission had accepted that 'living in a caravan was an integral and deeply-held part of the applicant's Gypsy lifestyle and that the traditional lifestyle of a minority could attract the guarantees concerning private life, home and family'.[54]

When the case was then taken to the Court, it found to the contrary that the governmental measures were proportionate, thus reversing the decision of the Commission. The Court did nevertheless confirm that a caravan must

---

[53] *Buckley/United* Kingdom, ECHR), 25 September 1995, available at www.echr.coe.int; 'Aménagement, environnement, urbanisme et droit foncier' (1997) 217 *Droit en Quart Monde* 13 note A Ottevaere; (1996) *Journal des tribunaux—Droit européen* 230; (1997) *NJB* 813; (1996) IV *Reports of Judgments and Decisions: European Court of Human Rights* 1271 and (1997) *Revue trimestrielle des droits de l'homme* 47, note O De Schutter. See also H O'Nions, 'The Right to Respect for Home and Family Life: the First in a Series of "Gypsy Cases" to Challenge UK Legislation' (1996) 5 *Web Journal of Current Legal Issues*, http://webjcli.ncl. ac.uk/1996/issue5/o'nions5.html; O De Schutter, 'Le droit au mode de vie tsigane devant la Cour européenne des droits de l'homme' (1997) 1 *Revue trimestrielle des droits de l'homme* 64.

[54] S Poulter, *Ethnicity, Law and Human Rights: the English Experience* (Oxford, Oxford University Press, 1998) 189.

be considered to be a home, and is therefore entitled to the protection of Art 8, even if illegally parked. Every interference with its legal position through planning laws has to be compatible with the rules laid down in the second paragraph of Art 8.

What seems to be an element of considerable importance in the reasoning of the Court, as well as in that of the Commission, is the question of whether or not there are sufficient alternatives. The specific constellation of facts in this case leaves open the question as to whether it would, or would not be disproportionate to prosecute people who camp on an unauthorised site when there is no real alternative.[55] As the applicant was not in real life subject to legal proceedings or threatened with eviction, the Court and Commission did not have to deal with this question.

The same matter was considered by the Commission in *Turner v United Kingdom*,[56] although it was only a subsidiary matter. The Commission in this case seems to have adopted the reasoning of the Court in the *Buckley* case insofar as it stressed the wide margin of appreciation that nation-states have, especially in planning matters. As the land involved was part of a designated heritage area, the accommodation considerations of the applicant, according to the Commission, could not prevail.

A negative answer was also given in the following five cases: *Chapman v United Kingdom*,[57] *Beard v United Kingdom*,[58] *Coster v United Kingdom*,[59] *Lee v United Kingdom*,[60] *and Jane Smith v United Kingdom*.[61] All five concerned 'Gypsies' who bought a piece of land on which to put their caravans, for which the permit was denied. While nevertheless parking there, the applicants were ordered to leave and were fined. In each of these cases the Court acknowledges that as to the rights protected under Art 8:

> the applicant's occupation of her caravan is an integral part of her ethnic identity as a 'Gypsy', reflecting the long tradition of that minority of following a travelling lifestyle. This is the case even though, under the pressure of development and diverse policies or from their own volition, many 'Gypsies' no longer live a wholly nomadic existence and increasingly settle for long periods in one place in order to facilitate, for example, the education of their children. Measures which affect the applicant's stationing of her caravans have therefore a wider impact than on the right to respect for home. They also affect her ability to lead her private and family life in accordance with that tradition.[62]

---

[55] *Ibid* at 191.
[56] *Turner/United Kingdom*, ECRM, 26 February 1997, available at www.echr.coe.int.
[57] *Chapman/United Kingdom*, ECHR, 18 January 2001, available at www.echr.coe.int.
[58] *Beard/United Kingdom*, ECHR, 18 January 2001, available at www.echr.coe.int.
[59] *Coster/United Kingdom*, ECHR, 18 January 2001, available at www.echr.coe.int.
[60] *Lee/United Kingdom*, ECHR, , 18 January 2001, available at www.echr.coe.int.
[61] *Jane Smith/United Kingdom*, ECHR, 18 January 2001, available at www.echr.coe.int.
[62] *Chapman*, above n 57 at 73; *Lee*, above n 60 at 75; *Jane Smith*, above n 61 at 80; *Coster*, above n 59 at 87; and *Beard*, above n 58 at 84.

In this particular case, however, the Court did not consider there to be a violation of these rights, partly because it was not persuaded that there alternatives were unavailable. The Court also mentioned that, because the applicant bought a piece of land to find a long-term residence for her caravan, 'it would appear that the applicant does not in fact wish to pursue an itinerant lifestyle... Thus the present case is not concerned as such with traditional itinerant Gypsy lifestyle'. However, seven judges suggested, in a joint dissenting opinion, that there was, in fact, a violation of Art 8 since the available alternatives were in this case too limited.[63] It thus did not seem to be a disagreement at the level of the principal matter, but rather one on the weighing of the very specific circumstances.

It was not until 2004, in *Connors v United Kingdom*,[64] that the Court held that there had been a violation of Art 8. The case concerned a 'Gypsy' family who used to lead a traditional travelling lifestyle but finally settled on a local gypsy site because of infinite harassment and compulsory moving. Even there, they suffered from excessive nuisance and lack of safety, so they decided to move into a rented house. They were, however, unable to adapt and again applied for a plot on the same site where they had lived before. The application was granted and after a while, the daughter occupied the adjacent plot with her partner. A dispute arose between the city council and the family. The argument escalated and the council gave notice to quit the plot. As the family disputed this decision, the council finally evicted the family following summary proceedings, without there being any alternative, relevant accommodation available.

In Court, it was not disputed that the eviction constituted an interference with the applicant's rights under Art 8. The only matter under discussion was whether this interference was necessary in a democratic society and proportionate in light of the aspired goal. Here, the Court first differentiated the present case from the preceding cases[65] on the ground that the margin of appreciation was to be interpreted rather more narrowly in the present case. It did not concern the question of general planning policy but procedural protection for a particular category of persons instead. The margin moreover varies according to the degree in which there is an intrusion in the personal sphere of the applicant. On the other hand, the Court did follow its former jurisprudence in stating that the vulnerable position of 'Gypsies' necessitates some special considerations and implies a positive obligation for the state to facilitate the 'Gypsy' way of life. The facts in this case made it appear that the situation in England was quite the opposite, as there were rather considerable obstacles in the way of 'Gypsies' pursuing an

---

[63] Joint dissenting opinion of Judges Pastor Ridruejo, Bonello, Tulkens, Stra, Nicka, Lorenzen, Fischbach en Casadevall.

[64] *Connors/United Kingdom*, ECHR, 27 May 2004, available at www.echr.coe.int.

[65] More precisely the *Buckley* and *Chapman* cases: *Connors*, above n 64 at 17 and 18.

actively nomadic lifestyle, while at the same time those who decide to take up a settled lifestyle were excluded from procedural protection. The procedure of eviction followed thus constituted a violation of Art 8 since there were not enough procedural safeguards and the interference was therefore not proportionate to the legitimate aim.

United States v Nicholas

Another interesting case, discussed at length by Sutherland, who was asked to appear as a cultural expert in it, is *United States v Nicholas*.[66] Sonny Nicholas, a so-called 'Gypsy', bought a Ford Mustang with the social security card of his younger nephew, who was, in fact, only five years old. The car dealer later on noticed this peculiar date of birth and asked Sonny to return the car. US legislation apparently makes the simple use of a false social security card a felony: 'a person who, with intent to deceive, falsely represents his or her number to obtain something of value or for any other purpose is a felon'.[67] The rationale behind this is that by doing so (false representation of numbers), one can easily attempt theft.

However, the underlying presupposition seems to be that one would not simply use another person's card as a matter of implied collective ownership. In fact, most people probably would not be inclined to do so and a 'general' perception corresponds with the one that is embedded in the law, namely that such a card is highly personal and individual. The issue at stake here was that such thinking was not necessarily applicable to 'Gypsies'. They do, in fact, have a rather different historical attitude towards identification cards then non-migratory people usually do. This legislation seems to presuppose a particular use of these cards, such that the use of another person's card necessarily implies a wrongful purpose. Because of this presupposed culturally determined behaviour, the law thus simply omits the condition of proof of a wrongful purpose to come to the definition of a felony. Yet the felonious intent should be proven and not so easily taken for granted.

The fact is that for 'Gypsies' there does not necessarily have to be such a linkage (the use of another person's card and the existence of any intent to commit a crime). The demonstration of this was precisely the role which the anthropologist was intended to play in this case. She was able to provide cultural understanding as to the 'Gypsy' worldview. Her testimony concerned the idea of collective property, as grounded in this particular

---

[66] A Sutherland, 'Complexities of U.S. Law and Gypsy Identity' in WO Weyrauch (ed), *Gypsy Law: Romani Legal Traditions and Culture* (Berkeley, University of California Press, 2001) 231–42.

[67] Statute 42 USC 408 (g) (2) as cited in Sutherland, above n 66 at 233.

cultural heritage. As a matter of cultural defence, the defendant claimed that his (innocent) behaviour was merely inspired by his cultural tradition. This means (and that is the third element of defence here) that this legislation affects one particular ethnic group in a disproportionate way, as the ascription of criminal liability corresponds to traditional 'Gypsy' behaviour, without there being any evidence of harm to someone or something in this, nor there being any attempt (intent) of harm in doing so. Thus, this legislation is ostensibly discriminatory because it 'irrationally and disproportionally' denies equal protection to 'Gypsies'. Consequently, it was argued that it was unconstitutional on the basis of the Fifth Amendment of the US Constitution. Notwithstanding these arguments, Sonny was convicted and given a custodial sentence.

MULTICULTURAL JURISPRUDENCE?

Although it is invoked in the courts, one can see that a defence based on Romani culture as such is no guarantee of success. The judge often has to decide on two aspects, two sides of the same coin. Is a specific cultural tradition to be taken into account when applying and interpreting a law (for instance, when dealing with the criminal concept of intent)? And is legislation that has a disproportionate impact on one ethnic group in particular to be considered legitimate? In order to reach substantive equality, it is often necessary to treat different situations differently. With regard to Romani, this has not always been the case. And when Romani culture is not taken into account as a differential factor, the aspired for equality remains formal only. After having sketched the primary outlines of the judicial position towards these questions above, I will now examine how far these responses do or do not provide insights into the Romani situation. First, I will do this for the two different legal contexts, after which I will offer some general observations concerning the concept of culture and the role of anthropology in legal proceedings.

Belgian Context

In Belgian legislation, living in a caravan is officially acknowledged as a mode of residence. The status of a nomadic habitat is considered equal to any other accommodation. Ideally then, this fundamental equation should also entail the granting in practice of the same protective rights. At the least, the constitutional right to proper housing should be equally guaranteed. In reality this does not always appear to be the case. By way of measures of urban planning and through regulation of one's domicile, certain traits of the nomadic lifestyle are subjected to serious pressure. But a true recognition of the nomadic home would require that the same guarantees are granted in the very concrete elaboration and application[68] of legislation relating to one's home. As we have seen in the preceding discussion, there is a lack of commitment with regard to these concrete measures, which is in striking opposition to the fundamental acknowledgement. Measures of urban planning do, however, also affect the constitutional right to proper housing and it is precisely because of a neglect of the specificity of the Romani situation that this right is not equally guaranteed. Another such example can be found in the rules pertaining to the confiscation of a caravan. Confiscating one's home implies respecting a certain procedure in which some protective rules are to be followed. A caravan may, however, be considered as 'moveable property'. Because one's home is implicitly assumed to be immovable property, the rules protecting one's dwelling therefore do not apply to a caravan and thus, no protective measures are granted. Hence it seems to be forgotten that, in order to grant such rights effectively, the implementation at the practical level hinges on this presumption.

As to the approach taken in the jurisprudence, I mentioned above the two Belgian cases where the court decided that it is the responsibility of the authorities to provide sufficient sites in the case of an eviction. This multicultural character came even more to the fore when the Justice of the Peace of Verviers stated that the constitutional right to proper housing implies housing that is in accordance with the cultural lifestyle of 'Gypsies' and thus cannot be met by simply providing a social welfare house. As was noted, this could already be called 'multicultural jurisprudence'.

Culture in this case does have a corrective effect, since a straightforward application of property and eviction laws would not allow such reasoning. However laudable such a jurisprudential incorporation may be, one can ask whether it is desirable to leave the inscription of this constitutional right into other legislation up to the judge. Perhaps an adaptation on the legislative level might be more appropriate to secure these rights. On the one hand, it might be very difficult to predict the exact extent to which differential treatment is necessary in order to achieve substantive equality. Since it mainly involves very concrete measures, one could probably say that a conscious jurisprudence might suffice and even is more apt to give a dynamic answer. On the other hand, the legislative apparatus must at least show a certain responsiveness toward these cultural features. When looking at the legislation, one sees not only that cultural difference is usually not accommodated but that, moreover, legislation often makes it impossible for the judge to accommodate it because the cultural aspect is penalised. In doing this, the legislator seems to choose the solution that is quite the opposite of accommodation,

---

[68] For an example of a (possibly) discriminatory application of communal regulations in relation to the Romani population, see Raad van State no 35.212, 19 June 1990, Arr Rv St 1990.

namely exclusion and repression. The highly symbolic value of criminal law[69] is in this case used to regulate inclusion and exclusion and to reaffirm societal values that are deemed to be of special importance.[70]

Even when inclusion is offered, it is offered in a conditional way and can only be realised when there is a willingness to conform.[71] When the government does provide sites to satisfy some basic needs of Romani people, the government can impose specific conduct requirements in order to grant the right to reside on such a site. A significant combination exists, however, when the providing of sites corresponds to enhanced policing powers of the government for those who do not wish to reside there, as was the former situation in England. Accommodation of minorities' culture does, however, inevitably imply a certain degree of disciplining into conformity, and of course incorporation in the legal system implies a willingness to comply with this inclusion. The Romani people have not always shown such willingness, as indicated by their reluctance as regards registration and by their suspicion towards nation-states in general. As an instrument for control, the law thus offers them the choice either to inscribe themselves into a regulated mode of nomadic habitat, thereby conforming with (spatial) normality, or to be totally outlawed, facing extra-governmental disciplinary powers as a consequence.[72]

European Context

When the Council of Europe declared in 1993 that 'Gypsies' are a true European minority, the wording provided an accurate characterisation of the matter involved: Romani people do indeed 'live scattered all over Europe', 'without a country to call their own' and they 'do not fit into the regular minorities definitions'.[73] When dealing with such a transnational

---

[69] See, eg, WO Weyrauch, 'The Unconscious Meanings of Crime and Punishment' (1999) 2 *Buffalo Criminal Law Review* 19 (Review of MG Duncan, *Romantic Outlaws, Beloved Prisons: the Unconscious Meanings of Crime and Punishment* (New York, New York University Press, 1996)).

[70] Cf D Cowan and D Lomax, 'Policing Unauthorized Camping' (2003) 2 *Journal of Law and Society* 283; Cf A Bancroft, 'No Interest in Land: Legal and Spatial Enclosure of Gypsy-Travellers in Britain' (2000) 4 *Space and Polity* 41.

[71] Cf Cowan and Lomax, above n 70.

[72] For England see, eg, Cowan and Lomax, above n 70 at 289; S Campbell, 'Gypsies: the Criminalisation of a Way of Life?' (1995) 1 *Criminal Law Review* 28; H O'Nions, 'The Marginalisation of Gypsies' (1995) *Web Journal of Current Legal Issues*, http://webjcli.ncl.ac.uk/articles3/onions3.html; P Niner, 'Accomodating Nomadism? An Examination of Accommodation Options for Gypsies and Travellers in England' (2004) 2 *Housing Studies* 154; ATP Smith, 'The Criminal Justice and Public Order Act 1994: the Public Order Elements' (1995) 1 *Criminal Law Review* 19.

[73] Parliamentary Assembly, Recommendation 1203 (1993) 'On Gypsies in Europe', as cited in M Danblaki, *On Gypsies: Texts Issued by International Institutions* (Midi-Pyrénées, Gypsy Research Centre CRDP, 1994) 55.

minority, it seems only natural to deal with the matter on a transnational level. And the ECHR offers the possibility to afford protection. More specifically, the human right to respect for one's private life, family life and home, as embedded in Art 8, does imply that the state is to take active steps in order to guarantee effective protection.[74] Article 14 also secures the equal enjoyment of, among others, this right.

The *jurisprudential* interpretation that the European Court has given to Art 8, moreover, fully confirms its applicability to the (semi-)nomadic dwelling of Romani people. As seen above, the Court first of all included culture as a distinctive factor[75] (including Romani culture)[76] and even an illegally parked caravan is to be considered a 'home' and thus entitled to the protection of Art 8.[77] As they are bound to have an effect on cultural identity, planning laws and measures that have an effect on the stationing of caravans should be in correspondence with Art 8.[78] The government has to avoid adopting detrimental measures and, furthermore, the positive obligation that Art 8 entails in these cases has been translated into the duty to provide an adequate and sufficient number of sites.[79]

So, although the European Court was willing to acknowledge the right to respect Romani culture, it only once decided that a violation of this right had occurred. In the other cases, the absence of any practical repercussions stands in a striking contrast with the recognition on the more fundamental level. What also seems to be remarkable is that the discrimination path has never really been successful. In *Connors v United Kingdom*, the alleged violation of Art 14 was not considered separately, in view of the established violation of Art 8. Previously, the European Court (and/or Commission) had not found a violation of Art 14 of the ECHR, for formal reasons in some cases, or because of an evaluation of the factual circumstances in others (there were enough alternatives). However, it is not that difficult to discern certain discriminatory elements. Following the dissenting opinion of Judge Pettiti in the *Buckley* case, one cannot deny that the totality of administrative rules with which Romani people have to comply place a particular burden on nomadic people that others do not have to bear.[80] As the concept of discrimination applied in Art 14[81] relies on the absence of

---

[74] Cf P De Hert, *Art. 8 EVRM en het Belgisch recht. De bescherming van privacy, gezin, woonst en communicatie* (Gent, Mys and Breesch, 1998) 287.

[75] *G/Norway*, above n 47, 3 October 1983, DR, nos 53, 30.

[76] *P/United Kingdom*, above n 48; *Beckers*, above n 49.

[77] *Buckley*, above n 53.

[78] *Buckley*, above n 53; *Chapman*, above n 57; *Beard*, above n 58; *Coster*, above n 59; *Lee*, above n 60; *Jane Smith*, above n 61.

[79] *P/United Kingdom*, above n 48; *Smith/United Kingdom (No 1)*, above n 51.

[80] Cf Dissenting opinion Judge Pettiti in *Buckley*, above n 53; T Gerbranda, 'Artikel 8 EVRM: geen recht op vrije standplaatskeuze woonwagen' (1998) 3 *NJCM-Bulletin* 312.

[81] See also ECHR, Art 1, Protocol 12.

an objective and reasonable justification for a difference in treatment,[82] one cannot escape a similar examination of the reasonableness, proportionality, etc, of the justification called upon. These considerations lie at the core of the matter involved since the cultural presuppositions that are implied in state legal systems do indirectly discriminate against certain populations. One thus has to ask oneself, case by case, to what extent such discrimination is objectively justified in the light of the interests concerned.

What is furthermore remarkable is the weighing of the rights under Art 8 against the governmental planning considerations.[83] In planning matters in general, the Court deems the margin of appreciation to be particularly wide. Where these were concerned, it thus led to the conclusion that the limitation of the right under consideration was legitimate. In *Connors v United Kingdom*, the situation was different, exactly because the case did not concern the planning policy in general but the procedural safeguards in the case of an eviction. As this is the most recent case, one hopes that it represents a more lenient approach toward the Romani situation in general, because one can ask why the result should be different when concerning planning policy in general. In considering that the nation-states are to take active steps in order to guarantee the rights under Art 8, one sees that, until *Connors*, this argument was not even really included in the reasoning of the Court. In applying the 'fair balance' test that corresponds with the 'positive obligations' perspective, the margin of appreciation, however, might not have been that wide and the weighing of the different interests involved might have resulted in a different balance.[84] It seems that the Court acknowledged the ideal of respect for Romani culture, but at the same time showed a limited willingness to intervene actively in this respect. This tendency will hopefully be modified in line with the *Connors* jurisprudence. A process of definitional limitation, somewhat similar to the earlier jurisprudence, can also be seen in the conception that the Court uses of Romani culture.

Jurisprudential Conception of Romani Culture

Essential Romani Culture: What Makes a True 'Gypsy'?

It seems that the European Court takes a rather limited concept of Romani culture into account. In *Smith v. United Kingdom (No 2)*, for instance, it did not answer the accusation that UK legislation criminalised the nomadic

---

[82] Cf OM Anardottir, *Equality and Non-Discrimination under the European Convention on Human Rights* (Den Haag, Martinus Nijhoff, 2003).

[83] In *Buckley*, above n 53 (see also dissenting opinion of Judge Pettiti) as well as in *Turner*, above n 56; Gerbranda, above n 80 at 312; De Hert, above n 74. Cf Bancroft, above n 70.

[84] Gerbranda, above n 80 at 311–12. See also dissenting opinion Judge Pettiti in *Buckley*, above n 53.

lifestyle.[85] The applicant could not prove herself to be a victim since she lived on an official site and she had not indicated any wish to leave. The mere existence of such legislation could not be the subject of a complaint. The mere existence of such legislation could, however, make a victim of the applicant since it effectively forced her to stay on one plot of land. When considering the side-effects of legal measures on practical behaviour, one has to take into consideration the fact that imprisonment, from a Romani perspective, is deemed to be very polluting and involves the crossing of many taboos, even to the degree that an individual might afterwards be expelled from the community for a certain (purification) period.[86] As such, it is simply not an option to risk imprisonment in order to be able to live nomadically.

Even more striking is the *Chapman* case, where the Court first said that:

> the applicant's occupation of her caravan is an integral part of her ethnic identity as a 'Gypsy', reflecting the long tradition of that minority of following a travelling lifestyle. This is the case even though, under the pressure of development and diverse policies or from their own volition, many 'Gypsies' no longer live a wholly nomadic existence and increasingly settle for long periods in one place in order to facilitate, for example, the education of their children. [The problem lies in this] it would appear that the applicant does not in fact wish to pursue an itinerant lifestyle... Thus the present case is not concerned as such with traditional itinerant 'Gypsy' lifestyle.

Simply because the applicant had bought a plot of land to put her caravan on, on a permanent base, the Court did not consider her a 'true' 'Gypsy'. The Court thus seemed to deny that any other than the 'real' nomadic lifestyle is genuine and worthy of protection. Contemporary nomadism can, however, just as well be semi-nomadism. The Court, moreover, did refer to this trend in other cases, and even acknowledged that it is often a result of a forced settlement policy. Even so, the Court did not seem to be inclined to apply the guarantees to these forms of lifestyle. In this way, the Court was essentialising Romani culture to a very high degree, and left very little possibility for change within this culture, thus rendering it somewhat static.

Again, it was only in the *Connors* case that the Court began to be truly responsive towards these contemporary tendencies. When reflecting on the difficulties that the authorities have in accommodating nomadic people, it mentioned that the recent trends only complicate their task, considering:

> the apparent shift in habit in the Gypsy population which remains nomadic in spirit if not in actual or constant practice. The authorities are being required

---

[85] *Smith/United Kingdom (No 2)*, above n 52.
[86] WO Weyrauch, *Gypsy Law: Romani Legal Traditions and Culture* (Berkeley, University of California Press, 2001) 235; see also A Renteln *The Cultural Defense* (New York, Oxford University Press, 2004) 120–21.

to give special consideration to a sector of the population which is no longer easy to define in terms of nomadism which is the raison d'être of that special treatment.

Actively nomadic or rather semi-nomadic, this distinction nonetheless did not prevent the Court from concluding that the concrete facts showed that the authorities in any event had failed to accommodate the gypsy lifestyle.

Power of Culture: Excluding the Others (Newcomers)

It is only Romani culture that is envisaged in the quoted jurisprudence, which is supposed to imply a certain (fixed) heritage and tradition. Yet there are people who choose to start living in a nomadic way in countries throughout Europe, be it the New Age Travellers in the United Kingdom, or the City Nomads of Antwerp in Belgium. They, too, claim to be entitled to respect for this chosen lifestyle. In the United Kingdom, they are included in the planning policy. This, however, does not seem to be the approach of the European Court. Particularly in *Beckers v. Netherlands* it became clear that a rather limited respect for nomadism was to be granted. As the applicant in that case was not part of a minority that could count on 'special' protection under Art 8, the measures taken by the Dutch authorities were not deemed to be disproportionate. The minorities Decree in Flanders also referred to a traditional way of life and mentioned the 'Gypsies' or their descendants in the first degree. This formed the legal basis for a selective policy in relation to, for instance, transit sites.[87] Although the minorities Decree did form a legal grounding for such a policy, one wonders what the justification is on a more fundamental level. To some extent, such a selective policy seems to imply that traditional people have more rights to nomadism then other people do, because it is their heritage. For other people it is just a choice.[88] Is such freedom of choice then to be opposed to a transcendent culture? Here, again, the Court relies on a certain ideology in relation to collective identity, regarding it as a given, that is common to all the members of the collectivity and in which no others are to be included.[89] The differential factor of cultural tradition is, however, not that unproblematic, for several reasons.[90] To begin with, the personal as

---

[87] In Antwerp, eg, a new transit site is being built, from which some 'New Age Travellers' had to be expelled. However, they also want to be able to live on the site. The admission policy is going to be based on mere appearance (personal communication).

[88] See also CJ Greenhouse, 'Constructive Approaches to Law, Culture and Identity' (1994) 5 *Law and Society Review* 1231.

[89] Cf J Ringelheim, 'Identity Controversies before the European Court of Human Rights: How to Avoid the Essentialist Trap?' (2002) 3 *German Law Journal*, § 2 http://www.german-lawjournal.com/article.php?id=167.

[90] Certain rights can, eg, be of particular importance for the Romani people, although this is not necessarily a matter of culture in every individual case: Haun, above n 23.

well as the material limitation of such a tradition is difficult.[91] The least
we can say is that, if the government wishes to guarantee an individual the
choice to live according to his or her cultural tradition, it is essential that
the measures taken in that regard be based on some understanding of this
culture. Anthropology might play a crucial role in this, although a delicate
one at times.

Role of Anthropological Knowledge in Multicultural Jurisprudence

A good illustration of the possibly ambivalent position of an anthropologist in the courtroom was given by Sutherland. As the author of '*Gypsies*':
the Hidden Americans, she was called to be an expert on 'Gypsy' culture in
the *Sonny* case. She concluded that one of the problems was the difficulty
that both the prosecution and the defence had in correctly understanding
the issue at stake.[92] The case therefore concerned some fundamental misunderstandings. As regards the problem of identification she explained that
there might be several civil names but only one 'Gypsy' name, based on
the extended kin group. Identification thus could have been established by
determining this 'Gypsy' name. This was, however, not deemed satisfactory,
as there had to be a civil name. But the US names are considered to be corporate property of the extended kin group and frequently borrowed from
each other. The same applies to social security numbers. As a consequence,
there is also a problem with birth certificates. Although the previous difficulties have lessened, the problem still remains, since these certificates mention only the civil name. All these issues are in themselves considered to be
highly suspicious and already seem to suggest criminal activities. A correct
understanding and contextualisation of information is thus indispensable.
Anthropological knowledge might hence play an important role as a plea
for respect in court cases such as these.

However, anthropological research can also be used against a minority culture, as in Sutherland's case. She found herself confronted with an
article that was used by the prosecution, entitled 'Gypsies, the People and
their Criminal Propensity'.[93] In this article, Sutherland herself was extensively quoted to back up bold statements about the criminal propensity of
'Gypsies'.[94] So her own research was used against *Sonny* in one and the
same case.

This shows how misuse of anthropological knowledge can very easily
throw the discipline back into its instrumental position of earlier days, as

---

[91] Cf A Renteln, *The Cultural Defense* (New York, Oxford University Press, 2004) 206–7
and 214–18.

[92] Sutherland, above n 66 at 235.

[93] T Getsay, 'Gypsies, the People and their Criminal Propensity' (1982) *Kansas State FOP
Journal* I, II and III.

[94] Sutherland, above n 66 at 238.

a way of confirming the already existing power relations.[95] Anthropology has, indeed, not always inspired a plea for respect but has sometimes served a political goal of dominance, especially through its link with colonial history.

In light of this tendency to cultural supremacy, the Romani reluctance as regards registration is not as outdated as it might seem. Cultural isolation as an internal mechanism of defence towards the outside world is in the end rooted in a documented history of prosecution and discrimination and it has, until now, proved to be a valuable instrument.[96] In modern society, it is often declared that cultural traditions deserve the highest possible respect. Such cultures, however, are also expected to 'integrate' to a certain minimum level, just as they are to be open towards the dominant society, and to let this larger society become acquainted with their inner practices and organisation. But evidently, knowledge still equals power. There is always the risk that information is misused in order to serve an improper political goal of submission. Another example of this can be found in Finnish police practices, who discovered that dogs had an unusual effect on Romani people, making them as 'amenable as sheep'.[97] Dogs are indeed of a defiling nature in Romani culture, and although the concrete basis for this was not appreciated, their use was to become an effective instrument for the police. Also, the fear of detention makes it much easier to elicit a confession,[98] which in itself might shed more light on statistics.

CONCLUSION

When considering the situation of the Romani people, one sees that their plight inspires the call for a multicultural jurisprudence. Although the right to respect for Romani culture is fundamentally acknowledged, the demands of their particular situation remain unanswered. In practice, however, most of the measures to be taken are essentially simple interventions. As such, it is possible for a society to incorporate this cultural lifestyle into its legal system without having to deal with too many problems. Equality can be achieved by creating the marginal conditions for Romani to live according to their own choice. Spatial enclosure in urban planning is one such

---

[95] AP Harris, 'Foreword' in WO Weyrauch (ed), *Gypsy Law: Romani Legal Traditions and Culture* (Berkeley, University of California Press, 2001) ix.

[96] Sutherland, above n 66 at 238; Haun, above n 23 at 156; F Bertram, 'The Particular Problems of (the) Roma' (1997) 1 *University of California Journal of International Law & Policy* 5; I Fonseca, *Bury Me Standing: the Gypsies and their Journey* (London, Vintage Press, 1996) 145–6.

[97] WO Weyrauch, 'Romaniya: an Introduction to Gypsy Law' in WO Weyrauch (ed), *Gypsy Law: Romani Legal Traditions and Culture* (Berkeley, University of California Press, 2001) 235.

[98] *Ibid.*

measure. A more fundamental reconceptualisation might be necessary in order not to discriminate against persons who are unwilling to conform to local culture.[99]

The measures to be taken are threefold. The principal acknowledgment should first inspire the state to make some very specific commitments, in particular to actively provide sufficient residing places and, as already mentioned, urban planning that takes the nomadic abode into account. Secondly, as regards the drafting of legislation, one should guard against the making of laws that have a disproportionate effect on one group of people only, especially when dealing with criminal law. Also, the regulations that concern housing matters and the issue of one's domicile should take nomadism into account, when, for instance, defining the conditions for a residential address and for a trading licence. Thirdly, the application and jurisprudential interpretation of these norms must support the principal acknowledgment of Romani culture by incorporating it into the jurisprudence, when necessary.

However undemanding these claims may seem, the stakes are relatively high since the consequences might be disproportionate when these measures are not taken. As described above, implicit processes of marginalisation do lead to criminalisation. Besides the principal ideal of respect for culture, a policy reason thus can be that failed assimilation is a vested criminalising factor.[100] In this respect, legal exclusion of the Romani culture can only reinforce their corresponding criminalisation. This would accordingly signify a twofold criminalisation: through legal definitions and instruments, on the one hand, and through the social exclusion that can be the outcome thereof, on the other.[101] While this chapter focused primarily on the first process, the second is not to be underestimated.

When considering these concerns from a policy perspective, one should also be aware of the important role of cultural knowledge. By using it in a constructive way, one can attain not only to the aspired multicultural jurisprudence, but also to a multicultural legislation as well. In order to achieve this, all levels of the law, even the law in action, have to be taken into account. The initial respect for the nomadic home as a culture-specific manifestation should as such lead to changes in the legal practices of the different parties involved. A less culture-biased formulation of legislation relating to housing matters, for instance, and an enhanced sensitivity to

---

[99] See, eg, WO Weyrauch, 'The Romani People: a Long Surviving and Distinguished Culture at Risk. Book Review' (2003) 3 *American Journal of Comparative Law* 687 (Review of I Hancock, *We are the Romani People: Ame Sam E Rromane Dzene* (Hertfordshire, University of Hertfordshire Press, 2002)).

[100] *Ibid* at 10. See also, eg, Durnescu, Lazar and Shaw, above n 4.

[101] The relationship between legal and social exclusion is multifaceted. Although legal exclusion can, and usually does, entail social exclusion, the same does not have to be true for legal inclusion, which can correspond to social exclusion, as stated above.

Romani culture in the jurisprudential application of such legislation, are important steps.

Anthropological knowledge might also raise awareness of the constant changes that emerge within these societies, which are most often a direct, though implicit, reaction to the society's way of approaching their culture. The fact that in relation to an ever-changing economic and social environment a culture changes, seems to be self-evident. From a policy perspective, one should thus guard oneself from approaching it as something static which forces people to remain traditional in the same way in perpetuity. For instance, as we saw earlier, the concept of 'nomadism' can change in relation to environmental factors. An anthropological comprehension of change can help guard against a static conception of certain cultural traits that could lead to fossilisation.

If legislation should avoid strained preservation of a traditional lifestyle, then the question, of course, arises of to what degree the government should support the maintenance of a traditional lifestyle. If no measures are taken, assimilation might indeed be achieved. Some emancipatory voices would also deem it to be to the good of the population as a wholel. Legal inclusion is indeed not such an unambiguous matter as it might seem. When trying to offer a free choice to live according to one's own cultural tradition, it remains important to make sure that there is a free choice for every individual within this tradition.[102] One aspect that is often considered to be problematic in regard to Romani culture is the educational situation of Romani children. Because of a variety of difficulties, Romani children do not enjoy an equal education, which might result in their being 'trapped' in their culture.[103] If granting respect for this culture would imply a continuation of Romani culture, legal inclusion of the global culture might mean social exclusion of future generations. In the final analysis, legal inclusion should try to embrace social inclusion through a weighing of the different interests involved.

---

[102] As to the freedom that is supposed to lie within this concept of choice, see also CJ Greenhouse, 'Constructive Approaches to Law, Culture and Identity' (1994) 3 *Law and Society Review* 1231.

[103] Cf Vlaams Minderhedencentrum, *Tussen school en wagen, onderwijs aan voyageurs, manoesjen en roms* (Brussel, Vlaams Centrum Woonwagenwerk, 2000).

9

Honor Killings and the Cultural Defense in Germany

SYLVIA MAIER

INTRODUCTION

Between October 2004 and June 2005, eight women were killed in Germany by their husband or brothers for allegedly bringing 'dishonour' to their families (Böhmecke, 2005: 19). Since 1996, more than 40 girls and women of Turkish or Middle Eastern origin who had lived in Germany for all, or most, of their lives were murdered for the same 'crime' (Böhmecke, 2005: 18). According to estimates by the United Nations, law enforcement and women's rights groups, more than 5,000 women around the world, and at least 100 women in Western Europe and North America, become victims of honour killings each year (United Nations General Assembly, 2002).[1] These so-called 'honour killings'—murders of women for allegedly bringing 'dishonour' to the family, community or religious faith—used to be limited to culturally conservative communities in the Middle East, South-East Asia and Southern Europe but, as of late, have become increasingly frequent in the Muslim diaspora of Western Europe, Canada and the United States.

Until recently, the public response to these crimes by the Muslim communities themselves as well as German politicians and law enforcement, has been rather muted. This was mainly in deference to claims by offenders that the need to punish women for social transgressions and to defend one's honour is a right and an obligation within Islamic culture. There was also concern by many Germans that criticism of such practices might be construed as xenophobia or intolerance, and, as such, play into the hands of racist right-wing extremists. Lately, however, in a post-9/11 political climate

---

[1] According to a report from *The Times* (London), Scotland Yard, after a recent upsurge in honour killings in the South Asian communities in England, was reopening 122 cases of suspicious deaths, suicides and disappearances of young women, see S Bird, 'Love Song Secret Drove Father to Kill Daughter', *The Times* (London), 7 December 2004, www.timesonline. co.uk/article/0,,2-1391940,00.html.

that highlighted many flaws in European integration policies, the murder of Dutch film-maker Theo van Gogh, and the prospect of Turkey's accession to the European Union, German courts have begun to reject cultural justifications of honour killings, just as women's rights groups, both mainly Muslim and German, and German policy-makers have become more vocal in their criticism of the pervasive violence against women in Muslim communities, ranging from abuse and forced marriages to honour killings. In particular, the high-profile killing of Hatun Sürücü, a 23-year-old German-Turkish woman in Berlin last year, catalysed opposition to honour killings and moved the question of the rights of women in Muslim communities into the spotlight. At the same time, it raised serious questions about the effectiveness and viability of Germany's integration policies.

In this chapter, I analyse the phenomenon of honour killings in Germany with a focus on the legal and political responses to these crimes. I argue that the juridical reaction to honour killings was emblematic of Germany's flawed approach to integration and multiculturalism (a hands-off differentialist integrationism that encouraged the establishment of 'parallel societies' of Muslim communities and resulted in a faulty understanding of cultural tolerance that let cultural sensitivities trump women's rights); but that as a result of intense lobbying campaigns by women's rights groups and several high-profile murder cases, honour killings are now punished with the full force of the law.

MULTICULTURALISM AND INTEGRATION POLICIES IN GERMANY

The prevalence of honour killings and the inconsistent response to these crimes by German law enforcement, policy-makers and Germany's Muslim communities is a reflection of that country's uneasy relationship with multiculturalism and, ultimately, its unwillingness to come to terms with the de facto cultural diversity within its borders.[2] It is the result of Germany's decade-long refusal to accept that the Turkish immigrants who came as 'guestworkers' in the 1960s, as well as their German-born children and grandchildren, were here to stay and, therefore, a coherent approach to cultural and religious diversity had to be devised.[3] Accepting that Germany

---

[2] More than three million Muslims from 41 countries live in Germany, making up approximately 2.6 per cent of Germany's population of close to 83 million. Turkish Muslims form the largest group, with smaller numbers hailing from the former Yugoslavia, the Middle East, as well as South and South-East Asia. Most live in the main urban centres in Germany, such as in Berlin, Frankfurt, Hamburg, Cologne, Hannover, and Stuttgart, with smaller communities in the southern German states of Bavaria and Baden-Württemberg. Only 15 per cent of Muslims (about 480,000) are German citizens.

[3] This was clearly expressed in the administrative regulations governing naturalisation, which stated unambiguously that 'the Federal Republic is not a country of immigration [and] does not strive to increase the number of its citizens through naturalization'. Roger Brubaker,

was, indeed, a 'country of immigration' meant that its ethno-cultural understanding of citizenship had to be abandoned; an understanding that (unlike France and the United States where membership in the polity is determined by the embrace of civic values such as liberty, equality, and individualism) determines belonging to the German community 'by blood', that is, by having German ancestors.[4] Naturally, that also meant that Germany had to abandon the myth of its ethno-cultural homogeneity. Such a suggestion was politically unthinkable (Brubaker, 1992).

Therefore, German politicians attempted to find a politically acceptable 'third way' to deal with the consequences of immigration and to accommodate its multi-ethnicity. This 'third way', a peculiar mixture of integrationism and differentialism, rejects both French and US versions of assimilationism, as well as British multiculturalism.[5] French assimilationism implies that all immigrants can become French by embracing the French language and civic culture; US assimilationism—the melting pot idea—entails the abandonment of old traditions and the creation of an entirely new US culture, whereas British multiculturalism, however reluctantly, tolerates and accommodates cultural diversity. Germany's 'third way' recognises that the 'germanization' of ethnic minorities is both politically impossible and morally indefensible for obvious historical reasons, that cultural diversity enriches society, and that minorities should be allowed to practise their culture, all the while ensuring that this means the support of a separate Turkish culture and not the mixing of cultures.[6] In practical terms, German multicultural policies—wisely—do not prohibit the wearing of the hijab by students, generally permit the exemption of Muslim girls from physical education classes, fund the teaching of Islam in public schools, encourage the foundation of Islamic research centres, and see German courts apply the Shari'a in cases involving Muslim family law. Furthermore, sincere efforts are underway to 'mainstream Islam' through the public incorporation of representative organisations and the institutionalisation of a 'dialogue of cultures' (Fetzer and Soper, 2004; Klausen, 2005).

This movement towards more inclusivist attitudes towards diversity was facilitated throughout the 1990s by closer European integration and the

---

Citizenship and Nationhood in France and Germany (Cambridge, MA, Harvard University Press, Cambridge, 1992) 77.

[4] Consequently, the attitude towards immigrants and cultural minorities, regardless of their willingness to assimilate into German culture, had to be negative.

[5] See, in particular, A Favell, *Philosophies of Integration: Immigration and the Idea of Citizenship in France and Britain* (Palgrave Macmillan, New York, 2001). Also, B Parekh *Rethinking Multiculturalism: Cultural Diversity and Political Theory* (Cambridge, MA, Harvard University Press, 2000).

[6] At times, German multiculturalism evokes notions of the US 'separate but equal' policy of the pre-civil rights era.

effects of globalisation which generated more contact with foreign cultures and customs. Furthermore, the replacement of the Christian-Democratic CDU party by a national 'red-green' coalition between the Social Democrats and the Green Party, both traditionally supportive of minority rights and diversity, and the close cooperation between this coalition and well-known moderate Germans of Turkish ancestry, such as Cem Özdemir, the first German-Turk to sit in the German Parliament, Özcan Mutlu, a Berlin city representative, and Dr Necla Kelek, a feminist sociologist, showed the possibility of a peaceful cultural hybridity and increased acceptance of Turks and Turkish culture—so much so that the Turkish döner[7] became the most popular snack food in Germany.

This is precisely where the problem lay. The embrace of all things Turkish became fashionable. Living in Kreuzberg, the district in Berlin with traditionally a large Turkish population, became *de rigeur* for upwardly mobile 'yuppies' and opinion-makers. The brilliant Turkish director, Fatih Akin, attained cult status. A small, modern Turkish middle-class emerged and closely cooperated with the local multiculturalism affairs departments in many German cities and local governments. In other words, German politicians patted themselves on the back and pointed to the success of German multiculturalism. However, the fact remained that most minority members (most importantly, Turks, born in Germany or not) were still not made to feel that they were truly a part of German society. For instance, it was not until the year 2000 that the German citizenship and naturalization laws were changed so that all children born on German soil automatically acquire German citizenship at birth provided one parent has been a legal resident for at least five years.[8] Furthermore, and very importantly, little attention was given to the consequences of the appalling educational under-achievement and sky-rocketing unemployment rates (up to 40 per cent) of young Turks living in Turkish urban ghettoes in German cities.

This widespread political and economic disenfranchisement, a sense of alienation, feelings of loss of power and status among young Turkish men—third generation and recent immigrant alike—had fuelled the radicalisation since the late 1980s of a small but vocal minority of Turks who soon found allies for their resentment of German and Western society, who they blamed (not always unjustifiably) for their plight, in radical Turkish nationalist groups or religious fundamentalist imams who longed for the establishment of a Muslim caliphate in Germany (Fetzer and Soper, 2004). Many imams counselled a return to traditional Islam, the rejection of all Western values as decadent and corrupting and, in particular, the close control of female behaviour as the easiest and most visible rejection of German

---

[7] A döner is warm pita bread or fluffy Turkish bread stuffed with grilled, spiced beef or lamb and a sour-cream-garlic sauce.

[8] The law also reduced the waiting period for naturalisation to eight years down from 15.

values. They found a ready audience in disenfranchised Turkish men (and numerous women) who lived on the margins of German (and often even Turkish) society (Heitmeyer *et al*, 1997). As a consequence, an idealised traditional Islamic and Turkish culture began to form the backbone of a thriving non-German counter-culture centred around recent immigrant communities from conservative parts of Turkey and established but alienated Turkish communities in working class ghettoes of Berlin, Hamburg and other cities. In these ghettoes, family honour and respect were the most precious commodities. The close-knit communities quickly established self-sustaining support networks, frequently with financial support from the Turkish and Saudi Arabian governments, with Turkish kindergartens, private schools, mosques, supermarkets, clothing stores, food markets and Turkish-language media. In other words, they created a 'parallel society' (Fetzer and Soper, 2004; Klausen, 2005).

The main characteristic of these 'parallel societies' is their strong patriarchal organisation and a high level of familial and social control, especially over women. As in most traditional societies, women are considered the repositories of a family's honour and any non-conforming behaviour on their part can sully the family's reputation. A family's honour depends on the chastity of its women, and therefore all females must be closely guarded in order to prevent any disastrous missteps (Cileli, 2002; Kelek, 2005).[9] Should a woman violate norms of acceptable behaviour, she may have to be killed because only the physical extermination of the offender can restore a family's honour. Studies of the background of victims of honour killings, as I shall discuss below in more depth, showed that, indeed, most victims, or their families, had come from a 'parallel society' background in Berlin, Cologne or Hamburg (Böhmecke, 2005: 20).

Why did the national and local governments stand idly by as these troublesome developments unfolded? A fateful aspect of Germany's 'third way' echoes the idea that 'Turks cannot and never will be Germans' and finds expression in a *laissez-faire* approach to internal community developments. German authorities were (and still are) hesitant to interfere in and sit in judgment of intra-cultural affairs, especially as they relate to 'family matters', as issues relating to the status of women are generally referred to. Until very recently, a second reason for the hesitance of well-meaning multiculturalists to take up the cause of women in light of the increasing fundamentalisation of some Turkish communities was a fear that any criticism of the mistreatment of women might be mistaken for xenophobia and play into the hands of right-wing extremist groups who had been responsible for several high-profile murders of Turks and asylum-seekers in the 1990s and

---

[9] See also the special issue 'Allah's Rechtlose Töchter' ('Allah's Powerless Daughters') in *Der Spiegel*, 15 November 2004, www.spiegel.de/sptv/thema/0,1518,327916,00.html.

enjoyed widespread support, especially in urban centres and East Germany. The German legal system as well, as we shall see below, was very sensitive to charges of racism and, in several cases of honour killings, courts took the cultural background of the offenders into account, convicting them of manslaughter instead of murder.

In sum, Germany's strategy to accommodate cultural diversity gives both too little and too much, with troublesome consequences for Turkish women.

THE CRIME OF HONOUR KILLINGS

Honour killings occur worldwide. According to the United Nations, between 5,000 and 10,000 women are killed annually by their husbands or close relatives for allegedly bringing a stain of dishonour to their families that only the killing—the physical extermination—of the woman can remove (Sev'er, 1999; Asamoah-Wade, 1999/2000; van Eck, 2003). Most of these crimes occur in Pakistan, Jordan, Afghanistan, Turkey and Palestine, but hundreds, perhaps thousands, of honour killings have occurred in the Muslim diaspora communities in the United Kingdom, Canada and continental Europe (Ruane, 2000; Arnold, 2001; van Eck, 2003; Mojab, 2004). It must be stressed, however, that honour killings are in no way limited to Muslim communities. Thousands of women are killed every year around the world by their husbands and (ex-)boyfriends for wanting a divorce, an extra-marital affair or similar perceived slights to the man's 'honour'. Yet these crimes are presented in the media and crime reports as 'family tragedies' or 'crimes of passion', although they are, in effect, honour killings.[10]

Honour killings, the most extreme form of honour-related violence against women in strictly patriarchal societies, are motivated by a wide variety of social, cultural, psychological factors. Women are killed for any number of 'offences', including pre-marital or extra-marital sex, refusal to marry a man the family has chosen for her, demanding a divorce, being a victim of rape or incest, dressing in an immodest 'Western' way, speaking with or smiling at a man, or wishing to continue an education or work outside the home: in short, for any behaviour through which a woman expresses her autonomy and that runs afoul of the social order in these patriarchal societies (Faqir, 2001; Douki, 2003; Kogacioglu, 2004; Rothwell, 2004; Böhmecke, 2005).

---

[10] Data from the German police crime statistics database indicate that in 2003, 49 per cent of 426 female victims of homicide or manslaughter were killed by someone in their family; almost 39 per cent of the 639 victims of attempted murder were assaulted by someone they knew. See also L Abu-Odeh, 'Comparatively Speaking: the "Honour" of the "East" and the "Passion" of the "West"' (1997) *Utah Law Review* 287.

This social order rests on clearly defined gender roles and gender behaviour. The woman's main role is to be a wife and mother, the man's to be the provider and 'protector' of the family's women. Likewise, it is his duty to protect and restore the family's 'honour'. A family's honour is dependent upon the behaviour and chastity of the women in the family, and a man's honour rests upon his ability to control the sexual behaviour of his wife, sisters or other female relatives. This means that a woman must remain a virgin until marriage and as a wife must be absolutely faithful to her husband and chaste in dress and action. Extra-marital sex for a married Muslim woman, if detected, means a likely death sentence. If a Muslim woman violates these rules of acceptable behaviour through her actions, real or imagined, her violations stain the family's honour which can only be erased by her physical eradication. In some countries, such as Pakistan, the woman must be killed publicly. Not doing so would mean an even more serious violation of the male honour. Ironically, most women who were killed for alleged sexual transgressions were determined in autopsies to still be virgins. A particularly cruel type of honour killings concerns girls who were killed because they have been raped by a family member or been the victim of incest. Instead of punishing the rapist, the girl is killed to keep up the appearance of family respectability (Faqir, 2001; van Eck, 2003; Rothwell, 2004; Mojab, 2004).

Honour killings are almost always committed by men, because it is only men who can restore a family's honour, although women often participate in the planning of the crime. Frequently, a victim's younger brother or cousin is chosen to kill because juveniles receive lower sentences. In Muslim countries, such as Jordan and Pakistan, where societal support for honour killings is quite high, punishments for killing in the name of honour are generally very lenient. Most legal codes specifically provide for much reduced sentences for honour killers, often only between six months and three years of incarceration. Considered an internal family matter, law enforcement authorities generally are unwilling to punish perpetrators at all, occasionally becoming complicit in presenting an honour killing as an accident or suicide. Once in prison, honour killers are treated like celebrities by their families, guards and other inmates, especially if they are underage, because in that case they have 'sacrificed' themselves for their family's honour. 'In the hierarchy of Turkish prisons honour killers rank at the top. And also in our [German] prisons they are celebrated like heroes. The family looks after them and honours their memory' (Lau, 'Kulturbedingte Ehrenmorde', 2005).[11] Attempts by reform-minded activists to outlaw honour killings and abolish the honour killing exemption have met with

---

[11] See also S Saywell, *Crimes of Honour* (Documentary, New York, First Run/Icarus Films, 1998).

mixed success. Bills that provided for the abolition of the honour exemption paragraph in the penal code—the infamous para 340—were rejected by the Jordanian Parliament several times, despite vocal support from the Royal family (Faqir, 2001; Human Rights Watch, 1999; Human Rights Watch, 2000; BBC News, 2000). Yet, in Pakistan, the country with the highest number of honour killings per annum (approximately 1,200: (Böhmecke, 2005) President Musharraf agreed to sign a Bill providing for murder charges for all honour killings over the vociferous opposition of Islamist parties who claimed that such a law would open the door to all sorts of immoral, Western behaviour by Muslim women (Joseph, 2002).

It is often claimed by defendants that honour killings are required or condoned by the *Q'uran*, the Muslim holy book. But this is emphatically not the case. The *Q'uran* prescribes clear rules of proper sexual behaviour for both women and men. While both sexes are encouraged to enjoy intimate relations and to please one another in marriage, pre-marital and extra-marital sex are prohibited for both men and women. In determining the proper punishment for sex outside marriage, the *Q'uran* distinguishes between pre-marital and extra-marital sex. The punishment for pre-marital sex for both women and men is generally 100 lashes. Adultery, on the other hand, is a very serious offence, and the punishment is usually death by stoning for both the man and woman (homosexual acts are punishable by death in all cases). However, the *Q'uran* stipulates clearly that four reliable male witnesses must have caught the offending couple *in flagrante delicto* and must accuse the offending couple in a public forum before a judge who then pronounces the sentence. Under no circumstances is vigilante justice without any corroborating evidence, ie, an honour killing, condoned or encouraged in the *Q'uran* or the *hadith*.[12]

In sum, honour killings are the ultimate form of social control over women by men. They are used as a punishment for and deterrence of behaviour that violates patriarchal notions of male honour and proper female (sexual) behaviour. They are widespread in the Middle East, especially in Pakistan and Jordan, and are becoming more frequent in the Muslim diaspora communities from Turkey, the Middle East and South-East Asia in Europe and North America.

Honour Killings in Germany

There are no definite numbers on honour killings in Germany. However, the most comprehensive report on honour killings in Germany currently

---

[12] The Feminist Sexual Ethics Project, *Special Focus: Islam. Honour Killings, Illicit Sex and Islamic Law*, www.brandeis.edu/projects/fse/Pages/honourkillings.html. See also Muslim Women's League, *Position Paper on 'Honour Killings'* (1999), www.mwlusa.org/publications/positionpapers/hk.html.

available, the study by the German women's rights group Terre des Femmes, on which this article draws heavily, indicates that since 1996, 49 girls and women of Turkish or Middle Eastern origin who had lived in Germany for all, or most, of their lives were victims of honour killings or survivors of an attempted honour murder (Böhmecke, 2005: 19).[13] Eight women were killed in honour murders just between October 2004 and June 2005. On 18 October 2004, a young German woman was stabbed to death in the middle of the street by her violent Turkish husband from whom she was separated (Agence France Presse, 2005). On 25 November 2004, 21-year-old Semra U,[14] a Turkish citizen, was stabbed to death by her Turkish ex-husband, a cousin, whom she had been forced to marry and who had beaten her severely. Four days later, Melek E,[15] another young woman of Turkish origin, who had been married for just four months, was stabbed to death by her husband Selahattin E because she had left him. On 4 January 2005, Meyrem Ö was strangled by her husband, who has since fled to Turkey (von Bullion, 2005). On 7 February 2005, Hatun Sürücü, 23 years old, was shot three times in the head by her brothers. She was killed because, according to some young German Turkish students, 'this whore behaved like a German woman' (Ramelsberger, 2005). 'Behaving like a German women' meant that Hatun had escaped a marriage that she had been forced to enter into at the age of 16, divorced her abusive husband, returned to Berlin with her young son, continued school, apprenticed as an electrician, wore Western clothes and went to parties. In June 2005, a 24-year-old Turkish man killed his 20-year-old sister with five shots because of her relationship with a 28-year-old German. Her family felt their honour had been sullied by her relationship (von Bullion, 'Ehrenmord Prozess Beginnt in Wiesbaden').

Of course, not all German Muslim women are at the same risk of becoming a victim of an honour killing. Whether a family will resort to violence against a female member largely depends on that family's level of social integration, their social and economic status, as well as their level of religiosity and region of origin. Evidence shows that most honour killings and forced marriages occur predominantly (but by no means exclusively) in socially and economically marginalized families with relatively low levels of education and difficult family circumstances. Additionally, the sense of a need to defend one's honour—violently, if necessary—is particularly high

---

[13] This section draws heavily on the only comprehensive source on honour killings in Germany: M Böhmecke, *Studie: Ehrenmord (Study: Honour Killing)* (Tübingen, Terre des Femmes, 2005).

[14] In Germany, the names of crime victims and offenders are generally not released to the public. Even court documents refer to the parties involved only by their first name and the initial(s) of their last name(s). On occasion, the news media learn the full name of the persons. Therefore, this article uses both initials and full names.

[15] The spelling of Turkish names varies in the German news media. In particular, the letters 'e' and 'a' are often used interchangeably.

in communities where the level of social control is very high; that is, if a family lives in close proximity to other families from the same village or region with strong ties to the original home country. Therefore, the lower a family's socio-economic background and level of integration into the larger society, the more close-knit their community, the higher their level of social conservatism, the higher the chance that 'honour' is that family's most important commodity, the higher the chance a woman will fall victim to an honour killing for non-norm-conforming behaviour (Böhmecke, 2005: 29)

> Traditionelle Regeln erleben unter Bedingungen von gesellschaftlicher Marginalisiereung und besonders in der Migration eine Renaissance. Wenn die Männer Angst haben, an den Rand gedrängt zu werden – durch Machtverlust, Identitätsverlust oder Männlichkeitsverlust – können Ehremorde wahrscheinlicher werden.[16]

According to Terre des Femmes, 77 per cent of honour murders in Germany occurred in families with a Turkish (or Kurdish) background and 10 per cent in Lebanese families (Böhmecke, 2005: 22); 62 per cent of victims were female and 38 per cent were male (Böhmecke, 2005: 23). Victims' ages peaked between 18 and 25 years (53 per cent), the age when girls become interested in boys, and between 31 and 40 years (24 per cent), when women might consider a divorce (Böhmecke, 2005: 27). The killers were mostly between 26 and 40 years old (45 per cent), with some as young as 15 to 18 (11 per cent) (Böhmecke, 2005: 28). A separation or divorce (44 per cent) and (alleged) extra-marital sex (32 per cent) were the main reasons given to justify an honour murder (Böhmecke, 2005: 24). The reason is that, as in some non-Muslim communities, divorce brings shame primarily on the woman's family, because any failed marriage is considered the result of the woman's failure to be a 'good wife'. Many women who were murdered had lived in Germany for many years and often had children who had been born in the country. The largest proportion of the honour killings was committed by an (ex-)husband or partner (36 per cent), followed by one or more brothers (28 per cent), the father (19 per cent), mother (4 per cent), other family members (9 per cent); 4 per cent of honour murders were contract killings (Böhmecke, 2005: 27). Data indicate that unmarried girls and women were most often killed by their brothers and fathers who are the 'guardians' of women's chastity and the family's good reputation, whereas married women who tried to leave an abusive marriage, even a forced marriage, were killed by their husbands.

---

[16] 'Traditional rules experience a renaissance under conditions of social marginalization, and particularly in migration. If men fear that they are being pushed to the margins—through a loss of power, loss of identity or loss of masculinity—honour killings can become more likely.'

HONOUR AND THE CULTURAL DEFENSE
IN GERMAN JURISPRUDENCE

Honour, Shame and Culture in German Law

German courts have had to adjudicate cases involving claims of 'honour' both as a cause for various offences, including homicide, and as a mitigating circumstance, for several centuries. Legal and social history abounds with stories of Prussian (and Austrian) officers and gentlemen killing and dying in duels fought over ever so slight offences to their most precious possession: their honour.[17] This bourgeois fixation on family honour and a good reputation (*guter Ruf*), remained even after the fall of the Wilhelminian empire and its militaristic social order. Reformulated into the inviolability (*Unantastbarkeit*) of human dignity and worth, the concept of honour was reaffirmed in law and policy after the Nazi Reich in which the most horrifying violations of human dignity were committed. Consequently, the concept of 'honour' continues to play a large role in German jurisprudence, particularly in cases of insult, libel and defamation.

According to commentaries by jurists and established jurisprudence, 'honour' is a 'person-related legal good' (*persönliches Rechtsgut*) that is inextricably linked with the right to be treated with dignity and respect. While the law states clearly that it is possible to violate the honour of individuals or groups,[18] it does not establish any subjective or objective standard by which to determine what constitutes violations of honour or reputation, which, of course, leaves the door wide open for spurious interpretations, as will be shown below. Very importantly, family honour as such is not protected because the family is not considered a single unit with a uniform will. Only the honour of individual members of a family is protected. Consequently, punishments of supposed violations of a *family's* honour as a result of the actions of a female member of the group are not legally sanctioned and the law does not protect violent retaliatory actions on the part of any member of the family. Self-defense has also been rejected as a justification by the courts. Additionally, according to the legal commentaries, conceptions of honour are outweighed by the rights of the women to life, freedom and bodily integrity (Bundestagsfraktion Bündnis90/Die Grünen, 2005).

---

[17] See, eg, T Fontane's *Effi Briest* or A Schnitzler's works *Liebelei (A Dalliance)*, *Leutnant Gustl (Lieutenant Gustl)* and *Das Weite Land (The Far Country)*.

[18] This is most clearly expressed, eg, in the so-called 'prohibition laws' (Verbotsgesetze) that make the denial, downplaying or justification of the Holocaust, as well as the dissemination of anti-Semitic or racist propaganda, a crime, as such acts would violate the memory of the Holocaust victims, and violate the honour and dignity of German Jews.

Honour Killings, the Cultural Defense and the Law

Honour killings or the cultural defense do not exist as categories in the German Criminal Code, the Strafgesetzbuch (StGB). According to § 211 of the StGB, murder is the killing of a person under specific conditions. As in US law, murder differs from manslaughter (§ 212). In German law, motives such as lust to kill, killing for sexual gratification, greed and other 'low' or 'base' motives (*niedrige Beweggründe*), to conceal another crime, or the mode of killing (eg, in a cunning and cruel way or with generally dangerous tools such as bombs or gas) serve to classify a crime as murder rather than manslaughter (Bundestagsfraktion Bündnis90/Die Grünen, 2005).

Whether killing someone to restore a family's honour qualifies as murder for base or low motives, rather than as manslaughter, has been at the core of the few cases on honour killings, and there is no unequivocal, consistent jurisprudence on either the state or federal level. The German Supreme Court, the Bundesgerichtshof (BGH), classifies as crimes with base motives those where the motive of the act would be condemned by community standards and constitute the 'lowest level of morality' (*stehen auf niedrigster moralischer Stufe*).[19] When making the determination of a base motive, the cultural background and alleged motive of the accused are normally considered; in other words, a cultural defense, even though not explicitly so named, may be presented (Bundestagsfraktion Bündnis90/Die Grünen, 2005).

While the cultural defense as such does not exist as a separate legal category, unlike the insanity defense or the provocation defense, in practical terms it means that for defendants from an ethnic or religious minority as for immigrants and migrants, the attitudes, values and beliefs of their community or country of origin are occasionally taken into consideration. Additional factors are usually considered, such as how long the accused has lived in Germany and his familiarity with the German value system (Bundestagsfraktion Bündnis90/Die Grünen, 2005: 12). Accordingly, defense attorneys have consistently argued that the desire to restore one's honour is not a base motive in many communities (indeed it may be morally *required* by a religion or particular culture), and hence killing someone to do so does not meet the standards of murder, but rather those of manslaughter, if that. Indeed, several defendants have been successful in presenting a cultural defense and have been convicted of manslaughter, which carries a much lower sentence, normally less than 10 years, rather than of murder, which carries 25 years' imprisonment (Germany prohibits the death penalty

---

[19] See, in particular, the key decision from 28 January 2004, 2 StR 452/03, in which the BGH rejected a cultural defence for honour killings and held that murderers who kill to restore their honour act out of base motives.

and 25 years count as a life sentence) (Bundestagsfraktion Bündnis90/Die Grünen, 2005).[20] In 2001, Emine Demirbrüken, the only woman of Turkish descent on the governing board of the Christian-conservative German CDU Party, deplored that 'the German judiciary deals way too leniently with these crimes' and Dr Necla Kelek, a German-Turkish feminist sociologist, asked 'How many more women have to die before this society wakes up?' (Lau, 'Wie Eine Deutsche', 2005).

On several occasions, murder charges for an honour killing or for attempted (honour) murders were downgraded to manslaughter or the accused was convicted of manslaughter only (Bundesgerichtshof 1StR 282/79, 28 August 1979). For this, there are three main reasons. First, prosecutors and judges accepted the justification that a crime was 'culturally determined' (*kulturbedingt*) and thus did not meet the criterion of a 'base motive' needed for a murder charge (Lau, 'Kulturbedingte Ehrenmorde', 2005). Secondly, according to German law, the accused has a right against self-incrimination and his closest relatives have a right to refuse to testify against him. Therefore, their wives—the mothers of the murdered girls—who often had direct knowledge of the murder plans, could not be compelled to give evidence against their accused husbands. Since premeditation could not be proved, the prosecution could only bring charges of manslaughter. Thirdly, on occasion, it is reported, the victim was reluctant to testify in court against her assailant and thus to bring additional shame on the family (Bundestagsfraktion Bündnis 90/Die Grünen, 2005: 13).

In 2002, the Landgericht (District Court) Frankfurt heard the case of a Turkish man who had stabbed his wife to death because she wanted to divorce him. He argued that his honour had so suffered by this affront that it could only be restored by killing his wife. The court accepted the honour defense and convicted him of the lesser charge of manslaughter. However, the German Bundesgerichtshof later overturned his manslaughter conviction as too lenient (Louis, 2004).

Likewise, another state court, the Landgericht Bremen, convicted three Kurdish men only of manslaughter in the case of a contract killing of a young Kurdish couple on the orders of a PKK boss. In their decision the judges said that a conviction for manslaughter rather than murder was more appropriate because 'the accused, as a result of the strongly internalised value system of their home country, were not aware that their motives would be viewed, from an objective perspective, as particularly morally offensive' (Louis, 2004).

The judgment in another case, an attempted honour killing, which was heard by the Landgericht Bochum, caused an uproar. A 41-year-old Afghan

---

[20] See, in particular, the judgment of the German Bundesgerichtshof 1StR 282/79, 28 August 1979.

physician, who had lived in Germany for 25 years, had repeatedly raped his wife. She had left him twice but returned to him both times upon pressure from her family. During the last rape, the defendant almost suffocated her by pressing a pillow over her face. The judge, Gerald Sacher, rejected the charge of attempted murder because, in his view, the accused, 'as a result of his culture and his tradition only had to overcome a low level of self-restraint' ('der Angeklagte musste nur eine niedrige Hemmschwelle überwinden') (Louis, 2004).

In recent years, however, courts and jurists have begun to set firm limits to the reach of a cultural defense. In no case has the cultural defense led to the acquittal of a defendant. In cases where defendants have lived in Germany for many years, the courts have rejected the 'honour' defense.[21] Jurists have also rejected claims that the particularly low status of women in the accused's society excused their killing, or that in some communities the head of the family, as the ultimate judge of the norm conformity of individual behaviour, has absolute power over the life and death of family members. Likewise, the argument that the absolute necessity of traditional gender or sexual behaviour (for instance, the insistence on a women's virginity until marriage or avoidance of interacting with non-*haram* men) excused murdering someone, was rejected, especially if that rule was enforced only against women but not men. Likewise, the courts have firmly followed the key legal principle of *ignorantia iuris non excusat neminem*. Claims that the accused did not know that killing somebody to restore a family's honour was a crime were firmly rejected (Bundestagsfraktion Bündnis90/Die Grünen, 2005: 12–13).

In February 2000, the German Bundesgerichtshof overturned a decision by the Landgericht Frankfurt that had convicted two Turkish men only of manslaughter after they had killed two people. The men had argued that they had a 'duty to take revenge' for the rape and subsequent suicide of the wife of one of the killers and murdered of a couple who were not forthcoming in divulging the whereabouts of the alleged rapist. The lower court accepted the men's argument that their cultural values demanded that, in order for the husband's and wife's honour to be restored, the rapist had to be killed. The accused conceded that the deaths of innocent people were deplorable, but their acts still did not meet the 'base motive' requirement to qualify for a murder conviction. The lower court agreed, but the BGH overturned.[22]

In March 2003, Latif Z, an Albanian Muslim who had lived in Germany for 14 years, killed his 16-year-old daughter Ulerika because she had rebelled against his tyranny, gone to parties, dressed in Western clothes, and fallen in love with a young man. Her father strangled her and dumped

---

[21] See the judgment of the German Bundesgerichtshof 2StR 452/03 (Zweiter Strafsenat), 28 January 2004, in which the court explicitly rejects a 'cultural defence'.

[22] Bundesgerichtshof 2 StR 550/99, judgment of 2 February 2000.

her body in a lake. Charged with murder, Latif Z argued that his deeply held cultural beliefs in the need to defend his honour and his conviction that men were superior to women had driven him to killing his daughter. The Landgericht Tübingen, a mid-size Southern German university town, rejected this argument and sentenced Latif Z to life imprisonment. Ulerika's mother now leads a campaign against honour killings in Germany (von Bullion, 'Ein Ehrenmord in Deutschland' http://www.zdf.de/ZDFde/inhalt/27/0,1872,2247643,00.html, last accessed 6 April 2006).

In its landmark decision of 28 January 2004, the Bundesgerichtshof upheld a decision by the Landgericht Frankfurt involving an honour killing by a Turkish husband of his German-Turkish wife. The man had stabbed his wife 48 times when she wanted to divorce him. He considered this an unforgivable assault on his honour, since a divorce from his wife, who was a German citizen, meant that he would have to return to Turkey. The killer then argued that, in his culture, killing his wife was his right and duty and demanded that the standards for determining his culpability be those of his home country and not those of Germany. The Landesgericht disagreed and convicted him of murder, calling his crime an expression of the lowest possible moral standards. The BGH agreed. The justices categorically rejected a cultural justification for an honour killing and unequivocally stated that the standard for judging any act are the values of the majority community:

> der Maßstab für die objektive Bewertung eines Beweggrunds [ist] jedoch den Vorstellungen der Rechtsgemeinschaft der Bundesrepublik Deutschland zu entnehmen, in der der Angeklagte lebt und vor deren Gericht er sich zu verantworten hat, und nicht den Anschauungen einer Volksgruppe, die sich den sittlichen und rechtlichen Werten dieser Rechtsgemeinschaft nicht in vollem Umfang verbunden fühlt.[23]

The impact of this judgment soon became clear. In the first case after this landmark decision, on 11 April 2005, a court in Esslingen in Baden-Württemberg sentenced a 19-year-old Turkish man to nine years' imprisonment for manslaughter, one year below the maximum penalty for a juvenile. He had stabbed the lover of his sister, who was in the process of divorcing her husband, 40 times, after he had refused to break off the relationship. The boy, who was a minor when the crime was committed, had confessed to the crime, but had argued that the need to restore the honour of his ultra-conservative family, which was sullied by his sister's impending divorce and the extra-marital relationship, compelled him to commit the murder (Agence France Presse, 2005).

---

[23] 'The standard for the objective determination of a motive must be derived from the values and ideas of the German community under the law [=German society] of which the accused is a resident and to whose courts he is answerable, and not from the values of an ethnic community that does not consider itself fully bound to the ethical and legal values of the German community under the law.'

Likewise, the killer of Hatun Sürücü, her youngest brother, received the highest possible sentence for juveniles, nine years in prison, in April 2006 from the Landesgericht Berlin. However, his two alleged accomplices, his two elder brothers, were acquitted because there was no proof of their direct involvement in the killing (von Bullion, 'Hohe Haftstrafe für den Täter', 2006).

These developments give rise to the hope that decisions that let a false deference to cultural difference trump a woman's right to live a self-determined life, are a thing of the past and that the legal battle against honour killings in Germany is largely won. Decisions by the German Bundesgerichtshof, especially the judgment of 28 January 2004, and those of several lower courts, have made clear that reduced sentences for cultural reasons in cases of honour crimes will no longer be tolerated. Most importantly, however, to remove any legal uncertainty, a Bill is currently being debated in the Bundestag, the German Parliament, which would *automatically* classify all honour killings as murder and thus give the prospect of a life sentence to serve as a true deterrent (von Bullion, 'Kristina Köhler Nimmt Kampf Gegen Ehrenmorde Auf', 2005).

The question that remains now is, what can and should be done to *prevent* honour crimes against women in the first place?

CONCLUSION: PREVENTING HONOUR KILLINGS

While precluding the use of a cultural defense for honour killings is a positive development, the emphasis must be on the prevention of honour crimes in the first place. How is this to be done? It is obvious that the battle against honour killings requires a long-term commitment and a multidimensional, coherent and coordinated approach by four equally important groups: (1) Muslim Turkish community leaders, both religious and secular; (2) moderate Muslims in Germany; (3) the German government; and (4) women's rights groups and activists, such as Terre des Femmes and Necla Kelek. Any effective campaign against honour murders must begin with the recognition that honour killings are not isolated incidents occurring in a socio-cultural vacuum. In fact, they are only the most brutal form of violence against women, a global problem that is insufficiently addressed by most governments, and includes sex-selective abortions, female infanticide, genital cutting, rape, physical assault and forced marriages. Nor are honour killings limited to the Muslim world. Portraying them as such is not only factually incorrect but also counter-productive in that it unnecessarily feeds the stereotype of 'all Muslim men are mistreating their women', thus playing into the hands of radical anti-Western religious groups and making the job of moderate Muslim-Turkish groups the more difficult. Furthermore, it would mask the fact that what are euphemistically labelled 'family tragedies' in non-Muslim German households (when, for instance, a husband kills his wife because she wanted to leave him) are, in fact, honour killings.

Muslim Turkish community groups and leaders, peaceful moderate Muslims that constitute the overwhelming majority of German Muslims, and the German governmental authorities on all levels will play the key role in the campaign to eradicate honour killings. It is incumbent upon Muslim leaders as respected elders of the community to make their condemnation of honour killings as a direct violation of the central tenets of the *Q'uran* absolutely clear, in public pronouncements, during Friday prayers and in Islamic schools. Pious Muslims, who reject the abuse of their faith as a justification for the suppression of women in the name of an archaic conception of honour, ought to leave no doubt that Islam does not allow or tolerate honour murders under any circumstances. The silence of many community leaders so far has been taken as a sign of tolerance and even tacit encouragement of honour killings (Lau, 'Kulturbedingte Ehrenmorde', 2005). Eren Unsal, a secular German-Turkish woman from the Turkish Federation in Berlin, deplored that 'there are many Islamic organizations here which don't approve of the lifestyle that Sürücü [the woman who was killed in February 2005] chose and which propagate very different values. They had to first think how their own communities would react if the condemnation came' (James, 2005). Nonetheless, in a positive development, the German DITIB, the Turkish-Islamic Union of the Institute of Religion with more than 110,000 members, funded by the Turkish government, said that it would finally discuss honour killings in Friday prayers and sermons. This is a step in the right direction. As the recent cartoon controversy has clearly shown, it is only the overwhelming majority of Muslim moderates, like those organised in DITIB, who can wrest control over how the image of Islam and Muslims is portrayed to the rest of the world away from radical fundamentalists, such as Metin Kaplan, the self-proclaimed 'caliph of Cologne'.

The task of the German government will be more far-reaching. Sense and sensitivity will be crucial. Most importantly, the national government needs to overhaul its approach to multiculturalism and cultural integration and do so in a close, on-oing dialogue with minority communities. The differentialist integrationism that permitted the establishment of separatist 'parallel societies' from which radical Islamist groups drew most of their support, ought to be supplanted by a British-style pragmatic integrationism that sees multiculturalism much as a fact of life and minorities not as unwanted guests who are 'different' but as equal members of the British polity. Much greater sensitivity ought to be shown to the cultural needs of Muslims and other religious minorities; for instance, prohibiting female Muslim public school teachers from wearing the hijab at work is an insult. Furthermore, the German government ought to continue its 'mainstreaming of Islam', that is, the public incorporation of representative organisations and the institutionalisation of a 'dialogue of cultures'.

Also, especially important for vulnerable women threatened with forced marriages back in their home countries, the laws governing residency permits for foreigners in Germany should be changed. Specifically, the right of the wife to stay in Germany ought to be decoupled from that of her husband. Terre des Femmes reports that dozens of Turkish women were unable to seek a divorce from their abusive husbands because, according to German law, if the marriage is dissolved within the first two years, the woman loses her right to stay in Germany and must return to her home country (Böhmecke, 2005: 28). Secondly, the length of time during which a foreigner with a German residency permit may leave Germany without losing the permit ought to be raised from six months to two years. Several cases were reported where young women were forced to marry in Turkey. When the women managed to contact German authorities, after more than six months had passed, they learned that they no longer had a right to reside in Germany and had to stay in Turkey (Böhmecke, 2005).

At the same time, the German government must make absolutely clear that a right to culture does not automatically trump human rights, and that state protection of cultural rights ends where they challenge a person's right to life and bodily integrity. The legal protection of Muslim women in Germany cannot be lower than that enjoyed by non–Muslim German women.

Finally, the work of women's rights groups and activists, such as Terre des Femmes, Necla Kelek and Serap Cileli, has been hugely influential in raising awareness about the pervasiveness of honour killings and shone the spotlight on the passivity of the Turkish communities and the German government in addressing this issue. As the German state and Turkish communities redefine the foundations of their co-existence, Turkey positions herself for membership in the European Union and a war is waged 'for Muslim minds', the need for their moral voices will be greater than ever.

10

A Critique of 'Loss of Face' Arguments in Cultural Defense Cases: a Comparative Study

CHER WEIXIA CHEN

In March 1988, New York State Supreme Court Justice Edward Pincus sentenced Dong Lu Chen,[1] a Chinese immigrant who killed his adulterous wife, to five years' probation on a reduced manslaughter charge. In the expert testimony, Prof Burton Pasternak[2] argued that the accused Dong Lu Chen had suffered a serious 'los of face' because of his wife's affair with another man, which drove him to kill her.

Yi Ching Chou was convicted of first-degree murder and sentenced to life in prison, for killing a popular Chinese restaurant owner.[3] Interestingly, both the defense and the prosecutor called an expert witness. These two expert witnesses, Hsien Sheng Ma and Freda Cheung, explained and used the concept of 'loss of face' in an almost opposite way.[4]

Chien-Chyun Lee was convicted of the felony murder of Jia Yann Chao and sentenced to life imprisonment.[5] Lee killed Chao when Chao refused to terminate an affair with Lee's ex-wife. The defense too mentioned 'loss of face' but the court refused to hear the expert testimony.[6]

---

[1] No 87-7774 (NY Sup Ct Dec 2, 1988). A copy of the transcript of the case was kindly provided by AD Renteln.

[2] According to Eugene Cooper, who is a Professor of Anthropology at the University of Southern California, Prof Pasternak has not served as an expert witness since this case, mostly because of the backlash this case caused.

[3] *Yi Ching Chou v Colorado*, No 99SC345, Supreme Court of Colorado, 1999 Colo LEXIS 783.

[4] See 'Killer Gets Life for Slaying at Food Court', *Denver Rocky Mountain News*, 2 June 1995, 30A.

[5] *Lee v The State*, No S92A0725, Supreme Court of Georgia, 262 G 593; 423 SE2d 249; 1992 Ga LEXIS 992; 92 Fulton County DR 3087.

[6] Eugene Cooper was the expert whom the defence attorney planned to call as the expert witness, but when he flew to Atlanta, the judge refused to let him testify. Interview with Prof Cooper, 10 December 2003.

New immigrants from various cultural backgrounds have posed a serious challenge to the US legal system. To solve this problem, the 'cultural defense' has therefore been proposed by many scholars as a necessary and legitimate solution.[7] However, this is a topic discussed mostly among Western academics. As an outsider to the dominant Western tradition, and a native Chinese born and raised in China and therefore an insider with respect to the cultural minority group involved, it is my hope that my analysis will contribute to this debate by offering some insights and a new perspective. This chapter has two principal objectives. First, it seeks to describe the problems associated with the use of 'cultural defense' in the US legal system through the examination of cases involving Chinese Americans. Since I am a native Chinese woman from mainland China, it will be more desirable and less controversial if I focus on Chinese Americans and speak from the perspective of a native Chinese person about the specific issue of 'saving face' in 'Chinese culture'. Secondly, by looking at similar cases in the Chinese legal system, I aim to recommend to US legal policy-makers a new policy which involves the comparative study of law. The proposal is based on the premise that the 'cultural defense' argument should at least be allowed to be presented to the court but should then be subjected to careful comparative analysis. This essay is based on interdisciplinary academic resources, in both English and Chinese.

LOSS OF FACE

Courts treated the 'loss of face' argument differently in these three cases. It succeeded in the *Chen* case, while it was not accepted in the *Lee* and the *Chou* cases. Obviously, Justice Pincus was convinced by the expert testimony that Chen's reaction was 'normal' according to the standard of 'an average Chinese man'. He held:

> Were this crime committed by the defendant as someone who was born and raised in America, or born elsewhere but primarily raised in America, even in the Chinese American community, the Court would have been constrained to find the defendant guilty of manslaughter in the first degree. But, this Court cannot ignore ... the very cogent forceful testimony of Doctor Pasternak, who is, perhaps, the greatest expert in America on China and interfamilial relationships.[8]

---

[7] 'A "cultural defense" is a defense employed by individuals who claim that their culture is so ingrained that it predisposes them to actions—actions which may conflict with the laws of their new homeland.' See AD Renteln, 'In Defense of Culture in the Courtroom' in RA Shweder, M Minow and HR Markus (eds), *Engaging Cultural Differences* (New York, Russell Sage Foundation, 2001) 196.

[8] Record at 301–2.

By contrast, in the *Lee* case, the judge was apparently not very interested in the expert testimony:

> We note that the defendant was permitted to testify to many aspects of Chinese culture, and therefore the jury had the benefit of much of the evidence the defendant sought to elicit from this expert.[9]

In fact, the court may be right to allow the accused to provide his cultural background while refusing to hear the expert testimony. This does not mean the court is unwilling to admit the 'cultural defense'. If the accused is able to employ a 'cultural defense', this is enough to assist the jury and the judges in understanding the whole case. The court in this case clearly tried to avoid over-reliance on the 'expert witness' and the possible controversy to which it may lead, as in the *Chen* case.

The utilization of the 'cultural defense' in the *Chou* case was even more contentious. Both the defense and the prosecution called an expert witness and elaborated on the 'loss of face'. In the end, the court did not accept the 'loss of face' claim as a defense for the murderer. Hsien Sheng Ma, an expert witness for the defense, testified that the 'loss of face' had driven the accused insane:

> 'Face' to the Chinese is your pride, respect, almost everything. If you lose face, you are in big trouble. Face is your life. Once you lose face, it's like a solider losing a gun ... if you lost your job and lose your fight, to the Chinese it's a big tragedy. If you can't find help, you go crazy.[10]

To the contrary, the expert witness for the prosecution, Dr Freda Cheung, refuted the defense argument, contending that 'the "loss of face" never justifies shooting a man in the heart. We never advocate violence to settle conflicts. We emphasize harmony. You want to settle it, so it does not result in violence'. Therefore, as regards 'loss of face', its meaning and its importance in a particular case is debatable. The 'cultural defense' in the *Chou* case was used to the fullest extent in the sense that both sides raised it and then tested it. The purpose of employing the 'cultural defense', to assist the jury and the judge in better comprehending the whole case, was achieved in this case; that is to say, the 'cultural defense' should be employed in court

---

[9] *Lee v The State*, above n 5. Professor Cooper also related to me a similar occasion: the judge held a conference which he attended, during which the judge explained that it was a case about self-defence, and asked him 'what is the role of culture here?'. Professor Cooper therefore did not need to attend court to testify as a 'culture expert' but flew back to Los Angeles. According to Prof Cooper, the judge also already had some knowledge of Chinese culture. Interview with Professor Cooper, 10 December 2003.

[10] H Pankratz, 'DA: Chinese Expert Knew Right from Wrong', *The Denver Post*, 9 March 1995, B–05.

proceedings because it helps the court, in practical ways, to solve the central issue in a given case. However, as to whether the court should adopt the 'cultural defense' as a factor to mitigate punishment, to make exemptions from policies, or to increase damage awards,[11] should be up to the judge and the jury to decide on a case by case basis.

Authenticity of 'Loss of Face' Defense

The concept of 'face' has been defined as 'something that is diffusedly located in the flow of events',[12] 'a psychological image that can be granted and lost and fought for and presented as a gift',[13] or 'the public self-image that every member of a society wants to claim for himself/herself'.[14] In ancient times, a Chinese warrior chief, after losing a battle, might commit suicide because he had lost face. While this may no longer occur, the concept of 'face' remains alive and well in China. Awareness of face and its impact is an extremely important cultural issue. From the scholarly works on face of both US and Chinese scholars, we can gain an insight into this cultural phenomenon.

A CULTURAL ANALYSIS OF 'LOSS OF FACE'

US Scholars on 'Loss of Face'

Among the earlier studies, Hsien-chin Hu's well-known essay is perhaps the first systematic analysis of the Chinese concept of *mianzi* (face).[15] Hu maintains that the word *mianzi* connotes a much wider range of meanings than can possibly be indicated by the English term 'face', and he further distinguishes between two kinds of face, reflected in two different terms in the northern Chinese dialect. The first kind indicates social prestige and is called *mianzi*. 'This is prestige that is accumulated by means of personal effort or clever maneuvering. For this kind of recognition ego is dependent at all times on its external environment.'[16] The second category is *lian*, which means 'the respect of the group for a man with a good moral reputation: the man who will fulfill his obligations regardless of the hardships involved,

---

[11] AD Renteln, 'The Use and Abuse of the Cultural Defense' (2005) 20 *Canadian Journal of Law and Society* 30.

[12] E Goffman, 'On Face-Work' (1955) 18 *Psychiatry* 213, 214.

[13] Y Lin, *My Country and My People* (Taipei, John Day, 1968) 199.

[14] P Brown and S Levinson, 'Universals in Language Usage: Politeness Phenomenon' in E Goody (ed), *Questions and Politeness: Strategies in Social Interaction* (Cambridge, Cambridge University Press, 1978) 66.

[15] See H Hu, 'The Chinese Concept of Face' (1944) 46 *American Anthropologist* 45.

[16] *Ibid* at 45.

who under all circumstances shows himself a decent human being'.[17] Unlike the former, which completely depends on others' evaluation, the latter 'is not only an external sanction for behavior that violates moral standards, but constitutes an internal sanction as well'.[18]

Hu argues that when a person commits a crime and has to be subject to the legal punishment for justice, he does not 'lose face' if this conduct is morally justified. He did not offer any example. However, this argument, on the one hand, reveals the reality of the occasional detachment of law and morality in the Chinese legal system. On the other hand, if applied to the cases mentioned above, it means that the three accused must be punished by the court, but they may get other compensation such as public sympathy in other social arenas.

While Hu's elaborate distinction between *mianzi* and *lian* has provoked further conceptual inquiries, most studies still emphasize face as being an aspect of social prestige (*mianzi*) and as having the function of regulating people's behaviour externally. The leading scholar on China studies, John Fairbank, represents the latter.[19] "'Face' has been a social matter. Personal dignity has been derived from right conduct and the social approval it has secured. "Loss of face" came from failure to observe the rules of conduct so that others saw one at a disadvantage.'[20] King has criticized this tendency to overlook the second kind of face (*lian*) and has rephrased the double meanings of face as a distinction between social face and moral face.[21] According to King, the moral face does not resort to an external environment or an audience in regulating a person's behaviour. On the contrary, moral face is based on a person's feelings of shame, a Chinese notion close to the Western concept of guilt, and thus serves as an internal moral constraint.[22]

Face, according to Stella Ting-Toomey, is a concept grounded in Confucianism. It 'means projected social image and social self-respect'. To cause someone to 'lose face' will lead to group disharmony.[23] Contact among group members flows smoothly as long as everybody's claim to face is supported. If not, the interaction would break down and the person who loses face would feel ashamed and embarrassed.[24] Various behaviours have

---

[17] *Ibid.*

[18] *Ibid* at 61.

[19] See JK Fairbank, *The United States and China*, 4th edn, (Cambridge, MA, Harvard University Press, 1979).

[20] *Ibid* at 135.

[21] AY King, '"Mian", "Chi" yu zhongguoren xingwei zhi fenxi' ('"Face", "Shame" and the Analysis of Behavior Patterns of the Chinese') in G Yang (ed), *Zhongguoren de xinli (The Psychology of the Chinese)* (Taipei, Guiguan Press, 1988) 325.

[22] *Ibid* at 335–8.

[23] S Ting-Toomey, *Communicating Across Cultures* (New York, Guilford Press, 1999) 75.

[24] E Goffman, 'On Face-Work' (1955) 18 *Psychiatry* 213; 'Embarrassment and Social Organization' (1956) 62 *American Journal of Sociology* 264. (Goffman, Apsler and Brown's articles (see below n 25) are focused on the Western concept of 'face', which again proves the concept of face is not unique to Chinese culture.)

been observed when people are embarrassed;[25] the most usual following a 'loss of face' is face-saving behaviour which does not entail a violent reaction, as in the three cases mentioned above.[26]

If we apply these 'face' theories to those cases, we unfortunately find that the expert opinions presented in the courtroom seem to lack the essence of the concept of 'face'. Who lost 'moral' face? Lee's ex-wife and Chen's wife did, since they did not follow social standards, and they were supposed to feel ashamed. Lee and Chen lost 'moral face' only after they killed the victims, rather than before the killing, which suggests the 'loss of face' theory is not applicable in these two cases as, before the killing, they had not lost face. Likewise, it is Hsieh rather than Chou who lost 'social face' since his social prestige had been damaged by that public dispute. It is also misleading to assume that only in China or Japan is the issue of 'face' important.[27] For example, face is sometimes key to international relations. The Cuban Missile Crisis of 1962 shows both Kennedy and Khrushchev paid fair attention to honouring 'face'. Additionally, as argued by Brown, face is vital in various negotiation processes, no matter whether it occurs in France or in China.[28]

Chinese Scholars on 'Loss of Face'

Ge Gao argues that *lian* (face) and *mianzi* (image) are essential to the Chinese self-concept and interpersonal relationship. 'Face need' governs a person's behaviour, and provides guidance as to when to disclose and not to disclose certain information. More importantly, 'face need' is a collective concern.[29]

David Yau-fai Ho,[30] a scholar from the University of Hong Kong, argues that suicide is repeatedly the ultimate way to save face after a very serious loss of face.[31] However, suicide as a means to saveface is not unique in the Chinese context.[32] Rather, face is universal.[33] Some common strategies

---

[25] R Apsler, 'Effects of Embarrassment on Behavior Toward Others' (1975) 32 *Journal of Personality and Social Psychology* 145; BR Brown, 'Face-saving Following Experimentally Induced Embarrassment' (1970) 6 *Journal of Experimental Social Psychology* 255.

[26] Brown, *ibid*.

[27] S Rosenberg, 'Face', available at www.beyondintractability.org/m/face.jsp.

[28] *Ibid*. See also B Brown, 'Face Saving and Face Restoration in Negotiation' in D Druckman (ed), *Negotiations: Social-Psychological Perspectives* (Beverly Hills, CA, Sage, 1977) 275.

[29] G Gao, 'Self and Other: a Chinese Perspective on Interpersonal Relationships' in WB Gudykunst *et al* (eds), *Communication in Personal Relationships Across Cultures* (Thousand Oaks, Sage Publications, 1996) 94–6. Also see AY King and MH Bond, 'The Confucian Paradigm of Man: a Sociological View' in WS Tseng and DH Wu (eds), *Chinese Culture and Mental Health* (Orlando, Academic Press, 1985) 29–45.

[30] DYF Ho, 'On the Concept of Face' (1975) 81 *American Journal of Sociology* 867.

[31] Eg, a 'captain found guilty of cowardly abandoning the ship and the crew to save his own life, priest caught in adultery, or a family disgraced by incestuous relationships'. *Ibid* at 873.

[32] Eg, 'the commander-in-chief beaten in the battlefield shoots himself to avoid the humiliation of being captured alive'. *Ibid*.

[33] *Ibid* at 881–2.

of saving face for another include avoiding criticizing anyone, especially superiors in public, using circumlocution and equivocation in any criticism of another's performance, and according greater social rewards to those skilled at preserving face for others.[34] These strategies are by no means particularly Chinese, however.[35] 'Face' is just a manifestation of basic desires derived from the fundamental nature of the existence of human beings.[36] It is a metaphor about not humiliating or embarrassing people in public. People in other cultures are just as concerned about public humiliation and try to avoid it as much as possible. Therefore, 'loss of face' is not an exclusively Chinese cultural notion. Obviously, neither Ho's nor other scholars' theories support Chen and Lee in their attempts to raise it as a special Chinese cultural phenomenon to excuse their misconduct.

However, it is fair to say that 'face' is a very important part of Chinese culture. CAJ,[37] a Chinese Academic Journals database constructed with the support of the Chinese government, includes 5,300 periodicals in full text and 700,000 full-text articles with 1 million abstracts and 2 million bibliographies added annually. A search in all categories by using the keyword 'face' was linked to 434 articles.[38] 'Face' is a word occurring in all kinds of fields, which to a great extent reflects the fact that it is an ingrained part of Chinese culture. Nevertheless, not many articles deal with the role of 'face' in Chinese law. Among them are two articles directly discussing 'loss of face' and 'law', which provides meaningful insights for those US cases involving the cultural defense of 'loss of face'. Although they are not about real legal cases, they still illustrate how Chinese scholars think about 'face' and 'law':

> The sheriff asked a butcher in front of many people to submit the tax he was supposed to give. The butcher felt he had lost face. Therefore he was so angry that he killed the sheriff with his blade. Both scholars agreed that the butcher should be punished by law, although it was true that the way the sheriff dealt with this issue needed improvement, ie, the sheriff should not have made the butcher lose face by humiliating him in public.[39]

---

[34] MH Bond and PWH Lee, 'Face Saving in Chinese Culture: a Discussion and Experimental Study of Hong Kong Students' in AYC King and RPL Lee (eds), *Social Life and Development in Hong Kong* (Hong Kong, Chinese University Press, 1981) 288–305.

[35] K Agyekum, 'The Socio-Cultural Concept of Face in Akan Communication' (2004) 12 Pragmatics and Cognition 71.

[36] T Hayashi, 'Reconstructing a Universal Theory of Politeness: Face, Politeness and the Model of Realization', available at www.nord.helsinki.fi/clpg/CLPG/Takuo%20Hayashi.pdf.

[37] See www.cnki.net.

[38] On 16 November 2003.

[39] See Y Tang, 'Xuefa, Shoufa, Zhifa' [('Study the Law, Obey the Law and Implement the Law') (1999) 11 *Anhui Taxation* 36. Also see H Wu, 'Bugai Fasheng de Beiju' ('Tragedy to be Avoided') (1999) 11 *Anhui Taxation* 36 (author's translation).

Even though the working method of the sheriff was problematic, there is no doubt that the butcher should be held legally responsible for his uncontrolled action. The butcher lost face, but he could by no means use this to avoid the legal sanction. To some extent, this legal fiction is similar to the *Chou* case. Within the Chinese context, an acceptable consequence was to put the butcher in jail even though he badly lost face. The butcher simply had no legal ground to avoid punishment. Chinese culture and law do not permit his conduct. If the *Chou* case had occurred in China, the only conceivable outcome would have been that Chou would have received the legal punishment he deserved. Moreover, Hsieh lost face more seriously than Chow. His 'loss of face' would not even have been taken into consideration to mitigate the sentence.

Culture is multidimensional. The 'loss of face' argument was presented in simplistic terms in the courtroom and other relevant facts were ignored, which is the main defect in the *Chen* case. This also explains why it caused such a public outcry. The problems in the *Chen* case were not only about whether women's rights should outweigh the 'cultural defense', but also about whether this is a defensible cultural argument (which I found largely unconvincing). Nonetheless, it appears that Justice Pincus was fascinated by this concept, and he even incorporated it into his legal reasoning,[40] which in part should be attributed to the successful testimony of Prof Pasternak.

PROBLEM OF 'EXPERT WITNESSES'

The *Chen* case demonstrates the potential danger of over-reliance on the 'expert witness'.[41] His or her role in these cases differed in terms of how they persuaded the judge and jury by their testimony. The *Chen* case is a significant example to demonstrate the extent to which a white anthropologist can affect the fate of a Chinese man. In the *Chou* case, judges appeared to be convinced by the expert testimony employed by the prosecution. But it seems the judge in the *Lee* case did not think there was a need to hear the expert testimony. The expert witness in the *Chen* case was Prof Pasternak, a well-known professor specializing in China issues. However, his work does not mean his view of Chinese culture is bias-free. As a matter of fact, at least for me, a native Chinese, his explanation as regards the violent reaction of an average 'Chinese man' to his wife's adultery[42] is exaggerated. His

---

[40] 'And if he does not obey and he violates any of these conditions, not only does he face jail, but his will be total loss of face.' See Record at 311.

[41] But for the anthropologist as expert witness, see L Rosen, 'The Anthropologist as Expert Witness' (1977) 79 *American Anthropologist* 555.

[42] When I shared this case with my Chinese friends, they were all shocked by Justice Pincus' decision. One male friend even made a joke, saying that, 'I should immigrate to America if my wife someday betrays me'. It seems that only in the United States, rather than in China, can a husband get away with murder.

account is possibly consistent with ancient Chinese culture but not with the current Chinese culture.

When *Brown v Board of Education* used the findings of a 'doll expert', it elevated the status of social scientists. However, uncertainty and controversy will always accompany the use of social science, as happened in the *Chen* case. The use of an 'expert witness' is vulnerable to abuse. As Prof Cooper has pointed out, some 'experts' are unscrupulous and are willing to say whatever the attorney wants about 'a culture' in return for payment.[43] Therefore, the consequence of the use of this sort of 'cultural defense' may not only bring about injustice but also the disdain of a certain cultural or ethnic group.[44] There has yet to be created a set of complete and effective regulations governing 'expert witnesses'. I would suggest, in fact, that to include the evidence of a legal scholar or lawyer familiar with the law in that specific country would be a fine supplement to an 'expert witness'. Although the 'expert witness' is usually an anthropologist or sociologist, the information obtained from a legal scholar or lawyer would be more law-oriented and his or her opinion about the positive law might be less contentious than the definition of 'culture' among anthropologists.

TOWARD A SOLUTION

The cultural defense can be a powerful defensive weapon and may be a legitimate means of reducing a penalty,[45] but judges and juries must continue to use it in a prudent, case-sensitive manner and recognize that culture is not the whole story, nor does the cultural issue at hand characterize the whole culture. Several proposals have been put forward to integrate the 'cultural defense' into the American legal system. According to one, those who wish

---

[43] L Rosen has argued that the contingent fee paid to an expert is one reason for concern about the impartiality of adversary witnesses. *Ibid* at 574.

[44] Many Chinese immigrants and Chinese Americans protested at the portrayal of China by Prof Pasternak in terms of the 'primitive', elemental oriental: 'Our culture does not give a man permission to kill his wife regardless of what the situation was at home'. Chen is 'either crazy or he's enraged ... It has nothing to do with his being Chinese or having a Chinese background ... It is not acceptable conduct'. See M Yen, 'Refusal to Jail Immigrant who Killed Wife Stirs Outrage; Judge Ordered Probation for Chinese Man, Citing his "Cultural Background"', *Washington Post*, 10 April 1989, A3. Chen, they say, 'would have been dealt with much more harshly by a Chinese court'. A man who accuses his wife of adultery 'goes to the court' but 'has no right to kill his wife. It is absolutely not part of Chinese culture'. See A Jetter, 'Fear is Legacy of Wife Killing in Chinatown; Battered Asians Shocked by Husband's Probation', *Newsday*, 24 November 1989, 4. 'This kind of thinking', argued S Hom of Queens College Law School, 'reinforces patriarchal and racial stereotyping ... which don't even exist in China today'. See D Woo, '*The People v. Fumiko Kimura*: But Which People?' (1989) 17 *International Journal of the Sociology of Law* 403, 423.

[45] For a detailed analysis for and against the use of the cultural defence, see AD Renteln, *The Cultural Defense* (New York/Oxford, Oxford University Press, 2004) Pt III.

to raise the 'cultural defense' have to show that 'the practice in question is an "authentic" part of their way of life and that the conduct of the person was influenced by the tradition'.[46] Kim also proposed that the Federal Rules of Evidence Rules 702 and 401 should guide the judges to decide the admissibility of expert evidence. Judges should determine the reliability and the relevance of the cultural evidence, which should be used only in cases where state of mind relates to the defendant's acculturation.[47]

In addition to allowing the presentation of the cultural background of the accused, one useful method to determine whether to adopt or reject the 'cultural defense' is by the comparative study of the positive law. According to the historical school of jurisprudence, law does reflect the morality and value system extant within a territory; that is to say, law embraces cultural values. Therefore, to compare how different legal rules deal with a phenomenon is more sensible than comparing how different cultures handle a similar case in the legal system. But it is simpler, more feasible and ultimately more desirable to compare positive law, rather than to put 'culture' on trial. As mentioned earlier, a legal scholar or lawyer knowledgeable about the law of that particular culture can assist the judge and jury in fully understanding that particular culture and its relationship with the local law, and therefore the entire case. After all, the 'cultural defense' is ultimately an issue existing within the legal system. This need for this sort of assistance was indicated in the *Chen* case. Both the prosecutor and the judge asked the expert witness Prof Pasternak about the status of marriage law and the legal consequence of divorce in China. But because Prof Pasternak was an anthropologist, he was not qualified and therefore unable to answer those questions. If a lawyer or a legal scholar acquainted with marriage law or family law in China had been present before the court, the outcome of this case could have been very different.

For example, as to the status of 'loss of face' in Chinese law, there have been many cases similar to the *Chen* case in China.[48] Angry husbands have killed their adulterous wives,[49] and have in consequence all been imprisoned or even subjected to the death penalty,[50] even though the husbands

---

[46] AD Renteln 'In Defense of Culture in the Courtroom' in RA Shweder, M Minow and HR Markus (eds), *Engaging Cultural Differences* (New York, Russell Sage Foundation, 2001) 207.

[47] See NS Kim, 'The Cultural Defense and the Problem of Cultural Preemption: a Framework for Analysis' (1997) 27 *New Mexico Law Review* 101, 140.

[48] See, eg, 'Gongan Zhangfu Shasi Tingzhang Qizi' ('Public Safety Husband Killed Judge Wife'), http://skb.hebeidaily.com.cn/200318/ca252854.htm. Also see www.china-woman.com/gb/zhuanti/cmsw/125.htm.

[49] Under such circumstances, it is called '*Dai LvMao*' ('wear green hats)' which means his wife has had an affair with another man.

[50] See   http://news.eastday.com/epublish/gb/paper148/20031123/class014800012/hwz1047482.htm.

had felt the loss of face. 'Loss of face' does not belong to a 'mitigation element'.[51] There are no grounds in Chinese law and culture to say that a violent reaction to adulterous wives is in any way acceptable.

How Does Chinese Law Deal with 'Loss of Face'?

Current Chinese criminal law does not break homicide down into categories such as murder, voluntary manslaughter and involuntary manslaughter, as US law does.[52] Instead, homicide is divided into two separate sections, homicide and negligent homicide. An interesting dichotomy exists in Chinese law, which distinguishes between serious offences and those offences covered by administrative regulations and practice. The most prominent administrative or 'non-crime' regulations are the Regulations of the PRC on Security Administration and Punishment (SAPR) adopted by the Standing Committee of the NPC in 1986. In many cases, a decision as to whether an offence will be tried as a crime or dealt with under the SAPR will be made according to the likely penalty or punishment to be imposed.[53] According to Chinese criminal law theory, four basic elements are required to establish criminal liability. These are (a) the subject: the person who performed the criminal act; (b) the subjective aspect: the person's intention or negligence; (c) the object: the type of crime, and (d) the objective aspect: the harm caused.[54] With regard to sentencing, there are several articles dealing with mitigation,[55] but 'loss of face' is not included among them.

Culture is not 'static, monolithic and misogynist'.[56] Culture evolves and changes. Chen argued that the traditional Chinese custom allows husbands to dispel their shame in this way when their wives have been unfaithful.[57] It is true that in ancient China, Chen's conduct might have been permissible and his wife's infidelity would have been blamed and sanctioned severely. However, that does not mean that this custom survived in the 1980s. The custom had in fact been continuously contested and then ultimately abolished. One finds no Chinese law allowing such conduct at the present time. Chen immigrated to the United States in the mid-1980s. According to Chinese criminal law in the 1980s, regardless of his wife's betrayal and his subsequent 'loss of face', he would have been

[51] PRC Criminal Code, art 16.
[52] See F Fan and Z Cao, *Fanzui Goucheng (Elements of a Crime)* (Beijing, Law Press, 1987).
[53] SAPR, art 2.
[54] See Fan and Cao, above n 52.
[55] Eg, PRC Criminal Code, art 16 stipulates that deaf-mutes or blind persons who commit crimes may receive lighter or mitigated sentences.
[56] L Volpp, '(Mis)Identifying Culture: Asian Women and the "Cultural Defense"' (1994) 17 *Harvard Women's Law Journal* 63.
[57] C Young, 'Equal Cultures—or Equality?', *Washington Post*, 29 March 1992, C5.

punished in China. Moreover, the 'loss of face' notion does not belong to any 'mitigating element' as designated in the Chinese code.

My argument is simply that the court should have checked to see how Chen's conduct would have been viewed in the modern Chinese legal system. If Justice Pincus or the other judges in the *Chou* and *Lee* cases had referred to the law or similar cases in the Chinese legal system, they would have been better able to judge the truth about claims and reach decisions closer to the truth about whether the claim was a genuine 'cultural defense'. Their decisions would therefore have been at less risk of being wrong if they had incorporated a comparative law approach to the assessment of cultural claims.

The suspicion surrounding the use of a comparative study of the positive law may lie in the attitude to, rather than possibly limited access to the legal information of, the culture at issue. Minority cultures have been considered as backward and barbarian and have been ignored for some time. Thus, it is not surprising if someone questions why the US legal system should pay attention to other legal systems from which these minority cultures come. This answer is that the comparative study of law can facilitate the efforts of policy-makers to improve their own legal systems.[58] To ignore and abandon such an effective means to solve legal problems present in our own legal system only demonstrates the 'legal parochialism' of US elites: they are completely unaware of the solutions adopted in other cultures, and therefore incapable of conceiving of legal reforms.[59]

CONCLUSION

Several years ago, a movie about a Chinese immigrant in the United States led to a media frenzy in China. This movie, entitled *Gua Sha*, is an absorbing movie interweaving the conflicts between the Chinese and US cultures. After immigrating to the United States from China, Datong and his family make their home in St Louis, but the family is suddenly thrown into turmoil. A cultural misunderstanding leads the Child Welfare Agency to threaten to take their young son away from them after Datong's father gave '*gua sha*' treatment[60] to his grandson in order to cure his stomach pain.[61] This movie achieved successful box office returns and nationwide media attention in

---

[58] R David and J Brierley, *Major Legal Systems in the World Today*, 2nd edn (London, Stevens and Sons, 1978) 5–8.

[59] R Kagan, *Adversarial Legalism* (Cambridge, MA/London, Harvard University Press, 2001) 251.

[60] *Gua sha* is a popular treatment for sunstroke by scraping the patient's neck, chest or back in traditional Chinese medicine.

[61] See http://ent.sina.com.cn/m/c/f/guasha.html.

China. It also caused a heated discussion. Many people who were thinking about living abroad or having to live abroad became quite concerned: 'Will I encounter such an incident after I arrive in the United States? Would I be prosecuted if I spank my rebellious son?'[62]

Cultural conflicts do trouble new immigrants and puzzle those who find themselves in the US legal system. Being empowered by the knowledge of the law probably is the only realistic way to avoid legal embarrassment for immigrants. The question of whether recent immigrants can raise the 'cultural defense', a kind of 'cultural rights' argument, has been extensively discussed. A leading scholar on cultural rights has a different point of view. He contends that only minorities who are not immigrants can enjoy 'cultural rights'.[63] However, to some extent, new immigrants are more likely to encounter predicaments in the new legal system as Chen did, since they have not been assimilated or integrated into the mainstream culture. As a result, they are more in need of the protection of 'cultural rights'.

In practice, this issue can be left to the discretion of the judge and jury. After all, it is inappropriate simply to draw a line between immigrants according to the respective length of their residence in the new homeland. Only a consideration of all aspects of a specific case can lead to a rational decision. Moreover, the central benefit to be derived from 'cultural defense' is to have the court focus on the ingrained influence of this culture on this particular person, no matter how long he or she has lived in the new homeland.

Although the US legal system has not yet formally adopted the 'cultural defense', it has been frequently applied in US courtrooms. Nonetheless, a false 'cultural defense' should not be allowed to penetrate the legal system. To determine whether the argument is genuine, careful scrutiny is necessary. A comparative analysis of a cultural practice in multiple legal systems can provide crucial information to both the judge and the jury to decide its authenticity. Only by ascertaining the validity of the claims advanced in cultural defense cases can the strategy be established as a legitimate one.

---

[62] See, eg, http://ent.sina.com.cn/r/m/35610.html.
[63] See W Kymlicka, *Multicultural Citizenship* (Oxford, Oxford University Press, 1995).

11

The Paradox of the Cultural Defence: Gender and Cultural Othering in Canada

MANEESHA DECKHA

THERE IS A cultural anxiety among feminists concerned with cultural and racial equality in pluralistic societies.[1] The anxiety typically arises in response to a situation where a man has committed an act of violence against his intimate female partner or child and there is the potential that he will play the 'culture card' as a method to absolve him from responsibility or, at least, mitigate his actions. Referred to as the 'cultural defence' in both instances, culture only hypothetically operates as a defence in the first. In the latter, culture is used to soften the impact of a conviction by reducing the penalty that would otherwise ensue. In Canada, the cultural defence operates more to reduce charges and sentences than to completely excuse an accused's conduct.[2] Although both Parliament and the courts have not instantiated a formalised cultural defence,[3] and regardless of the precise role culture plays, the mention of it in this type

---

[1] I borrow here from Joan Williams' term, 'commodification anxiety', which she uses to describe cultural resistance to granting property rights in certain entities such as human bodies. Commodification anxiety reflects a concern that certain entities should be kept separate from the market sphere and divorced from market discourse in order to protect human flourishing. By 'cultural anxiety', then, I am referring to an aversion to cultural discourse to describe certain phenomenon. J Williams, *Unbending Gender: Why Work and Family Conflict and What to Do About It* (New York, Oxford University Press, 2000) 118.

[2] CM Wong, 'Good Intentions, Troublesome Applications: the Cultural Defence and Other Uses of Cultural Evidence in Canada' (1999) 42 *Criminal Law Quarterly* 367, 368, 372. The cultural defence does not arise only in the situations in which a woman has suffered harm; Canadian cases involving the cultural defence have arisen in other contexts. However, for the purposes of this chapter, I will only discuss the defence as it has arisen in cases involving harm to women, as such cases present the most pressing issues for a post-colonial critical race feminist analysis.

[3] *Ibid* at 367–9.

of criminal context has been a cause of concern for critical race feminists.[4] Sonia Lawrence and Pascale Fournier have most recently written about the phenomenon of the cultural defence with respect to two high profile Canadian cases involving 'immigrant' communities.[5] Sherene Razack has recently written about mitigation of sentences for cultural reasons in cases involving Aboriginal individuals.[6] These scholars articulate two principal concerns. First, there is a persistent anxiety as to how majoritarian courts portray and misrepresent marginalised cultures so as to reproduce colonial discourses about non-Western peoples. Secondly, critical race feminists are concerned that the end result of culturally sensitive laws and sentencing is the diminishment of the value of the lives of marginalised women and children and the harm done to them through family violence.

In this chapter, I will discuss the trends in the cases involving non-Aboriginal sexual and family violence in Canada to show how judges are 'making sense' of culture.[7] I argue that, despite the impoverished understanding of culture in Canadian courtrooms that critical race feminists have identified, it is possible and desirable for the law to factor culture into assessments of guilt and punishment without diminishing the harm done to the female and child victims of sexual and family violence. I do not canvass all the arguments for and against the cultural defence here, nor do I survey all the cases in Canada that have dealt with it.[8] Instead, I concentrate on what critical race feminists should do about cultural defences in the context of sexual and family violence in the non-Aboriginal context, taking recent cases as illustrative examples. In particular, I offer some additional arguments focusing on the conceptual links between culture and violence

---

[4] By 'critical race feminists', I refer to feminist legal academics who make race and gender, if not other social markers of identity, priorities in contextualising and interrogating legal narratives. See, eg, A Wing, *Critical Race Feminism: a Reader* (New York, New York University Press, 1996).

[5] See Fournier, below n 11; Lawrence, b note 12.

[6] See Razack, below n 13. For the work of another insightful Canadian critical race feminist, see Wong, above n 2.

[7] The cultural dimensions of legal analyses where Aboriginal complainants and defendants are involved are unique given the nature of colonial encounters suffered by Aboriginal peoples in Canada. Canadian courts, through a growing awareness of the failures of the criminal justice system vis-à-vis Aboriginal peoples, have addressed cultural considerations more consistently and with direction, at times, from the Criminal Code as to the appropriateness of applying culturally distinct measures, eg, diversion and/or sentencing circles. See Criminal Code, RSC, 1985, c C-46, s 718.2(e). The complexities of this analysis merit more sustained attention than I can give here, which is why the parameters of this chapter focus on the non-Aboriginal context. For an analysis of the problems in the cultural adjudication of Aboriginal peoples in the context of cultural defence, see Razack, below n 13. For an analysis of the problems of courts attempting to define the cultures of Aboriginal people in general, see J Borrows, 'Sovereignty's Alchemy: an Analysis of Delgamuukw v. British Columbia' (1999) 37 *Osgoode Hall Law Journal* 537; and J Borrows, 'Frozen Rights in Canada: Constitutional Interpretation and the Trickster' (1998) 22 *American Indian Law Review* 37.

[8] For a fairly recent article that does do both of these things, see Wong, above n 2.

for retaining the concept of the cultural defence in law. I then suggest an approach, which I have elsewhere referred to as the 'refined differentiated' approach to receiving cultural claims in law,[9] and apply it to two recent cases of sexual and family violence in British Columbia to consider how culture should have been received in those instances. I turn first to an exploration of the anxiety that the cultural defence is causing for critical race feminists.

CULTURAL ANXIETY

As noted above, the anxiety that critical race feminists experience when contemplating even this incarnation of the cultural defence takes two forms. The first is a discursive problem of representation and conceptualisation. Judges in Canada still primarily come from the dominant cultural groups in Canada, that is male, white and European, of British origin in English-speaking Canada and French origin in French-speaking Canada. Majoritarian cultural values thus heavily influence their worldviews, including what they 'know' about other cultures, especially those classified as non-Western.[10] Given this context, it is not surprising that many decisions result in reductive representations of the concept of culture and, in particular, non-Western cultures.

Discursive Harm

The first reductive move in representing cultures which authors such as Pascale Fournier,[11] Sonia Lawrence[12] and Sherene Razack[13] note in Canadian judicial decisions involving family violence within racialised communities, is the ease with which courts talk about the culture of a group as a monolithic whole. In doing so, the law reflects modernist ideas of culture as reified and totalised phenomena, largely bereft of internal contestation, differences

---

[9] M Deckha, 'Is Culture Taboo?: Feminism, Intersectionality, and Culture Talk in Law' (2004) 16(1) *Canadian Journal of Women and the Law* 14.

[10] Of course, cultural reductionism is not the only problem that a judiciary stacked with majoritarian values breeds. Jenny Nedelsky has noted the problems in judicial comprehension, given a male-dominated judiciary, of physical violence against women in assaults where culture is understood to be absent. She argues for a greater diversification of the judiciary in Canada. J Nedelsky, 'Embodied Diversity and the Challenges to Law' (1997) 42 *McGill Law Journal* 91.

[11] P Fournier, 'The Ghettoisation of Difference in Canada: "Rape by Culture" and the Danger of a "Cultural Defense" in Criminal Law Trials' (2002) 29 *Manitoba Law Journal* 81.

[12] S Lawrence, 'Cultural (In)sensitivity: the Danger of a Simplistic Approach to Culture in the Courtroom' (2001) 13 *Canadian Journal of Women and the Law* 107.

[13] S Razack, *Looking White People in the Eye: Gender, Race, and Culture in Courtrooms and Classrooms* (Toronto, University of Toronto Press, 2001).

or disputes among its members. The trend in traditional anthropological ethnography has been to create a binary between the Western cultural background of the anthropologist and the non-Western peoples he or she studied through 'native informants'.[14] The post-colonial inflections into anthropology as a discipline wrote against this history to focus instead on the partialities of suggested universals or 'truths' about a certain culture by highlighting the situatedness of the Western 'knowledge-maker' and the power dynamics that inform that position. Post-colonial cultural anthropology examines the situatedness of cultural claims, and the ways in which cultural elites create 'traditions' that do not resonate or reflect the experiences of other cultural members.[15] By discussing 'culture' as uniformly experienced by all within it, the law glosses over the tension and fissures that mark most, if not all, cultural groups.

An anxiety about essentialism lies at the core of the concern over homogeneity. Cultural essentialism takes that which is properly dynamic, evolving and the contested terrain of multiple interpretations and turns it into something fixed, static and exclusionary of different interpretations as to what counts as a *cultural* 'tradition' or 'practice'.[16] Both Lawrence and Fournier have demonstrated how essentialism permeated the court's construction of culture in *Lucien*.[17] A further example may be seen in the 2004 Ontario Court of Appeal case of *R v Liu*, which upheld the conviction of a husband charged with the murder of his wife. Both the victim, Fengzhi Huang, and the defendant, Liu, were ethnically Chinese; the court does not indicate how long they had been living in, or whether even they were born in, Canada. *Liu* is an interesting case because it is an example where the accused sought to avoid cultural evidence being adduced on his behalf because of the obstacles it created for his defence. A letter with two Chinese characters scrolled in Liu's blood had been found at the crime scene and the accused had objected to the admissibility of expert evidence that testified that the two characters symbolised loyalty and righteousness. This interpretation of the characters became a liability for Liu because of the Crown's theory that Liu had sexually assaulted his wife and then murdered her after finding out about her infidelity. Liu insisted that the letter was a statement of love created in the hope of reconciliation and ending their arguments.

---

[14] R Coombe, 'Contingent Articulations: Critical Cultural Studies of Law' in A Sarat and T Kearns (eds), *Law in the Domains of Culture* (Ann Arbor, University of Michigan Press, 1997); V Kirby, "Feminisms, Reading, Postmodernisms: Rethinking Complicity' in S Gunew and A Yeatman (eds), *Feminism and the Politics of Difference* (Boulder, West View Press, 1993) 29–30.

[15] *Ibid.*

[16] R Kapur, *Erotic Justice: Law and the New Politics of Postcolonialism* (London, Glass House Press, 2005).

[17] Below n 34.

In characterising the admissibility of the expert evidence, the trial court had this to say:

> Loyalty and righteousness are values enshrined in the Chinese culture and embraced at every level of life. In Chinese culture, loyalty and righteousness are viewed as the most important values, akin in importance to Western notions of democracy and freedom. Divorce runs contrary to the values of loyalty and righteousness, as mandated by Confucian tradition.[18]

China is the most populous country in the world, with many distinct ethnic, regional and class groups. To even speak of a uniform 'Chinese culture' is a precarious claim, but the court has no anxiety itself in contrasting 'Chinese culture' with 'Western notions'. They do not hesitate to construct China as a land where support for democracy or freedom is absent, with the West as a political scape where loyalty and righteousness do not resonate as values. On appeal, the court did not nuance its handling of this cultural dimension of the case, but rather reiterated the emphasis on Chinese culture by contrasting it with Canadian society,[19] even though 3.5 per cent of Canadians were found to be ethnically Chinese in the 2001 census.[20]

As Uma Narayan notes, when this type of essentialism operates within gendered narratives, it conveys distorted views of what it means to be a man or a woman in particular cultures and the roles and values that accompany these gender performances. She describes the problem as it pertains to discussions of racialised persons, including women marked as 'non-Western':

> The project of attending to differences among women across a variety of national and cultural contexts then becomes a project that endorses and replicates problematic and colonialist assumptions about the cultural differences between 'Western culture' and 'Non-Western cultures' and the women who inhabit them. Seemingly universal essentialist generalizations about 'all women' are replaced by culture-specific essentialist generalizations that depend on totalizing categories such as 'Western culture', 'Non-Western cultures', 'Western women', 'Third World women', and so forth ... They depict as homogenous groups of heterogeneous people whose values, interests, ways of life, and moral and political

---

[18] *R. v Liu* [2002] OJ no 5078, per McKinnon J, para 5.

[19] *R. v Liu* [2004] OJ no 4221, para 21 where the court stated that the expert evidence about the letter 'was necessary because otherwise the cultural significance of the letter would have been lost on a Canadian jury'.

[20] See 'Canada's Ethnocultural Portrait: the Changing Mosaic', available at www12.statcan. ca/english/census01/products/analytic/companion/etoimm/canada.cfm#chinese_largest_ visible_minority. For a US example of a binary construction involving the United States and China, see Wong, above n 2 at 374–5, noting that in the case of People v Dong Lu Chen, (1988) No 87-7774 (NY Sup Ct), the court characterised 'American' and 'Chinese' as being two 'utterly distinct categories" despite the lack of testimony or other evidence for the court's characterisation of Chinese society.

commitments are internally plural and divergent ... (C)ultural essentialism often conflates socially dominant cultural norms with the actual values and practices of a culture.[21]

When cultural essentialism operates, we are offered a picture or snapshot of a culture that is always already complete, discrete and readily identifiable from a global circuit of cultural exchanges. It is not simply that cultures are presented as monolithic, but that we assume there is an inherent core to the culture comprised of certain features or practices. Moreover, we assume that these practices or features unify cultural members despite the differences that might deeply divide or stratify a society and despite the fact that there are members of that group who do not carry out the practices said to be emblematic of their culture.[22]

Are we to assume that these latter members have lost their culture or that the culture has not been properly preserved? As Narayan and others have argued, such an understanding would be simplistic. It is better to regard statements such as 'US culture is violent' as an essentialist interpretation of what the United States is, not an accurate one, that is in need of history and politics to complete a contextual understanding.[23] For such a statement to make sense to us, we must gloss over pacifist elements of US society, as well as violent elements in other cultures. As Narayan notes, the objective is not to prove that violent practices or features are non-existent in the United States or that we are all the same and part of the human family.[24] Cultures persist and differences can and do exist between people who grow up in one country as opposed to people who grow up in another. The point is, however, that it is more likely than not that it is a particular segment of US society in terms of time, place, gender, class, age, etc, that is violent, rather than all Americans regardless of these qualifications of social location.

A second central reductive feature in how Canadian courts understand culture raised in defence of family violence charges follows from the previous two and is, arguably, the focus of feminist cultural anxiety surrounding the discursive harm that results through conventional conceptualisations of culture. The concern is prompted by the fact that the essentialist and monolithic accounts of non-Western cultures are primarily *negative* ones where non-Western cultural 'traditions' are made synonymous with bad

---

[21] U Narayan, 'Essence of Culture and a Sense of History: a Feminist Critique of Cultural Essentialism' (2000) 13(2) *Hypatia* 86, reprinted in U Narayan and S Harding (eds), *Decentering the Center: Philosophy for a Multicultural, Postcolonial, and Feminist World* (Bloomington, Indiana University Press, 2000) 81–2.

[22] A Dundes Renteln, 'The Use and Abuse of the Cultural Defense' (2005) 20(1) *Canadian Journal of Law and Society* 47, 63–4.

[23] U Narayan, 'Restoring History and Politics to 'Third-World Traditions' in U Narayan (ed), *Dislocating Cultures: Identities, Traditions, and Third-World Feminism* (New York, Routledge, 1997) 42.

[24] Narayan, above n 21 at 96.

behaviour.[25] Part of the work that cultural essentialism accomplishes is that it 'assumes and constructs sharp binaries between "Western cultural" and "Non-Western cultures" or between "Western culture" and particular "Other" cultures'.[26] The effect of this is not just inaccuracy, but a positioning of Western cultures as superior to non-Western cultures, especially with respect to gender relations and the treatment of women.[27] Non-Western cultures are thus 'Othered' in a process in which negative characterisation advances colonial narratives of social progress that place the West as the exemplar of civilisation and non-Western cultures as 'civilisationally backward'[28] and desirous of cultural rehabilitation through the inculcation of Western values.[29] Further, this understanding of cultures continues to imagine the racialised male body, in particular the black male body, as dangerous and savage and thus inherently—almost naturally—aggressive.[30] At the same time, it imagines racialised non-Western females as passive and submissive and/or sexually experienced and lascivious, all of whom invariably experience 'their' cultures as oppressive due to an inherent misogyny.[31] The non-Western body becomes an Other onto which the West projects and thus establishes its own subjectivity by presenting 'their' practices as incomprehensibly foreign, exotic and, in general, backward with respect to liberal values.[32] Through the normative regulatory regime of colonialism as a backdrop, the cultural defence 'promotes the essential "other-ing" that it claims to erase'.[33]

Lawrence and Fournier discuss how recent cases involving sexual or intimate violence in Canada entrench this reductive and discursively harmful picture of non-Western cultures as homogeneous, essentialist and backward. Both scholars focus on the case of *R v Lucien*, which involved the gang rape of an 18-year-old black girl, identified only as MO.[34] MO had met the two accused, Patrick Lucien and Evens Shannon, at a club in Montreal. After dancing with Shannon for most of the night, MO accompanied the accuseds back to their apartment. After eating something, she indicated her desire to leave. The two accused then raped her in succession with the other assisting

---

[25] L Volpp, 'Blaming Culture for Bad Behavior' (2001) 12 *Yale Journal of Law and the Humanities* 89.

[26] Narayan, above n 21 at 82.

[27] A McClintock, *Imperial Leather: Race, Gender and Sexuality in the Colonial Contest* (London, Routledge, 1995).

[28] Kapur, above n 16.

[29] L Volpp, 'Feminism Versus Multiculturalism' (2001) 101 *Columbia Law Review* 1181; Coombe, above n 14.

[30] b hooks, *Yearning: Race, Gender, and Cultural Politics* (Toronto, Between the Lines, 1990).

[31] G Anzaldua, *Making Face, Making Soul/Haciendo Caras: Creative and Critical Perspectives by Feminists of Color* (San Francisco, Aunt Lute Foundation Books, 1990); Fournier, above n 11.

[32] Volpp, above n 29; Kapur, above n 16.

[33] Wong, above n 2 at 373.

[34] *R. c Lucien* [1998] AQ no 8 (cour du Quebec), as cited in Fournier, above n 11.

in restraining her while one was raping.[35] The defendants were convicted of sexual assault pursuant to s 272(1)(d) of the Criminal Code.[36]

The facts of the case are unremarkable. *Lucien* became a prominent case in Quebec when the French-Canadian female trial judge said the following about the actions of two unremorseful black men with Haitian origins convicted of mutually raping an 18-year old black girl:

> Evens Shannon, confident in his charm, did not take into account the hesitations and reticence of the young girl after she accepted to go to his place. The two accomplices then took her consent for granted. They behaved like two young roosters craving for sexual pleasure without any regard for the young woman. Despite their resentment for her, despite the pride of young males who cannot admit having committed a serious insult to the victim by not respecting her choice to leave at a certain moment, they nevertheless thought about the incident and gained a little more maturity since it became judicial ... In this case, the absence of remorse of the two accused seems to me to arise more from a particular cultural context with regard to relations with women than to a real problem of a sexual nature.[37]

This extract from the judgment reflects all of the reductive discursive elements discussed above. It imagines Haitian culture (the particular 'cultural context') as one that involves blatant disrespect for women. It imagines young Haitian men as naturally sexual animals, as unable to contain their desire as roosters. It is only after the Western legal system becomes involved to interrupt their biological instincts, that the court concludes that they are able to think beyond the traditions they grew up with to entertain the possibility that their actions might be morally reprehensible. We are encouraged to view these non-Western men as nature- and tradition-bound. This paradox, that the men are both *naturally* and *culturally* sexually predatory, is consistent with colonial understandings of non-Westerners, especially blacks, as at once highly sexual, 'closer to nature' or 'primitive' and 'ruled by custom or dictate'.[38] What is more, they are presumed to follow the values of 'Haitian culture' despite the fact that they had both been living outside of Haiti for a significant amount of time. Notably, Shannon had just arrived in Canada after living in the United States for 11 years. Interestingly, the court does not explain his actions through references to US culture and its sexual objectification of women. Instead, it is the non-Western culture that is represented as 'bad for women'. White Western culture emerges as the egalitarian-seeking spaces that these non-Western cultures make toxic.

---

[35] *Ibid* as described by Fournier, above n 11.
[36] Above n 11.
[37] Quoted in Fournier, above n 11 at paras 14, 16.
[38] Coombe, above n 14; Fournier, above n 11 at para 16.

Similar modes of Othering, as Fournier discusses, are present in *R v Ammar Nouasria*.[39] This case involved a Muslim man who was convicted of four separate counts of sexual violence against his spouse's daughter from a previous marriage when she was between the ages of nine and 11. The violence, which transpired through 20 incidents and was enabled by threats and coercion, involved sexual touching, fellatio and anal intercourse, but not penile vaginal intercourse. As in *Lucien*, the accused was without remorse, yet managed to persuade the judge to recognise a mitigating factor from a particular understanding of Islam.[40] Ammar Nouasria was effectively rewarded by the court for doing everything except 'complete vaginal intercourse' because of the cultural premium the court understood to be placed on the victim's virginity as a Muslim girl.

As Fournier notes, here the difference between religion and culture is effaced as Islam becomes the stand-in for culture.[41] Islam, a religion whose meanings, like other religions, is mediated by gender, age, class, ability and culture, assumes an essential meaning—that it values virginity. While the court does not cast Islam, as the emblem of harmful non-Western values, in the traditional Orientalist paradigm of being associated explicitly with poor treatment of women,[42] Islam is nevertheless used to soften the effect of the egregiousness of the defendant's actions. We are left to infer that it would tolerate, or not as strongly condemn, the sexual violence the accused did commit (the indicator of backwardness) while we leave uninterrogated the assumption that the accused was acting according to this religious/cultural dictate in not committing penile vaginal intercourse (the indicator of tradition-boundedness).

Other examples of simplistic cultural conceptualisations in non-Aboriginal sexual violence cases exist.[43] While not all judicial decisions accept impoverished accounts of culture, these cases are worrying in that they indicate that law has not kept pace with trends in post-colonial critique. This is not particular to the Canadian context. Leti Volpp, among others, has detected

---

[39] *R. v Ammar Nouasria* (13 January 2004) 500 01 003139 927 (cour du Quebec).

[40] *Ibid*, as discussed by Fournier, above n 11 at paras 32–33.

[41] Fournier, above n 11.

[42] L Abu-Lughod, 'Do Muslim Women Really Need Saving? Anthropological Reflections on Cultural Relativism and its Others' (2002) 104 *American Anthropologist* 783.

[43] In *R v Kanagarajah*, a case that Lawrence discusses above n 12, the court essentialised and exotified the Sri Lankan Tamil community as one that beats and burns teenage girls for talking to boys outside their families. In Kanagarajah, two 14-year-old Tamil refugee girls were burned with an iron and beaten with a stick by their uncle and two elder male cousins, see A Findlay, 'Bail Nixed in Torture Case: Two Girls Allegedly Burned for Talking to Boys', *Toronto Sun*, 19 February 1999, in Lawrence, above n 12 at 108. In the very recent case of *R. v Quashie*, involving an appeal from two convictions of sexual assault and sexual assault causing bodily harm, the Ontario Court of Appeal summarily described the victim as 'adher[ing] to traditional Nigerian cultural values, which precluded sex before marriage'. See *R. v Quashie* [2005] OJ no 2694, per Gillese J at para 4 (hereinafter *Quashie*).

these problems in cultural defences presented to US judges.[44] The problem of representation is also not constricted to *legal* representations. Indeed, the frequency with which culture is misrepresented and reductively understood is related to the colonial narratives of non-Western cultures that continue to inhabit the mainstream Western cultural imagination. Jack Shaheen has noted, for example, how representations of Arabs in Hollywood films, a cultural medium acutely familiar to Canadians, perpetuate Orientalist myths that Other Arabs in a myriad of ways.[45] Uma Narayan's work on the parallels between dowry murders in India and domestic violence murders in the United States highlights the sensationalist and slimly researched media accounts that attribute dowry deaths to an unyielding patriarchal 'Indian culture', but explains domestic violence as the fault of maladjusted individuals and not 'US culture'.[46] As Narayan notes, even when the broader economic and social context is adverted to in analysing the causes of intimate or sexual violence, for example, we (Westerners and post-colonial critics alike) have generated 'a fairly widespread tendency in discussions of "Third-World issues" to engage in ... a "schizophrenic analysis", where religious and mythological "explanations" must be woven in willy-nilly, even if they do no real "explanatory work"'.[47] Ratna Kapur confirms the same discursive trends in the global Violence Against Women campaigns.[48]

Again, this is not to suggest that there is no relationship between intimate or sexual violence and culture. As I argue below, there is. Rather, it is to underline the repeated ways in which non-Westerners are seen as tradition-bound and products of 'their culture' that are, in turn, violent and oppressive toward women, in ways in which those identified as 'Western' are

---

[44] Volpp, above n 25 and n 29.

[45] J Shaheen, 'Reel Bad Arabs: How Hollywood Vilifies a People' (2003) 588 *American Academy of Political and Social Science Annals* 171.

[46] U Narayan, 'Cross-Cultural Connections, Border-Crossings' and 'Death by Culture' in U Narayan, *Dislocating Cultures: Identities, Traditions, and Third-World Feminism* (New York, Routledge, 1997). Narayan discusses the cultural explanation proffered by Elisabeth Bumiller in a chapter of her New York Times Bestseller, *May You be the Mother of a Hundred Sons: a Journey Among the Women of India* (New York, Fawcett Columbine, 1990) for dowry deaths. Narayan chose this book not 'because it is uniquely problematic' but because of its phenomenal reception in North American popular culture as a treatise on the 'situation of Indian women'. Indeed, the 'truth factor' of Bumiller's text was not restricted to popular culture. It was on the syllabus as one of four books to be reviewed in my introductory course on Third World Politics as an undergraduate. Narayan herself notes that '(i)t is a book [she has] seen in college bookstores, including the bookstore in which [she] teach[es]' (at 105). Narayan analyses how current day violence against women is explained devoid of temporal, regional, class or religious specificity through monolithic and ill-suited invocations of ancient Hindu 'traditions' as the cause of such violence (at 106–9). The 'death by culture' explanation makes sense only to an audience ignorant of the diverse, changing and otherwise complex nature of Indian society, which is why similar simplistic accounts of domestic violence do not resonate in the United States.

[47] Narayan, *ibid* at 111.

[48] Kapur, above n 16.

not.[49] Casting colonised peoples as 'traditional' and less civilised, whether because of how they treat women or some other propped up indicator of barbarity, is a familiar colonial trope.[50] It is this function of perpetuating discourses of colonisation and imperialism that continue to imagine non-Western cultures as unchanging, monolithic and gender equality-adverse that critical race feminists rightly find so distressing when culture is introduced into a legal proceeding.

Bodily Harm

The second manifestation of cultural anxiety moves from the impact on the culture to the impact for the victims of the intimate or sexual violence, typically women and children. This concern would exist even if the first problem of representation did not. That is, even if the law replaced its modernist understandings of culture, and non-Western cultures in particular, with sophisticated post-colonial frameworks for the articulation of cultural defences, the expressivity of the diminished punishment—what it says about the value of certain bodies—persists. When judges consider culture in sentencing individuals convicted of intimate or sexual violence, out of a multicultural sensibility or not, the effect may be a reduced sentence. From a critical race feminist perspective, however, this type of responsiveness toward cultural pluralism undermines, rather than advances, cultural equality since any accommodation of culture that reduces the defendant's responsibility subordinates the (typically) minority women and children who are the ones harmed by the defendant's actions.

In *Lucien*, the court imposed a sentence of 18 months which was to be served in the community as the sentence for a 'gang rape'. Both Lucien and Shannon were able to live in their own homes as long as they observed a curfew between 10.30 pm and 6 am and performed 100 hours of community service.[51] This stands in stark contrast to the maximum penalties of 14 years' imprisonment for a conviction under s 272(1)(d) and (2)(b), the relevant provisions of the Criminal Code.[52] In *R v Ammar Nouasria*, where the accused was convicted of four counts of sexual misbehaviour toward a child to whom he stood in a position of trust as stepfather, he faced a maximum term of imprisonment of 10 years for each offence. Instead, he was sentenced, concurrently, to 23 months in prison with a year of probation.[53]

---

[49] CT Mohanty, 'Under Western Eyes: Feminist Scholarship and Colonial Discourses' in R Lewis and S Mills (eds), *Feminist Postcolonial Theory: a Reader* (New York, Routledge, 2003) 49.

[50] *Ibid* at 53.

[51] Fournier, above n 11 at para 10, discussing *Lucien*.

[52] As discussed by Fournier, above n 11 at para 12.

[53] *Ibid* at para 33.

As Fournier notes, the latter sentence is particularly striking since the victim was a child and a fiduciary relationship existed between the accused and the child, prime aggravating factors where sentencing is concerned.[54] Conversely, remorse, the impaired mental capacity of the accused, or progress in sought out psychotherapy, all of which are factors that serve to mitigate sentences in sexual offences involving children, were absent.[55]

The concern in these cases is not simply that courts are attempting (to impute best intentions) a culturally sensitive, although misrepresentative, contextualisation of a person's actions that is devoid of a gendered analysis. Rather, it is the contribution of a degendered cultural analysis to a *legal* tradition of devaluing the impact of sexual violence on women, particularly where the bodies assaulted are racialised ones, which is the problem.[56] The reception and application of sexual assault laws has always been a burdened area of legal discourse from a feminist perspective due to sexist stereotypes about female sexuality.[57] As bell hooks and others have noted, the sexist legal discourse is also infused, however, with racist and classist stereotypes that order women's bodies into different categories with varying assessments of the harm that ensues if a particular type of woman is assaulted.[58] Marginalised female bodies are typically at the bottom of this hierarchy.[59] Given this background to sexual violence against racialised women, a failure to consider the gendered impact when 'culturalising violence', as Razack terms it,[60] raises concerns about racism and classism enabling the ease with which courts render gender absent in decisions.[61] That contextual factors such as racism, poverty and culture are taken into account for the benefit of the racialised male accused, rather than the racialised female or juvenile victim, is no coincidence.

In highlighting this disparity in terms of who within a culture stands to benefit from a cultural defence, many critical race feminists are equally alive to the problem of excessive incarceration of racialised communities, especially Aboriginal individuals, in Canada and elsewhere,[62] with some promoting the abolition of prisons altogether due to the acutely oppressive dynamics of current prison-industrial complexes.[63] This need not be

---

[54] Fournier, above n 11 at 106–7; Criminal Code, RSC, 1985, c C-46, s 718.2(a)(ii)–(iii).

[55] Fournier, above n 11 at para 32.

[56] Razack, above n 13.

[57] Fournier, above n 11.

[58] For exotification and commodification of sexualities for pleasure and experience see b hooks, 'Getting a Bit of the Other' in b hooks, *Black Looks: Race and Representation* (Toronto, Between the Lines, 1992) 23–4; Kline, below n 65.

[59] hooks, above n 58 at 62.

[60] Razack, above n 13.

[61] *Ibid.*

[62] Razack, above n 13.

[63] J Sudbury, 'Introduction: Feminist Critiques, Transnational Landscapes, Abolitionist Visions' in J Subdury (ed), *Global Lockdown: Race, Gender, and the Prison-Industrial Complex* (New York, Routledge, 2005).

an argument necessarily for more incarceration, but a call to conceptualise culture as a complex and fiercely gendered phenomenon, such that a lenient sentence on account of culture may be the furthest thing imaginable from an anti-racist initiative.

Having articulated the two main reasons that worry critical race feminists about the prospect of routinising cultural defences in the legal system, the next section turns to the possibility of avoiding these problems of discursive and bodily harm, and recuperating culture as an appropriate tool for a critical race feminist analysis.

CULTURAL CLAIMS AND ADJUSTMENTS

Critical race feminists are, of course, in favour of cultural equality, but believe that the cultural defence is a step towards racialised sexism. Instead, they underscore 'the need to introduce a more gendered vision in our efforts to situate and conceptualise racial groups'[64] through a theory of intersectionality that foregrounds the multiple forces of power operating within our institutions, legal or otherwise, to better address the experiences of marginalised women and without Othering non-Western cultures.[65] Put simply, courts must eschew binary analytics and attend to both race and sex, as well as other constructs of difference, when engaging with culture.[66] This section outlines why and how this may be done.

Keeping Culture

This emphasis on better and more critical contextualisation, an emphasis which I share, invariably keeps culture and cultural discourse within our courtrooms. The cultural anxiety that feminists have highlighted is real, rather than imagined, and in need of redress. But it is possible to address intimate or sexual violence through a framework that takes into account culture when contextualising a situation of violence without subordinating the racialised women and children who are often its victims. Indeed, it is difficult to imagine a discussion of violence that does not attend to culture. When we say that violence is not cultural, to disarm cultural relativist

---

[64] Fournier, above n 11 at para 21.

[65] Wong, above n 2 at 394. Intersectionality is a theory that directs attention to the multiple and mutually constitutive dimensions of one's identity to understand how one experiences any given social condition and/or hierarchy. See K Crenshaw, 'Mapping the Margins: Intersectionality, Identity Politics and Violence Against Women of Color' (1994) 43 *Stanford Law Review* 1241; and M Kline, 'Race, Racism and Feminist Legal Theory' (1998) 12 *Harvard Women's Law Journal* 115.

[66] hooks, above n 58 at 62–4.

arguments that would tolerate violent practices to honour 'cultural' traditions or even to avoid the simplistic cultural explanations that Narayan and others properly highlight, we risk casting violence as biological; a view of violence as natural or genetic is also a dangerous one.

First, to the extent we want to resist colonial discourses that associate certain cultures with higher degrees of violence,[67] imposing a biological discourse may have a fortifying effect exactly in this direction if the history of evolutionary biology in constructing races and sanctioning racism is any indication.[68] This concern that behaviour will receive a biological explanation is heightened in our current climate, with a revivified faith in genetic determinism through the surge in research in genetic testing and the human genome.[69]

A second, more disquieting, reason to keep culture and violence associated, is the power of cultural discourses based on nature or genetics, more so than culture, to excuse behaviour. Part of the resistance and aversion to the cultural defence that exists stems from the conviction that certain behaviour is reprehensible irrespective of whether one has been socialised and enculturated to accept and perpetuate that behaviour. The message is clear: culture should not be a euphemism for violence. But it would seem that this message would have to be all the more emphasised if violence was understood as non-cultural and thus, by definition, biological or natural. This is because the argument for excusing behaviour would be reinforced if the *cause* of the behaviour were understood as biological. How could we fault someone for carrying out his (deliberate use of the pronoun here) genetic programming? We may take that stand with respect to 'cultural programming', the argument would proceed, but it would be futile to oppose behaviour that is the natural function of and inherent to an individual. If someone's 'natural' or 'innate' functioning is to engage in a certain practice, then the moral blameworthiness generally required for criminal sanction is lost.

Consider that historically, in Europe, non-human animals were tried for 'bad behaviour' including the killing of humans.[70] Today the idea seems ridiculous to us because of our cultural understandings of the role of criminal law, punishment and the cognitive limits, although varied, of non-human animals.[71] It is for the same reason regarding intent and the

[67] R Emerson Dobash and RP Dobash, *Women, Violence and Social Change* (New York, Routledge, 1992) 217; hooks, above n 58 at 65–77; Crenshaw, above n 65 at 93–102.

[68] McClintock, above n 27.

[69] L Andrews and D Nelkin, 'Homo Economicus: Commercialization of Body Tissue in the Age of Biotechnology' (1998) 5 *Hastings Center Report* 30.

[70] K Tester, *Animals and Society: the Humanity of Animal Rights* (London, Routledge, 1991) 72–3.

[71] I do not wish to be seen here as endorsing the conventional view regarding species difference: that there are sharp distinctions based on 'defects' of reason, or otherwise, between humans and all other animals, that justify the current attribution of legal and moral personhood

capacity to govern oneself within appropriate limits that we do not try children under a certain age.[72] It is not difficult to extend this reasoning to the adult human if we understood human reactions as completely naturally determined. It would be similar to establishing a law against breathing, eating or urinating! It would appear that no intellectual or political headway emerges in de-emphasising the social and cultural forces underlying violent behaviour. Instead, we might actually risk creating an even more formidable opponent in biological relativism and genetic determinism to sanction violent behaviour.

Apart from the risk of slipping into 'biology as destiny' discourses about violence, it is also appropriate to associate violence with culture because the ways in which violence operates—its modes, perpetrators, victims and effects—are all deeply informed by ideas of difference and the power locations that shape them. I am mindful of the cultural anxiety critical race feminists harbour that reintroducing culture as an explanation for most, if not all, forms of human-on-human violence will be a strategy that is/may be misread by mainstream white Canadians. It may very well translate, given indefatigable stereotypes equating violence with racialised masculinities, into a message that certain minority cultures are violent and are in need of a 'cultural adjustment'. As Razack succinctly states, talking culture can indeed be a 'tricky business' given the discourses of racism and colonialism infecting the project.[73] But leaving culture out of our analyses of violence and Canadian courtrooms seems to entail an equally undesirable result. As Leti Volpp has noted, to exclude culture from legal discourse is to be complicit in the charade that the law has no culture, when in actuality it espouses majoritarian cultural values.[74] Instead of harnessing the opportunity, however slim, to redefine culture from a reductive liberal notion to a nuanced post-colonial one, foregoing cultural discourse out of distress for the contours it will assume leaves a binary between majority and minority cultures intact. And what is perhaps even more worrisome is that the binary remains unstated.

The fear that Volpp's attempt to progressively reshape a term or concept politically will instead fall flat and cement conventional and problematic understandings is a familiar one in legal feminism. Here, a parallel to other feminist debates over terminology and concepts is useful. As noted

to the former and the abject object status or property to the latter. For an excellent critique of our conventional understandings of non-human animals, see G Francione, *Animals, Property and the Law* (Philadelphia, Temple University Press, 1995) 36–8; and C Adams and J Donovan (eds), *Animals and Women: Feminist Theoretical Explorations* (Durham, Duke University Press, 1995).

[72] See Criminal Code, RSC, 1985, c C-46, s 13.
[73] Razack, above n 13 at 60, 85.
[74] L Volpp, '(Mis)Identifying Culture: Asian Women and the "Cultural Defense"' (1994) 17 *Harvard Women's Law Journal* 57.

above,[75] the term 'cultural anxiety' borrows from Joan Williams' term 'commodification anxiety', which is meant to encapsulate the fear that commodification (converting entities into fungible units in the market) will corrode that entity or a valuable human relationship that it sustains.[76] Margaret Jane Radin's work has been of pioneering stature in setting out the possible perils of commodification in realms such as family, love and human bodies.[77] Williams and others, while acknowledging that 'Radin is right that excessive commodification can threaten human flourishing' have argued that 'women's key problem has been too little commodification, not too much'.[78]

Williams is directly addressing the unremunerated nature of the domestic labour of primary care-givers who are usually women. She queries the fairness of family property laws that delay the division of matrimonial property to the point of marital breakdown. If we really believed that the at-home worker was contributing to the ability of the market worker to earn his wage/salary, should we not, she asks, divide the wage/salary earned by the market worker and vest a share immediately, at the point of earning, to the at-home primary care-giver?[79] Williams notes that the negative reply to this argument is animated by the concern that by making this currently radical change in the law the home will be 'sullied' by market discourse.[80] Williams' argues that this:

> commodification anxiety glosses over an important point: The issue is not *whether the family wage will be owned but who will own it*. Note the unstated assumption that having wives' work give rise to entitlements will import strategic behavior into the family sphere, while having husbands' work give rise to entitlements raises no such problem. Husbands' work takes place in the market, so it 'naturally' is commodified.[81]

Williams draws attention to the extant commodification in the domestic sphere to argue that the debate over whether that sphere should be commodified is misplaced. Williams encourages feminists exhibiting commodification anxiety to shift their focus from worrying about commodification to thinking about how commodification can best be carried out with respect to the domestic sphere for women, given that it already exists. The parallel to cultural anxiety is that culture already exists within the legal

---

[75] Williams, above n 1.

[76] *Ibid* at 118.

[77] MJ Radin, 'Market Inalienability' (1987) 100 *Harvard Law Review* 1849; MJ Radin, *Contested Commodities* (Cambridge, MA, Harvard Univeristy Press, 1996) as noted by Williams, above n 1.

[78] Williams, above n 1 at 118.

[79] *Ibid* at 118.

[80] Williams, above n 1 at 118.

[81] *Ibid*.

system: it is the hegemonic one. Instead of worrying about whether or not the law should talk about culture, it is preferable to recognise that culture already permeates legal reasoning and work to reshape the configurations of the conversations in ways that promote the interests of women and other marginalised groups.

To help illustrate this point, consider for a moment two cases. One is *R v MC*, a case involving physical and sexual assault of an Indian-Canadian woman by an Indian man whom she had very recently married through an arranged marriage.[82] The other is the recent Ontario Court of Appeal decision in *R v Quashie*,[83] where the court reviewed the reasoning of the jury and the sentencing judge that took the Nigerian culture into account to the benefit of the female rape victim. In *R v MC*, the court used culture to recognise the heightened nature of the victim's suffering given that she would soon be divorced from the defendant and experience difficulty in remarrying within her community because of purported views about the remarriageability of divorced women. In *Quashie*, the fact that the complainant was 'a naïve young woman from a different culture who viewed [the sexual assaults] with shame' helped put her actions in a credible light for the court.[84] The sentencing judge also adverted to culture to recognise the particularly serious implications for the victim given the judge's view that she 'she was ashamed to speak with her father and lost her former close relationship with her brother' because 'Nigerian society would look down on a family whose daughter engaged in premarital sex'.[85]

These are not situations where the accused relied on a cultural defence. Rather, the court averted to the 'culture' of the couple to contextualise the harm suffered by the victim. Is this not a move toward contextualisation that feminists would support on the theory that we cannot grasp the impact of family violence on a victim without knowing her particular social location, especially how she thinks and feels about herself, perceptions indelibly influenced by the culture in which she lives? Of course, what feminists need to prevent are the simplistic accounts of culture from informing these cultural discussions as they do in these two cases. It would be problematic to contextualise victim impact statements and then hand down significant sentences, and thus register a valuation of the lives and wellbeing of female victims of violence by men in their families, but continue to invoke impoverished understandings of a particular culture. In *R v MC*, the court did just this:

> Most particularly, this complainant because of her membership in the East Indian community has especially suffered. To begin with, it was clear from the evidence

---

[82] [1994] OJ no 4348 (Gen Div).
[83] *Quashie*, above n 43.
[84] *Ibid* at para 80.
[85] *Quashie*, above n 43 at para 85.

that it is a tradition in that community that problems, including problems that amount to criminal activity, are dealt with privately, within the family. I gather it is frowned upon in that community to take these matters outside of that context and bring them to the attention of legal authorities. Of course, the Court must support, and does support, the complainant in reaching out to the institutions which are in place to protect every citizen against criminal acts. The Court must make it clear that crime will not be condoned in any community.

As well, because of cultural beliefs, this woman who is absolutely without fault, will not be viewed as an appropriate candidate for marriage because there is an assumption in her community that if she is divorced, as she unquestionably will be, that is somehow her fault and she is unworthy to be anyone's wife. Nothing, of course, could be further from the truth, but that fact does not change and undoubtedly will not change deep-seated cultural beliefs. So she has had to display rather remarkable courage in reaching outside of her community for the help of the system and in facing its continuing condemnation in respect of acts for which she, herself, bears no fault whatever.[86]

The court constructs the 'East Indian community' as a monolith marked by a 'tradition' to cover up criminal behaviour and to castigate and ostracise women who divorce. How South Asians, now in excess of one billion, might differ as to cultural ideas of family issues, state responsibility, criminal activity, marriage, divorce and the men and women who engage in these activities, is ignored. The statement is strikingly general and essentialist. What is more, it is the Canadian state as the institution to which the woman has reached out that must save her by 'mak(ing) it clear [to the 'East Indian community'] that crime will not be condoned in any community'.[87] The narrative is deeply implicated in the liberal cultural belief of liberal values saving non-Western women from their patriarchal cultures.[88] The court reproduces discursive structural violence of colonialism as it attempts to acknowledge the emotional harm the woman has experienced. The better route would have been to recognise the harm the victim suffered because of her perception (whether real or imagined) that she was now unmarriageable, but particularise the claims about divorced women that generated her perception of her chances at remarriage. The victim impact could have thus been contextualised without resorting to reductive understandings of Other cultures. To abandon culture talk in this situation for fear that courts will continue to imagine non-Western peoples in essentialised ways, would be to negate an important element of the harm to victims of family violence: their culturally informed perceptions of their identities and future possibilities.

---

[86] Above n 83 at paras 9, 10.
[87] *Ibid.*
[88] Kapur, above n 16.

Which Cultural Claims Should Count

For all these reasons, it seems desirable to include culture in our conversations of intimate or sexual violence.[89] And this means deconstructions of the majority as well as minority cultures, rather than the sanction of violent practices in any culture or the privileging of violent majoritarian cultural norms or behaviours and the targeting of minority ones. But including culture in legal conversations also means permitting some cultural claims that, while not crudely claiming that the subordination of women and children are part of an accused's culture, nonetheless seek to contextualise the mens rea, or address the sentencing hearing, by offering cultural evidence of why the defendant acted in a particular way. How may we ensure that this occurs without undermining the human rights of internally vulnerable cultural members?[90]

Elsewhere I have offered a model of how this may be done.[91] Under the framework I propose, drawing from Volpp's work in this area, a court would be able to receive and consider cultural defences that do not rely on sexist, racist or other discriminatory values or otherwise fail to particularise their cultural claims. This approach would be responsive to the valid aspirations toward a critical cultural pluralism without tolerating inegalitarian arguments. The approach identifies the harmful element in cultural discourse as that which is actually or foreseeably subordinating of vulnerable members of a cultural group. It does not classify essentialism qua essentialism as a harm and will permit cultural claims that, although qualified, are nevertheless essentialist as long as that essentialism or any other feature of the claim does not place vulnerable cultural insiders, such as women and children, in a worse position than before the claim was articulated.

It is instructive to illustrate the approach with a few examples. Consider the recent (as-of-yet unreported) *Atwal* case. In early spring of 2005, Rajinder Singh Atwal was convicted by a British Columbia Supreme Court jury of second-degree murder for the death of his teenage daughter, Amandeep, in July 2003. The family was Sikh and the motive for the murder was widely reported as Atwal's inability to accept that his 17-year-old daughter was dating and planning to move to Prince Rupert from the family home in Kitimat, BC with her non-Sikh boyfriend.[92] Amandeep and her boyfriend had been dating in secret for about three years because she feared

---

[89] This is not to contradict arguments by feminists concerned about the problematic traditional multicultural view of culture to change our terminology from 'culture' to 'cultural'. See R Dhamoon, '"Cultural" versus "Culture"' (unpublished manuscript on file with author).

[90] Dundes Renteln, above n 22 at 66.

[91] Deckha, above n 9.

[92] J Armstrong, 'Death of a Secret Lover', *Globe and Mail*, 3 March 2005, available at www.diversitywatch.ryerson.ca/media/cache/secretlover_globe_mar3.htm.

her parents' reaction to the fact that she was dating a non-Sikh man. Her parents came to know of the relationship following a car crash involving the couple in June 2003. Amandeep had initially planned to move to Prince Rupert, another small town in British Columbia, to escape the resistance she received from her family to dating her 19-year-old boyfriend. She left a note for her parents to that effect. Her mother asked her to stay, but her father let her go, only to pick her up in Prince George a few days later for a family trip to Vancouver.[93] Amandeep and her father were alone, purportedly returning to Prince George in the car, when her father stabbed her 11 times. He then drove to a nearby hospital where Amandeep later died. Atwal had told medical personnel that the injuries were self-inflicted.[94]

The sentence for second-degree murder in Canada is an automatic life sentence with a chance of parole.[95] Atwal received a sentence of 16 years for the murder. By newspaper accounts, the sentencing hearing did not permit any cultural arguments and Atwal's lawyer did not lead any. The approach I am suggesting would have permitted the victim's father to tell the court that his anger at his daughter's actions was culturally influenced (when are our emotions not?) and this information could inform the context by which he is judged. The representation of culture should not be a monolithic, essentialist one, but particularised and nuanced, although some amount of essentialism is likely to result. The approach I put forward would tolerate this but it would not permit the explanation that it is a cultural 'tradition' to kill one's daughter who 'disgraces' her intimate or sexual honour in this way. This would be the case even if what Mr Atwal did were sanctioned by a nuanced view of his cultural background (which it is not). This is because this 'tradition' (even if it were one)[96] would be a highly gendered one upholding sexist values, ie, that it is permissible to harm one's daughter for transgressing gender behavioural codes. It is true that we might, in a comparable situation, be penalising an individual who acted according to certain social expectations and thus 'did not know any better' and does not deserve moral condemnation through a criminal conviction. Yet this concern, to the extent it is one, must yield to the goal of devising laws that do not countenance discrimination or inequality.

---

[93] L Sin and A Turner, 'Tragic Killing of "Sweet Girl" Stuns Kitimat', *The Province*, 3 August 2003, available at www.primetimecrime.com/Recent/murder_Atwal.htm.
[94] 'Father Guilty of Murdering Daughter', *CBC News*, 4 March 2005, available at http://vancouver.cbc.ca/regional/servlet/View?filename=bc-atwal20050305.
[95] 'B.C. Father Guilty of Killing Daughter in Fit of Rage', *CBC News*, 4 March 2005, available at www.cbc.ca/story/canada/national/2005/03/04/atwal-jury050304.html.
[96] The coverage of this case confirms points articulated above of how violence within racialised communities is seen as cultural and linked to broader phenomenon to which a connection might not necessarily exist. The *Toronto Star*, a leading Canadian newspaper, ran an opinion piece that characterised the crime as an 'honour killing' involving a 'South Asian' family. See Amar Khoday, '"Honour Killings" Hide Racist Motives', *Toronto Star*, 8 March 2005, available at www.diversitywatch.ryerson.ca/media/cache/atwal_star_mar8.htm.

And, of course, the same approach should adhere in legal analyses of majoritarian violent practices. For an example of how the approach would work in this situation, consider another situation of family violence, namely, the child spanking case recently decided by the Canadian Supreme Court. In *Children and Youth Foundation v Canada*,[97] the applicant Canadian Foundation for Children, Youth and the Law sought a declaration that s 43 of the Criminal Code, which permits parents to use reasonable force to discipline their children, was unconstitutional.[98] The applicant contended, among other arguments regarding vagueness and overbreadth, that s 43 violates ss 7, 12 and 15 of the Canadian Charter of Rights and Freedoms.[99] Section 7 of the Charter ensures that 'everyone has the right to life, liberty and security of the person and the ability not to be deprived thereof except in accordance with the principles of fundamental justice';[100] s 12 is Canada's protection against 'cruel and unusual treatment or punishment';[101] s 15 is the main Canadian equality guarantee. It states that 'every individual is equal before and under the law and has the right to the equal protection and equal benefit of the law without discrimination and, in particular, without discrimination based on race, national or ethnic origin, colour, religion, sex, age or mental or physical disability'.[102] By permitting a defence to assault for parents, guardians and teachers for a range of corporal punishment against children's bodies, the Canadian Foundation for Children, Youth and the Law argued that s 43 violated Canadian children's security of the person. Since the defence to assault was only applicable to violence against children, the Foundation also argued that it violated children's equality rights vis-à-vis adults and their equal claim to personhood.

The majority, with three judges dissenting, disagreed, thus affirming the decisions of the lower courts. Based on the evidence led, the majority accepted the fact that corrective use of force was a legitimate parenting tool in certain circumstances. Writing for the majority, McLachlin CJ interpreted the section to permit corrective corporal punishment in certain circumstances. Under the majority's interpretation of the section, it is only force that is not aimed at the head, implemented in a sober and rational mood, without assistive devices, by parents, and on children who are capable of understanding the beating and who will not develop anti-social

---

[97] *Children and Youth Foundation v Canada*, 2004 SCC 4, 16 CR (6th) 203 (hereinafter *Children and Youth Foundation*).

[98] Section 246 states the following: 'Every schoolteacher, parent or person standing the in the place of a parent is justified in using force by way of correction toward a pupil or child, as the case may be, who is under his care, if the force does not exceed what is reasonable under the circumstances'.

[99] Canadian Charter of Rights and Freedoms, Sch B to the Canada Act 1982 (UK) 1982.

[100] *Ibid* s 7.

[101] *Ibid*.

[102] *Ibid* s 15.

behaviour because of it, that is permitted.[103] In anticipating the concerns raised by the minority decision, McLachlin CJ suggested that the section did not violate the dignity of children, but enabled parents to discipline their children in their best interests without 'breaking up families' through criminalising parents.[104]

At no part of the judgment, does the majority analyse child spanking as a 'Canadian tradition'. McLachlin CJ also refrains from discussing parenting practices as shaped by cultural values despite the ample evidence, which Arbour J canvassed in dissent, that what counted as reasonable for different courts was linked to 'public policy issues and one's own sense of parental authority' and thus 'always entail(s) an element of subjectivity'.[105] In documenting the widespread force against children that has counted as 'reasonable' under s 43 in Canada, Arbour J detailed the cultural contingencies of the legal definition of 'reasonableness'. She wrote:

> Corporal punishment is a controversial social issue. Conceptions of what is 'reasonable' in terms of the discipline of children, whether physical or otherwise, vary widely, *and often engage cultural and religious beliefs as well as political and* ethical ones. Such conceptions are intertwined with *how other controversial issues are understood*, including the relationship between the state and the family and the relationship between the rights of the parent and the rights of the child. Whether a person considers an instance of child corporal punishment 'reasonable' may depend in large part on his or her *own parenting style and experiences*.[106]

Unlike the majority, Arbour J's dissent identifies the subjective nature of parenting and how our cultural backgrounds help to form the ideas about parenting, including the discipline of children, that we hold. In doing so, she suggests that the mundane and quotidian practice of parenting—something that *all* Canadian parents do—is a cultural practice that can result in violence and indignities against children.[107]

The refined differentiated approach I propose would continue Arbour's dissenting line of reasoning to firmly cast child spanking as a cultural practice and s 43 as a provision that entrenches this mainstream cultural practice through the law. With s 43 struck down, a parent accused of assault could, of course, raise a cultural defence. But the differentiated approach would recognise children as a vulnerable group, contextualise the disciplining of children to the history of patriarchal discipline in the domestic

---

[103] *Children and Youth Foundation*, above n 97 at para 40.
[104] *Ibid* at para 62.
[105] *Children and Youth Foundation*, above n 97 at para 183.
[106] *Ibid* at para 185 (emphasis added).
[107] She would have found the section unconstitutional for vagueness and referred the matter back for legislative drafting. *Children and Youth Foundation*, above n 97 at para 194.

sphere,[108] and thus characterise the cultural claim as one that subordinates children since it seeks to inflict unwanted pain on their bodies. Instead, again, of abandoning culture talk, the approach works to undo the colonial suppositions that only non-Western peoples have an ethnicity or culture, while liberal states are guided by reason.

What these two examples illustrate is the ability of culture and the idea of the cultural defence to inform critical race feminist analyses of legal proceedings involving sexual or family violence. The perils of 'talking culture' may be managed to open up a way of attending to culture that disrupts modernist narratives of who has it and who does not, and which cultures are bad and which are ideal. Thus, far from justifying the abandonment of cultural analysis, being responsive to the ways in which the law genders and racialises complainants and defendants in sexual and family violence cases could actually necessitate keeping culture within legal discourse. This is not to deny that problems with the cultural defence will still persist. As Wong worries, the colonial trappings of traditional anthropology where the 'Western' expert establishes what is and what is not an 'authentic' part of the 'traditions' of 'non-Western' peoples will still likely inform the reception of evidence in legal proceedings.[109] As she further notes, the cultural defence may, similar to affirmative action, become a symbol of a two-tiered justice system that prompts a backlash from those insisting on 'one law for all'.[110] But, as with affirmative action, the fear of backlash against it or the spectre of white middle class liberals defining and operationalising such programmes are insufficient reason to dispense with such programmes if they are otherwise good social policy. For the reasons canvassed above, including those relating to the drawbacks of dissociating culture from violence, it is good social policy to retain the cultural defence in law.

CONCLUSION

The anxiety that critical race feminists experience when culture enters mainstream legal venues by way of the cultural defence is legitimate and understandable. Canadian courts have not been particularly adept at incorporating post-colonial critiques of culture into legal discourse in situations of sexual and family violence. In a context of systemic racism, racially regressive ideas of non-Western cultures and peoples prevail in sexual and family violence cases to the detriment of racially marginalised women.

---

[108] A McGillivray, 'Child Physical Assault: Law, Equality and Intervention' (2003) 30 *Manitoba Law Journal* 133, 135–41.

[109] Wong, above n 2 at 377.

[110] This phrase has been recently articulated in the debate over religious, and in particular, Shari'a family arbitrations in Ontario. See Natasha Bhakt, *Arbitration, Religion and Family Law: Private Justice on the Backs of* Women, NAWL Working Paper (March 2005).

Discarding culture as a discursive tool, however, is not a desirable response to the cultural defence dilemma. To dissociate culture from violence would do violence to the concept of violence itself, as well as preclude legal scripts that can undo colonial understandings of what constitutes culture and who has it. Instead of abandoning the cultural defence, critical race feminists should encourage the specification and historicisation of cultural claims that do not subordinate vulnerable cultural members. While this approach would permit some level of essentialism, and thus a potentially problematic way of domesticating otherwise fluid identities, it would reject claims that seek to justify discursive, bodily or structural violence. In this way, it is possible to recuperate the cultural defence and culture as legitimate concepts for legal analysis and, in doing so, approximate the vision of a critical culturally pluralistic Canada.

IV

Legal Actors

12

Dealing with the Ethnic Other in Criminal Law Practice: a Case Study from the Netherlands

BRENDA CARINA OUDE BREUIL

INTRODUCTION

O N A COLD winter day, 1999, a young Moroccan-Dutch boy named Yussef[1] rushes into the building of the Child Protection Board. He wants to speak to Leyla, the employee who handles his case. His mother has received a letter about a child protection measure. Yussef does not understand it; he is afraid that 'they' will take him away from home and put him in an institution. He is not aware that his mother voluntarily called in the help of the Child Protection Board, as she can no longer control Yussef's violent outbreaks. Leyla hurries in and tells Yussef that she has no time now; he will have to wait for his appointment. 'Your mother can explain why we are intervening in your life', she adds. At the mention of his mother, Yussef becomes very angry, shouting that Leyla will be 'in trouble' if she messes with his life and threatening to set the building on fire. He eventually leaves, complaining and making obscene gestures.

Six months after the incident, Leyla's supervisor insists that the Child Protection Board ('the Board') will not give in to this so-called 'culturally inspired' aggressive behaviour. He finds the lack of responsibility displayed by Yussef and his mother, and the former's openly expressed aggression against this Dutch institution and Dutch people in general, 'typically Moroccan'. Should the Board adapt its working methods to the cultural backgrounds of clients? According to the supervisor, 'they' (clients with non-Dutch origins) must abide by 'our' Dutch norms and laws as well. As far as fundamental norms and values are concerned, such as the rights of

---

[1] For reasons of anonymity, the names in this example are fictitious. The incident took place during the author's fieldwork and was followed up as part of the research. See Oude Breuil, 2005: 169–72.

women and children, he is not willing to conform to other cultures 'in any way' (Oude Breuil, 2005: 1).

This incident shows the interaction between a criminal law institution and its ethnic minority clients at its problematic extreme. It is not representative of intercultural contacts in the Board's practice; they generally go more smoothly. It does, however, illustrate how the open question in this book—to what extent, if at all, should cultural imperatives mitigate punishment?—may become more complicated when confronted with the everyday realities of multicultural law enforcement. In everyday practice, down-to-earth questions arise such as: what should be understood as 'culturally imperative'? Is Yussef's aggressive behaviour an aspect of his Moroccan background, or rather of his successful integration into a Dutch big city's street culture? Who are 'they' in the supervisor's worldview and to whom belong 'our' Dutch norms and laws? And what does adaptation to clients' cultures concretely look like?

In this chapter I approach the 'multicultural riddle' (Baumann, 1999) of cultural imperatives in criminal law practice from an empirical angle. I draw from my fieldwork at the penal division of the Child Protection Board in the Netherlands, from 1999 up to 2002.[2] The Board is a criminal law institution under the responsibility of the Minister of Justice. It consists of a civil division, concerned with child adoption cases, cases of child rearing problems etc, and a penal division which is concerned with children from 12 to 18 years of age who are suspects in criminal cases. My research dealt with the penal division only. Since the late 1970s, the workers of this division have seen their client population become increasingly culturally diverse[3] (this applies to other institutions in the Dutch criminal law chain as well). They were (and still are) confronted daily with practical intercultural dilemmas, such as language problems or divergent cultural norms and values.

The research consisted of fieldwork in two phases. First, I interviewed (and observed the working techniques of) over 50 employees at seven offices of the Board, spread around the Netherlands (Amsterdam, Rotterdam, The Hague, Utrecht, Almelo, Breda and Groningen). I tried to answer the

---

[2] This research was part of the research programme 'Multiculturality and the Administration of Justice', coordinated by Prof Dr F Bovenkerk and Dr Y Yeşilgöz at the Willem Pompe Institute for Criminal Law and Criminology of Utrecht University.

[3] The cultural diversity of the client population is hard to substantiate, since registering ethnicity was for a long time not allowed in Dutch government institutions. However, a calculation taken among the 22 Board offices in 2001 (Van Es and Bakker, 2001) showed that clients who were not autochthonous Dutch, were most often born in Surinam (233 cases), the Dutch Antillean Islands (127 cases), Morocco (117 cases) and Turkey (89 cases). Note that these figures only show where clients were born. Second-generation migrant children, who are born in the Netherlands, but whose parents (one or both) are not (Korf, 2001) are not included here.

question of how Board employees dealt with the cultural diversity of their client populations. The second phase of fieldwork consisted of case studies of 20 juveniles and their parents, from five ethnic groups, and focused on the question how *they* experienced the Board interventions and the way eventual cultural obstacles were dealt with.[4]

The experiences of Board employees and clients of their intercultural contacts may afford insights here, because they show that whatever normative position is adopted on whether to let culture influence criminal law enforcement or not, everyday praxis may always throw a 'monkey wrench in the works'. No matter how we think executive employees *should* handle a case of a client from an ethnic minority group, it is still another question whether they actually *do* it that way. It is therefore useful to pay attention to the praxis of multicultural law enforcement. Although the Board has its own specific Board '(sub)culture', many of its intercultural dilemmas are not unique. They might be comparable to those of other criminal law institutions, inside and outside the Netherlands.

DEALING WITH THE CLIENT'S CULTURE

Adapting the Rules for the Sake of Culture...

One of the main tasks of the executive employees of the Board's penal law division is writing social inquiry reports about the children who have to appear in court. These reports serve to inform the judge about the living conditions of the child in court and recommend a punishment or protection measure that best fits the situation. Board employees also coordinate the activities of different institutions that assist with the carrying out of child protection measures. Moreover, Board employees coordinate community service orders; they arrange for training and working locations, keep in contact with supervisors at the spot, and check the successful completion of the community service order.

When asked about cultural obstacles in their contacts, most Board employees are cautious in their answers. They are afraid to be considered racist[5] if they attribute problems to clients' cultural backgrounds and prefer to look at every client as an individual, rather than a representative of a culture. However, this probably reflects how employees would like to see and deal with culture and their desire to be politically correct, rather than basing their judgment on lived experience; for when asked further, most employees do have examples of difficulties they label 'cultural'. The great

---

[4] The research findings are reported in Oude Breuil, 2005 (dissertation).
[5] Wikan (2004: 27 and 209) also pays attention to the influence of social workers' fears of being labelled 'racist' in the way they handle ethnic minority cases.

majority of them, moreover, think that *they*—not the client—are primarily responsible for overcoming these difficulties; after all, they say, 'we are the professionals'. They thus try to pay due attention to cultural backgrounds in their meetings and, if necessary, adapt their working techniques. A ministerial memorandum of 1997 supports such attempts; it states that Board employees should pay attention, in their social inquiry reports, to 'individual, sometimes also culturally determined ... characteristics of the client' (Ministry of Internal Affairs and Ministry of Justice, 1997: 45).

Cultural imperatives should thus be taken into account. How that should be done is a different question. How, for example, should a Board employee deal with communication problems, not only when clients or parents do not speak Dutch, but also when being confronted with mimicry, expressions, a narrative style, etc with which employees are not acquainted? How should clients who do not trust the Board because of the negative image of government institutions in their countries of origin be approached? How should an employee react if a client refuses, because of religious beliefs, to shake the hand of a female Board member or to conduct his community service order in a children's farm where pigs walk around?[6] And what should employees, finally, do when the standard intervention methods available to them conflict with clients' beliefs or practices? The latter is most relevant here, since it relates to the question of mitigating punishment. As I will illustrate below, employees change existing rules surrounding child protection measures and/or community service orders because they experience these measures as ineffective in certain ethnic minority families or consider them culturally insensitive.

One such problematic intervention methods is 'sexuality training'. This form of punishment can be imposed by the judge on sex offenders in order to teach them to behave in ways that are sexually respectful towards others. Board employees have had the experience that many Islamic parents resist this training. They find it taboo to talk openly about sex and are afraid it will harm their child. When advising the judge to impose this training, Board employees have to weigh its importance for the child against the will of the parents. This consideration might lead to putting aside a useful intervention method to ensure the continued cooperation of the parents.[7]

---

[6] For more on communication difficulties between executive employees and their clients in criminal law practice, see, eg, Bal, 1988; Oude Breuil, 2005; Van Rossum, 1998; Shusta *et al*, 1995 and Yeşilgöz, 1995. For more on distrusting clients from ethnic minority groups, see Oude Breuil, 2005. On difficulties that arise from diverging etiquette, norms and values, see also the above-mentioned authors.

[7] Wikan (2004) gives several other examples in which the will of the parents is given preference over the assumed needs of the child. In this case, however, it is not so easy to disentangle the needs of the child from those of the parents. Studies have shown that children generally succeed better in their community service order or training if parents are fully behind the imposed (form of) punishment (Hakkert, 1999).

Other strategies to deal with 'culturally insensitive' regulations are reactions to what employees call 'a deviating time perception' among some of their clients. As one Board employee explained, she would never schedule an appointment with a gypsy client before 10 am because 'gypsies don't wake up before sunrise'. Although this strategy may not interfere with Board standards too much, others do. Consider the example of an employee supervising an Antillean-Dutch client who always arrived late for his community service. Normally, this would be reprimanded with a 'yellow card'; when arriving late a second time, a 'red card' would be handed out, and the case would go back to court. The employee, however, allowed this client to make up the time from his late arrival at the end of every work day, without any yellow or red cards being distributed. His reason for doing so was that the boy had grown up with less strict ideas about time, and therefore could not help being unacquainted with the strict Dutch time schedule. In short, he deserved an extra chance.[8]

A final intervention method that places Board employees in a dilemma, is the child protection measure of 'guardian tutelage'. This measure can be imposed by the judge if the family situation imperils the child's safe development. The family guardian will then take over part of the parents' authority and try to ameliorate family conditions. According to several Board employees, some Turkish 'closed families'[9] do not accept the authority of a social worker or family guardian because they are not used to government interference in family affairs. Board employees doubt whether they should advise this intervention method when a family fits the profile. They are afraid that the guardian will not gain access to the family. Three Board employees, therefore, offered such families a last chance to solve their problems on their own. They drew up a contract which stipulated the actions the family had to undertake to ameliorate the home conditions. If the family did not abide by the contract within a certain period of time, the legal proceedings for appointing a family guardian would be resumed.

Employees using this strategy were positive about it; the families appreciated the extra chance and took the contract seriously.[10] However, the underlying assumption that 'the culture of the client' causes an intervention problem can be seriously questioned. In July 2002, a family drama in the southern town of Roermond shocked the Netherlands. A father of

---

[8] Culturally sensitive as this example might seem, I doubt whether in the long run the boy really benefitted from condoning his supposed 'culturally inspired' behaviour; other Dutch institutions, or a future employer for that matter, might not be so patient and tolerant.

[9] They specifically refer to 'traditional' Turkish families, meaning Turkish families in which the parents are first-generation Islamic migrants who come from rural areas.

[10] Notwithstanding, the contract method often did not bring about the necessary change and most families were still were appointed a family guardian. However, they found this guardian tutelage easier to accept after the 'contract method' had been tried and they cooperated better (Oude Breuil, 2005: 57).

six set his house to fire, killing his children and severely injuring his wife. The many organisations assisting the family (including the Board) had not been able to prevent this accident from happening. An independent study concluded that the organisations not only failed to cooperate sufficiently, but were unable to establish effective communication and interaction with the family. They were mostly talking *about*, and not *with* the family, it was stated (Inspectie Jeugdhulpverlening en Jeugdbescherming Regio Zuid, 2002). Culture could not have been the problem here, since the family was autochthonous Dutch. Clearly, the Board and other institutions do not only have problems penetrating Turkish families. The idea that the clients' culture is the main pitfall is thus dubious. As the independent research suggests, it might even be used as an excuse for hidden, structural problems within the organisations and the criminal law system.

Besides the question whether 'culture' is really the problem in this and other intercultural contacts, we might want to take a look at how Board employees perceive 'culture'. A closer look at two common perceptions of culture in the social sciences illuminates their underlying ideas and the effect of these ideas on intercultural interaction.

...But What is Culture? Essentialism and Constructivism Applied

In many Board strategies dealing with clients' cultural backgrounds, we can recognise a perception about culture that has been called *essentialist* by social science scholars (see, for example, Baumann, 1999: 81–96; Ghorashi, 2003: 210–11 or Wikan, 2002: 72–3). This can best be illustrated by looking at the standard Board questionnaire used to take social inquiry interviews. The client is asked, for example: 'Do you consider yourself Dutch or ...?' (Doreleijers *et al*, 1999: appendix BARO: 11). In the blanks, employees must fill in the client's cultural background. A question for the parents asks: 'Do you raise your child according to Dutch or to your own culture?' (Doreleijers *et al*, 1999: appendix BARO: 9).

In both questions, a choice must be made between their 'own' culture (the one the parents grew up with)[11] and the 'new' or 'Dutch' culture. This sort of question reflects an approach in which 'culture' is considered to be the property of an ethnic group. 'Cultures' are in this view clearly distinguishable, reified essences or things. They are conceived of as stable and uniform sets of norms, values, knowledge, habits, etc that members of a group share. Moreover, the question seems to support the view that when migrants get to know more than one culture—or in Binsbergen's words: have more than

---

[11] Wikan (2004) shows convincingly that many second-generation migrant children do not consider their parents' system of cultural beliefs to be 'their own'; they often perceive the dominant culture in the country they live in, as 'their own'.

one 'cultural orientation' (Binsbergen, 1999)—these different 'cultures' will remain separate entities. The client's behaviour can thus easily be labelled as 'Dutch' or 'Moroccan' and these cultures used to explain the behaviour.

More *constructivist* thinkers (Baumann, 1999; Ghorashi, 2003; Wikan, 2002) would seriously object to such a vision. According to them, it is not possible to make such clear demarcations between 'cultures'; different cultural influences may well mix and form an amalgam of norms, values, knowledge and habits the person can draw from as the situation demands. According to them, people are not determined by the culture they grew up in; they constantly construct and reconstruct their cultural framework while going through their lives. Someone might thus feel Dutch in one situation and Moroccan in another, or both at the same time, maybe even without differentiating between Dutch and Moroccan values. The 'or–or questions' in the Board's instrument do not allow for such hybrid personalities. They only allow for one cultural orientation at a time, or at best for schizophrenic combinations of two clearly separated cultural orientations.

We can recognise essentialist thinking in the reaction to the Antillean-Dutch late-arriving client. Even though the employee acted out of genuine motives and 'cultural sensitivity'—he wanted to prevent placing the Dutch conception of time above other ways of perceiving time—he employed a very static idea of culture, ruling out the possibility of cultural values changing in a new cultural context. This essentialist vision conflicts with ethnographic studies of migrant populations (see, eg, Yen Le Espiritu, 2003; Halleh Ghorashi, 2003; Clyde Mitchell, 1956; Aihwa Ong, 1999 and 2003), which show that when cultural ideas, values and habits deterritorialise from their original environment and reterritorialise in the country of arrival, they do change, simply because their frame of reference—the physical and social surroundings—have changed.

Not all Board employees look at culture in an essentialist way, nor do those who do, always do it, nor do they *consciously and intentionally* do it. Most executive employees simply try to establish pragmatic, workable solutions to the intercultural problems they daily face; they lack time to seriously think them through. We can thus recognise more constructivist ways in dealing with culture as well. Some Board employees, for example, challenged the essentialist idea of ethnic groups as being homogeneous. They pointed to the fact that there are often as many differences *within* an ethnic group as *between* such groups. This observation is mirrored by research findings in ethnographic studies. Thomas Hylland Eriksen (1998: 103–30), for example, showed in his study on Mauritian multicultural society how people made alliances across ethnic group boundaries by emphasising what he called 'common denominators': aspects of life that they had in common, notwithstanding their ethnic differences. Gerd Baumann writes about 'cross-cutting cleavages' (1999: 84) and shows that people not only categorise and form groups on the basis of ethnicity, but also on the basis of characteristics that cut across ethnic boundaries. One can think of gender, age, nationality, education, social-economic class, political alliances and so on.

Eriksen (1998) and Baumann (1999) both conclude that searching for common denominators or cross-cutting cleavages has a positive influence on cooperation between members of different ethnic groups. Some Board employees have reached the same conclusions, as can be observed in their conversations with clients. They tend to emphasise a characteristic or goal that they have in common with their clients or parents. One employee, for example, told his client that he, too, had been arrested when he was still young, while another told the parents that he had children too, and knew how hard it is to educate them.

Another intercultural coping strategy that we might mark as being based on a more constructivist approach of culture was used by the Board employee who handled the case of a Somali-Dutch, Islamic client, convicted of (moderate) indecent assault. The employee wanted to recommend sexuality training but the boy's parents severely objected to the training for reasons already discussed. Had the employee approached culture in an essentialist way, he would probably have chosen to propose another kind of punishment. There is, after all, no going back on innate, unchanging cultural values. However, when confronted with the argument that the training could not be reconciled with their religious beliefs, this employee asked the parents to explain these beliefs. He wondered what part of the training—or, for that matter, what part of Dutch intervention methods and underlying values—might be so objectionable for these (and probably other) people. He found out that the parents had serious misconceptions about the training. They thought, for example, that the training room would be filled with pictures of naked bodies and contraceptives. Once these false ideas were disproved, the parents agreed that their son could complete the training, even encouraging him.

This employee clearly did not approach culture as a thing that explains behaviour, as essentialists do, but as the thing *to be explained*. He actively questioned culture—not only the clients' but also his own. Such reflection on autochthonous Dutch norms, values, penal habits, etc was, however, quite unique during my fieldwork. Most Board employees never considered the fact that they themselves brought cultural values into the contact as well.[12] However, in cross-cultural contacts there are always two parties involved: the ethnic other as well as the ethnic self. That goes for Board practice as well. Although at first glance Board rules, procedures and

---

[12] The observation need not surprise us: in many intercultural contacts the dominant ethnic group attributes a (mostly 'exotic') culture to the ethnic other while overlooking its 'culturally loaded' self (see, eg, Eriksen, 2002: 87–90; Gupta and Ferguson, 1997).

practices might seem rational, neutral and 'culture-free', even universal at times, I will argue here that they are not.

DEALING WITH THE BOARD'S CULTURE

Cultural Specific Board Mores

It might be unusual to consider the employees of a criminal law institution as some sort of 'ethnic group' and to label their norms, values, knowledge and habits as 'culture'. Ethnicity has, in anthropology, long been considered a 'primordial' phenomenon, a property of a group, which determines who belongs to that group and who does not. It had been preceded by the concept 'tribe' (Eriksen, 2002: 10–11). In this sense, it can hardly apply to a group of people who happen to work for the same organisation.

However, in the historical development of the concept, the emphasis came to be put less on the 'cultural stuff' (Barth, 1998) that groups share, and more and more on the *process of drawing boundaries* to make a difference between oneself and the other, between insiders and outsiders. As Thomas Hylland Eriksen put it: 'ethnicity is essentially an aspect of a relationship, not a property of a group' and 'only in so far as cultural differences are perceived as being important, and are made socially relevant, do social relationships have an ethnic element' (Eriksen, 2002: 12). Ethnicity and culture are here approached in an instrumental way: not the 'cultural stuff' itself is what we should focus on, but the way it is used to create a feeling of belonging to one group and differentiating oneself from another'. In this sense, it applies to Board practice as well: the knowledge, practices, traditions, shared history and rituals are perceived by most employees as being important and are made socially relevant in their contact with clients.[13]

Moreover, the 'ethnic group' of employees is far more homogeneous than ethnic minority groups will ever be: the members have a certain age (children and the elderly are excluded) and educational level, belong almost entirely to the same socio-economic class and are, to a certain extent, ethnically homogeneous as well (the autochthonous Dutch group is largely overrepresented). The homogeneity is strengthened by the disciplining force of work-related rules, regulations and behavioral expectations—even by a distinct architecture of the buildings in which the Board is housed.

---

[13] I may be rightfully accused of reifying and essentialising Board culture here. However, this approach mirrors how most Board employees, as well as employees in other criminal law institutions, perceive their clients' cultural backgrounds. Board culture is presented here in an essentialised way for the sake of the argument. Considering a corporate group as an ethnic group is not new, however: Abner Cohen (1974) considered London stockbrokers as an ethnic group because of their shared identity and their largely endogamous marriage patterns (they married within the same socio-economic class).

The Board clearly has its own territory, demarcated by the architecture, spatial arrangements and rules inside the buildings. Board buildings are usually big, impressive and modern, with front doors protected with intercoms and (sometimes) cameras, which indicate the exclusiveness of the organisation: not everybody can just walk in. Inside the buildings, most hallways and offices are inaccessible for clients and visitors; Board employees can open them with magnetic keys. Some of the consulting rooms have bars placed under the table that will sound an alarm if kicked against. This is a safety system for employees who are threatened by clients. These attributes and architecture express a wish to separate, to a certain extent, Board employees—the insiders—from clients and other outsiders.

The specificity of the Board is not only visible in its material culture. As in court (see, eg, Bal, 1988; Hoefnagels, 1977; Komter, 1998; Van Rossum, 1998) a specific language and way of speech are used within the organisation, that deviate from 'normal' speech. Words and expressions are used that are never heard of in clients' everyday lives. There even exists a 'language and concept book' (Zuur, 2001) within the organisation, to explain the jargon to the Board insiders. Even though most employees do not use jargon when talking to a client, their way of speech is still recognised by the latter as different and specific. Observe, for example, the remarks made by an 18-year-old Moroccan-Dutch client on his encounter with a Board employee: 'It was a very weird conversation, as if it were a match. She said something and then she sat back, like: "I tell this and now it is your turn". Almost like a game ... ping pong or something'.

Just as Board members wonder about their clients' cultural habits, norms and values, so do clients about those adopted on the Board's territory. Talking about feelings to a stranger, considered 'normal', daily routine by Board employees, was considered 'strange' and 'foreign' by children who came in contact with the Board. Clients' parents did often not share the Board's norm of children's supposed and encouraged independence. Addressing Board letters (eg, informing the child about her or his community service) explicitly to the child and not to the parents, or demanding that children cancel their appointments independently when unable to come, were Board strategies that parents neither understood nor appreciated. Board norms, for example on childhood, that were normal to its employees, were thus considered abnormal and 'Board typical' by parents and their children.

Moreover, executive Board employees adhere to some organisational values (although sometimes rather unwillingly) which might seem the outcome of universal, rational processes of organisational expansion and professionalisation at first sight, but appear as particularistic, irrational and sometimes even hostile to clients and their parents. The common objectified approach to the client, for example, comes across as an unnatural way of approach to children. Some children in this research said that this approach made them feel like 'a number in a row' instead of a unique individual. Their feeling is reflected in Board terminology in, for example, the annual reports: the interactions of Board employees with clients for the purpose of writing a social inquiry report are clinically referred to as 'realised production'.

All in all, clients and their parents may well experience Board employees in the same way as many employees experience them: as the representatives of an ethnic group that they do not belong to and whose language, habits, norms, values, etc they do not, or only partly, understand. The Board comes across as a strange, maybe 'exotic' and sometimes frightening culture that is difficult to understand and therefore distrusted by many.

Dutch Board Culture versus Non-Dutch Clients?

The obscurity of the criminal law system and the Board's inaccessible culture are reflected in the children's lack of understanding of what the Board is about and where it fits in the criminal law system. Even after having been in contact with the organisation and having its function and goals explained to them, they did not know why the organisation was involved in their case, what its tasks and work methods were, or what the responsibilities of the Board employees or their own rights and obligations were. Only one of the 20 children interviewed could accurately explain one of the main functions of the Board. Some children and parents attributed their lack of understanding to the number of organisations they had encountered on their way through the criminal law system; they could not 'see the wood for the trees' and, as far as the Board was concerned, were unable to differentiate the organisation from the other institutions involved in their case.

Remarkably, autochthonous clients experienced this problem just as much as clients from ethnic minority groups did.[14] It is therefore a simplification to state that clients' foreign cultures clash with Dutch Board mores. Rather, Board-specific, subcultural values collide with an enormous diversity of values of the culturally and in other respects heterogeneous client population. The Board system of meaning clearly is not universally applicable and therefore not self-evident, logical nor legitimate from the point of view of clients whose frames of reference—culturally, socially or otherwise—differ from it.

As a result, the children and parents in this research generally felt insecure about the rules they had to follow and the behaviour expected from

---

[14] Because of the small number of case studies, this finding cannot be generalised beyond this group of informants. However, considering that variation in age, ethnicity, seriousness of the offence, sort of family and recidivism has been assured in choosing the case studies, the chance that they are exceptions to the rule is quite small.

them. They felt powerless in their contact with the Board, as illustrated by a 14-year-old autochthonous-Dutch client: 'They just play with your feelings, but they don't care. They think: we will decide what will happen [to you]. You can't do anything'. Several children and parents mentally withdrew from the contact. They answered Board employees' questions as briefly as possible, plainly lied, threw Board letters away unread or did not respond to invitations. Complaints about Board interventions were kept internally instead of being voiced and formally treated. Two children in the research population withdrew from the contact physically as well, by walking out of their interviews with Board employees. It must be obvious that in this way, children's and parents' involvement in their own legal proceedings, and thereby their perception of the legitimacy of criminal law practice, is imperilled (see also Oude Breuil and Post, 2002).

DISCUSSION: HOW TO DEAL WITH THE ETHNIC OTHER?

In this chapter, I have rephrased the central question of this book—should cultural imperatives mitigate punishment?—to the empirical question whether or not cultural backgrounds are actually being taken into account in criminal law practice and how that is done. Employees of the Dutch Child Protection Board do indeed encounter cultural obstacles in their interaction with clients from ethnic minority groups and sometimes over-come these obstacles by changing rules and regulations surrounding child protection measures and community service orders.

When they do so with an underlying, essentialist perception on culture—considering ethnic minority groups as homogeneous entities—they risk stereotyping their clients. This is illustrated by the supervisor's observation (at the beginning of this contribution), ascribing lack of responsibility and aggression towards everything that is Dutch, to Moroccan culture.[15] An essentialist view on culture, moreover, under-emphasises the fact that cul-tural values and habits change and denies hybrid forms of cultural identity. Clients are, so to speak, socially and culturally incarcerated: they are put in a limited and stereotyped cultural space.[16] Their agency—more precisely: their capacity to think independently of their ethnic group, change cultural values and ideas over time and act upon their changed ideas—is thereby

---

[15] Stereotyping allows employees of criminal law institutions to quickly categorise children and the latter's living conditions—a welcome advantage in a sector that is striving for more efficiency and productivity.

[16] The idea of 'social and cultural incarceration' of the ethnic other derives from Arjun Appadurai's 'spatial incarceration of the native' (Appadurai, 1988: 36–7), which refers to the tendency in anthropological studies to describe cultural units as bounded by territory and confine ethnic others within these boundaries.

overlooked. Whereas the client is viewed as a passive receiver, a cultural 'dope', caught inside her or his values, the Board employee is considered to be able to put his cultural values aside and adapt him or herself to the client's culture. By culturally incarcerating clients, the Board thus places itself in a superior position, making children and parents feel powerless in the process.

A constructivist view, on the other hand, takes culture as 'the thing to be explained', not the final answer. It leaves more room to talk about norms and values, deepen knowledge and negotiate space for compromise. Board members who apply such a constructivist view have less risk of ending up in an 'us–them' polarity and might find common ground in their contacts with parents and children.

Organisations such as the Board, however, have an interest in defining their problems with clients of ethnic minorities as a problem of the latter's culture, as well as defining thereby culture in an essentialist way. When the client's culture is perceived as unchangeable, static, prescribed in the clients' genes, the organisation can hardly be blamed for not being able to interact and communicate fluently with ethnic minority families. Clients' cultures may then function as an excuse for shortcomings within the organisation itself or the system that it is part of.

The Board cases presented here answer the question about the role of culture in criminal law practice with a counter-question: whose culture is so problematic anyway? Even though it is generally assumed that clients' cultures are the central question in this multicultural riddle, this study shows that criminal law institutions such as the Board have their own particular rules, shared knowledge, rituals, and symbols that may also be hard to understand, by autochthonous and ethnic minority clients alike. We might even argue that when confronted with a criminal law institution that is so hard to understand, presenting oneself as an uninitiated member of a different, exotic 'tribe' can be a logical and sensitive strategy of positioning oneself. The findings in this case study suggest at least that it might be important to invest more energy in informing children and parents about the criminal law system, rather than focusing on adapting this system to the cultural values of ethnic minority groups.

When asking whether cultural imperatives should influence the way people are treated within criminal law practice, we should also realise that culture might not be so imperative as we like to believe. Culture is not fixed: neither the minorities' culture nor the culture in criminal law institutions such as the Board. It is constantly in flux, created and recreated by the thoughts and actions of all involved. By socially and culturally incarcerating ethnic others and ethnic selves, we do not do justice to this complex reality.

13

Cultural Defence and Societal Dynamics

ERIK CLAES AND JOGCHUM VRIELINK

[L]aw, rather than a mere technical add-on to a morally (or immorally) finished society, is, along with a whole range of other cultural realities from the symbolics of faith to the means of production, an active part of it.

Clifford Geerz[1]

INTRODUCTION

IN RECENT DECADES 'Western' societies have witnessed a marked increase in the number of cases in which cultural aspects appear to play a prominent role. Though still relatively few in numbers these 'cultural offences'[2] enjoy wide attention in both the media and academic research. This is not only due to the sensational nature of many of these crimes. Cultural offences also pose a serious problem to the criminal justice system by throwing into question broadly shared and taken for granted assumptions about fundamental legal concepts such as free will and criminal responsibility.

Within the study of law and jurisprudence, cultural offences have typically received a very specific type of attention,[3] which focuses on the possibility and desirability of taking the cultural backgrounds of a perpetrator

---

[1] C Geertz, *Local Knowledge: Further Essays in Interpretive Anthropology* (New York, Basic Books, 1983) 218.

[2] For the purposes of this chapter, 'cultural offences' will be understood as violations of norms that are defined in the criminal law of a country or region, that are strongly related to the cultural background of the perpetrator. This concept, the anthropological and behavioural assumptions underlying it and the myriad of problems associated with it, are themselves not subjected to analysis in this chapter.

[3] The issue has, of course, also received attention from other academic disciplines, most notably criminology and anthropology.

of an action into account in the criminal procedure,[4] the so-called 'cultural defence'.[5]

One thing that these analyses tend to have in common is that the legal 'pros and cons' are discussed in complete abstraction from the dynamic societal context in which the debate on cultural defence takes place. This may in itself not come as much of a surprise, since this tendency is characteristic of the vast majority of legal scholarship: law and culture are considered as distinct realms of action that are only marginally related. Lawyers are inclined to neglect that law itself is a dynamic cultural phenomenon constantly interacting with other cultural practices and trends. As a result of this, 'legal' problems tend to be analysed in isolation from culture and especially from its dynamics and trends.[6] Taking the influence of the dynamic nature of society at large into account tends to be the furthest thing from a lawyer's mind.

This chapter is an attempt at redressing this neglect. As such, we wish to raise the question of what kind of societal trends are playing (or could play) a role in the elaboration of legal arguments pro and contra 'cultural offence'. How and to what extent do these trends bear on these arguments? And what happens to (the nature and validity of) the arguments in the legal debate on cultural defence when the undeniable fact of societal dynamics is taken into consideration? Underlying these questions is also a normative concern to allow the law to carve out a deliberative space to take these forces into account and critically assess them.

---

[4] One can, and in some cases should, distinguish the informal use of cultural evidence from a formal(ised) cultural defence. This distinction will, however, not be made in the following, as it has limited relevance to our argument and would only serve to complicate it. As such, we employ the term 'cultural defence' to cover both notions, thereby referring to a situation in which a person seeks to introduce evidence of his specific cultural background in an attempt to either exculpate himself from liability or mitigate his punishment. As to the distinction between a formal and informal cultural defence and its implications, see especially SM Tomao, 'The Cultural Defense: Traditional or Formal?' (1996) 10 *Georgetown Immigration Law Journal* 241.

[5] See for some examples of the type of analysis to which we refer Harvard Law Review Editors, 'The Cultural Defense in the Criminal Law' (1985–86) 2 *Harvard Law Review* 1293; JM Sams, 'The Availability of the "Cultural Defense" as an Excuse for Criminal Behavior' (1986) 16 *Georgia Journal of International and Comparative Law* 335; TF Goldstein, 'Cultural Conflicts in Court: Should the American Criminal Justice System Formally Recognize a "Cultural Defense"?' (1994) *Dickinson Law Review* 141; AJ Gallin, 'The Cultural Defense: Undermining the Politics Against Domestic Violence' (1994) 35 *Boston College Law Review* 723; VL Sacks, 'An Indefensible Defense: On the Misuse of Culture in Criminal Law' (1996) *Arizona Journal of International and Comparative Law* 523; M Fischer, 'The Human Rights Implications of a "Cultural Defense"' (1998) 6 *Southern California Interdisciplinary Law Journal* 663.

[6] At the most lawyers have raised the question of how cultural defence strategies (are likely to) affect society. The question of how trends and movements in society might influence the legal debate on cultural offences has, however (to our knowledge) not been considered in legal analyses. In other words, the dialectical nature of the dynamic entanglement of law and society at large tends to be ignored. See generally, N Mezey, 'Law as Culture' (2001) 13 *Yale Journal of Law and the Humanities* 35.

In the following we will first provide a general overview of the main legal arguments that are put forward in the debate surrounding the cultural defence. Subsequently we shall attempt to assess whether and to what extent societal dynamics may have an impact on the relevance of these arguments and their relative weight. Two major conflicting societal trends will be analysed in this regard: 'cultural relativism', on the one hand, and the growing impact of a 'culture of control' on the other.[7] We will finish with a proposal to widen the focus in the debate: to the question 'what are the best legal arguments in the debate surrounding the cultural defence in the criminal law' should be added another one, namely 'how should the impact of societal dynamics on legal arguments and principles be properly managed by the criminal law'.

PRINCIPLES AND ARGUMENTS IN THE DEBATE

One obvious way to provide an overview of the debate on cultural defence would be to categorise legal principles according to whether they either plead in favour of or against a cultural defence in criminal proceedings. The problem with such a strategy, however, is that it is difficult, if not impossible, to sort out what principles and arguments belong to what side of the discussion. Often the same principles and concepts are used to serve the views of both 'friends and foes' of a cultural defence.

In order to address this problem, we will therefore adopt an alternative strategy. We will start from the main goals, values or principles that steer the debate in legal cultures governed by the rule of law, and attempt to reconstruct how these same 'ingredients' are actually used and annexed in the debate by both proponents and opponents. Our aim in doing this has nothing to do with establishing whether the 'pros' or the 'cons' have the upper hand. This, as mentioned above, is typical for the large majority of legal scholarship, and we do not intend to repeat it here. Our goal is merely to analyse the legal discourse as it is and demonstrate the ways in which it twists and turns. Such a strategy is in line with the main concern of our chapter. It will naturally lead us to transcend the 'superficial'[8] legal debate and to pose anthropological questions such as: how come the same legal principles and penal goals at once push the debate in seemingly opposite directions? And what kind of societal forces are responsible for this phenomenon?

---

[7] We draw the concept and its underlying analysis from D Garland, *The Culture of Control: Crime and Social Order in Contemporary Society* (Oxford, Oxford University Press, 2001).

[8] The term 'superficial' should in no way be read in its common pejorative meaning, but rather in its literal sense as arguments pertaining to the surface. Our analysis holds no pretence of being more 'profound' in any intellectual sense than the legal analyses to which we refer.

Before embarking on our analysis, some notes of humility are in order. First, in the light of the general aim and prospective nature of our contribution, our analysis will be kept rather limited (or even simplified). Secondly, we will try to (only) present arguments that are common to the criminal laws of most states governed by the rule of law, and as such also steer clear from more technical issues that are typical of any particular criminal justice system.

Arguments in the Debate

Criminal Responsibility

A main cluster of arguments in the debate is related to the legal (un)acceptability of a cultural defence and centres around issues of criminal responsibility and mens rea. Arguments in relation to these issues provide the primary motivation for admitting cultural evidence, according to proponents of one form or another of cultural defence.[9] The specific form that this argument takes varies greatly depending on the particular legal system, the type of culture offence that is involved, and the specific contexts of individual cases.[10] However, despite all their differences, the underlying reasoning comes down to the fact that cultural backgrounds allegedly can and do in some cases either negate the requisite criminal responsibility to find a defendant guilty of a particular crime, or at least work to diminish a defendant's degree of culpability and therefore should serve to mitigate his punishment.

As such, the main legal motivation for admitting cultural evidence from this point of view basically consists in an attempt to bridge a (perceived) gap in the criminal law between moral and legal responsibility.[11]

Opponents respond to this argument in several different ways. Many of these counter-arguments consist in stressing the lack of accuracy in determining someone's state of mind with regard to the cultural defence, and the possibilities of manipulation and fraud that the use of cultural evidence would thereby open up.[12] Another response, however, entails a different interpretation

---

[9] AD Renteln, 'A Justification of the Cultural Defense as a Partial Excuse' (1993) 2 *Southern California Review of Law and Women's Studies* 443; Harvard Law Review Editors, above n 5 at 1294–95; Sams, above n 5 at 338–45; NS Kim, 'The Cultural Defense and the Problem of Cultural Preemption: a Framework for Analysis' (1997) *New Mexico Law Review* 103; J Sing, 'Culture as Sameness: Toward a Synthetic View of Provocation and Culture in the Criminal Law' (1999) *Yale Law Journal* 1849.

[10] Depending on these latter facts and contexts, pleas for admitting cultural evidence have been made (and sometimes accepted) on the following grounds: ignorance of law; consent; intoxication; automatism; mistake of fact; self-defence; provocation; duress; diminished capacity and (temporary) insanity.

[11] Renteln, above n 9.

[12] Goldstein, above n 5; JP Sams, above n 5 at 346–7; Kim, above n 9 at 115; Fischer, above n 5 at 689.

or emphasis in the concept of criminal responsibility altogether. Opponents often hold that criminal responsibility should—perhaps not exclusively, but as much as possible—be determined by the (criminal) act rather than the particular mindset of the perpetrator. In order for someone to be held criminally responsible, this view holds that in general it should at most be established whether an individual intended to commit the act that is defined as a crime.[13]

Deterrence

Arguments in relation to 'deterrence' also play an important role in the 'cultural defence' debate. Deterrence comes in two forms: specific and general. Specific deterrence is concerned with the influence of punishment on the particular perpetrator of a crime. General deterrence is interested in the effect of punishment on other people's future actions.

The opponents maintain that deterrence constitutes a(nother) main objection to the foregoing argument for taking culture into account in determining someone's criminal responsibility, since doing so is perceived to pose problems for the deterrent effect of the criminal law. Opponents argue that accepting exonerating cultural evidence conflicts with both basic forms of deterrence. First, it allegedly defeats the criminal law's objective of deterring the same individual from committing a similar crime in the future (specific deterrence). A person punished for breaking a law would normally be less likely to misbehave again. In the absence of punishment or where the punishment is mitigated due to one's cultural background, the specific deterrent effect will respectively either be absent or substantially reduced.[14]

Secondly, the cultural defence is also believed to detract from the law's general deterrent effects. General deterrence tends to be perceived as more effective when punishment for committing proscribed acts is certain. As such, when one's cultural background might serve as an excuse or as mitigating circumstances, members of cultural minority groups might be less deterred by the law.[15] When cultural evidence might serve to lift or lessen criminal responsibility, others are likely to believe the defence will also work for them, thus removing the incentive to conform to the law. This might serve to increase uncertainty as to what constitutes criminal behaviour, especially among immigrants. This confusion might in turn lead to an

---

[13] Depending of course on the specific (nature of the) offence involved.

[14] DL Coleman, 'Individualizing Justice through Multiculturalism: the Liberals Dilemma' (1996) 5 *Columbia Law Review* 1137.

[15] Goldstein, above n 5 at 160–1; Gallin, above n 5 at 737–8; Sams, above n 5 at 348–50; Kim, above n 9 at 112; Coleman, above n 14 at 1137; Sacks, above n 5 at 541. Sacks argues that this has in fact been demonstrated in cases where a cultural defence was accepted.

increased disobedience of those rules. The cultural defence may then not only fail to deter crime, 'it may even encourage it'.[16]

Proponents take issue with these allegations. For one thing, they argue that the concern about maintaining deterrence by uniformly applying traditional modes of punishment is unjustified since the criminal law is also able to maintain its deterrent effects despite the availability of other defences.[17] More fundamentally, however, they argue that the opponents' argument is beside the point, since deterrence in this traditional sense has a rather limited value in relation to cultural offences. When (as proponents believe) acts are indeed dictated or mandated by a defendant's cultural background and his peer group, (the threat of) traditional punishment is said to have low deterrence value at best. Moreover, it is argued that deterrence in this context is rendered invalid when it would result in punishing someone who does not morally deserve it. As such, the goal of deterrence and the modes of punishment ought to be 'rethought' in this context.[18] Rather than simply persisting in administering 'medicine' that will not work, other modes of punishment should be worked out that can and will serve to prevent recidivism and which promote reinsertion and reintegration of perpetrators of cultural offences into mainstream society.

Legality

Another principle that surfaces now and then in the discussions about the cultural defence is that of legality. This principle entails that no conduct may be held criminal unless it is precisely described in a (preceding) criminal law. Here again, the different dimensions of this principle allow both opponents and proponents to instrumentalise it for their respective purposes.

Opponents, for one thing, believe the principle of legality pleads against the acceptance of exonerating cultural evidence. They hold that the principle in essence requires that rules of law are attributed with 'objective meanings', that are determined and declared by competent officials, and that only *those* meanings of the rules constitute the law. As such, it is argued, it conflicts with the principle of legality to treat a defendant as if the law were as *he* thought it to be. In accepting exonerating cultural evidence, the cultural backgrounds and ideas of the defendants and his community would be placed above the law as declared by the officials.[19] In this sense, then,

---

[16] Goldstein, above n 5 at 161. Compare: M Galenkamp, 'Tolerantie in de Nederlandse strafrechtspleging: is er ruimte voor een cultureel verweer?' in M ten Hooven (ed), *De lege tolerantie. Over vrijheid en vrijblijvendheid in Nederland* (Amsterdam, Boom, 2001) 198.

[17] Harvard Law Review Editors, above n 5 at 1304.

[18] DC Chiu, 'The Cultural Defense: Beyond Exclusion, Assimilation, and Guilty Liberalism' (1994) *California Law Review* 1053; Harvard Law Review Editors, above n 5 at 1303.

[19] Sams, above n 5 at 351.

the principle serves to provide at once a legitimate basis for fighting crime and a need for strict and uniform enforcement.

Proponents are of the opinion that this interpretation of the principle of legality fails to do justice to its 'proper' aspirations. They point rather to the constraints that the principle of legality poses on state action. The requirement of strict interpretation of penal statutes, for instance, (that is generally regarded as a derivative or corollary of the principle of legality) might serve as a basis for allowing exonerating cultural evidence when it is (potentially) relevant in negating or diminishing the legally required mens rea. A second way in which the principle of legality is said to offer room for a cultural defence is through the demands it places on states in rendering the norms that are laid down in their criminal statutes accessible for all. To the extent that newcomers with a different cultural background have not been provided with access to these norms nor with information about them, it is sometimes argued that they should not then be held responsible in the light of the requirements of the principle of legality.

Discrimination and Equal Treatment

A final 'family' of arguments that is used in the debate surrounding the 'cultural defence' is based on principles of equal protection and non-discrimination. As was the case with the other arguments, proponents and opponents offer vastly different interpretations of these principles. Depending on these interpretations, equality arguments are variously regarded as either pleading against or, on the contrary, in favour of accepting cultural evidence. A basic distinction in equality arguments is that between those concerning defendants and those concerning victims.

Equality and Defendants

With regard to defendants, opponents often advance that the cultural defence amounts to discrimination against those who do not have the 'moral luck' to excuse their behaviour in the light of their cultural backgrounds. In general, a person's cultural background will not exculpate him from criminal responsibility or mitigate his sentence. Thus, it is argued, it amounts to a form of discrimination when only a certain class of people is able to utilise this specific defence, if their cultural backgrounds 'accidentally' provide an explanation for their conduct. 'Non-cultural' uses of state of mind defences tend to be of a much more general nature, equally available to anyone regardless of cultural backgrounds. The exonerating acceptance of cultural evidence as such is said to violate the rights of equal protection of criminal defendants for whom the defence was unavailable but who were otherwise in a similar situation as defendants that would be entitled to use it. Therefore, allowing a cultural defence would serve to undermine the principle that people should be treated equally before the law.[20]

This problem is said to be further enhanced by a myriad of definitional problems about for whom the defence should be available and under what circumstances. The absence of a firm basis for distinguishing disparate phenomena increases the risk of unequal treatment of those who are 'seemingly dissimilarly, but actually similarly situated'.[21]

Proponents, however, argue that the accusation of discrimination is spurious, since the principle of non-discrimination first of all requires that the (categories of) persons that are being compared are in fact alike. Precisely this is disputed by proponents of a cultural defence. According to them the relevant category of comparison should not be the 'regular' offender for whom a cultural defence is unavailable, but rather offenders for whom a traditional (application of a) defence is available. It is these categories that are in fact argued to be alike in relevant ways, for both are believed by proponents to have a reduced degree of criminal responsibility, or even an absence thereof. Allowing cultural defences in one form or another should then simply be regarded as providing minority defendants with the ability to invoke state of mind defences on an equal footing in ways that are relevant to them.

If anything, then, proponents argue that the principle of (substantive or material) equality actually requires, or at least allows for, the possibility of a cultural defence.[22] Definitional problems, although acknowledged, are generally not considered much more problematic than is the case for traditional (applications of) defences.

Equality and Victims

Finally, regarding the victims there is a somewhat analogous situation. Opponents of the cultural defence maintain that allowing exonerating cultural evidence violates the principle of equal protection of the victims that are involved.[23] Successful use of a cultural defence is often said to imply

---

[20] Sacks, above n 5 at 543; N Rimonte, 'A Question of Culture: Cultural Approval of Violence Against Women in the Pacific-Asian Community and the Cultural Defense' (1991) 57 *Stanford Law Review* 1326; 'Goldstein, above n 5 at 162; Sams, above n 5 at 350–1; Coleman, above n 14 at 1098–9; JC Lyman, 'Cultural Defense: Viable Doctrine or Wishful Thinking?' (1986) *Criminal Justice Journal* 116; Galenkamp, above n 16 at 197.

[21] Sacks, above n 5 at 544. See also Kim, above n 9 at 114–15; Fischer, above n 5 at 688–9.

[22] The arguments on this point of course differ significantly between those advocating for the institutionalisation of a formal cultural defence and those arguing for the (informal) acceptance of a 'cultural defence' within traditional defences. They do share a stress on substantive rather than formal equality. See Tomao, above n 4. See also Galenkamp, above n 16 at 195; S Bloemmink, 'Cultureel verweer' in G Anders, S Bloemink and NF Van Manen (eds), *De onvermijdelijkheid van rechtspluralisme* (Nijmegen, Ars Aequi Libri, 1998) 67; Sing, above n 9 at 1878–80.

[23] When of course there *are* victims involved.

that the victims involved have less protection than victims of similar crimes receive in the absence of a cultural defence. As a consequence, the victims of these crimes are denied (equal) justice or might even be said to be victimised a second time through the possibility of a cultural defence.[24]

In this way, it is often argued that the cultural defence operates to condone or perpetuate human rights violations, especially since the strategy allegedly is most often used in order to justify crimes committed against women and children. Therefore, when sentences or charges are reduced on the basis of this defence, it sends the message that these acts are condoned.[25]

Proponents argue, first, that the portrayal of cultural offences as solely targeting women and children is inaccurate and based on essentialist and categorical ideas about victimhood.[26] Secondly, proponents again differ with opponents about the relevant category of comparison (see above). Again, while opponents compare the victims' situation with that of victims of 'regular' crimes, proponents maintain that the comparators should be victims of crimes in which a traditional defence was available. In the latter case, proponents fail to see discrimination. On the contrary, since cultural backgrounds are believed by proponents to (potentially) negate one's criminal responsibility (just as other states of mind for which there are traditional defences), it is only logical that equality between victims of these crimes precisely requires that this be taken into account in both situations. If not, it could amount to reverse discrimination against the victims of perpetrators for whose crimes a traditional defence was accepted as compared with victims of cultural offences.

Conclusion

All in all, then, most if not all legal principles and goals that are relevant in the debate surrounding the cultural defence provide arguments both for and against a cultural defence, depending on one's particular interpretations and emphases. All main legal principles, from 'criminal responsibility' to 'equality', leave space for diverging interpretations and uses.

Lawyers could easily neutralise this ambivalence by arguing that diverging uses of these principles do not preclude that some uses lead to better arguments and, in the end, to a more defensible position: 'a right answer'.[27]

---

[24] Coleman, above n 14 at 1144.

[25] Sacks, above n 5 at 534; Goldstein, above n 5 at 162–3; Gallin, above n 5 at 725 and 735; Fischer, above n 5 at 662–3; SM Okin, 'Is Multiculturalism Bad for Women?' in SM Okin (ed), *Is Multiculturalism Bad for Women?* (Princeton, Princeton University Press, 1999) 19.

[26] L Volpp, 'Talking "Culture": Gender, Race, Nation, and the Politics of Multiculturalism' (1996) *Columbia Law Review* 1573 at 1583–5; L Volpp, 'Feminism Versus Multiculturalism' (2001) *Columbia Law Review* 1181.

[27] The best known proponent of this thesis in legal philosophy is, of course, R Dworkin, he also coined the term, see R Dworkin, *A Matter of Principle* (Oxford, Clarendon Press, 1996).

Perhaps this is indeed the case in the debate on cultural defence. But then one should raise the question why despite this alleged possibility of a right answer, the legal discussion on the cultural defence is far from being settled and has in fact lost none of its intellectual vigour. One reasonable explanation, which brings us to the main hypothesis of our chapter, could be that the driving force behind the legal controversy about the cultural defence is not confined to an intellectual commitment to truth and justice. The vigour of the debate and the ambivalent use of the same legal concepts and principles could betray the presence and impact of broader competing societal dynamics that vie over the minds of lawyers, politicians and legal theorists. These dynamics are not primarily driven by a commitment to truth and justice, but rather by a will to survive and prevail.

Such an explanation, if made plausible, is not without practical consequences. If we agree on the idea that lawyers are under the obligation to settle the discussion on cultural defence by means of the most justifiable arguments and the best interpretation of the law's values and principles, then they have a responsibility to identify these societal dynamics and to assess them critically. Such a commitment would prevent legal principles and concepts being completely delivered over to cultural forces, and would, accordingly, better allow for a deliberative space in which the quality of arguments would steer the discussion, instead of the sheer 'will to power'.

In what follows we would like to lend support to such a commitment by first sketching two societal dynamics or trends against which the debate on cultural offence takes place: cultural relativism and a 'culture of control'. Subsequently, we will try to make plausible that the struggle between these dynamics is in part responsible for the divergent shapes that legal principles and values take in the afore-mentioned debate.

SOCIETAL DYNAMICS

Preliminary Remarks

Both cultural relativism and the culture of control can be seen as a response to some major changes in late modern society: globalisation, migration and multiculturalism, the decline of the welfare state, the rise of mass media and political populism, new technological possibilities and corresponding risks, and last but not least global terrorism. Common to these trends is, furthermore, that their response to the late-modern predicament is coloured by a set of values and ideas which are characteristic of Western democracies and of modern Western history, such as tolerance, individual autonomy and authenticity, the inadmissibility of human suffering, relativism and instrumentalism.[28,29] Moreover, these trends are supported by similar 'power strategies':[30] that is, strategies to impose certain cultural habits and dispositions on the law, its actors (professionals, citizens) and institutions, as well as strategies of denial and repression of other cultural meanings and values.

Cultural Relativism

Consider first the trend of cultural relativism.[31] One of the most important characteristics and challenges of Western societies is surely their multicultural nature. Especially in urban regions, different ethnic groups are living together under the same societal context, while at the same time often diverging considerably in lifestyles, ethical codes and values. How to deal with these differences? As a response to this question, modern societies developed a collective attitude, cultural relativism, which in its essence comes down to a positive embracing of multicultural pluralism and a self-critical attitude to one's own cultural predispositions (anti-ethnocentrism). This attitude has a long history and can be retraced to a set of values and concepts that are characteristic of modern Western societies.

The idea of taking a self-critical attitude toward one's own cultural predispositions is profoundly influenced by epistemological scepticism: Modern intellectual culture is shaped by a shared belief that we do not have objective normative standards to assess moral positions and arbitrate between them.[32] Consequently, we do not have any standard or reason to prioritise our values over competing normative practices.

The idea of embracing multicultural pluralism is closely linked with ideals and values such as subjectivism and tolerance. Subjectivism, first, entails a belief in the relativity of ethical codes and practices. To quote

---

[28] This is not to say that these values and ideas are limited to these societies or that the latter hold a monopoly on them of any kind.

[29] Our notion of societal trends is closely related to C Taylor's idea of 'social imaginaries' and N Lacey's notion of 'cultural practices and discourses'. Lacey defines the latter as 'a relatively systematic set of values, understandings, expectations or conventions expressed or realised within a relatively structured field of linguistic or other conduct'. See: N Lacey, 'Contingency and Criminalisation' in I Loveland (ed), *Frontiers of Criminality* (London, Sweet & Maxwell, 1995) 9.

[30] We borrow the notion of power strategies from the Foucauldian approaches in critical criminology. See, eg, S Cohen, *Visions of Social Control: Crime, Punishment and Classification* (Cambridge, Polity Press, 1985). For strategies of denial (on state level), see S Cohen, *States of Denial: Knowing about Atrocities and Suffering* (Cambridge, Polity Press, 2002).

[31] What follows is a descriptive reconstruction of cultural relativism as it is enacted in late-modern society. We are concerned with an analysis of the philosophical coherence and the moral defensibility of this trend. For an excellent philosophical analysis of cultural relativism, see B Williams, *Ethics and the Limits of Philosophy* (London, Fontana Press, 1985) ch 9.

[32] C Taylor, *Philosophical Arguments* (Cambridge, MA, Harvard University Press, 1997).

Charles Taylor: 'When it comes to moral values, we all just ultimately have to plump for the one which feel best to us'.[33] From this follows a positive affirmation of cultural differences: other cultural practices have a right to exist, as long as they feel best for some.

Secondly, tolerance refers to a democratic ideal of respect for persons with different lifestyles and conceptions of the good life. Cultural difference should be embraced positively here, because it is essential to citizens' obligation to give each other equal respect as a full person. Denying a person in his right to cultural difference implies denying him as a person.[34]

As already suggested, it is important to underline here that in Western societies, cultural relativism also comes with a nexus of power strategies. As a societal dynamic, cultural relativism comes along, first, with a strategy of imposing itself on an institutional level in order to give a public and authoritative voice to its message of scepticism, subjectivism and tolerance.[35] The criminal law with its highly symbolic concepts such as criminal punishment, legal wrongdoing and criminal responsibility, but also with the strong ritual dimension of the criminal trial, is an ideal target for such a power strategy.[36] Criminal law, criminal justice and penal institutions are the perfect forums to publicly express the values of cultural relativism. Given the power of the criminal law to alter cultural habits,[37] it can also serve as a powerful instrument to change ideas and attitudes in society.

This brings us to a second power strategy that is involved with the societal trend of cultural relativism. It is a strategy of conquering institutions in order to discipline social behaviour in accordance with the values of cultural relativism. Again, the criminal law with its capacity to represent and exert coercive power through its institutions and its penal apparatus, is a pole of attraction for such type of strategy.[38]

A final power strategy also focuses on the coercive nature of public institutions in order to repress or deny diverging interpretations of moral reasoning (that sits ill with epistemological scepticism), or other values such as the right to life, the value of equal respect, the inadmissibility of human suffering (which might all impose constraints on a positive embracing of cultural pluralism and on anti-ethnocentrism). The criminal law serves then

---

[33] *Ibid* at 34. See also C Taylor, *The Ethics of Authenticity* (Cambridge, MA, Harvard University Press, 1992).

[34] See W Kymlicka, *Multicultural Citizenship* (Oxford, Oxford University Press, 1995).

[35] For the cultural dimension of criminal law and criminal punishment, see D Garland, *Punishment and Modern Society* (Oxford, Clarendon, 1990).

[36] On the symbolic dimension of criminal law and punishment, see *ibid* at 193. Garland here defines punishment as 'a cultural artefact, embodying and expressing society's cultural forms'.

[37] Or at least given the (public and institutional) aim of doing so.

[38] See, for the classical analysis of disciplinary techniques through the criminal law and penal institutions, M Foucault, *Surveiller et punir. Naissance de la prison* (Paris, Gallimard, 1975).

as a useful instrument to withdraw public attention from these diverging values and conceptions of moral reasoning.

Culture of Control[39]

Before examining the potential impact and effects of cultural relativism and its power strategies on the debate surrounding cultural defence, it is worthwhile to draw our attention to another societal trend called the culture of control. This trend draws its dynamics in part from three major changes in late-modern societies: there is first the massive insecurity with regard to employment touching all professional levels of society, which is triggered and reinforced by a globalising economy. The second major change is the daily projection through mass media of the idea of life quality: a comfortable, entertaining and glamorous lifestyle. The third change is the undeniable rise of global risks, which form a threat to our quality of life, and even to human life itself. These global risks result to a great extent from new technological inventions that have recently set the stage for evolving global terrorism. A final change that is worth noting here is the decline of nation-states who have proved (and are proving) to be incapable of addressing the fear and insecurities of their citizens, of efficiently organising social solidarity among them, and of fulfilling their longing for a comfortable life.

These aspects of late-modern society have triggered a complex set of cultural practices, habits and techniques. Despite their variety, these practices are linked to each other by a common structure. First, they are aimed at controlling and managing risk behaviour, risk situations and risk-full categories of persons. Secondly, these practices are driven by a desire of powerful social classes to safeguard the indispensable (material, intellectual) resources for the leading of a comfortable individual life. Thirdly, these strategies serve to adapt modern societies to the irremediable shortcomings of the nation-state in managing the problems of our time.

Some practices expressing a culture of control contain a dynamic of 'responsabilising' citizens to manage themselves, risk situations and the risk-full behaviour of fellow citizens.[40] Or, to put it somewhat differently: citizens are under the obligation now to control (prevent) their own victimhood. Other practices are of a more expressive nature; they are called into existence to rhetorically convince citizens that in the end the state 'has everything under control' and that the state is taking care of and listening attentively to the suffering voice of the victim. Often, these practices

---

[39] Our analysis of the culture of control is based upon Garland, above n 7.

[40] Garland speaks of 'responsibilisation strategies' (D Garland, 'The Limits of the Sovereign State: Strategies of Crime Control in Contemporary Society' (1996) 36 *British Journal of Criminology* 452.

are simply designed to regulate existential anxiety: they give expression to collective emotions of moral indignation and despair by transforming risk-full and harm-causing acts into criminal wrongs of aliens, monsters, predators and psychopaths.[41]

This culture of control is, of course, also shaped in its design by a set of values and modes of reasoning which are familiar to modern history. The drive to obsessively maintain and protect the quality of life is unthinkable without positively affirming individual self-fulfilment, subjectivism and the value of ordinary, private life. The urge to control every potential danger which may create victims is guided by an extreme sensibility for human suffering.[42] And, finally, the unfolding of complex programmes and techniques of risk control is inspired by a naive belief in technological possibilities and instrumental reasoning. Everything is under control once we are furnished with the appropriate technique to identify risk situations, to profile risk groups, to point to types of risk behaviour, and to prescribe codes of prevention.

Similar to the societal trend of cultural relativism, a culture of control is supported by a web of power strategies that are strongly attracted by the concepts and institutions of the criminal law. The first power strategy manifests itself in efforts to control the public scene in order to reflect and shape the existential fears of 'Westerners', and to reinforce a feeling of the familiar Us against the Alien Others. The criminal law, by virtue of its expressive medium of criminal punishment, is an excellent instrument to rhetorically reaffirm the power of a weakened nation-state, to express collective emotions of moral indignation, to offer a focus to undetermined existential 'angst' and to construct the offender as a dangerous criminal who, through the alleged atrocities he has committed, has placed himself beyond the limits of humanity.

The second power strategy consists in repressing the inner contradictions underlying a culture of control. In the words of David Garland:

> Convinced of the need to re-impose order, but unwilling to restrict consumer choice or give up personal freedoms; determined to enhance their own security, but unwilling to pay more taxes or finance the security of others; appalled by unregulated egoism and anti-social attitudes but committed to a market system which reproduces that very culture, the anxious middle classes today seek resolution for their ambivalence in zealously controlling the poor and excluding the marginal.[43]

---

[41] B Hudson, *Justice in the Risk Society: Challenging and Re-affirming Justice in Late Modernity* (London, Sage, 2003).

[42] C Taylor, *Sources of the Self: the Making of the Modern Identity* (Cambridge, MA, Harvard University Press, 1989).

[43] See Garland, above n 7 at 195.

The criminal law and its penal apparatus, with their power to control and exclude, and with their potential to express publicly collective beliefs and social imaginaries, are an ideal medium through which such strategies of occulting inner contradictions could be processed.

SOCIETAL DYNAMICS AND THE DEBATE
ON CULTURAL DEFENCE

How do the trends of cultural relativism and the culture of control weigh on the debate on cultural defence? To what extent do they explain that most of the legal principles in the debate at once pull in opposite directions? In what follows we will try to examine these issues by revisiting two of the legal principles or concepts around which the controversy on cultural defence is centred: criminal responsibility and equality of victims. We restrict the elaboration to these two principles in order to avoid undue repetition of highly analogous reasoning. However, the following applies *mutatis mutandis* to the other principles discussed in the second part above as well.

Criminal Responsibility

To explain why the discussion is still not settled on the issue of whether to give criminal responsibility either a more action-centred or a person-centred interpretation, one could reasonably point to cultural relativism and the culture of control, competing with each other in order to impose their values on the concepts and institutions of the criminal law.

As already mentioned, the trend of cultural relativism is supported by a power strategy to impose the values of cultural tolerance, epistemological scepticism and subjectivism. Once the law and its practitioners are subjected to this power strategy, they are inclined to render a person-centred shape to the concept of criminal responsibility and apply this conception of responsibility to cultural offences. Such a conception protects the defendant in his subjective valuing of his culture, and makes him totally or partly immune against being publicly accountable for the wrong he committed. Making criminal responsibility dependent on the mental state of the offender protects the defendant from being censured and punished for the actions he committed. It creates an ideal legal context through which the equal value of cultures can be expressed. A person-centred conception of responsibility can also suitably be used to discipline the victim and citizens in their capacity of potential victims: such a conception would help in making them believe that their sentiments of moral indignation are relative to their culture, and will prove inappropriate when they encounter opposing cultural practices and beliefs. Finally, a person-centred responsibility that focuses on the state of mind of the offender helps to divert attention away from the suffering, the loss of dignity and the moral indignation of the victims and their relatives. Repressing this reality is important, if one wants cultural relativism's belief in the equal value of diverging cultural practices and in anti-ethnocentrism to be sustained.

Once this trend of cultural relativism enters the scene of the criminal law, it encounters opposition from another trend: the afore-mentioned culture of control. In contrast with the former, a culture of control tends to bring to the fore values such as the suffering and loss of dignity of the victim, the (collective) moral indignation and even the will to revenge. These values are expressive of a pervasive existential anxiety which large categories of people are living with. They fear to lose their chances of self-fulfilment and of a high quality of life due to harmful and risky behaviour of others. They expect the nation-state to prevent and to control this kind of behaviour.

Entering the debate on cultural defence, and attacking this notion on the grounds of an action-centred conception of responsibility, creates an ideal forum for a culture of control to exercise its power. Making persons who commit cultural offences responsible for their offences in accordance with the seriousness of the crime or—better yet—punishing them even more harshly helps in diverting the attention away from the person of the offender and shifting it exclusively to the person of the victim, to his suffering and loss of dignity.

Such an 'action-responsibility' allows criminal punishment to play a central symbolical role in the criminal process. Through the imposition of severe criminal punishment, the state can communicate to their anxious citizens that everything is under control. Punishing perpetrators of a cultural offence by means of an action-centred conception of responsibility also creates an ideal context in which the offender could be represented as an alien towards whom we bear no obligations of solidarity, an alien who is now 'justly' deprived of his right to question the legitimacy of our obsession with safeguarding our 'cosy' designed individual lives.

Equality of Victims

The potential ambiguity of the principle of equal protection of victims can be explained in a similar fashion. Again, the radically different directions that this principle can take could be (partially) explained by the culture of control and cultural relativism vying for dominance in the sphere of the criminal law.

As said, the culture of control tends to stress the suffering and loss of dignity of (instrumentally construed) victims and a (collective) moral indignation at acts that constitute a threat to a controlled and predictable societal ordering. Focusing heavily on the formal inequality and injustice that arises between victims of cultural offences as compared to victims of other, 'mainstream', offences provides a culture of control with appropriate means for furthering its aims and establishing its control over the criminal law. A one-sided focus on the victims and an accompanying discourse on human rights violations, and the atrocious, 'backward' nature of many cultural offences, allows the state first to provide a convenient focus for societal fears in an age of growing xenophobia and fear of terrorism, and subsequently to publicly demonstrate that it can control this 'threat to civilisation'. Furthermore, it again—and even more markedly—serves to divert societal and legal attention away from the person of the offender, sometimes even to the point of rendering him irrelevant to attaining a 'just' outcome, shifting it exclusively to the person of the victim and considerations of the 'general' interest. The interests of the defendant are thereby effectively neglected and repressed.

A trend towards cultural relativism would be prone to pull the debate in the opposite direction, and 'colour' the principle of equality of victims in a wholly different fashion. Core values of the trend of cultural relativism would serve to seek categories of comparison for victims of cultural offences that allow the cultural background of a defendant to figure largely in the criminal process. As such, the trend of cultural relativism will render more plausible the comparison of victims of cultural offences with those of victims of crimes for which the defendant (successfully) invoked traditional exonerating evidence, thereby reiterating the values of cultural relativism.

Furthermore, this switch of victim-categories of comparison can again serve to discipline society as well as the victims involved. Victims are thereby 'taught' that their legal expectations should be adjusted depending not only on traditional, cultural specific or 'ethnocentric' conceptions of lack of criminal responsibility, but also—and on an equal footing—depending on the cultural backgrounds of their wrongdoers.

Finally, a move towards greater cultural relativism in society might again serve to repress opposing interpretations and streams of thought. This is done not only by one-sidedly focusing on certain victim-categories as comparison but also by deconstructing and rendering suspect the conception of victimhood characteristic of opposing arguments. The latter are attacked and discredited as being, among other things, 'decontextualised', 'ethnocentric' and 'part of a conservative backlash'. The public might thereby be deflected away and discouraged from these competing interpretations, and from the reality of the suffering of victims of cultural offences and their relatives.

CONCLUSION

To conclude, one could adequately summarise this chapter by pointing out two guiding ideas that we have tried to illustrate through a critical analysis of the debate on cultural defence. The first concerns the idea that law is a cultural phenomenon and that, consequently, legal issues, legal principles and arguments are often the reflection of broader societal dynamics, which are supported by a nexus of power strategies. Law cannot be divorced from culture and its dynamics despite the efforts, or rather the pretences, to do so by lawyers.[44] As such, all interpretations and arguments about law are necessarily cultural interpretations.[45]

In our chapter we have tried to demonstrate this cultural sensitivity of the law in the debate surrounding the cultural defence.[46] We did so in three steps. The first step consisted in drawing attention to the ambivalence of the legal principles on which the discussion is grounded. The second step entailed showing how this vigour and ambivalence are (partially) connected with a struggle between at least two cultural trends: cultural relativism and the culture of control. The final step entailed the retrieval of a nexus of power strategies that are bound up with the afore-mentioned societal dynamics.

The second guiding idea of our chapter is related to a belief that the law can only live up to its potential to produce the most defensible position in a legal issue if it is, first, conscious of the cultural dynamics to which it is subjected, and if it secondly tries to 'tone down' or even impose normative constraints on these dynamics as far as their impact on the law in concerned.

As long as lawyers, in their ambition to find the right answer for pressing legal issues, continue to ignore the ways in which the law is influenced by and reflects particular cultural trends and forces, this latter potential remains unexploited. Or to put it more affirmatively: if lawyers are willing to act upon the cultural forces that often subconsciously shape their attitudes, and if they wish to carve out a deliberative space allowing for the most justifiable positions to prevail in the debate, then a twofold responsibility weighs upon them. First, they should carefully map these cultural trends and their impact on legal arguments and principles, and they ought secondly to uncover the underlying power strategies of these trends in order to critically assess them.

[44] Nor can culture be divorced from law. See Mezey, above n 6.

[45] This is not to say that law and society are wholly indistinguishable from one another. With the possible exception of the more radical reaches of academic post-modernism, one would be hard-pressed to dispute that there is an important distinction between a particular society and its trends, on the one hand, and the (practice of) law in that society, on the other. The necessary interconnections between the two do not make law indistinguishable from society, nor do they rob the practice of law of intrinsic value(s).

[46] Our attempt to confront this assumption with the legal discussion on the cultural defence is not arbitrary. This discussion, at least at first sight, appears to be a particularly apt subject for analysis, since it itself so explicitly deals with 'culture'. This, in a sense, is likely to serve as a 'multiplier' for the sensitivity and responsiveness to wider cultural dynamics in society.

Within the confines of this chapter we cannot offer a full-fledged answer on how to deal properly with the cultural forces that impact upon the debate surrounding the cultural defence. However, our critical analysis of the twin trends of the culture of control and cultural relativism, despite its limitations, might offer at least three preliminary reference points that might better enable lawyers to implement the afore-mentioned responsibilities.

A first reference point entails articulating the values which are suppressed by either of these cultural trends and rectifying our view on the topic: solidarity, right to life and physical integrity and freedom, the inadmissibility of human suffering, tolerance, the right to cultural difference, etc. A second point requires that the leading concepts and principles (responsibility, legality, deterrence, equality, etc) of the debate be evenly reconstructed in the light of all the values that are at stake in the debate on cultural defence. A final suggestion would be that one at least avoids taking positions in the debate on the cultural defence that are entirely and one-sidedly tributary to one of the cultural trends we sketched above.

These reference points might contribute to giving genuine legal effects to an insight widely accepted among anthropologists , namely that the law is not 'merely a technical add-on to a morally (or immorally) finished society' but rather 'an active part of it'.[47]

---

[47] C Geertz, *Local Knowledge: Further Essays in Interpretive Anthropology* (New York, Basic Books, 1983) 218.

14

The Anthropologist as Expert Witness: the Case of a Murder in Maine

JOHN L CAUGHEY

INTRODUCTION

IN THIS CHAPTER I will consider the role of the anthropologist, or other cultural studies scholar, who serves as an expert witness at a cultural defense trial. In presenting the general significance of culture to the matter at issue, this legal actor plays an important part in such trials. Using my own experience at a murder trial as an illustrative case, I will orient the chapter towards a variety of practical issues that confront those of us who are or may be asked to serve in this expert witness role. I will consider how anthropologists should respond to an invitation to serve and I will offer suggestions on how we should proceed if we agree to participate. I will suggest that a particular kind of comparative, person-centred ethnographic approach is fundamentally important to presenting cultural evidence ethically and effectively. I will also suggest that the issues that come up in a practical examination of this expert witness role are of importance to all of us who are concerned about the complexities of using cultural evidence in trials.

As an anthropologist with interests in South Asian cultures, I have done fieldwork in Pakistan and India and interviewed South Asian immigrants to the United States. Married to an Indian woman, I am also married into an Indian family. Given these connections, I have received several requests to serve as an expert witness in trials involving Indian immigrants to the United States. My involvement in the case I will describe here began in the summer of 1997 when a defense attorney phoned and asked me to serve as an expert witness at a murder trial in Maine. There was no doubt that Nadim Haque, an immigrant from Raniganj, India, had murdered his Anglo girlfriend/fiancée and that he would be imprisoned for somewhere between 20 and 50 years. The trial would have to do with whether this was 'murder' (premeditated first-degree murder) or 'manslaughter' (a spontaneous killing with provocation and/or in an extreme state of mind) and with other issues pertinent to the kind of prison sentence Haque should receive. In trying to persuade me to serve, the lawyer said that the murder was 'spontaneous' and 'completely out of character', that Haque was 'a nice guy', and that while he would and should be imprisoned for many years, he did not deserve the maximum ('life') sentence that the prosecution would seek to impose.[1] My presentation of cultural evidence, he said, might help keep Haque from 'being screwed by the all white jury'. He also suggested that the prosecuting attorney would try to pick apart any cultural evidence I presented and that this would be an interesting 'test of your acumen'. I was sceptical but I said I would consider participating if he sent me the file on the case. I had no desire to get involved in such a tragic situation and no relish for battling with a practised prosecuting attorney. But having reviewed the case material, I did feel that certain cultural issues might be pertinent to understanding what happened and I reluctantly agreed to participate.

Two days before I was scheduled to testify, I flew up to Maine, consulted with the defense attorneys, and interviewed Haque in the Auburn jail. He seemed so young, not a hardened criminal or sociopath. He reminded me of my nephews. He also still seemed in love with the woman he had killed. How could this terrible murder have happened? We discussed his background in India, and his experiences in the United States. The next day, in *voir dire* session, I testified before the judge but not the jury about the role that cultural adjustments and misunderstandings seemed to me to have played in the events that led up to the murder. In the end—as is often the case in US courts—the judge excluded this cultural testimony. He did this despite the fact that many of those involved with the trial who had heard my testimony recognized that culture was an important issue. Even the prosecuting attorney stated that, 'To some degree culture may explain what happened'.

PARTICIPATION IN CULTURAL DEFENSE TRIALS

Given that trials like this are difficult, adversarial, disturbing and depressing, and that our testimony may be challenged and excluded anyhow, why not reject invitations to serve in cultural defense trials? Why put yourself into the midst of something so difficult and messy, tragic and ugly, in the contentious circumstances of a trial? Here I think the answer is that as cultural studies scholars we have an obligation to sometimes climb down

---

[1] Unless otherwise noted, quotations in this chapter are from my interview and observational notes before and during the trial. A complete transcript of the trial, *State of Maine v Nadim Haque*, is available in the courthouse in Auburn, Maine.

from the ivory tower and get involved in the messy areas where what we are supposed to be experts about is tangled up in legal questions. If we know about cultural issues that may be important to very high stakes decisions about guilt and innocence, sentencing and imprisonment, we should seriously consider our responsibility to offer what we can by way of cultural understanding. Getting involved in trials may also help us (as it certainly did me) to learn more about the cultural matters we study and how they may play out in court. This kind of engagement may also raise our awareness about an important international debate on the relevance of culture to legal decisions and the ethical, philosophical and social justice issues that permeate this debate.

In considering invitations to trials, another issue is one's philosophical and ethical stance to the cultural defense itself. From a cultural perspective, all trials involve culture. A trial is a cultural ritual, crime a cultural construct, and the court a cultural apparatus that represents and enforces the dominant culture's values and perspectives. But this is precisely why cultural evidence may often be important. In the United States, your typical white middle class judge and jury are unlikely to know much about the depth and pervasiveness of cultural conditioning. As cultural studies scholars we understand that everything we think, feel and do is influenced by culture, but this is often not well understood outside our fields. Also, the average judge and jury, entangled in their own often ethnocentric, middle class US assumptions and beliefs, are unlikely to have much knowledge about the beliefs and practices of cultures outside the US mainstream. When the individual under trial is an immigrant from another society or a member of a minority group in the United States, and where an understanding of this unfamiliar cultural influence is important to determining what happened, cultural evidence should be admitted and considered. As Alison Renteln argues, the weight of international law, which supports the 'right to culture', our ideals of respecting cultural diversity and freedom in a pluralistic society, and the considerable evidence that members of minority communities have often been systematically mistreated by the US legal system, all provide a strong rationale for the need to bring cultural evidence into certain trials.[2]

However, some cultural studies scholars argue against the cultural defense. They do so, first, on the grounds that the term masks naive notions of cultural determinism, the culture-made-me-do-it excuse. The answer here is what we need to bring to trials is our most sophisticated professional understanding about how culture influences human thought and behaviour. Critics also suggest that when cultural evidence has been admitted it has too often been wrongly used as an excuse, particularly to

[2] A Renteln, *The Cultural Defense* (New York, Oxford University Press, 2004).

rationalize violence against women or children.[3] It is true that this has more than sometimes been the case (as is evident in some of the cases discussed in this volume). While this is highly reprehensible, it seems to me that it constitutes a serious misuse of cultural evidence, not a reason to exclude cultural evidence. Other cases indicate that cultural evidence can be used appropriately in instances where, were this defense not available, severe forms of injustice would likely have been imposed by US courts.[4] Furthermore, if we are concerned about using cultural understandings accurately in a way that promotes rather than blocks social justice, we have an obligation to get involved in order to try and make this happen. We who study cultural systems and their influences on behaviour are precisely the people who are most likely to ensure that cultural evidence is not abused.

TACTICS IN CULTURAL DEFENSE TRIALS

So if we agree to serve in a cultural defense case, and social justice issues are a prime concern, how should we proceed? One question here involves our role in relationship to the defense (for it is typically the defense that will ask us to serve) including the need to combine our own independent cultural assessments and some degree of neutrality with what the defense will want of us. This is difficult as we move from scholarly traditions of cultural inquiry into the very different cultural worlds of US courts. We will be interested in using cultural evidence to understand what happened with the desire that justice will be done in the court case. This is not the orientation of the defense attorney who is asking us to serve. US trials are highly adversarial. You are being called by the defense because they want to make every effort that they can to minimize guilt and culpability in relation to the legal definitions being applied. US trials are interpretive battle zones. The prosecution wants to spin every piece of evidence as hard as they can to maximize guilt and culpability, while the defense does the opposite.[5]

Given this, several tactics need to be kept in mind. First, we need to do some preliminary research on the case before accepting an expert witness role. In some instances we may conclude that cultural issues are not relevant

---

[3] T Goldstein, 'Cultural Conflicts in Court: Should the American Criminal Justice System Formally Recognize A "Cultural Defense"?' (1994) 99 *Dickinson Law Review* 162.

[4] A Renteln, 'The Use and Abuse of the Cultural Defense' (2005) 20 *Canadian Journal of Law and Society* 47.

[5] L Korobkin, 'Narrative Battles in the Courtroom' in M Garber, P Franklin and R Walkowitz (eds), *Field Work* (New York, Routledge, 1996); cf L Rosen, 'The Anthropologist as Expert Witness' (2005) 79 *American Anthropologist* 569.

to the crime under examination. I have rejected several invitations when I learned enough about the situations to see that, in my view, there was absolutely no legitimate basis for bringing cultural evidence into the trial. We need to be careful here, however, for defense attorneys, who are unlikely to know much about culture in general and about the particular cultural orientations of immigrant or minority individuals in particular, may not initially see how cultural evidence may be pertinent.

If we are convinced that cultural factors may be relevant to *understanding* what happened in a given case, we still need to research this as thoroughly as possible and to prepare strategic ways to present the evidence. This includes the complex problem of working out the extent to which we and the defense attorneys believe that cultural understanding may provide legally mitigating evidence in this trial. An issue that is tangled up here involves the very term 'cultural *defense*'. If we take the term in its literal form it sounds like we mean that cultural evidence will automatically constitute a defense, that the introduction of cultural evidence will make the defendant either not guilty or less guilty than would otherwise be the case. Unfortunately, this is a fairly common assumption. For example, throughout his important 1996 article on the cultural defense, Michael Winkelman continually seems to assume that cultural evidence will always and invariably constitute an excuse, that is, a mitigating or exculpating influence on assessments of a defendant's behaviour.[6] I believe the situation is much more complex. Just because cultural influences may have been at play in whatever happened in a given case, this does not necessarily mean that the person is not guilty or less culpable in terms of the standards of the local court or in terms of whatever additional legal and ethical frames of reference we may bring to bear on matters at issue in the trial.

A key issue here is the extent to which the legal system of the local court provides openings (including precedents) for the use of cultural evidence in the matter under trial. If it does not but if culture seems not only relevant but to provide a potentially significant mitigating influence, it may be useful to consult with the defense attorney about whether international law, the procedures used in other courts (such as those of another nation, including the law of the society from which an immigrant hails), or the customary law of the pertinent community/minority culture are perhaps more oriented to and practised in bringing cultural evidence to bear on the particular issue at hand. Such an approach may help in the case under consideration and may also be useful in the setting of precedents for future culture defense trials.

---

[6] M Winkelman, 'Cultural Factors in Criminal Defense Proceedings' (1996) 55 *Human Organization* 154.

CULTURAL EVIDENCE

If we believe that cultural issues are not only relevant but potentially excul-pating or mitigating factors, we will still need to work with the defense in considering how best to present cultural evidence in a way that will be heard by the judge and jury. There is some debate here about who is best qualified to serve as an expert witness on culture, an anthropologist who has studied the culture under consideration or a knowledgeable person—perhaps a respected elder—from within the community. My sense is that it may be best to use both. A knowledgeable elder, or some equivalent, may be an extremely convincing person to certify the validity of customs or to speak to the experiences of immigrants. However, knowing a culture is not the same as being a scholarly expert on its particular characteristics. We may speak a language fluently without being a convincing expert on its linguistic structure. Anthropologists can offer perspectives and information that usefully supplement what a knowledgeable insider can provide. Not only do we study culture, we are used to teaching about the importance of its influence on human thought, feelings and behaviour. This is useful since an important part of what is likely to be needed is to persuade a judge and jury that culture is a significant influence on the issues of the trial. Also, as experts on a particular culture or kind of culture experience, we are used to articulating this knowledge and backing it up with scholarly references. As persons with PhDs we have a certain kind of caché in this society as 'experts' that provides authority for presenting cultural evidence effectively.

Such concerns point to another significant issue we need to attend to should we agree to serve as an expert witness. There is often another problem in the use of 'cultural' in the terms '*cultural* defense' or *cultural* evidence. What kinds of cultural information and evidence should we as scholar/expert witnesses bring into cultural defense trials?

In some cases, such as those involving issues like attire, treatment of animals, burial customs, and the like, what may be at issue is a cultural practice or custom. Here, it may sometimes be sufficient to establish the existence and force of a widespread cultural custom. However, even in these matters and certainly in a majority of criminal cases, what is on trial is not a cultural custom but a particular individual. So we do not just need to know about the culture of the community, we need to know about the particular defendant in the criminal case and his or her relationship to the culture. Here, it is not usually appropriate for us simply to state that the person is a member of a culturally organized society or community and to assume that this person's beliefs, assumptions and state of mind are unproblematically representative of 'the culture' of this community.[7]

---

[7] Goldstein, above n 3 at 166.

In both the literature and in presentations in court cases, there is often insufficient attention to the particular cultural location of the particular defendant under consideration. Again, Winkelman's article is, unfortunately, representative of this trend. In his discussion he presents essentialised formulations of the beliefs and customs of minority cultures and then appears to assume that the individual members whose cases he is concerned with are unproblematic, representative persons whose beliefs and behaviour will be automatically and fully governed by a single unitary culture. He speaks, for example, of how a defendant's beliefs and values reflect that fact that he or she is an individual of 'Mexican culture', 'Hispanic culture' or 'Latin American culture'.[8] This is a big problem. While there may be a few general orientations that characterize many (but far from all) men or women with Mexican culture, just as there may be some such orientations for many men and women of US mainstream culture, it is easy to see that this is not necessarily the case for any particular individual from the United States or Mexico, let alone everyone from Latin America. An over-simplified approach to the individual and culture ignores and obscures the enormous cultural variation and complexity that characterizes even small communities, let alone nation-states and culture areas. Fortunately, there are other approaches, including a body of work in life history, cultural biography and person-centred ethnography that provides a more sophisticated and relevant approach to the ways culture influences individual behaviour.[9]

First of all, it is important to *locate* an individual within his or her cultural background. People occupy very different positions within any society or community, in terms of gender, age, status, class, caste, race, social position, religious affiliation, etc. Individuals in particular social positions may be quite differently influenced and constrained by that community's culture. For example, even within mainstream US society, an individual's understandings and actions are influenced by a variety of distinctive cultural traditions relating to class, occupation, ethnicity and religion.[10] Similarly, Nadim Haque is not some typical representative of Indian culture: he is a young man of a particular region, city and caste, a person with a particular kind of relationship to Islam, the eldest son of a particular kind of Indian family. Secondly, it is important to understand how and to what extent the person is influenced by several cultural traditions. As implied

---

[8] Winkelman, above n 6 at 157–8.

[9] On life history and person-centred ethnography, see J Caughey, *Negotiating Cultures and Identities: Life History Issues, Methods, and Readings* (Lincoln, University of Nebraska, 2006); A Cole and J Knowles, *Lives in Context: the Art of Life History Research* (Walnut Creek, Altamira, 2001); R Levy and D Hollan, 'Person Centered Interviewing and Observation' in H Bernard (ed), *Handbook of Method in Cultural Anthropology* (Walnut Creek, Altamira, 1998).

[10] L Weber, *Understanding Race, Class, Gender, and Sexuality* (New York, McGraw Hill, 2001).

above, the individual in any society is typically influenced by particular traditions within his or her home community and sometimes by traditions from outside his home community. That is, individuals are sometimes partially or quite completely bicultural or multicultural. This is true of many individuals in our globalizing society and it is especially likely to be true of immigrants to the United States or persons from minority communities within the United States—the very people who are likely to be under consideration in cultural defense cases. Such people typically are engaged with and influenced by some mainstream US traditions, as well as those of their home community. Haque had spent more than three years in the United States prior to the murder. He was not isolated in an immigrant enclave, he had become familiar with some traditions of US mainstream culture, he was a college student, and he had some white American friends. He had also become intensely and intimately involved with a girlfriend/fiancée, Lori Taylor, who was not another Indian immigrant, but a member of US mainstream society. He had entered into an intense form of US male-female relationship. Here, as in other such cases, we may need to explore how the social interactions leading up to a crime involve the relationships of persons operating with very different cultural understandings.

We cannot get very far in understanding the way culture influences an individual without exploring this kind of information: we need to know their specific location within their home community, their degree of multiculturalism, and the particular relationship they have with the particular cultural traditions that are most pertinent to the state of mind and behaviour under consideration in a trial. No doubt such matters are complex, no doubt experts, whether anthropologists or members of a cultural community, may disagree on particular cultural influences. But we live in a multicultural world and if we are seriously concerned about understanding individual conduct and states of mind, cultural evidence is often crucial. And while some aspects of cultural influence are not only complex but ambiguous, others are very clear and quite amenable to ethnographic understanding. In order to present such influences in court we need to bring the most sophisticated understanding we can to exploring how cultural issues have affected the individual whose behaviour we are considering.

One implication of this is that we should insist that our willingness to participate in a trial is contingent on being given several opportunities to interview the defendant before our appearance in court, so that we can seek to locate this individual within his or her repertoire of cultural influences and formulate our best understanding of how and to what extent cultural factors may have influenced the state of mind and behaviour of the defendant.

Another implication is that it will usually be useful to meet with the defense team to discuss strategy and to consider how best to present our cultural evidence in relation to that of other expert witnesses, including members of the defendant's community and psychiatrists. While I had a decent opportunity to discuss some of these matters with the defense attorney, I think we could have done a better job if my testimony had been better coordinated with that of the psychiatrist who served as expert witness and who also presented cultural evidence, along with his sense of Hague's psychological state. Given our different orientations, we may be able to help the psychiatrist coordinate what he or she knows with cultural information and the psychiatrist may help us with what he or she will say about how cultural matters are intertwined with the particular individual's personal psychology, emotional reactions, state of mind, etc.

ANTHROPOLGICAL TESTIMONY

Anthropological testimony is likely to consist of two parts. In the first, the defense attorney calls us to the stand and, with his or her lead questions, which can be discussed and worked out in advance, we offer our testimony on cultural evidence. After questions useful in establishing our credentials (academic degrees and appointments, fieldwork, publications, etc), at least two different levels of presentation may be useful. First, we may need to do some explication on the nature of culture and its pertinence to issues under consideration, something that may not be well understood by judges, lawyers and jury members. Then we need to address the ways culture influences the particular defendant's thoughts, emotions and actions.

In the *Haque* case, the question was the manner and extent to which cultural evidence might help us understand how a loving romantic relationship between these 'two gentle people' ended up in a brutal murder. Clearly, the simplest idea of the cultural defense did not apply. It is as completely unacceptable in the Indian culture Haque came from, as it is in our society, to kill one's fiancée, no matter what the provocation or circumstances. However, from my research on the case, including my interview with Nadim, I did come to believe that cultural adjustment played a significant part in the state of mind that led to this seemingly inexplicable murder.

The defense attorney asked me a series of questions that allowed me to describe research on cultural adjustment, including the large body of evidence that shows that individual migrants often experience extreme cognitive and emotional strain in adjusting to an unfamiliar culture, including frustration, confusion, anxiety, disorientation, depression, loss and anger. I noted, for example, that research on peace corps volunteers suggests that 40 per cent of people who are trained for a sojourn in an unfamiliar culture are unable to adjust.[11] I also sought to make a connection with 'state of

---

[11] P Pederson, *The Five Stages of Culture Shock: Critical Incidents Around the World* (Westport, Greenwood Press, 1995).

mind' by noting that psychiatry recognizes 'culture shock' to be a form of temporary mental disturbance. Drawing on the research literature, I said that the likelihood of severe culture adjustment problems depends on a variety of factors. These, I suggested, include the extent to which the dominant culture of the home and host cultures are similar or different, the extent to which guidance and support is available from those who have made the transition, the degree to which the person feels he is doing well in the new society, the extent of religious support, and the stability or instability of the immigrant's relations with persons in the new society. I suggested that all of these put Nadim in a vulnerable position. The culture of his home community is vastly different from what he was trying to adjust to in Maine; he had little family and Indian community support in making the transition; he was not doing well in college; he had little religious support (there was no mosque in the area); and, as it turned out, he became involved in a secret but very intense and very unstable emotional relationship with Lori Taylor, his Anglo girlfriend/fiancée. It is the cultural nature of this relationship that helps us see how this murder could have occurred.

Growing up in US culture, Lori was familiar with and practised in US dating and courtship rituals. In this system one meets someone, one dates them, and one thinks, 'might this be the one to marry?' And then, if the magic goes, you break up, feel temporarily down, and then move on and start dating someone else. Is this a *cultural* practice? Absolutely. In moving from one relationship to another, Americans are following a basic middle class US cultural courtship script—a script that is completely absent in many other societies, including the one Haque is from.

Now consider Nadim Haque. He saw himself as only temporarily here in this strange US world. As the oldest son in a close Indian family, he knew he had strong family obligations, he fully expected to return to India to meet them. There, he would enter the family business (managing a Hindi movie theatre), support his parents and sisters, and eventually have a marriage arranged for him by his older relatives. Once this marriage is set, he fully expected it to last a lifetime, there would be no other relationships. In his world there was no dating. Young men and women were kept separate. Marriages are not the product of dating and individual choice. While there may be a very occasional 'love marriage' (and while Hindi movies glorify romance), almost all marriages are arranged by family elders. At age 26, Haque had never dated, never had a girlfriend, never had an affair, never participated in anything like what he was about to get caught up in.

Nadim and Lori met at school. One day, she gave him a ride home. They became friends, they were attracted to each other, they fell in love, and they became lovers. It must have been a very intense affair. Lori was very taken with Nadim. He was completely smitten by Lori. He had never been in love, never had an affair—and now this overwhelming emotional and sexual experience. Caught up in the emotional intensity of this affair and under the influence of Indian and US cultural myth-dreams of love, they both thought, 'This is it. We should get married'. For a time, they both imagined that this is what they would do. But they kept their plans secret, afraid to even mention the relationship to their respective families because they knew they would strongly disapprove. Committed to this intense relationship, Nadim was willing to go against his family and to give up his entire background.

Then, Lori began to get second thoughts as she contemplated what it would be like to be married to Nadim in India or the United States. Nadim worried about all this from his point of view—giving up his heritage, violating his family's expectations—but he had made the commitment. And then Lori started to pull away, she became more distant. Nadim felt the anguish of doubt, 'What is going on?' This has been the best thing in his life. Trying to save the relationship, he bought Lori an American engagement ring. She accepted the ring and the relationship was back on. But, soon, again, she seemed less than fully committed. And then she started talking about their being 'so different'. What did she mean by that? And then she started talking about how they should stop seeing each other for a while.

There is something Lori knows about of which Nadim has no knowledge or experience. The kind of courtship rituals Americans practice—moving from one relationship to another before settling on a particular spouse, involves a peculiar kind of cultural learning. We learn, of course, how-to-do-it dating and relationship scripts, what to say and do and how to express our emotions. But we also learn something else that is peculiarly important to this practice. We learn how to break up. True, it is almost always difficult, especially the first time. But starting as teenagers, Americans usually go through this dating, breaking up, starting again with someone else routine again and again. We learn how to manage a break-up and the primitive emotions it evokes. We learn that it only temporarily *seems* to be the end of the world. That soon enough someone else will seem appealing. We get help from our friends, they support us—they help us see that the person from whom we are now separating has multiple flaws. They remind us of other possibilities, they tell us what it was like for them—how they got through it and found someone better, etc. Lori knows this. Nadim has not a clue. And he has no friends to offer help of this kind. It feels like this is the end of the word.

There was some concern at the trial that Lori was particularly unkind to Nadim in a way that involved some provocation, even by the rather harsh practices of US dating break-ups. How could she take his engagement ring and start seeing someone else? Actually it looks like she was having trouble letting go, in part because she cared about him and in part out of concern about his situation in the United States. She knew how much he had come to depend on her emotionally, that he had so few resources and supports here, that without her he was lost. She had found someone new, but she was afraid for Nadim. He seemed in such bad shape, he wasn't eating, he wasn't sleeping.

As a person of colour in white America, as an Indian who grew up in the aftermath of British colonial racism, Nadim wondered what Lori meant when she said their relationship must end because they were 'too different'. While Lori did not mean it this way, these words struck Nadim as an extremely hurtful, frustrating, ethnocentric, and possibly racist expression of rejection. Nadim was in despair. As he said to one of his American college professors, 'My whole world has come to an end'. He stopped eating, stopped sleeping, brooded constantly, and eventually decided that he had to resolve the situation. He wanted to kill himself, he wanted to kill Lori, he thought of killing himself in front of her. He bought a knife, he went to see Lori one last time. They talked, they fought, 'We are just too different!' Lori told him. And then he killed her with the knife.

In killing Lori, Nadim killed his beloved. He destroyed her young life and devastated her family and friends. At the same time he also ruined his own life and devastated his own family—a truly awful, disastrous action. Cultural factors certainly do not excuse this violent crime. However, they are relevant to making some sense of how it could have happened in a situation that is otherwise very difficult to understand. Cultural evidence like this, the defense wanted to argue, was important to understanding how this tragic killing happened.

The prosecution disagreed and they worked to exclude cultural evidence. In this case, as in other trials, in the second part of expert witness testimony, the prosecuting attorney is given an opportunity to cross-examine an expert witness. Typically, the prosecuting attorney will seek to discredit cultural testimony by questioning our credentials, attacking our procedures, and disputing the relevance of culture to the case. In the *Haque* case, the prosecuting attorney used all these techniques. For example, she asked me questions the answer to which she already knew ('You are not a psychologist, sir?' 'You are are not a psychiatrist?') in order to suggest that not having the expertise of these more accepted expert witness positions weakened or negated my qualifications to testify. In order to counter such tactics, it may be useful to try and establish in part one of the testimony what qualifications anthropologists believe are necessary to understand a particular culture or type of immigrant experience such as advanced training in anthropology, extensive experience with people of a given community, membership in the community, knowing the pertinent languages, etc. Such characteristics can then be used to suggest that psychologists and psychiatrists may lack such credentials. It may also be useful to counter an aggressive attorney's attack by asking, for example, if he or she speaks Hindi, has ever lived in India, or has ever made a transition into an unfamiliar society. This may help to reaffirm our own expertise and to undermine the attorney's qualifications to speak about or question the cultural matters at hand.

In the *Haque* case the judge (viewed as conservative by the defense) declined to admit the cultural evidence that I presented and it was completely excluded from the trial. While the judge and the attorneys did continue to refer to cultural issues, including Nadim's lack of familiarity with the highly emotional practices of US romantic relationships, they could not fully utilize my testimony and the jury never heard it.

I think this was a mistake. Haque was guilty of a terrible crime. But why did it happen? The judge himself spoke of the murder as unusual and difficult to understand, but by denying the admission of cultural evidence he excluded information that helps make sense of what happened, information that is, therefore, relevant to making informed decisions about whether this was murder or manslaughter. Should Haque, an individual with no record of violence or criminal conduct, have received the maximum life sentence, one that would be given to a murderer with a past history of violent criminal conduct and no mitigating factors, or should he have received a somewhat lesser sentence? This is a difficult decision and one the jury needed to determine. But without cultural evidence that even the prosecuting attorney believed helped to explain what happened, the jury was denied access to a significant aspect of the case. In the end, the judge and jury concluded that Haque was guilty of murder and he was sentenced to the maximum prison term. The defense appealed, partly on the grounds that cultural evidence was not admitted. The appeal was denied. Haque will be imprisoned for 50 years and deported to India on his release in 2047.

CONCLUSION

Depending on the situation, our testimony as an expert witness may not end our involvement in a cultural defense case. In his concluding statement, the defense attorney predicted that the *Haque* case would continue to affect those of us who were involved long after the trial was over. It certainly did me. Even after the appeal was denied, the case continued to disturb me and I spent a good deal of time reviewing the case material and trying to understand it further. Some of what I have presented in this chapter involves understandings I only came to long after the trial. My involvement in the case also led me to continue my research on immigration and culture in ways that are different from how this would have otherwise developed. Finally, the trial brought me into relationship with the ongoing international debate about the cultural defense. This I have come to feel is an extremely important issue which anthropologists should be more aware of and more engaged with than we currently are.

In conclusion, I think cultural evidence is often, though not always, needed to illuminate what happened in US cases involving immigrants or people of minority communities. As with the *Haque* case, such cultural evidence may be essential to understanding what happened and hence to a fair trial. We anthropologists, I believe, have an obligation to participate in cases where culture is relevant and we have an important role to play in seeking to persuade courts about the reality and power of culture to influence thoughts, perceptions, state of mind and behaviour. However, while cultural evidence may be important to understanding what happened, it does not necessarily constitute a defense, in the sense of mitigating or exculpating evidence. This is something to be determined by research and consultation with legal experts and ultimately must be decided by the judge and jury. In order to provide useful cultural evidence, we as cultural studies scholars need to reject simplistic formulations that falsely portray individuals as unproblematic perfect representatives of uniform single unitary cultures and to draw instead on approaches such as those in life history and person-centred ethnography that help us explore the complex ways in which multiple cultural influences and specific situations affect a particular individual's state of mind and behaviour. This will help the judge and jury decide if and to what extent cultural factors constitute mitigating evidence in this particular case. Finally, engagement in cultural defense trials is important because it brings anthropologists into direct connection with the ongoing international debate that lies behind such trials, that is, the debate about the nature and extent to which cultural evidence is pertinent to legal, social justice issues. Without our engagement in this debate, key aspects of the complex ways in which culture influences human thought, emotion and behaviour are likely to be overlooked, misunderstood or neglected.

Conclusion

ALISON DUNDES RENTELN AND MARIE-CLAIRE FOBLETS

A LTHOUGH COURTS HAVE entertained arguments based on cultural
factors for centuries, this practice has largely escaped the notice of
scholars and policy-makers. Gradually, the phenomenon of culture
conflict in legal proceedings has attracted attention. To date, much of
what has been published on the subject of the cultural defense has been
geographically limited to North America. This book adds to the existing
scholarship with analytic essays that document the role of cultural defenses
in legal systems in Western Europe, Australia, South Africa, as well as the
United States and Canada. As the question of justice is a matter of concern
for academics in all fields, we are fortunate to have contributions from
scholars in various disciplines such as anthropology, jurisprudence, political
science and law. We feel it is a virtue of this collection that it is both cross-
national and interdisciplinary.

In contrast to other studies of the cultural defense, the scope of this
project extends beyond criminal law. Although many cultural conflicts
fall within the domain of the criminal law, others are adjudicated through
asylum law, child welfare law, constitutional law, employment law, family
law, private international law and zoning law. The reason for this is that
although norm transgressions have been divided somewhat arbitrarily into
separate fields of law, culture conflicts do not neatly fit these categories.
Furthermore, sometimes the same case will involve a criminal matter, eg,
child abuse, and also a civil law matter, ie, whether to remove a child from
the home and place the child in protective custody. This collection demonstrates the importance of recognising that legal responses to culture conflict
involve many fields of law.

Many of the essays reflect a concern about the potential misuse of the cultural defense. There is a perception that courts are ill-equipped to interpret
cultural claims and that they sometimes rely too heavily on the testimony
of expert witnesses. In legal systems where experts receive a fee for their
testimony, there is a risk that they may be tempted to misrepresent aspects
of a tradition for financial gain. Chen, for instance, makes this observation
in her treatment of 'saving face' cases. It is unclear whether preventing this
sort of abuse requires the involvement of multiple experts in a particular
case so they can provide a sort of check on the veracity of one another's testimony, the official participation of a single court-appointed expert who will

at least in theory be objective in presenting cultural evidence, or the establishment of a certification system managed by professional associations. To address this concern, some have called for the creation of a code of ethics for experts, seeing this as particularly necessary in cultural defense cases. While it is not obvious at this time which policy should be adopted, the role of experts in multicultural jurisprudence merits further consideration.

Another worry expressed in the collection is that the cultural defense will inevitably reinforce stereotypes about groups. This is the oft-mentioned fear that lawyers will resort to 'essentialising' or 'racialising' the identities of litigants for strategic purposes. Indeed, many of the contributors are obviously ill at ease when it comes to the formal presentation of group characteristics in the context of court cases. Deckha's chapter, for instance, highlights this particular risk, even though she ultimately embraces the cultural defense. A related fear is that media coverage of legal proceedings will give members of the public the mistaken impression that anyone who belongs to the ethnic minority group in question possesses the pertinent trait or follows the tradition relevant in the given case. While this over-simplification is false and even ridiculous, there is a danger that the way in which journalists cover cultural defense cases may unfortunately shape public perceptions of minority groups. The media should be circumspect about how they describe the facts in a given case, so it is clear that only one specific individual was influenced by a cultural imperative in a particular context.

At the heart of the matter is a concern that the cultural defense is predicated on the notion that cultural factors *determine* the behaviour of legal actors. In fact, the cultural defense is based on the idea that culture *predisposes* individuals to act in ways that conform to their cultural upbringing. This does not mean that individuals who move from one society to another have been programmed like robots to act in particular ways. They may, in fact, consciously reject traditions. But enculturation does influence both perception and behaviour. So, the premise of the cultural defense is that individuals have learned a way of life that depends on a particular worldview. Moreover, enculturation has long-term effects, so that individuals who are accustomed to reacting to particular insults are likely to continue to be offended by them, even years after they migrate across borders. Individuals who cross borders will often adhere to traditional techniques of socialising children, believe in the necessity of preparing meat for consumption in accordance with religious tenets, and subscribe to notions of honour concerning the behaviour of young girls. While some prefer to focus on whether these cultural practices are desirable, the point of the cultural defense is to highlight the reality that individuals have had it instilled in them that these are proper ways to behave. Consequently, as we have seen, it is unrealistic to expect individuals to shed aspects of their cultural identities in a short period of time, particularly in the absence of any formal state intervention of a serious nature.

The question of whether litigants should have the right to present evidence regarding their cultural background is separate from the question of whether courts should ever mitigate criminal sentences in cultural defense cases. From the cases presented, it is clear that courts (whose judges are not from the litigants' backgrounds) are often incapable of understanding what motivated the behaviour of defendants without the benefit of cultural evidence. Emphasising the need for the contextual analysis of legal questions is wholly consistent with a major tenet of the law and society movement. For example, the meaning of the provocation defense and the meaning of the best interests of the child standard must be interpreted in their cultural context. According to the law and society approach, one cannot accurately comprehend the meaning of acts without considering them in light of the pertinent cultural considerations.

Having understood what transpired in a case involving an unfamiliar cultural tradition, a judge may nevertheless decide to impose full punishment, without any mitigation whatsoever. Moreover, as Siesling and Ten Voorde noted, a judge may also, in light of the cultural factors, decide to impose a *harsher* penalty than would ordinarily be given. The cultural defense, to the extent it is allowed, ensures the consideration of cultural factors. It does not necessarily affect the ultimate disposition, and, if it does affect it, may not necessary result in a reduction in punishment. As a number of contributors to this volume have concluded, the decision as to the proper outcome can only be made on a case-by-case basis.

The underlying philosophical issue is what equal protection of the law means in a case involving a cultural defense. Does the idea of equal protection require identical treatment; or rather does it mean that a person must be treated differently in order to be treated equally? In cases in which all involved are from the dominant culture, contextual information is less likely to be needed for the court to render a just decision. However, in cases in which individuals come from other cultural or religious backgrounds, judges will lack the requisite information and means by which to interpret the significance of conduct if there is no attempt to explain the cultural context in which defendants or parties acted. Consequently, the premise of the cultural defense is that equal protection of the law should be construed as requiring the presentation of evidence regarding an individual's cultural background or the meaning of the tradition in question.

The related issue is that being treated equally within a culturally hegemonic judicial system is problematic. As contributors suggest, the notion of what constitutes 'reasonable' behaviour varies from one society to the next; hence, if we consider, for example, the 'reasonable person' standard, it is misleading to pretend that there is an objective standard against which the conduct of the cultural defendant is judged. The 'objective' reasonable person is the persona of the majority culture. Consequently, if we acknowledge that the rules of the national legal system reflect the values of the dominant culture, then being treated 'equally' in a legal system built on culturally biased standards is almost meaningless.

In some of the cases considered in this volume there was disagreement within the group as to the validity of the custom. There is no question that courts face difficult challenges when there is a trend within the cultural community toward rejecting a custom. It is by no means clear how much of a consensus must exist for it to be proper for the court to consider the tradition an authentic part of the group's way of life. (Presumably there need not be 100 per cent agreement.) There are also questions about who should be able to invoke the cultural defense; some are inclined to say only first-generation immigrants.

While the contributors to this book make no claim to have solved all of the problems associated with the use of the cultural defense, they have made clear that legal systems must come to grips with this important challenge. The extent to which countries are prepared to allow cultural defenses may depend on societal trends underway. For example, the extent to which citizens enthusiastically welcome immigrants is likely to correlate with greater acceptance of the defense. Some like Claes and Vrielink suggest that the legitimacy of the defense may hinge on societal dynamics. Additional comparative empirical data on the degree to which legislatures and courts accept the cultural defense will enable us eventually to assess the accuracy of this claim. We trust this volume is a step in this direction.

We have seen that there are dangers associated with the use of a new type of defense. That is unfortunately inevitable. But it is our view that the potential for abuse is not a basis for rejecting a defense that can yield greater understanding in courts if used with care. Jurists certainly must be vigilant to prevent the possible misuse of the defense, just as they must with other defenses like the insanity defense. But we should not throw the baby out with the bathwater.

Although the cultural defense was for a long time a topic beneath the radar screen, it has captured the attention of jurists in the twenty-first century. This book demonstrates the importance of having scholars across the globe analyse the role that cultural defenses play in their own legal systems. It is our hope that this collection will encourage even more academics, judges and policy-makers in other parts of the world to investigate how cultural defenses are used in their jurisdictions. Through the comparative analysis of polices, we may eventually come to understand how best to approach the challenges posed by cultural defenses in court. Multicultural justice requires no less.

Scientific Bibliography

FINDING REFERENCES ON THE CULTURAL DEFENSE

As standard legal references do not contain the cultural defense among their key words, it can be challenging to identify relevant scholarship. The most productive strategy is to do computer searches combining 'culture' or 'cultural' or 'ethnic' within several words of 'crime', 'criminal', 'offense', 'sentence' or 'mitigate'. Truncating words like 'mitigat!' is advisable so the researcher finds sources with all forms of the word in the title or abstract. Another tactic is to look for sources on particular groups known to have traditions that clash with the law. This might include Gypsies/Roma, the Hmong, Jews, Muslims, Rastafarians, Sikhs. As particular issues such as drugs often generate culture conflict, looking for references on specific controversial substances may yield results. Scholarship that examines the tensions between folk law and state law, legal pluralism, and religious freedom may be relevant for the analysis of cultural defenses.

Some indexes are extraordinarily helpful. In particular, scholars will benefit from the *Index to Foreign Legal Periodicals*, compiled at Boalt Hall, School of Law, University of California, Berkeley. Anthropological tools such as *Anthropology Plus* and the *UNESCO International Bibliography of Social and Cultural Anthropology* are also quite useful as they contain subject references.

Although one might expect to find cultural defense material in political theory scholarship that focuses on multiculturalism, the vast majority of this work does not contain the sort of empirical data sought by serious social scientists. Publications in the field of constitutional law that analyze religious liberty usually offer well-known national judicial decisions. Because of the emphasis on case that higher courts hand down, there is a tendency to ignore interesting lower court decisions. As social scientists would be eager to analyze cases at a whatever level, it is a pity to overlook some of the cases.

Another difficulty is that some of the most fascinating cultural defence cases are unpublished. This means it is unlikely one can find them in published case reports. Because individuals at Lexis or Westlaw, or other legal databases services, may opt to include them in the databases, despite their lack of precedential value, researchers may come across wonderful examples there.

For some, there is greater interest in the individuals who play a crucial role in the cases. Social scientists often participate in legal proceedings as expert witnesses. Researchers interested in the presentation of cultural evidence will want to hunt for scholarship in applied anthropology, sociology and other journals in the social sciences. As some of the best cases are unpublished, talking to legal actors may help researchers locate fascinating cases. Police, attorneys, court interpreters, judges and expert witnesses often know about significant cases that are beneath the radar screen.

Those hunting for examples of culture conflict would also do well to read newspapers, including both popular and legal press. Legal databases contain many newspapers and a well-designed search should enable researchers to find many relevant cases. Contacting journalists is worthwhile, too, as they often have additional background information on important lawsuits.

Abu-Lughod, L, 'Do Muslim Women Really Need Saving? Anthropological Reflections on Cultural Relativism and its Others' (2002) 104 *American Anthropologist* 783

Abu-Odeh, L, 'Comparatively Speaking: the "Honour" of the "East" and the "Passion" of the "West"' (1997) *Utah Law Review* 287

Acton, TA, 'A Three Cornered Choice: Structural Consequences of Value-Priorities in Gypsy Law as a Model for a More General Understanding of Variations in the Administration of Justice' (2003) 3 *American Journal of Comparative Law* 639

Adams, CJ and Donovan, J (eds), *Animals and Women: Feminist Theoretical Explorations* (Durham, Duke University Press, 1995)

Adviescommissie Vreemdelingenzaken, *Tot het huwelijk gedwongen. Een advies over preventieve, correctieve en repressieve maatregelen ter voorkoming van huwelijksdwang* (Den Haag, 2005)

Agence France Presse, 'Neun Jahre Haft für Ehrenmord in Esslingen. Gericht Bleibt Knapp Unter Höchststrafe', 11 April 2005, www.123recht.net/article. asp?a=12657&p=1

Agyekum, K, 'The Socio-Cultural Concept of Face in Akan Communication' (2004) 12 Pragmatics and Cognition 71

Alexander, LA, 'Justification and Innocent Aggressors' (1987) 33 *Wayne Law Review* 1177

Amirthalingam, K, 'Negotiating Law, Culture and Justice', *The Drawing Board*, 2 July 2004, www.econ.usyd.edu.au/drawingboard/digest/0407/amirthalingam. html

——'Women's Rights, International Norms and Domestic Violence: Asian Perspectives' (2005) 27 *Human Rights Quarterly* 683

Amnesty International, *Pakistan, Violence Against Women in the Name of Honour*, AI Index: ASA 33/17/99 (1999)

——*Pakistan, Insufficient Protection of Women*, AI Index ASA 33/006/2002, (2002)

Anardottir, OM, *Equality and Non-Discrimination under the European Convention on Human Rights* (Den Haag, Martinus Nijhoff, 2003)

Andrews, L and Nelkin, D, 'Homo Economicus: Commercialization of Body Tissue in the Age of Biotechnology' (1998) 5 *Hastings Center Report* 30

Anon, 'Sexual Mutilation Horror, or Hoax?', *Channel 2 CBS Los Angeles*, Associated Press, 23 January 2003

——'Federal Court Convicts Phony African "Princess" of Falsehoods' (2003) 9 *International Law Update* 1, available on Lexis/Nexis

——*Hidden Slaves: Forced Labor in the United States* (Berkeley, Human Rights Center, 2004)

Anzaldua, G, *Making Face, Making Soul/Haciendo Caras: Creative and Critical Perspectives by Feminists of Color* (San Francisco, Aunt Lute Foundation Books, 1990)

Appadurai, A, 'Putting Hierarchy in its Place' (1988) 3 *Cultural Anthropology* 1

Apsler, R, 'Effects of Embarrassment on Behavior Toward Others' (1975) 32 *Journal of Personality and Social Psychology* 145

Ardèvol, E, 'Vigencias y cambio en la cultura de los Gitanos' in T San Román (ed), *Entre la marginación y el racismo. Reflexiones sobre la vida de los Gitanos* (Madrid, Alianza, 1986)

Armstrong, J, 'Death of a Secret Lover', *Globe and Mail*, 3 March 2005

Arnold, KC, 'Are the Perpetrators of Honour Killings Getting Away with Murder? Article 340 of the Jordanian Penal Code Analyzed under the Convention on the Elimination of All Forms of Discrimination Against Women' (2001) 16 *American University International Law Review* 1343

Asamoah-Wade, Y, 'International Column: Women's Human Rights and "Honour Killings" in Islamic Countries' (1999/2000) 8 *Buffalo Women's Law Journal* 21

Asens, J, 'La criminalització del moviment okupa' in *Okupació, repressió i moviments socials* (Barcelona, Edicions Kasa de la Muntanya–Diatriba, 1999)

Ashworth, A, 'The Doctrine of Provocation' (1976) 35 *Cambridge Law Journal* 292
——*Sentencing and Criminal Justice*, 3rd edn (London, Butterworths, 2000)

Australian Law Reform Commission, *Aboriginal Customary Law: Recognition*, Discussion Paper no 17 (1980)
——*The Recognition of Aboriginal Customary Laws*, Report no 31 (1986)
——*Multiculturalism and the Law*, Report no 57 (1992)
——*Sentencing of Federal Offenders*, Issues Paper no 29 (2005)
——*Same Crime, Same Time: Sentencing of Federal Offenders*, Report no 103 (2006)

Azon, F, 'Los movimientos migratorios y los juzgados españoles' (2002) VI(119) *Scripta Nova, Revista Electrónica de Geografía y Ciencias Sociales*, Universidad de Barcelona 111, www.ub.es/geocrit/sn/sn119111.htm

Bagaric, M, 'In Defence of a Utilitarian Theory of Punishment: Punishing the Innocent and the Compatibility of Utilitarianism' (1999) 24 *Australian Journal of Legal Philosophy* 95

Bal, PL, *Dwangkommunikatie in de rechtszaal. Een onderzoek naar de verbale interactie tussen rechter en verdachte tijdens de strafzitting van de politierechter* (Arnhem, Gouda Quint, 1988)

Ballard, R, 'Common Law and Uncommon Sense: the Assessment of "Reasonable Behaviour" in a Plural Society', www.art.man.ac.uk/CASAS/pdfpapers/commonsense.pdf

Banach, E, 'The Roma and the Native Americans: Encapsulated Communities within Larger Constitutional Regimes' (2002) 3 *Florida Journal of International Law* 353

Bancroft, A, 'No Interest in Land: Legal and Spatial Enclosure of Gypsy-Travellers in Britain' (2000) 4 *Space and Polity* 41

Barber, S, 'La ocupación de inmuebles del artículo 245.2 del Código Penal' (1999) V *Sentencias de TSJ y AP y otros Tribunales* (BIB 1999\793)

Barry, B, *Culture and Equality: an Egalitarian Critique of Multiculturalism* (Cambridge, MA, Harvard University Press, 2001)

Barth, F (ed), *Ethnic Groups and Boundaries: the Social Organization of Cultural Difference* (Boston, Little, Brown and Company, 1969; reprint, Prospect Heights, IL, Waveland Press, 1998)

Barzaili, G (ed), *Law and Religion* (Aldershot, Ashgate, 2007)

Basile, F, *Immigrazione e reati 'Culturalmente Motivate' : Il Diritto Penale Nelle Società Multiculturali Europee* (Milano, CUEM, 2008).

Bauböck, R, 'The Crossing and Blurring of Boundaries in International Migration: Challenges for Social and Political Theory' in R Bauböck and J Rundell (eds),

Blurred Boundaries: Migration, Ethnicity and Citizenship (Ashgate, Aldershot, 1998) 17.

Baucells, J, *La ocupación de inmuebles en el Código Penal de 1995* (Valencia, Tirant lo Blanc, 1997)

—— 'L'ocupació d'inmobles en el nou Codi Penal' in *Okupació, repressió i moviments socials* (Barcelona, Edicions Kasa de la Muntanya–Diatriba, 1999)

——*La delincuencia por convicción* (Valencia, Tirant lo Blanc, 2000)

——'El derecho penal ante el fenómeno inmigratorio' (2005) 13 *Revista de Derecho y Proceso Penal* 45

Baumann, G, *The Multicultural Riddle, Rethinking National, Ethnic, and Religious Identities* (New York, Routledge, 1999)

BBC News, 'Royals Lead Honour Killing Protest', 14 February 2000, http://news.bbc.co.uk/1/hi/world/middle_east/642591.stm

Beger, R. and Hein, J, Immigrants, Culture and American Courts: a Typology of Legal Strategies and Issues in Cases involving Vietnamese and Hmong Litigants' (2001) 26 *Criminal Justice Review* 38

Bennett, A and Kahn-Harris, K, 'Introduction' in *After Subculture* (Basingstoke, Palgrave Macmillan, 2004)

Berman, M, 'Justification and Excuse, Law and Morality' (2003) 53 *Duke Law Journal* 13

Bernardi, A, 'El derecho penal entre globalización y multiculturalismo' (2002) 8 *Revista de Derechos y proceso penal* 13

Berton, J, 'But He was Just Taking Orders', *East Bay Express*, 16 June 2004

Bertram, F, 'The Particular Problems of (the) Roma' (1997) 1 *University of California Journal of International Law and Policy* 1

Bhakt, N, *Arbitration, Religion and Family Law: Private Justice on the Backs of Women*, NAWL Working Paper (March 2005)

Bielefeld, S, 'The Culture of Consent and Traditional Punishments under Customary Law' (2003) 7 *Southern Cross University Law Review* 140

Binder, G, 'Twentieth-Century Legal Metaphors for Self and Society' in A Sarat *et al* (eds), *Looking Back at Law's Century* (New York, Cornell University Press, 2002)

Binsbergen, W van, *Culturen bestaan niet. Het onderzoek van interculturaliteit als een openbreken van vanzelfsprekendheden* (Rotterdam, Erasmus University, 1999)

Bird, S, 'Love-Song Secret Drove Father to Kill Daughter', *The Times* (London), 7 December 2004, www.timesonline.co.uk/article/0,2-1391940,00.html

Björling, B *et al*, *European Conference Report, Honour Related Violence within a Global Perspective: Mitigation and Prevention in Europe* (Stockholm, 2004)

Blay, S, 'The International Covenant on Civil and Political Rights and the Recognition of Customary Law Practices of Indigenous Tribes: the Case of Australian Aborigines' (1986) 19 *Comparative and International Law Journal of Southern Africa* 199

Bloemmink, S, 'Cultureel verweer' in G Anders, S Bloemink and NF Van Manen (eds), *De onvermijdelijkheid van rechtspluralisme* (Nijmegen, Ars Aequi Libri, 1998)

Böhmecke, M, *Studie: Ehrenmord* (Tübingen, Terre des Femmes, 2005), www.frauenrechte.de/tdf/pdf/EU-Studie_Ehrenmord.pdf

Bond, MH and Lee, PWH, 'Face Saving in Chinese Culture: a Discussion and Experimental Study of Hong Kong Students' in AYC King and RPL Lee (eds), *Social Life and Development in Hong Kong* (Hong Kong, Chinese University Press, 1981) 288–305

Bornmann, E, Van Eeeden, R and Wentzel, M (eds), *Violence in South Africa: a Variety of Perspectives* (Pretoria, Human Sciences Research Center, 1998)

Borrows, J, 'Frozen Rights in Canada: Constitutional Interpretation and the Trickster' (1998) 22 *American Indian Law Review* 37

——'Sovereignty's Alchemy: An Analysis of Delgamuukw v. British Columbia', 37 *Osgoode Hall L.J.* 537–596

Botha, T, *South African Police Service: Special Investigations, Witchcraft and Related Crimes* (unpublished document, 1999)

Bovenkerk, F, *Hedendaags kwaad. Criminologische opstellen* (Amsterdam, Meulenhoff, 1992)

——'Essay over de oorzaken van allochtone criminaliteit' in J Lucassen and A De Ruyter (eds), *Nederland multicultureel en pluriform?* (Amsterdam, Askant, 2002) 209

——'Drie lessen over het criminaliseren van minderheden' in R Gowricharn (ed), *Falende instituties, Negen heikele kwesties in de multiculturele samenleving* (Utrecht, Forum en Uitgeverij De Graaff, 2006) 89

Bradfield, R, 'The Demise of Provocation in Tasmania' (2003) 27 *Criminal Law Journal* 322

Braithwaite, J, *Crime, Shame and Reintegration* (New York, Cambridge University Press, 1989)

——'Restorative Justice' (1999) 25 *Crime and Justice: a Review of Research* 1

——*Restorative Justice and Responsive Regulation* (Oxford, Oxford University Press, 2002)

Branigin, W and Farah, D, 'Asylum Seeker is Impostor, INS Says', *Washington Post*, 20 December 2000, A1.

Brems, E, 'De nieuwe grondrechten in de Belgische Grondwet en hun verhouding tot het internationale, inzonderheid het Europese recht' (1995) 12 *Tijdschrift voor Bestuurswetenschappen en Publiek Recht* 619

Briggs, CL and Mantini-Briggs, C, '"Bad Mothers" and the Threat to Civil Society, Race, Cultural Reasoning and the Institutionalization of Social Inequality in a Venezuelan Infanticide Trial' (2000) 25 *Law and Social Inquiry* 299

Broeck, JV, 'Cultural Defence and Culturally Motivated Crimes (Cultural Offences)' (2001) 9 *European Journal of Crime, Criminal Law and Criminal Justice* 1

Bronitt, S and Amirthalingam, K, 'Cultural Blindness: Criminal Law in Multicultural Australia' (1996) 21 *Alternative Law Journal* 2

Bronitt, S and McSherry, B, 2nd edn, *Principles of Criminal Law* (Sydney, Law Book Company, 2005)

Broster, J and Bourne, H, *Amagqirha: Religion, Magic and Medicine in Transkei* (Cape Town, 1981)

Brown, B, 'The "Ordinary Man" in Provocation: Anglo-Saxon Attitudes and "Unreasonable Non-Englishmen"' (1964) 13 *International and Comparative Law Quarterly* 203

——'Face Saving and Face Restoration in Negotiation' in D Druckman (ed), *Negotiations: Social-Psychological Perspectives* (Beverly Hills, CA, Sage, 1977)

Brown, BR, 'Face-Saving Following Experimentally Induced Embarrassment' (1970) 6 *Journal of Experimental Social Psychology* 255

Brown, D et al, *Criminal Law: Materials and Commentary on Criminal Law and Process of New South Wales* (Sydney, Federation Press, 1990)

Brown, P and Levinson, S, 'Universals in Language Usage: Politeness Phenomenon' in E Goody (ed), *Questions and Politeness: Strategies in Social Interaction* (Cambridge, Cambridge University Press, 1978)

Brubaker, R, *Citizenship and Nationhood in France and Germany* (Cambridge, MA, Harvard University Press, 1992)

Bundestagsfraktion Bündnis 90/Die Grünen, *Menschenrechtsverletzungen im Namen der Ehre. Dokumentation des Öffentlichen Fachgesprächs vom 13. April 2005* (Berlin, Bundestagsfraktion Bündnis 90/Die Grünen, 2005), www.gruene-bundestag.de/cms/publikationen/dokbin/89/89963.pdf

Burchell, J and Milton, J, *Cases and Materials on Criminal Law* (Cape Town, Juta, 1997)

Burke, A, 'Man Who Said Wife Abused Him Guilty in Killing', *Daily News*, 26 March 1994

Calvo Buezas, T, *¿España racista? Voces payas sobre los Gitanos* (Barcelona, Anthropos, 1990)

Cameron, E, 'Judicial Accountability in South Africa' (1990) *South African Journal on Human Rights* 251

Campbell, S, 'Gypsies: the Criminalisation of a Way of Life?' (1995) 1 *Criminal Law Review* 28

——*Called to Heal: Traditional Healing Meets Modern Medicine in Southern Africa Today* (Johannesburg, Zebra Press, 1998)

Canadian Commission for UNESCO, 'A Working Definition of "Culture"' (1977) 4 *Cultures* 78

Carstens, PA, 'The Cultural Defence in Criminal Law: South African Perspectives' (2004) 2 *De Jure* 312

Castles, AC, *An Australian Legal History* (Sydney, Law Book Company, 1982)

Castro Argüelles, MA, 'El vinculo conyugal como requisito para acceder a la pensión de viudedad. Ineficacia del matrimonio por el "rito" gitano' (1999) IV *Arzandi Social* 2754

Caughey, J, *Negotiating Cultures and Identities: Life History Issues, Methods, and Readings* (Lincoln, University of Nebraska, 2006)

Chabria, A, 'His Own Private Berkeley', *Los Angeles Times Magazine*, 25 November 2001, 22–3, 40

Chavunduka, G, 'The Reality of Witchcraft' (2001) *African Legal Studies* 163

Chisholm, BJ, 'Credible Definitions: a Critique of U.S. Asylum Law's Treatment of Gender-Related Claims' (2001) 44 *Howard Law Journal* 427

Chiu, D, 'The Cultural Defense: Beyond Exclusion, Assimilation, and Guilty Liberalism' (1994) 82 *California Law Review* 1053

Chorney, J, 'Investigation into Interpreter in Landlord Sex Case; Translator may have Encouraged Alleged Victims to Exaggerate Testimony', *Oakland Tribune*, November 2001

Cileli, S, *Wir Sind Eure Töchter, Nicht Eure Ehre* (Michelstadt, Neuthor Verlag, 2002)

Clarkson, CMV and Keating, HM, *Criminal Law: Text and Materials*, 5th edn (London, Sweet and Maxwell, 2003)

Clinton, OL, 'Cultural Differences and Sentencing Departures' (1993) 5 *Federal Sentencing Reporter* 348

Coetzer, PWW, Carstens, P and Klopper, H, 'Some Medical Forensic Aspects of Cultural Practices' in PWW Coetzer, P Carstens, C Fosseus and CF Blok (eds), *Clinical Forensic Medicine and Medical Jurisprudence* (2001)

Cohen, A, *Two-dimensional Man* (London, Tavistock, 1974)

Cohen, S, 'Symbols of Trouble' in K Gelder (ed), *The Subcultures Reader* (London, Routledge, 1980)

——*Visions of Social Control: Crime, Punishment and Classification* (Cambridge, Polity Press, 1985)

——*States of Denial: Knowing about Atrocities and Suffering* (Cambridge, Polity Press, 2002)

Cole, A and Knowles, J, *Lives in Context: the Art of Life History Research* (Walnut Creek, Altamira, 2001)

Coleman, DL, 'Individualizing Justice through Multiculturalism: the Liberal's Dilemma' (1996) 96 *Columbia Law Review* 1093

Colman, AM, 'Crowd Psychology in South African Murder Trials' (1991) *American Psychologist* 1070

Comaroff, J and Comaroff, JL, *Ethnography and the Historical Imagination* (Boulder, Westview, 1992)

Commonwealth of Australia Office of Multicultural Affairs, *National Agenda for a Multicultural Australia* (AGPS, 1989)

Coombe, R, 'Contingent Articulations: a Critical Cultural Studies of Law' in A Sarat and T Kearns (eds), *Law in the Domains of Culture* (Ann Arbor, University of Michigan Press, 1997)

Corrado, ML, *Justification and Excuse in Criminal Law: a Collection of Essays* (New York, Garland Publishing, 1994)

Cotterrell, R, *Law, Culture and Society: Legal Ideas in the Mirror of Social Theory* (Aldershot, Ashgate, 2006)

Cowan, D and Lomax, D, 'Policing Unauthorized Camping' (2003) 2 *Journal of Law and Society* 283

Cowan, J, Dembour, MB and Wilson, RA, 'Introduction' in *Culture and Rights* (Cambridge, Cambridge University Press, 2001)

Crawford, J, 'International Law and the Recognition of Aboriginal Customary Law' in B Hocking (ed), *International Law and Aboriginal Human Right* (Law Book Co, 1988)

Crenshaw, K, 'Mapping the Margins: Intersectionality, Identity Politics and Violence Against Women of Color' (1994) 43 *Stanford Law Review* 1241

Dalton, V, 'Australian Deaths in Custody and Custody-related Police Operations 1999' in *Trends and Issues in Crime and Criminal Justice*, no 153 (Australian Institute of Criminology, 2000)

Daly, K and Hayes, H, 'Restorative Justice in Conferencing in Australia' in *Trends and Issues in Crime and Criminal Justice*, no 186 (Australian Institute of Criminology, 2001)

Danblaki, M, *On Gypsies: Texts Issued by International Institutions* (Midi-Pyrénées, Gypsy Research Centre CRDP, 1994)

Darden, MD, 'Return to Europe? The Czech Republic and the EU's Influence on its Treatment of Roma' (2004) 4 *Vanderbilt Journal of Transnational Law* 1181

David, R and Brierley, J, *Major Legal Systems in the World Today*, 2nd edn (London, Stevens and Sons, 1978)

Davis, D *et al*, *Fundamental Rights in the Constitution* (Cape Town, Juta, 1997)

De Hert, P, *Art. 8 EVRM en het Belgisch recht. De bescherming van privacy, gezin, woonst en communicatie* (Gent, Mys and Breesch, 1998)

De Lucas, J, 'La sociedad multicultural. Problemas juridicos y políticos' in MJ Añón, R Bergalli, M Calvo and P Casanovas (eds), *Derecho y Sociedad* (Valencia, Tirant lo blanch, 1998)

De Muniz, PJ, 'Introduction' in JI Moore (ed), *Immigrants in Courts* (Seattle, University of Washington Press, 1999) 3De Pasquale, S, 'Provocation and the Homosexual Advance Defence: the Deployment of Culture as a Defence Strategy' (2002) 26 *Melbourne University Law Review* 110

De Schutter, O, 'Le droit au mode de vie tsigane devant la Cour européenne des droits de l'homme' (1997) 1 *Revue trimestrielle des droits de l'homme* 47

De Stefano, AM, 'Fraud Charge in Genital Mutilation Asylum Case', *Newsday*, 10 September 2002, A13

De Winter, R, 'Godsdienst als alibi' (1996) 1 *Nederlands Juristenblad* 1

Deckha, M, 'Is Culture Taboo?: Feminism, Intersectionality, and Culture Talk in Law' (2004) 16(1) *Canadian Journal of Women and the Law* 14

Delhez, P, 'Le droit au logement des gens du voyage: une revendication incongrue' (1997) 3 *Droit en Quart Monde* 3

Department of Immigration and Multicultural and Indigenous Affairs, *The People of Australia: Statistics from the 2001 Census*, www.immi.gov.au/research/publications/people_of_australia.pdf

Devlin, P, *The Enforcement of Morals* (Oxford, Oxford University Press, 1965)

Dhamoon, R, '"Cultural" versus "Culture"' (unpublished manuscript)

Diamond, AS, 'Review of *The Law of Primitive Men: A Study in Comparative Legal Dynamics* by EA Hoebel, and *The Judicial Process among the Barotse of Northern Rhodesia* by M Gluckman' (1956) *International and Comparative Law Quarterly* 624

Diamond, BL, 'Social and Cultural Factors as a Diminished Capacity Defense in Criminal Law' (1978) 6 *Bulletin of the American Academy of Psychiatry and the Law* 195

Dobash Emerson, R and Dobash, RP, *Women, Violence and Social Change* (New York, Routledge, 1992)

Dolman, MM, *Overmacht in het stelsel van de strafuitsluitingsgronden*, PhD Thesis University of Amsterdam, (Nijmegen, Wolf Legal Publishers, 2006)

Donders, Y, *Towards a Right to Cultural Identity?* (Antwerpen, Intersentia, 2002)

Doreleijers, ThA, Bijl, B, van der Veldt, MC and van Loosbroek, E,, *BARO. Standaardisatie en protocollering basisonderzoek strafzaken Raad voor de Kinderbescherming* (Amsterdam, Vrije Universiteit Amsterdam/Nederlands Instituut voor Zorg en Welzijn, 1999)

Douki, S et al, 'Violence Against Women in Arab and Islamic Countries' (2003) 6 *Archives of Women's Mental Health* 165

Downs, H and Walters, B, *We Want Our Children Back*, 20/20, ABC, 18 August 1995, transcript #1533, available on Nexis

Dressler, J, 'New Thoughts about the Concept of Justification in the Criminal Law: a Critique of Fletcher's Thinking and Rethinking' (1984) 32 *UCLA Law Review* 65
——'Justifications and Excuses: a Brief Review of the Concepts and the Literature' (1987) 33 *Wayne Law Review* 1155

Du Toit, E, *Straf in Suid-Afrika* (Johannesburg, Juta, 1981)

Dundes, A, *Two Tales of Crow and Sparrow: a Freudian Folkloristic Essay on Caste and Untouchability* (Lanham, Rowman and Littlefield, 1997)

Durnescu, I, Lazar C and Shaw, R, 'Incidence and Characteristics of Rroma Men in Romanian Prisons' (2002) 3 *Howard Journal of Criminal Justice* 237

Dworkin, R, *Taking Rights Seriously*, 4th edn (London, Duckworth, 1978)

——*A Matter of Principle* (Oxford, Clarendon Press, 1996)

Editorial, 'A Defence of Consent to Indigenous Customary Punishment' (2003) 27 *Criminal Law Journal* 229

Ehrlich, E, *Fundamental Principles of the Sociology of Law* (trans WL Moll, Cambridge, Harvard University Press, 1936)

Entzinger, H, 'Shifting Paradigms: an Appraisal of Immigration in the Netherlands' in H Fassmann and R Münz (eds), *European Migration in the Late Twentieth Century, Historical Patterns, Actual Trends and Social Implications* (Aldershot, Edward Elgar, 1994) 93

Epstein, A, 'The Reasonable Man Revisited: Some Problems in the Anthropology of Law' (1973) 7 *Law and Society Review* 643

Eriksen, TH, *Common Denominators: Ethnicity, Nation-building and Compromise in Mauritius* (Oxford/New York, Berg, 1998)

——(ed), *Ethnicity and Nationalism: Anthropological Perspectives* (Chicago, Pluto Press, 2002)

Es, JL van and Bakker, M, *Allemaal anders. Intercultureel werken in het raadsonderzoek* (Rotterdam, Raad voor de Kinderbescherming, 2001)

Espiritu, Y Le, *Home Bound: Filipino American Lives Across Cultures, Communities and Countries* (Berkeley, CA, University of California Press, 2003)

European Committee on Migration, *Report on the Situation of Gypsies in Europe* (CDMG, 1995)

Evans, J, 'Muti Murders: Ritual Responses to Stress' (1991) 8 *Indicator South Africa* 46

Ewick, P and Silbey, S, *The Common Place of Law: Stories from Everyday Life* (Chicago, University of Chicago Press, 1998)

Eycken, M, 'De Roma afkomstig uit Slowakije plaatsen België en Europe voor hun verantwoordelijkheid' in M Eycken (ed), *Het recent Euro-nomadisme, Roma-zigeuners in een 'nieuwe beweging'?* (Brussels, Cultuur en Migratie, themanummer, 2001)

Fairbank, JK, *The United States and China* (Cambridge, MA, Harvard University Press, 1979)

Fan, F and Cao, Z, *Fanzui Goucheng (Elements of a Crime)* (Beijing, Law Press, 1987).

Faqir, F, 'Intrafamily Femicide in Defence of Honour: the Case of Jordan' (2001) 22 *Third World Quarterly* 65

Faure, V, 'Notes on the Occult in the New South Africa' (2001) *African Legal Studies* 170

Favell, A, *Philosophies of Integration: Immigration and the Idea of Citizenship in France and Britain* (New York, Palgrave Macmillan, 2001)

Fedler, J and Olckers, I, *Ideological Virgins and Other Myths* (Pretoria, Justice College, 2001)

Feinberg J, 'The Classic Debate' in J Feinberg and J Coleman, *Philosophy of Law* (Belmont, CA, Wadsworth, 2000)

Feldman, MW, 'Cultural Evolution: Theory and Models' in NJ Smelser and PB Baltes (eds), *International Encyclopedia of the Social and Behavioral Sciences* (Oxford, Pergamon, 2001) vol V, 3057

Feminist Sexual Ethics Project, *Special Focus: Islam: Honour Killings, Illicit Sex and Islamic Law*, Fact Sheets, www.brandeis.edu/projects/fse/Pages/honourkillings.html

Ferwerda, HB and Van Leiden, I, *Eerwraak of eergerelateerd geweld. Naar een werkdefinitie* (Den Haag, WODC, 2005)

Fetzer, J and Soper, C, *Muslims and the State in Britain, France and Germany* (New York, Cambridge University Press, 2004)

Fierens, J, 'Logement familial et droit au logement' in P Delnoy, Y-H Leleu and E Vieujean (eds), *Le logement familial* (Diegem, Story-Scientia, 1999)

Findings from the Multi-Agency Domestic Violence Murder Reviews in London (December 2005) 21, www.met.police.uk/csu/pdfs/MurderreportACPO.pdf

Findlay, A, 'Bail Nixed in Torture Case: Two Girls Allegedly Burned for Talking to Boys', *Toronto Sun*, 19 February 1999

Finnane, M, '"Payback", Customary Law and Criminal Law in Colonised Australia' (2001) 29 *International Journal of the Sociology of Law* 293

Fischer, M, 'The Human Rights Implications of a "Cultural Defense"' (1998) 6 *Southern California Interdisciplinary Law Journal* 663

Fitzpatrick, P, *The Mythology of Modern Law* (London, Routledge, 1992)

Fletcher, GP, 'The Right Deed for the Wrong Reason: a Reply to Mr Robinson' (1975) 23 *UCLA Law Review* 293

——*Rethinking Criminal Law* (Boston, Little, Brown and Co, 1978)

Foblets, M-C, 'Cultural Delicts: the Repercussion of Cultural Conflicts on Delinquent Behaviour. Reflections on the Contribution of Legal Anthropology to a Contemporary Debate' (1998) 3 *European Journal of Crime, Criminal Law and Criminal Justice* 187

——*Juridische aspecten van de multiculturele samenleving. Knelpunten en uitdagingen voor het beleid, Pre-advies Nederlandse Vereniging voor Rechtsvergelijking* (Deventer, Kluwer, 2005)

Fonseca, I, *Bury Me Standing: the Gypsies and their Journey* (London, Vintage Press, 1996)

Foucault, M, *Surveiller et punir. Naissance de la prison* (Paris, Gallimard, 1975)

Fournier, P, 'The Ghettoisation of Difference in Canada: "Rape by Culture" and the Danger of a "Cultural Defense" in Criminal Law Trials' (2002) 29 *Manitoba Law Journal* 81

Francione, G, *Animals, Property and the Law* (Philadelphia, Temple University Press, 1995)

Fraser, B, 'Aboriginal Fishing Strategy in Western Australia' (2004) 5(29) *Indigenous Law Bulletin* 10

Freiberg, A, 'Problem-Oriented Courts: Innovative Solutions to Intractable Problems?' (2001) 11(1) *Journal of Judicial Administration* 8

Friedman, LM, *The Legal System: a Social Science Perspective* (New York, Russell Sage Foundation, 1975)

Fuller, LL, *The Morality of Law* (rev edn, New Haven, Yale University Press, 1967)

Galenkamp, M, 'Tolerantie in de Nederlandse strafrechtspleging: is er ruimte voor een cultureel verweer?' in M ten Hooven (ed), *De lege tolerantie. Over vrijheid en vrijblijvendheid in Nederland* (Amsterdam, Boom, 2001)

——'De multiculturele samenleving in het geding; op zoek naar fundamenten' (2002) 28 *Justitiële Verkenningen* 75

——'Religieuze overtuigingen en het discriminatieverbod. Enkele bedenkingen bij het leerstuk van interpretatieve terughoudendheid' (2005) *Trema* 251

Gallin, AJ, 'The Cultural Defense: Undermining the Politics Against Domestic Violence' (1994) 35 *Boston College Law Review* 723

Gao, G, 'Self and Other: a Chinese Perspective on Interpersonal Relationships' in WB Gudykunst *et al* (eds), *Communication in Personal Relationships Across Cultures* (Thousand Oaks, Sage Publications, 1996)

García Arán, M, 'Introducción' in J Baucells, *La ocupación de inmuebles en el Código Penal de 1995* (Valencia, Tirant lo Blanc, 1997)

Garland, D, *Punishment and Modern Society* (Oxford, Clarendon, 1990)

——'The Limits of the Sovereign State: Strategies of Crime Control in Contemporary Society' (1996) 36 *British Journal of Criminology* 445

——*The Culture of Control: Crime and Social Order in Contemporary Society* (Oxford, Oxford University Press, 2001)

Garssen, J, Nicholaas, H and Sprangers, A, *Demografie van de allochtonen in Nederland* (Centraal Bureau voor de Statistiek, 2005)

Gay-Y-Blasco, P, 'A "Different" Body? Desire and Virginity among Gitanos' (1997) 3 *Journal of the Royal Anthropological Institute* 517

Geertz, C, *Local Knowledge: Further Essays in Interpretive Anthropology* (New York, Basic Books, 1983)

Gendercide Watch, *Case Study: 'Honour' Killings and Blood Feuds*, www.gendercide.org/case_honour.html

Gerbranda, T, 'Artikel 8 EVRM: geen recht op vrije standplaatskeuze woonwagen' (1998) 3 *NJCM-Bulletin* 312

Getsay, T, 'Gypsies, the People and their Criminal Propensity' (1982) *Kansas State FOP Journal* I, II and III

Ghorashi, H, *Ways to Survive, Battles to Win: Iranian Women Exiles in the Netherlands and the United States* (New York, Nova Science Publishers, 2003)

Girasoli, N, 'Roma/Gypsies and Immigration Issues in the EU' (2000) 1/2 *Revue des affaires européennes (Law and European Affairs)* 128

Glaberson, W, 'Perjury Conviction in Asylum Case', *New York Times*, 16 January 2003, B4

Goldstein, TF, 'Cultural Conflicts in Court: Should the American Criminal Justice System Formally Recognize a "Cultural Defense"?' (1994) *Dickinson Law Review* 141

'Gongan Zhangfu Shasi Tingzhang Qizi (Public Safety Husband Killed Judge Wife)', http://skb.hebeidaily.com.cn/200318/ca252854.htm

Gordon, NA, 'The Implications of Memetics for the Cultural Defence' (2001) *Duke Law Journal* 1809

Greenawalt, K, 'The Perplexing Borders of Justification and Excuse' (1984) 84 *Columbia Law Review* 1897

Greenhouse, CJ, 'Constructive Approaches to Law, Culture and Identity' (1994) 5 *Law and Society Review* 1231

Griffey, V, 'Reddy to be Sentenced Today: Lawyer's Defense Utilizes Cultural Context', *Daily Californian*, 19 June 2001

Grönfors, M, 'Institutional Non-Marriage in the Finnish Roma Community and its Relationship to Rom Traditional Law' (1997) 45 *American Journal of Comparative Law* 305

——'Institutional Non-Marriage in the Finnish Roma Community and its Relationship to Rom Traditional Law' in WO Weyrauch (ed), *Gypsy Law: Romani Legal Traditions and Culture* (Berkeley, University of California Press, 2001)

Gross, A, 'Beyond Black and White: Cultural Approaches to Race and Slavery' (2001) *Columbia Law Review* 640

Gross, H, *A Theory of Criminal Justice* (New York, Oxford University Press, 1979)

Gruenbaum, E, *The Female Circumcision Controversy: an Anthropological Perspective* (Philadelphia, University of Pennsylvania Press, 2001)

Gunther, J, *Inside Africa* (New York, Harper, 1995)

Gupta, A and Ferguson, J, 'Beyond "Culture": Space, Identity, and the Politics of Difference' in A Gupta and J Ferguson (eds), *Culture, Power, Place: Explorations in Critical Anthropology* (Durham NC, Duke University Press, 1997) 33–51

Gutmann, A, 'The Challange of Multiculturalism in Political Ethics' (1993) 22 *Philosophy and Public Affairs* 171

Gutwirth, S and De Hert, P, 'Een theoretische onderbouwing voor een legitiem strafproces' (2001) 31 *Delikt en Delinkwent* 1048

Habermas, J, *Between Facts and Norms: Contributions to a Discourse Theory of Law and Democracy* (Cambridge, Polity Press, 1996)

——'The Politics of Recognition in a Democratic State' in J Habermas, *The Inclusion of the Other: Studies in Political Theory* (C Cronin and P De Creiff (eds), Cambridge, MA, MIT Press, 1998) 203

Hakkert, A, *Ouders en reacties op jeugdcriminaliteit. Een verkenning van de mogelijkheden van de ouderlijke betrokkenheid* (Den Haag, Ministerie van Justitie, DPJS, 1999)

Hammond-Tooke, WD, *Rituals and Medicines: Indigenous Healing in South Africa* (Johannesburg, Donker, 1989)

Hancock, I, 'A Glossary of Romani Terms' in WO Weyrauch (ed), *Gypsy Law: Romani Legal Traditions and Culture* (Berkeley, University of California Press, 2001)

Harouel, J-L, 'Sociology of Culture' in NJ Smelser and PB Baltes (eds), *International Encyclopedia of the Social and Behavioral Sciences* (Oxford, Pergamon, 2001) vol V, 3179

Harris, AP, 'Foreword' in WO Weyrauch (ed), *Gypsy Law: Romani Legal Traditions and Culture* (Berkeley, University of California Press, 2001)

Hart, HLA, *The Concept of Law* (Oxford, Clarendon Press, 1961)

——*Punishment and Responsibility* (New York, Oxford University Press, 1968)

Harvard Law Review Editors, 'The Cultural Defense in the Criminal Law' (1985–86) 2 *Harvard Law Review* 1293

Haun, A, 'The Long Road: the Roma of Eastern and Central Europe and the Freedom of Movement and Right to Choose a Residence' (2000) 1 *George Washington International Law Review* 155

Hawkins, S, 'Caught, Hook, Line and Sinker: Summary of the AJAC Report into Aboriginal Fishing Rights in NSW' (2004) 4 *Indigenous Law Journal* 4

Hayashi, T, 'Reconstructing a Universal Theory of Politeness: Face, Politeness and the Model of Realization', www.nord.helsinki.fi/clpg/CLPG/Takuo%20Hayashi.pdf

Heijder, A, *Kritische zones in de strafrechtswetenschappen* (Deventer, Kluwer, 1970)

Heitmeyer, W, Müller, J and Schröder, H, *Verlockender Fundamentalismus: Türkische Jugendliche in Deutschland* (Suhrkamp, Frankfurt am Main, 1997)

Herranz, R, 'Desobediencia civil, ocupación y derecho a la vivienda' (2000) *Actualidad jurídica Aranzadi* 435

Herreros, T, 'El moviment okupa a finals del segle XX' in *Okupació, repressió i moviments socials* (Barcelona, Edicions Kasa de la Muntanya–Diatriba, 1999)

Herring, J, 'Provocation and Ethnicity' (1996) *Criminal Law Review* 490

Hildebrandt, M, 'Slachtofferschap en de legitimatie van het strafrecht' (1998) 27 *Rechtsfilosofie en rechtstheorie* 1

——'Punitieve handhaving en sociale cohesie in een multiculturele samenleving' in P Cliteur and V Van den Eeckhout (eds), *Multiculturalisme, cultuurrelativisme en sociale cohesie* (Den Haag, Boom Juridische uitgevers, 2001) 303

Hirsch Ballin, EMH, 'De positie van minderheden in ons rechtsbestel' in NJH Huls and HD Stout (eds), *Recht in een multiculturele samenleving* (Zwolle, WEJ Tjeenk Willink, 1993) 21

Ho, DYF, 'On the Concept of Face' (1975) 81 *American Journal of Sociology* 867

Hoefnagels, GP, *Rituelen ter terechtzitting. Een voorstudie van emoties, attituden en interakties tijdens het strafproces ter terechtzitting om te komen tot een methode van strafprocesvoering* (Deventer, Kluwer, 1977)

Holland, WA, *Gewetensbezwaren en strafuitsluitingsgronden* (Arnhem, Gouda Quint, 1989)

Holmquist, KL, 'Cultural Defense or False Stereotype? What Happens when Latina Defendants Collide with the Federal Sentencing Guidelines' (1997) 12 *Berkeley Women's Law Journal* 45

Honour Related Violence within a Global Perspective: Mitigation and Prevention in Europe, European Conference Report, Stockholm, 7–8 October 2004, www.kvinnoforum.se/english/

Hooks, B, *Yearning: Race, Gender, and Cultural Politics* (Toronto, Between the Lines, 1990)

——'Getting a Bit of the Other' in b hooks, *Black Looks: Race and Representation* (Boston, South End, 1992)

Horder, J, *Provocation and Responsibility* (Oxford/New York, Oxford University Press, 1992)

——'Criminal Law and Legal Positivism' (2002) 8 *Legal Theory* 212

Horowitz, DL (1986) 'Justification and Excuse in the Program of the Criminal Law' 49 *Law and Contemporary Problems* 109–126.

Howard, C, 'What Colour is the "Reasonable Man"?' (1996) *Criminal Law Review* 41

Hu, H, 'The Chinese Concept of Face' (1944) 46 *American Anthropologist* 45

Hu, W, 'Woman Fleeing Mutilation Savors Freedom', *New York Times,* 20 August 1999, B4

Hudson, B, *Justice in the Risk Society: Challenging and Re-affirming Justice in Late Modernity* (London, Sage, 2003)

Huisman, W, 'Culturele delicten. De rol van de culturele achtergrond van de verdachte in het strafproces' (1995) 5 *PROCES* 80

Human Rights Committee, *General Comment No 23 on Article 27 of the Covenant,* CCPR/C/21/Rev.1/Add.4, 25 April,1994

Human Rights Watch, () *Jordanian Law Excuses Murder* (11 August 1999), http://hrw.org/english/docs/1999/08/11/jordan1012.htm

——*Jordanian Parliament Supports Impunity for Honour Killings,* Fact Sheet (27 January 2000), www.hrw.org/press/2000/01/jord0127.htm

Hund, J, 'Witchcraft and Accusations of Witchcraft in South Africa: Ontological Denial and Suppression of African Justice' (2000) *Comparative and International Law Journal of Southern Africa* 366

——'African Witchcraft and Western Law: Ontological Denial and the Suppression of African Justice' (2001) 2 *African Legal Studies* 22

Husak DN, *Philosophy of Criminal Law* (Totowa, NJ, Rowman and Littlefield, 1987)

ICEM–Ministerie van de Vlaamse Gemeenschap, *Jaarrapport 2001 inzake het Vlaamse beleid naar etnisch-culturele minderheden* (Brussels, ICEM–Ministerie van de Vlaamse Gemeenschap, 2002)

Inspectie Jeugdhulpverlening en Jeugdbescherming Regio Zuid, *Casus Roermond nader onderzocht* (Den Bosch, 2002)

James, K, Interview with Eren Unsal, 'Honor Killings Plague Germany's Turkish Community', *Morning Edition*, National Public Radio Atlanta, 29 March 2005

Janssen, J, *Je eer of je leven? Een verkenning van eerzaken voor politieambtenaren en andere professionals* (Elsevier Overheid, 2006)

Jetter, A, 'Fear is Legacy of Wife Killing in Chinatown; Battered Asians Shocked by Husband's Probation', *Newsday*, 26 November 1989, 4

Johnson, C, 'Crimes Usual in India, Reddy Says', *San Francisco Chronicle*, 16 June 2001

Johnston, E, *Royal Commission into Aboriginal Deaths in Custody: National Report* (AGPS, 1991)

Joseph, R, 'Musharraf Targets Abuse of Pakistani Women', *Washington Times*, 16 August 2002

Judicial Studies Board, *Handbook on Ethnic Minority Issues* (London, 1994)

Junger, M, *Delinquency and Ethnicity: an Investigation on Social Factors relating to Delinquency among Moroccan, Turkish, Surinamese and Dutch Boys* (Deventer, Kluwer, 1990)

Junger-Tas, J and Van der Zee-Nefkens, AA, *Een observatie-onderzoek naar het werk van de politie-surveillance* (WODC, Den Haag, 1977)

Kadish, SH, 'Excusing Crime' (1987) 75 *California Law Review* 257

Kagan, R, *Adversarial Legalism* (Cambridge, MA/London, Harvard University Press, 2001)

Kant, I, *Groundwork of the Metaphysic of Morals* (HJ Paton (trans), New York, Harper and Row, 1964)

Kanwar, J, 'Preserving Gypsy Culture through Romani Law in America' (2000) 4 *Vermont Law Review* 1265

Kapur, R, *Erotic Justice: Law an d the New Politics of Postcolonialism* (London, Glass House Press, 2005)

Kassindja, F and Bashir, LM, *Do They Hear You When You Cry?* (New York, Delta, 1998)

Kearnley, S and Overington, C, 'Digging in at the Beach', *The Australian*, www.theaustralian.news.com.au/common/story_page/0,5744,17563468%255E601,00.html

Kelek, N, *Die Fremde Braut* (Köln, Kiepenheuer and Witsch, 2005)

Kelk, C, 'Het algemeen menselijk karakter van de overmacht' (2006) *Delikt en Delinkwent* 821

Kettle, M, 'Feminist Cause was Fraud', *The Guardian*, 21 December 2000

Khoday, A, '"Honour Killings" Hide Racist Motives', *Toronto Star*, 8 March 2005

Kim, K and Hreshchyshyn, K, 'Human Trafficking Private Right of Action: Civil Rights for Trafficked Persons in the United States' (2004) 16 *Hastings Women's Law Journal* 23

Kim, NS, 'The Cultural Defense and the Problem of Cultural Preemption: a Framework for Analysis' (1997) *New Mexico Law Review* 101

King, AY, '"Mian", "Chi" yu zhongguoren xingwei zhi fenxi ("Face", "Shame", and the Analysis of Behavior Patterns of the Chinese)' in G Yang (ed), *Zhongguoren de xinli (The Psychology of the Chinese)* (Taipei, Guiguan Press, 1988) 75

King, AY and Bond, MH, 'The Confucian Paradigm of Man: a Sociological View' in WS Tseng and DH Wu (eds), *Chinese Culture and Mental Health* (Orlando, Academic Press, 1985) 29

Kirby, V, '"Feminisms, Reading, Postmodernisms": Rethinking Complicity' in S Gunew and A Yeatman (eds), *Feminism and the Politics of Difference* (Boulder, West View Press, 1993)

Klausen, J, *The Islamic Challenge: Politics and Religion in Western Europe* (NewYork, Oxford University Press, 2005)

Kline, M, 'Race, Racism and Feminist Legal Theory' (1998) 12 *Harvard Women's Law Journal* 115

Knoops, GGJ, *Psychische overmacht en rechtsvinding, Een onderzoek naar de strafrechtelijke, forensisch-psychiatrische en psychologische grenzen van psychische overmacht*, PhD Thesis Leiden (Deventer, Gouda Quint, 1998)

Kogacioglu, D, 'The Tradition Effect: Framing Honour Crimes in Turkey' (2004) 15 *Difference: a Journal of Feminist Cultural Studies* 118

Kohnert, D, 'Magic and Witchcraft in the Democratisation of South Africa' (2001) *African Legal Studies* 177

Komter, ML, *Dilemmas in the Courtroom: a Study of Trials of Violent Crime in the Netherlands* (Mahwah, NJ, Erlbaum, 1998)

Kool, R *et al*, *Vrouwelijke genitale verminking in juridisch perspectief. Achtergrondstudie. (Rechtsvergelijkend) onderzoek naar de juridische mogelijkheden ter voorkoming en bestrijding van vrouwelijke genitale verminking* (Zoetermeer, Commissie Bestrijding Vrouwelijke Genitale Verminking, 2005)

Korf, DJ, 'Witte allochtonen en zwarte autochtonen; etniciteit en criminaliteit in Nederland' (2001) 31 *Delikt en Delinkwent* 531

Korobkin, L, 'Narrative Battles in the Courtroom' in M Garber, P Franklin and R Walkowitz (eds), *Field Work* (New York, Routledge, 1996)

Kroeber, AL and Kluckholn, C, *Culture: a Critical Review of Concepts and Definitions* (Cambridge, MA, The Museum, 1952)

Kurhi, E, 'Civil Suits Against Lakireddy are Settled', *The Berkeley Voice*, 9 April 2004, A1, A9

Kvinnoforum, *Honour Related Violence: European Resource Book and Good Practice* (Stockholm, Kvinnoforum, 2005)

Kymlicka, W, *Multicultural Citizenship* (Oxford, Oxford University Press, 1995)

Labaca Zabala, ML, 'La familia polígama y pensión de Viudedad' (2004) 22 *Sentencias de TSJ y AP y otros Tribunales*

Labuschagne, JMT, 'Geloof in Toorkuns: 'n morele dilemma vir die strafreg' (1990) *South African Journal for Criminal Justice* 246

——'Geloof in towery, die regsbewussynsdraende persoonlikheid en die voorrasionele onderbou van die regsorde: 'n Regsantropologiese evaluasie' (1998) *South African Journal of Ethnology* 78

Lacey, N, 'Contingency and Criminalisation' in I Loveland (ed), *Frontiers of Criminality* (London, Sweet and Maxwell, 1995)

——*Unspeakable Subjects: Feminist Essays in Legal and Social Theory* (Oxford, Hart Publishing, 1998)

Lacey, N, Wells, C and Quick, O, *Reconstructing Criminal Law*, 3rd edn (London, Butterworths, 2003)

Lal, V, 'Sikh Kirpans in California Schools: the Social Construction of Symbols, Legal Pluralism, and the Politics of Diversity' (1996) 22 *Amerasia Journal* 57

Lau, J, 'Kulturbedingte Ehrenmorde', *Die Zeit* (Hamburg), 3 March 2005, Politik 1

——'Wie eine Deutsche', *Die Zeit* (Hamburg), 9 March 2005, www.zeit.de/2005/09/Hatin_S_9fr_9fc_9f_09

Lawrence, S, 'Cultural (In)sensitivity: the Danger of a Simplistic Approach to Culture in the Courtroom' (2001) 13 *Canadian Journal of Women and the Law* 107

Leader-Elliott, I, 'Sex, Race and Provocation: In Defence of Stingel' (1996) 20 *Criminal Law Journal* 72

Lee, C, *Murder and the Reasonable Man* (New York, New York University Press, 2003)

Lee, HK, 'Guilty Plea Seen in Sex Smuggling Case in Berkeley', *San Francisco Chronicle*, 22 June 2002, A15

Lee, IC and Lewis, M, 'Human Trafficking from a Legal Advocate's Perspective: History, Legal Framework and Current Anti Trafficking Efforts' (2003) 10 *University of California Davis Journal of International Law and Policy* 169

Lee, R, 'The Rom-Vlach Gypsies and the Kris-Romani' in WO Weyrauch (ed), *Gypsy Law: Romani Legal Traditions and Culture* (Berkeley, University of California Press, 2001)

Levine, KL, 'Negotiating the Boundaries of Crime and Culture: a Sociological Perspective on Cultural Defence Strategies' (2003) 26 *Law and Social Inquiry* 39

Levy, R and Hollan, D, 'Person Centered Interviewing and Observation' in H Bernard (ed), *Handbook of Method in Cultural Anthropology* (Walnut Creek, Altamira, 1998)

Lew, M, *The Humanity of Jewish Law* (Soncino Press, 1985)

Lewis, J, 'The Outlook for a Devil in the Colonies' (1958) *Criminal Law Review* 661

Lijphart, A, *The Politics of Accommodation, Pluralism and Democracy in the Netherlands* (Berkeley, CA, University of California Press, 1975)

Lin, Y, *My Country and My People* (Taipei, John Day, 1968)

Lindsay, S, 'Killer Gets Life for Slaying at Food Court', *Denver Rocky Mountain News*, 2 June 1995, 30A

Lloyd, P, 'The Case of Mrs. Adesanya' (1974) 4 *RAIN: Royal Anthropological Institute News* (Sept/Oct) 2

Loenen, T, 'Het gelijkheidsbeginsel en andere grondrechten in de multiculturele samenleving. Ontwikkelingen sinds 1983' (2003) 28 *NJCM-Bulletin* no 3a

Löfgren, N, 'Aboriginal Community Participation in Sentencing' (1997) 21 *Criminal Law Journal* 127

Louis, C, 'Kampf der Tödlichen Ehre' in *Emma* (Köln, Nov/Dec 2004), www.emma.de/561.html

Ly, C, 'The Conflict Between Law and Culture: the Case of Hmong in America' (2001) *Wisconsin Law Review* 471

Lyman, JC, 'Cultural Defense: Viable Doctrine or Wishful Thinking?' (1986) *Criminal Justice Journal* 87

Macaulay and Other Indian Law Commissioners, *A Penal Code Prepared by the Indian Law Commissioners* (Union, NJ, Lawbook Exchange Ltd, 2002)

Machiels, T, *Keeping the Distance or Taking the Chances* (Brussels, ENAR, 2002)

MacKinnon, C, *Toward a Feminist Theory of the State* (Cambridge, MA, Harvard University Press, 1989)

Macklem, T and Gardner, J, 'Provocation and Pluralism' (2001) 64 *Modern Law Review* 815

Maddock, K, 'Note' (1992) XXI *Commission on Folk Law and Legal Pluralism Newsletter* 64

Magnarella, PJ, 'Justice in a Culturally Pluralistic Society: the Cultural Defense on Trial' (1991) 19 *Journal of Ethnic Studies* 65

Malkin, M, 'Mutilating the Truth', *Washington Times*, 20 September 2002

Marchetti, E and Daly, K, 'Indigenous Courts and Justice Practices in Australia' in *Trends and Issues in Crime and Criminal Justice*, no 277 (Australian Institute of Criminology, 2004)

Marcos del Cano, AM, 'Inmigracion y el derecho a la propia cultura' in M Minot (ed), *Justicia, migración y Derecho* (Madrid, Dykinson, 2004)

Marech, R, 'Slavery Abounds in U.S., Rights Group Says', *San Francisco Chronicle*, 24 September 2004, A3

Margulies, P, 'Identity on Trial: Subordination, Social Science Evidence, and Criminal Defense' (1998) 51 *Rutgers Law Review* 45

Martin, DA, 'Adelaide Abankwah, Fauziya Kasinga, and the Dilemmas of Political Asylum' in DA Martin and PH Schuck (eds), *Immigration Stories* (New York, Foundation Press, 2005)

Marzulli, J, 'Her Mutilation Tale is a Fake, Say Feds', *Daily News*, 10 September 2002, 10

Matras, Y, *Problems Arising in connection with the International Mobility of the Roma in Europe* (CDMG, 1996), www.social.coe.int/en/cohesion/action/publi/roma/matras.htm

Maynard, R, 'Racial Anger on the Brew', *Straits Times*, 13 December 2005, 18

McCall, M, *Deaths in Custody in Australia: 2003 National Deaths in Custody Program Annual Report* (Australian Institute of Criminology, 2004), www.aic.gov.au/publications

McClintock, A, *Imperial Leather: Race, Gender and Sexuality in the Colonial Contest* (London, Routledge, 1995)

McGillivray, A, 'Child Physical Assault: Law, Equality and Intervention' (2003) 30 *Manitoba Law Journal* 133

McNamara, L, *Regulating Racism: Racial Vilification Laws in Australia*, Institute of Criminology Monograph Series no 16 (Sydney, 2002)

McRobbie, A, *The Uses of Cultural Studies* (London, Sage Publications, 2005)

Menski, WF, 'Immigration and Multiculturalism in Britain: New Issues in Research and Policy', www.art.man.ac.uk/CASAS/pdfpapers/osakalecture.pdf

Merry, SE, 'Changing Rights, Changing Culture' in J Cowan, MB Dembour and R Wilson (eds), *Culture and Rights* (Cambridge, Cambridge University Press, 2001)

Meyer, LH *et al* (eds), *Rights, Culture and the Law* (Oxford, Oxford University Press, 2003)

Mezey, N, 'Law as Culture' (2001) 13 *Yale Journal of Law and the Humanities* 35

Mihalik, J and Cassim, Y, 'Ritual Murder and Witchcraft: a Political Weapon' (1992) *South African Law Journal* 138

Ministry of Internal Affairs and Ministry of Justice, *Criminaliteit in relatie tot de integratie van etnische minderheden* (The Hague, Ministry of Internal Affairs, 1997)

Minnaar, A, 'Witchpurging and Muti Murder in South Africa' (2001) *African Legal Studies* 1

Minnaar, A *et al*, 'Witch Killing with Specific Reference to the Northern Province in South Africa' in E Bornman, R Van Eeden and M Wentzel (eds), *Violence in South Africa: a Variety of Perspectives* (Pretoria, Human Sciences Research Center, 1998)

Mitchell, JC, *The Kalele Dance: Aspects of Social Relationships among Urban Africans in Northern Rhodesia*, Rhodes-Livingstone Papers no 27 (Manchester, Manchester University Press, 1956)

Mohanty, CT, 'Under Western Eyes: Feminist Scholarship and Colonial Discourses' in R Lewis and S Mills (eds), *Feminist Postcolonial Theory: a Reader* (New York, Routledge, 2003)

Mojab, N (ed), *Violence in the Name of Honour: Theoretical and Political Challenges* (Istanbul, Bilgi University Press, 2004)

Moran, M, *Rethinking the Reasonable Person: an Egalitarian Reconstruction of the Objective Standard* (Oxford, Oxford University Press, 2003)

Morgan, J, 'Equality Rights in the Australian Context: a Feminist Perspective' in P Alston (ed), *Towards an Australian Bill of Rights* (CIPL and HREOC, 1994)

Morgan, J and Graycar, R, *The Hidden Gender of Law* (Federation Press, 2002)

Morse, R, 'Whistle-Blower Ready for Justice', *San Francisco Chronicle*, 27 January 2002, A2

Mrozek, T, 'Accused Wife Killer to Claim Mental Abuse', *Los Angles Times*, 7 May 1993, B1

——'Cultural Defense in Wife's Death', *Los Angeles Times*, 4 March 1994, B3

——'Prosecutor Says Accused Killer Lied', *Los Angeles Times*, 18 March 1994, B4

Mullally, S, 'Feminism and Multicultural Dilemmas in India: Revisiting the Shah Bano Case' (2004) 24 *Oxford Journal of Legal Studies* 671

Murphy, DE, 'I.N.S. Says African Woman Used Fraud in Bid for Asylum', *New York Times*, 21 December 2000, B3

Murray, YM, 'The Battered Woman Syndrome and the Cultural Defense' (1995) 7 *Federal Sentencing Reporter* 197

Muslim Women's League, 'Position Paper on "Honour Killings"' (1999), www.mwlusa.org/publications/positionpapers/hk.html

Narayan, U, '"Cross-Cultural Connections, Border-Crossings", and "Death by Culture"' in U Narayan, *Dislocating Cultures: Identities, Traditions, and Third-World Feminism* (New York, Routledge, 1997)

——'Restoring History and Politics to "Third-World Traditions"' in U Narayan (ed), *Dislocating Cultures: Identities, Traditions, and Third-World Feminism* (New York, Routledge, 1997)

——'Essence of Culture and a Sense of History: a Feminist Critique of Cultural Essentialism' (2000) 13(2) *Hypatia* 86, reprinted in U Narayan and S Harding (eds), *Decentering the Center: Philosophy for a Multicultural, Postcolonial, and Feminist World* (Bloomington, Indiana University Press, 2000)

Nedelsky, J, 'Embodied Diversity and the Challenges to Law' (1997) 42 *McGill Law Journal* 91

Neff, KM, 'Removing the Blinders in Federal Sentencing: Cultural Difference as a Proper Departure Point' (2003) *Chicago-Kent Law Review* 445

Nel, CJ, Verschoor, T, Calitz, FJW and Van Rensburg, PHJJ, 'Die belang van 'n Antropologiese perspektief by toepaslike verhore van oënskynlike motieflose moorde' (1992) *South African Journal of Ethnology* 85

Nelken, D, 'Law in Action or Living Law? Back to the Beginning in Sociology of Law' (1984) 4 *Legal Studies* 157

——*Comparing Legal Cultures* (Aldershot, Dartmouth, 1997)

Nelson, C, 'Consistently Revealing Inconsistencies: the Construction of Fear in the Criminal Law' (2004) 48 *Saint Louis University Law Journal* 1261

New South Wales Law Reform Commission, *Partial Defences to Murder: Provocation and Infanticide*, NSWLR Report (1997) 83

Nielsen, J and Martin, G, 'Indigenous Australian Peoples and Human Rights' in D Kinley (ed), *Human Rights in Australian Law* (Federation Press, 1998)

Niner, P, 'Accomodating Nomadism? An Examination of Accommodation Options for Gypsies and Travellers in England' (2004) 2 *Housing Studies* 141

Nomoyi, NC, 'Necklacers Speak Out on Hunting Down and Demolishing Transgressors', paper presented at the Research Internship Sala, Human Sciences Research Council, Pretoria, 1995

Nys, M, 'Les Tsiganes: ces exclus de l'Europe' (1995) 6 *Droit en Quart Monde* 3

Odediran, TC, 'The Adelaide Abankwah Immigration Furore', *TransSahara News* (2003)

Okin, SM, 'Is Multiculturalism Bad for Women?' in SM Okin (ed), *Is Multiculturalism Bad for Women?* (Princeton, Princeton University Press, 1999)

Ong, A, *Flexible Citizenship: the Cultural Logic of Transnationality* (Durham NC, Duke University Press, 1999)

——*Buddha is Hiding: Refugees, Citizenship, the New America* (Berkeley, CA, University of California Press, 2003)

O'Nions, H, 'The Marginalisation of Gypsies', *Web Journal of Current Legal Issues* (1995), http://webjcli.ncl.ac.uk/articles3/onions3.html

——'The Right to Respect for Home and Family Life: the First in a Series of "Gypsy Cases" to Challenge UK Legislation' (1996) 5 *Web Journal of Current Legal Issues*, http://webjcli.ncl.ac.uk/1996/issue5/o'nions5.html

Ottevaere, A, 'Le droit des tsiganes à la protection sociale. La culture du voyage au pays des sédentaires' (1996) 7 *Sociaalrechtelijke Kronieken* 313

Oude Breuil, BC, *De Raad voor de Kinderbescherming in een multiculturele samenleving* (Den Haag, Boom Juridische Uitgevers, 2005)

Oude Breuil, BC and Post, M, 'De praktijk van openbaarheid, of waarom cricket zo moeilijk te begrijpen is' in A Beijer, CH Brants, L Van Lent and CM Pelser (eds), *Openbare Strafrechtspleging* (Deventer, Kluwer, 2002) 159–80

Pankratz, H, 'DA: Chinese Expert Knew Right from Wrong', *Denver Post*, 9 March 1995, B–05

Parekh, B, *Rethinking Multiculturalism: Cultural Diversity and Political Theory* (Cambridge, MA, Harvard University Press, 2000)

Paz, O, 'The Sons of La Malinche' in O Paz, *The Labyrinth of Solitude: Life and Thought in Mexico* (Lysander Kemp (trans), New York, Grove Press, 1961)65

Pederson, P, *The Five Stages of Culture Shock: Critical Incidents Around the World* (Westport, Greenwood Press, 1995)

Pettman, J, 'Learning about Power and Powerlessness: Aborigines and White Australia's Bicentenary' (1988) 29(3) *Race and Class* 69

Phillips, A, 'When Culture Means Gender: Issues of Cultural Defence in English Courts' (2003) 66 *Modern Law Review* 510

Piret, JVAG, 'Multiculturalisme, gelijkheid en openbare orde in een liberale rechtsstaat' in JVAG Piret (ed), *De precisie van het lezen. Liber Amicorum M. Weyemberg* (Brussels, VUB Press, 2003) 279

Pogany, I, *The Roma Café: Human Rights and the Plight of the Romani People* (London, Pluto Press, 2004)

Poulter, S, 'Foreign Customs and English Criminal Law' (1975) 24 *International and Comparative Law Quarterly* 136

——*Ethnicity, Law and Human Rights: the English Experience* (Oxford, Oxford University Press, 1998)

Pound, R, 'Mechanical Jurisprudence' (1908) 8 *Columbia Law Review* 605

Presencia Gitana (Equipo de Estudios), *Los Gitanos ante la Ley y la Administración* (Madrid, Editorial Presencia Gitana, 1991)

Quraishi, M, *Muslims and Crime: a Comparative Study* (Aldershot, Ashgate, 2006)

Rachels, J, *The Elements of Moral Philosophy*, 4th edn (New York, McGraw-Hill, 2003)

Radin, MJ, 'Market Inalienability' (1987) 100 *Harvard Law Review* 1849

——*Contested Commodities* (Cambridge, MA, Harvard University Press, 1996)

Ramelsberger, A, 'Vogelfreie Frauen', *Süddeutsche Zeitung* (München), 21 February 2005, Politik 1

Ramirez-Heredia, J, *Matrimonio y boda de los Gitanos y de los "Payos"* (Barcelona, Centro de Producción Editorial y Divulgación Audiovisual, 2005)

Razack, S, *Looking White People in the Eye: Gender, Race, and Culture in Courtrooms and Classrooms* (Toronto, University of Toronto Press, 2001)

Remmelink, J, 'De overtuigingsdader' in *Honderd jaar rechtsleven. De Nederlandse Juristen-Vereniging 1870–1970* (Zwolle, Tjeenk Willink, 1970) 179

Renteln, AD, 'Women and the Courts: a Justification of the Cultural Defense as Partial Excuse' (1993) *Southern California Review of Law and Women's Studies* 437

——'Is the Cultural Defense Detrimental to the Health of Children?' (1994) 7 *Law and Anthropology* 27

——'Cultural Rights and Culture Defence: Cultural Concerns' in NJ Smelser and PB Baltes (eds), *International Encyclopedia of the Social and Behavioral Sciences* (Oxford, Pergamon, 2001) vol V, 3116

——'In Defense of Culture in the Courtroom' in RA Shweder, M Minow and HR Markus (eds), *Engaging Cultural Differences* (New York, Russell Sage Foundation, 2002) 194–215

——'Visual Religious Symbols and the Law' (2004) 47 *American Behavioral Scientist* 1573

——*The Cultural Defense* (New York, Oxford University Press, 2004)

——'The Use and Abuse of the Cultural Defense' (2005) 20 *Canadian Journal of Law and Society* 47

Renteln, AD and Dundes, A (eds), *Folk Law: Essays in the Theory and Practice of Lex Non Scripta* (Madison, University of Wisconsin Press, 1995)

Rice-Oxley, M, 'Britain Examines "Honour Killings"', *Christian Science Monitor* (Boston), 7 July 2004, www.csmonitor.com/2004/0707/p06s02-woeu.html

Rimonte, N, 'A Question of Culture: Cultural Approval of Violence Against Women in the Pacific-Asian Community and the Cultural Defense' (1991) 57 *Stanford Law Review* 1311

Ringelheim, J, 'Identity Controversies before the European Court of Human Rights: How to Avoid the Essentialist Trap?' (2002) 3 *German Law Journal,* www. germanlawjournal.com/article.php?id=167

Robinson, PH, 'A Theory of Justification: Societal Harm as a Prerequisite for Criminal Liability' (1975) 23 *UCLA Law Review* 266

——*Structure and Function in Criminal Law* (Oxford, Clarendon Press, 1997)

Roche, D, *Restorative Justice* (London, Ashgate, 2000)

——*Accountability in Restorative Justice* (Oxford, Oxford University Press, 2003)

Rose, L, 'The Anthropologist as Expert Witness' (1977) 79 *American Anthropogist* 555

Rose, R, 'Sinti and Roma as National Minorities in the Countries of Europe', www. geocities.com/Paris/5121/sinti-roma.htm

Rosen, L, 'The Anthropologist as Expert Witness' (1977) 79 *American Anthropologist* 555

Rosenberg, S, 'Face', www.beyondintractability.org/m/face.jsp

Rossum, W van, *Verschijnen voor de rechter. Hoe het hoort en het ritueel van Turkse verdachten in de rechtszaal* (Amsterdam, Uitgeverij Duizend and Een, 1998)

Rothwell, N, 'Death to Bad Girls', *The Australian* (Sydney), 7 August 2004, 29–34

Rozemond, K, 'Beledigende uitspraken over homoseksuelen en de functie van de vrijheid van godsdienst en vrijheid van meningsuiting in een democratie' (2001) *Delikt en Delinkwent* 441

Ruane, R, 'Comment: Murder in the Name of Honour: Violence Against Women in Jordan and Pakistan' (2000) 14 *Emory International Law Review* 1523

Russell, D, 'Why Did Chanti Die?' (2000) 30 *Off Our Backs* 10

Sacks, V, 'An Indefensible Defense: On the Misuse of Culture in Criminal Law' (1996) *Arizona Journal of International and Comparative Law* 523

Sadurski W, *Giving Desert its Due: Social Justice and Legal Theory* (Boston, D Reidel, 1985)

Saltman M, *The Demise of the Reasonable Man: a Cross-Cultural Study of a Legal Concept* (Edison, NJ, Transaction Publishers, 1991)

Sams, JM, 'The Availability of the "Cultural Defense" as an Excuse for Criminal Behavior' (1986) 16 *Georgia Journal of International and Comparative Law* 335

Samuels, A, 'Legal Recognition and Protection of Minority Customs in a Plural Society in England' (1981) *Anglo-American Law Review* (now *Common Law World Review*) 241

San Román, T, *La diferencia inquietant: vells i noves estrategias culturals dels Gitanos* (Barcelona, Universidad Autonoma de Barcelona, 1994)

Saywell, S, *Crimes of Honour* (Documentary, First Run/Icarus Films)

Schweder, RA, 'Culture: Contemporary Views' in NJ Smelser and PB Baltes (eds), *International Encyclopedia of the Social and Behavioral Sciences* (Oxford, Pergamon, 2001) vol V, 3151

Seidman, RB, 'The Inarticulate Premiss' (1965) 3 *Journal of Modern African Studies* 805

——'Witch Murder and *Mens Rea*: a Problem of Society under Radical Social Change' (1965) 28 *Modern Law Review* 46

Sev'er, A, 'Culture of Honour, Culture of Change: a Feminist Analysis of Honour Killings in Rural Turkey' (1999) 7 *Violence Against Women: an International and Interdisciplinary Journal* 964

Shah, P, *Legal Pluralism in Conflict: Coping with Cultural Diversity in Law* (London, Cavendish Publishing, 2005)

Shaheen, J, 'Reel Bad Arabs: How Hollywood Vilifies a People' (2003) 588 *American Academy of Political and Social Science Annals* 171

Sheehy, E, Stubbs, J and Tolmie, J, 'Defending Battered Women on Trial: the Battered Woman Syndrome and its Limitations' (1992) 16 *Criminal Law Journal* 369

Sherwin, RK (ed), *Popular Culture and Law* (Aldershot, Ashgate, 2006)

Sheybani, M-M, 'Cultural Defense, One Person's Culture is Another's Crime' (1987) 9 *Loyola of Los Angelos International and Comparative Law Journal* 751

Shusta, RM, Levine, DR, Harris, PR and Wong, HZ, *Multicultural Law Enforcement: Strategies for Peacekeeping in a Diverse Society* (Upper Saddle River, NJ, Prentice-Hall, 1995)

Shute, S *et al* (eds), *A Fair Hearing? Ethnic Minorities in the Criminal Court* (Devon, Willan Publishing, 2005)

Siesling, M, *Eerwraak in Veghel? Een nieuwe betekenis voor culturele achtergronden in het Nederlandse strafrecht* (unpublished, 2002)

——'The International Conference on Honour Related Violence' (2005) 5 *PROCES* 191

——*Multiculturaliteit en verdediging in strafzaken, Een onderzoek naar de manier waarop in het Nederlandse strafrecht ruimte wordt gevonden voor het verwerken van de culturele achtergrond van de verdachte*, PhD Thesis, Utrecht (Den Haag, Boom Juridische Uitgevers, 2006)

Siklova, J and Miklusakova, M, 'Law as an Instrument of Discrimination: Denying Citizenship to the Czech Roma' (1998) 2 *East European Constitutional Review*, /www.law.nyu.edu/eecr/vol7num2/special/denyingcitizenship.html

Simester, AP and Sullivan, GR, *Criminal Law: Theory and Doctrine*, 2nd edn (Oxford, Hart Publishing, 2003)

Simpson, AWB, *Legal Theory and Legal History: Essays on the Common Law* (Hambledon Press, 1987)

Sin, L and Turner, A, 'Tragic Killing of "Sweet Girl" Stuns Kitimat', *The Province*, 3 August 2003

Sing, J, 'Culture as Sameness: Toward a Synthetic View of Provocation and Culture in the Criminal Law' (1999) *Yale Law Journal* 1845

Smith, ATP, 'The Criminal Justice and Public Order Act 1994: the Public Order Elements' (1995) 1 *Criminal Law Review* 19

Smith, JC, 'Case and Comment: Homicide—*R v Smith*' (2000) *Criminal Law Review* 1005

——*Smith and Hogan Criminal Law*, 10th edn (London, LexisNexis Butterworths, 2002)

Smith, KJM, 'Duress and Steadfastness: In Pursuit of the Unintelligible' (1999) *Criminal Law Review* 363

Snel, E, *De vermeende kloof tussen culturen* (Lecture Twente University, 2003)

Snyman, CR, *Criminal Law* (Butterworths, SA, 2002)

Sociaal en Cultureel Planbureau, *Sociaal Cultureel Rapport 1998, 25 jaar sociale verandering* (Den Haag, Sdu, 1998)

Srebnik, AG and Levy, R (eds), *Crime and Culture* (Aldershot, Ashgate, 2005)

Strang, H, *Restorative Justice Programs in Australia: a Report to the Criminology Research Council* (2001), www.aic.gov.au/crc/reports/strang/report.pdf

Strang, H and Braithwaite, J (eds), *Restorative Justice: Philosophy to Practice* (London, Ashgate, 2000)

Strijbosch, F, 'Eerwraak, onderzoek en strafrecht' (2001) *Nederlands Juristenblad* 883

Stubbs, J and Tolmie, J, 'Falling Short of the Challenge? A Comparative Assessment of the Australian Use of Expert Evidence on the Battered Woman Syndrome' (1999) 23 *Melbourne University Law Review* 709

Sudbury, J, 'Introduction: Feminist Critiques, Transnational Landscapes, Abolitionist Visions' in J Subdury (ed), *Global Lockdown: Race, Gender, and the Prison-Industrial Complex* (New York, Routledge, 2005)

Sutherland, A, 'Complexities of U.S. Law and Gypsy Identity' in WO Weyrauch (ed), *Gypsy Law: Romani Legal Traditions and Culture* (Berkeley, University of California Press, 2001)

Tang, Y, 'Xuefa, Shoufa, Zhifa (Study the Law, Obey the Law and Implement the Law)' (1999) 11 *Anhui Taxation* 36

Taylor, C, *Sources of the Self: the Making of the Modern Identity* (Cambridge, MA, Harvard University Press, 1989)

——*The Ethics of Authenticity* (Cambridge, MA, Harvard University Press, 1992)

——*Philosophical Arguments* (Cambridge, MA, Harvard University Press, 1997)

Tempelman, S, 'Constructions of Cultural Diversity, Multiculturalism and Exclusion' (1999) 47 *Political Studies* 17

Ten Voorde, J, 'Het zwaarder straffen bij culturele delicten. Feit of fictie?' (2004) 84 *PROCES* 3

——*Cultuur als verweer. Een grondslagentheoretisch onderzoek naar de ruimte en grenzen van culturele diversiteit in enige leerstukken van materieel strafrecht*, PhD Thesis, Erasmus University, Rotterdam (Nijmegen, Wolf Legal Publishers, 2007)

——'Godsdienstige overtuigingsdelicten beoordeeld. Het leerstuk van interpretatieve terughoudendheid in het licht van de strafrechtelijke gedraging' in PHPHMC van Kempen, T Kraniotis and G van Roermund (eds), *De gedraging in beweging. Handelen en nalaten in het materiële strafrecht, strafprocesrecht en sanctierecht* (Nijmegen, Wolf Legal Publishers, 2007) 143

Ter Heijde, J, *Vrijheid, Over de zin van straf. Een bijdrage tot de ontwikkeling van een klinische criminologie* (Den Haag, Bakker/Daamen, 1965)

Tester, K, *Animals and Society: the Humanity of Animal Rights* (London, Routledge, 1991)

't Hart, AC, 'Criminal Policy in the Netherlands' in J Van Dijk *et al* (eds), *Criminal Law in Action: an Overview of Current Issues in Western Societies* (Gouda Quint, Arnhem, 1986) 73

——*Openbaar Ministerie en rechtshandhaving, Een verkenning* (Arnhem, Gouda Quint, 1994)

——*Mensenwerk? Over rechtsbegrip en het mensbeeld in het strafrecht van de democratische rechtsstaat*, Mededelingen Koninklijke Nederlandsche Academie van Wetenschappen (Amsterdam, Noord-Hollandsche Uitgevers Maatschappij, 1995)

——'Rechtsbegrip en multiculturele samenleving' in AC 't Hart, *De meerwaarde van het strafrecht, Essays en annotatie* (Den Haag, Sdu, 1997) 293

——'Grondslagen van een multiculturele samenleving' in R Welters (ed), *Grenzeloze selectie, 75 jaar Katholieke Universiteit Nijmegen* (Nijmegen, Uitgeverij KU Nijmegen, 1999) 149

——'Twee perspectieven' in *Hier gelden wetten! Over strafrecht, Openbaar Ministerie en multiculturalisme* (Deventer, Gouda Quint, 2001) 185

Thio, Li-ann, 'Recent Constitutional Developments: of Shadows and Whips, Race, Rifts and Rights, Terror and *Tudungs*, Women and Wrongs' (2002) *Singapore Journal of Legal Studies* 328

Tholomé, L, 'L'article 23 de la Constitution n'est pas un simple déclaration de principe' (2000) 4 *Echos du Logement* 121

Thomas, DA, *Principles of Sentencing: the Sentencing Policy of the Court of Appeal Criminal Division*, 2nd edn (London, Heinemann, 1979)

Thornberry, P, *International Law and the Rights of Minorities* (Oxford, Clarendon Press, 1991)

Timmer, W et al, *Pilot 'Eer gerelateerd geweld in Haaglanden en Zuid-Holland-Zuid'*, tweede tussenrapportage (Den Haag, Politie Haaglanden, 2005)

Timmerman, J, 'When her Feet Touch the Ground: Conflict between the Roma Familistic Custom of Arranged Marriage and Enforcement of International Human Rights' (2004) 2 *Journal of Transnational Law and Policy* 475

Ting-Toomey, S, *Communicating Across Cultures* (New York, Guilford Press, 1999)

Tomao, SM, 'The Cultural Defense: Traditional or Formal?' (1996) 10 *Georgetown Immigration Law Journal* 241

Torry, WI, 'Multicultural Jurisprudence and the Culture Defense' (1999) 44 *Journal of Legal Pluralism* 127

Tugend, T, '"Cultural Defense" Plea Gets Sentence Lowered', *Jerusalem Post*, 29 March 1994, 3

Tyler, T, *Why People Obey the Law* (New Haven, Yale University Press, 1990)

United Nations General Assembly, *Working Towards the Elimination of Crimes Against Women Committed in the Name of Honour, Report of the Secretary-General*, UN GAOR 57th Session, UN Doc A/57/169 (2002)

Van den Broeck, J, 'Cultural Defence and Culturally Motivated Crimes (Cultural Offences)' (2001) 9/1 *European Journal of Crime, Criminal Law and Criminal Justice* 1

Van den Heever, JA and Labuschagne, JMT, 'Geloof in towery en die dekonkretiseringsproses' (1996) *Obiter* 310

Van der Hoeven, E, *Allochtone jongeren bij de jeugdpolitie I* (Den Haag, CWOK, 1985)

——*Allochtone en autochtone jongeren bij de jeugdpolitie II* (Den Haag, CWOK, 1986)

Van der Sloot, BP, 'Moeten rechters lijken op de Nederlandse bevolking? Over de wenselijkheid van descriptieve representatie door de rechterlijke macht' (2004) *Trema* 49

Van Eck, C, *Purified by Blood: Honour Killings Amongst Turks in the Netherlands* (Amsterdam, Amsterdam University Press, 2003)
——'Een geval van eerwraak in Veghel (Nederland)' (2002) *Delikt en Delinkwent* 162
Van Rossum, W, *Verschijnen voor de rechter, Hoe het hoort en het ritueel van Turkse verdachten in de rechtszaal* (Amsterdam, Duizend and Een, 1998)
Van Vliet, 'Amal of de tedere hand van de opvoeder' in *Crimineel Jaarboek* (Breda, Papieren Tijger, 1995) 169
Van Walsum, S, 'Het machtskarakter van het cultuurdebat' (1992) 2 *Nemesis* 12
Van Wyk, B, Van Oudtshoorn, B and Gericke, N, *Medicinal Plants in South Africa* (Pretoria, Briza Publications, 1997)
Verdier, R, 'Le système vindicatoire. Esquisse théorique' in *La vengeance: études d'ethnologie, d'histoire et de philosophie* (Paris, Cujas, 1980) vol 1
Visweswaran, K, 'Family in the US India Diaspora', *South Asian Women's Forum*, 19 March 2001, www.sawf.org/newedit/edit03192001/womensociety.asp
Vlaams Minderhedencentrum, *Tussen school en wagen, onderwijs aan voyageurs, manoesjen en roms* (Brussels, Vlaams Centrum Woonwagenwerk, 2000)
——*Voyageur, Manoesj, Rom: Cultuur, historiek, woonwagenwerk* (Brussels, Vlaams Minderhedencentrum, 2002)
Vlemminx, FMC, 'Mogen in deze tijden sympathieën zwaarder wegen dan constitutionele zuiverheid?' (2002) 34 *Nederlands Juristenblad* 1696
Volpp, L, '(Mis)identifying Culture, Asian Women and the "Cultural Defense"' (1994) 17 *Harvard Women's Law Journal* 57
——'Talking "Culture": Gender, Race, Nation, and the Politics of Multiculturalism' (1996) *Columbia Law Review* 1573
——'Blaming Culture for Bad Behavior' (2001) 12 *Yale Journal of Law and the Humanities* 89
——'Feminism Versus Multiculturalism' (2001) 101 *Columbia Law Review* 1181
Von Bullion, C, 'In den Fängen einer Türkischen Familie', *Süddeutsche Zeitung* (München), 25 February 2005, www.sueddeutsche.de/,tt4m2/ausland/artikel/506/48458/
——'Kristina Köhler nimmt Kampf gegen Ehrenmorde auf', 15 June 2005, www.kristina-koehler.de/presse/mitteilungen/20050615/kristina_koehler_nimmt_kampf_g/
——'Hohe Haftstrafe für den Täter—Freispruch für Zwei Angeklagte', 13 April 2006, www.faz.net/
——'"Ehrenmord"-Prozess Beginnt in Wiesbaden', www.heute.de/ZDFheute/inhalt/25/0,3672,3918073,00.html
——'Ein Ehrenmord in Deutschland'
Von Hirsch, A, *Past or Future Crimes* (New Brunswick, NJ, Rutgers University Press, 1985)
Vrij, A, *Misverstanden tussen politie en allochtonen, sociaal-psychologische aspecten van verdachten* (Amsterdam, VU Uitgeverij, 1991)
Waldman, A, 'Woman Fearful of Mutilation Wins Long Battle for Asylum', *New York Times*, 18 August 1999, B3
Walgrave, L, 'Extending the Victim Perspective Towards a Systemic Restorative Justice Alternative' in A Crawford and J Goodey (eds), *Integrating a Victim Perspective within Criminal Justice* (London, Ashgate, 2000)
Walker, L, *The Battered Woman Syndrome* (New York, Springer, 1984)

Walzer, M, 'New Tribalism', (1992) *Dissent* 164

Wanderer, NA and Connors, CR, 'Culture and Crime: Kargar and the Existing Framework for a Cultural Defense' (1999) 47 *Buffalo Law Review* 829

Wang, A, 'Beyond Black and White: Crime and Foreignness in the News' (2001) 8 *Asian Law Journal* 187

Wasik, M, *Emmins on Sentencing*, 4th edn (London, Blackstone Press, 2001)

Watt, JM and Breyer-Brandenwijk, MG, *The Medicinal and Poisonous Plants of South Africa* (Edinburgh, 1932) 20

Wayland, SV, 'Religious Expression in Public Schools: Kirpans in Canada, Hijab in France' (1997) 20 *Ethnic and Racial Studies* 545

Weber, L, *Understanding Race, Class, Gender, and Sexuality* (New York, McGraw Hill, 2001)

Wetenschappelijke Raad voor het Regeringsbeleid, *Nederland als immigratiesamenleving* (Den Haag, Sdu, 2001)

Weyrauch, WO, 'The Unconscious Meanings of Crime and Punishment' (1999) 2 *Buffalo Criminal Law Review* 19

——'Romaniya: an Introduction to Gypsy Law' in WO Weyrauch (ed), *Gypsy Law: Romani Legal Traditions and Culture* (Berkeley, University of California Press, 2001)

——*Gypsy Law: Romani Legal Traditions and Culture* (Berkeley, University of California Press, 2001)

——'The Romani People: a Long Surviving and Distinguished Culture at Risk, Book Review' (2003) 3 *American Journal of Comparative Law* 679

Weyrauch, WO (ed), 'Gypsy Law Symposium' (1997) 2 *American Journal of Comparative Law* 225

Wiersinga, H, 'Dossier van een verloren zaak' (1993) 23/6 *Delikt en Delinkwent* 528

——'Gevallen van eerwraak in Nederland en het beslissingsmodel van de strafrechter' (2001) *Ontmoetingen (Voordrachtenreeks van het Lutje Psychiatrisch-Juridisch Gezelschap)* 7

——*Nuance in benadering. Culturele factoren in het strafproces* (Boom Juridische Uitgevers, 2002)

Wikan, U, *Generous Betrayal: Politics of Culture in the New Europe* (Chicago, University of Chicago Press, 2002)

Williams, B, *Ethics and the Limits of Philosophy* (London, Fontana Press, 1985)

Williams, G, *Human Rights under the Australian Constitution* (Oxford, Oxford University Press, 1999)

Williams, J, *Unbending Gender: Why Work and Family Conflict and What to Do About It* (New York, Oxford University Press, 2000)

Wing, A, *Critical Race Feminism: a Reader* (New York, New York University Press, 1996)

Winkelman, M, 'Cultural Factors in Criminal Defense Proceedings' (1996) 55 *Human Organization* 154

Wolswijk, HD, 'Cultuur en strafbaarheid' (2004) 5 *RM Themis* 257

Wong, CM, 'Good Intentions, Troublesome Applications: the Cultural Defence and Other Uses of Cultural Evidence in Canada' (1999) 42 *Criminal Law Quarterly* 367

Woo, D, '*The People v. Fumiko Kimura*: But which People?' (1989) 17 *International Journal on Sociology and Law* 403

——'Cultural "Anomalies" and Cultural Defenses: Towards an Integrated Theory of Homicide and Suicide' (2004) 32 *International Journal of the Sociology of Law* 279

Woodman, GR, 'Some Realism about Customary Law: the West African Experience' (1969) *Wisconsin Law Review* 128

——'Judicial Development of Customary Law: the Case of Marriage Law in Ghana and Nigeria' (1977) 14 *University of Ghana Law Journal* 115

——'Unification or Continuing Pluralism in Family Law in Anglophone Africa: Past Experience, Present Realities, and Future Possibilities' (1988) 4 *Lesotho Law Journal* 33

——'How State Courts Create Customary Law in Ghana and Nigeria' in BW Morse and GR Woodman (eds), *Indigenous Law and the State* (Dordrecht, Foris, 1988)

——'Non-State, Unbounded, Unsystematic, Non-Western Law' in M Chiba (ed), *Sociology of Law in Non-Western Countries*, Oñati Proceedings no 15 (Oñati, International Institute for the Sociology of Law, 1993)

——'Ideological Combat and Social Observation: Recent Debate about Legal Pluralism' (1998) 42 *Journal of Legal Pluralism* 21

——'Accommodation between Legal Cultures: the Global Encounters the Local in Ghanaian Land Law' (2001) *Recht in Afrika* 57

——'Why There can be No Map of Law' in R Pradhan (ed), *Legal Pluralism and Unofficial Law in Social, Economic and Political Development*, papers of the XIIIth International Congress, 7–10 April, Chiang Mai Thailand (Kathmandu, ICNEC, 2003)

——'The One True Law, or One Among Others? The Self-Image of English Common Law', paper delivered at the XIVth International Congress of the Commission on Folk Law and Legal Pluralism, Fredericton, Canada, 26–29 August 2004

Woolf, M, 'Anti-terror Police Told to Target Asians', 13 September 2005, *The Independent Online Edition*, http://news.independent.co.uk/uk/politics/article312202.ece

Wormhoudt, RH, 'De culturele achtergrond van Turkse justitiabelen en strafrechtspleging. Een oriëntering' (1986) 6 *PROCES* 163

——'Culturele achtergronden: strafuitsluitingsgronden?' (1986) 12 *PROCES* 329

Wu, H, 'Bugai Fasheng de Beiju (Tragedy to be Avoided)' (1999) 11 *Anhui Taxation* 36

Yen, M, 'Refusal to Jail Immigrant who Killed Wife Stirs Outrage; Judge Ordered Probation for Chinese Man, Citing his "Cultural Background"', *Washington Post*, 10 April 1989, A3

Yen, RJ, 'Racial Stereotyping of Asians and Asian Americans and its Effects on Criminal Justice: a Reflection on the Wayne Lo Case' (2000) 7 *Asian Law Journal* 1

Yeo, S, 'Power of Self-Control in Provocation and Automatism' (1992) 14 *Sydney Law Review* 3

——'Editorial: Recognition of Aboriginal Criminal Jurisdiction' (1994) 18 *Criminal Law Journal* 193

——'Native Criminal Jurisdiction after Mabo' (1994) 6 *Current Issues in Criminal Justice* 9

——'Sex, Ethnicity, Power of Self-Control and Provocation' (1996) 18 *Sydney Law Review* 304

——*Criminal Defences in Malaysia and Singapore* (Malaysia, LexisNexis Malayan Law Journal, 2005)

Yeo, SMH, 'Provoking the "Ordinary" Ethnic Person: a Juror's Predicament' (1987) 11 *Criminal Law Journal* 96

——'Recent Australian Pronouncements on the Ordinary Person Test in Provocation and Automatism' (1990–91) 33 *Criminal Law Quarterly* 280

Yeşilgöz, Y, *Allah, Satan en het recht. Communicatie met Turkse verdachten* (Arnhem, Gouda Quint, 1995)

Yi, M, 'Guilty Plea in Smuggling of Girls: Landlord Gets 5 Years in Prison', *San Francisco Chronicle*, 8 March 2001, A21

——'Berkeley Landlord Jailed for 8 Years', *San Francisco Chronicle*, 21 June 2001, A15

Young, C, 'Equal Cultures—or Equality?', *Washington Post*, 29 March 1992, C5

Zuur, G, *Raad in taal. Taal- en begrippenboek voor de Raad voor de Kinderbescherming* (Amsterdam, Raad voor de Kinderbescherming, 2001)

Index